JUVENAL'S TENTH SATIRE

Juvenal's Tenth Satire

Paul Murgatroyd

LIVERPOOL UNIVERSITY PRESS

First published in 2017 by
Liverpool University Press
4 Cambridge Street
Liverpool
L69 7ZU

This paperback edition first published 2021

British Library Cataloguing-in-Publication data
A British Library CIP record is available

ISBN 978-1-78694-069-8 cased
ISBN 978-1-80085-681-3 paperback

Typeset by Carnegie Book Production, Lancaster

optimae socrui

Charlotte Woodbridge Winship

(1923–2014)

Contents

Preface

This is not a commentary on Juvenal 10: there are enough of those already, some of a high quality, on which I have drawn frequently and gratefully; it is a critical appreciation of the poem that examines it on its own and in context, and tries to make it come alive as a piece of literature. I offer one man's close reading of X as poetry, concerned with literary criticism rather than philological minutiae, not discussing textual problems unless they have a substantial effect on interpretation, and, to avoid inordinate clutter, not including constant references to material already adequately covered by commentators (anyone who needs more elucidation than that provided below by me is directed to those scholars). There is not much on well-worn topics like the *persona* and the influence of rhetoric. Over the last 30 years or so there has been a very welcome broadening of insights into Juvenal's satire. Out of all this I have concentrated on the lines of approach which I find most illuminating and useful and areas in which I feel I have the most to contribute. Doing full justice to them entails passing lightly or in silence over critical stances and theories which I find less fruitful and unconvincing, so as not to make this monograph even longer and more complicated. So I often address the issues of distortion and problematizing and also style and diction. I also devote much time to intertextuality and to humour, wit and irony. In particular I hope to build on the work of scholars like Martyn, Jenkyns and Schmitz, who see in J. a consistently skilful and sophisticated author, and to produce something new – a whole book demonstrating a high level of expertise on J.'s part sustained throughout a long poem (rather than intermittent flashes). My investigation of 10 has led me to conclude that J. is an accomplished poet and provocative satirist, a writer with real focus, who makes every word count; and my (admittedly less probing) exploration of the other *Satires* confirms that assessment. I offer, of course, just a personal evaluation of a notoriously slippery and intriguing author, highlighting aspects that I find of interest and note; and readers are encouraged to engage critically with the views expressed below, to take them further and to pursue other lines of inquiry which they themselves find appealing. This book is aimed at senior undergraduates and above. I have included translation and explanation of references so that Classics students will find the book easier to use and in order to reach scholars and students interested in satire outside of Classics departments.

I base my text on Housman's 1931 edition. Apart from minor matters of orthography (v for u) and punctuation (the starts of sections are not indented) the following are the variants from Housman: no inverted commas after *hominem* and before *sed* in 10.69; *mitius id sane. quid? non et stigmate dignum / credidit?* instead of *mitius id sane quod non et stigmate dignum credidit:* at 10.183f.; *ille* instead of *ore* at 10.197; and inverted commas around *nil ergo optabunt homines?* at 10.346.

Finally, I would like to thank Dr Chris Kelk for his extremely meticulous proofreading and in particular Dr Martin Winkler, who offered much appreciated support, gave generously of his great expertise in the field of satire and made many helpful suggestions and corrections.

CHAPTER ONE

Overview

Juvenal's tenth *Satire* is concerned with prayer, and has a simple and clear structure. In the introduction, at 1–55, comes the main thesis (because humans cannot distinguish between true blessings and their opposite they pray for pointless, excessive and harmful things) with a few short examples (such as petitions for wealth) by way of illustration. The 'proof' of that thesis comes in the main part of the poem, which provides much longer examples of such misguided prayers – for political power (56–113), eloquence (114–32), military glory (133–87), a long life (188–288) and beauty (289–345). Finally, the conclusion (346–66) rounds off the satire by telling us what we can pray for (the genuine blessings of 356–62), but adds that we don't need to pray for them (we can acquire them by our own efforts), mocks the process of sacrifice and questions the whole concept of prayer (and divinity).[1] This piece also addresses the whole concept of individual aspiration, and the value systems of individualism in and aside from society.

This is one of the most famous and fascinating of J.'s *Satires*, one which raises several major issues still very pertinent to us today (see below). It is a poem which had a definite contemporary relevance (for example, the lines on political power and military glory had an obvious bearing on the imperial court and the imperial generals Trajan and Hadrian), but there is also a universality to what J. wrote here. It is a rich and exciting read, packed with ideas and problems. It both stimulates and infuriates, with its various possible shades of sincerity, and its perplexing and involving blend of seriousness and humour, common sense and cynicism, perceptiveness and blinkered bigotry. It has a long reception history and has been translated and adapted by many writers,[2] most notably by Samuel Johnson in his *Vanity of Human Wishes* (some of the more notable versions will be touched on in later chapters).

The poem has also attracted a lot of scholarly attention down the years. In more recent times there have been some interesting developments in criticism of it and it has evoked a wide range of reactions, interpretations and evaluations. Coffey (131f.) sees the piece as a straightforward expatiation on the futility of most prayers, combining grave nobility and cynical wit. According to Ferguson (276f.), gentle laughter predominates, and in the end, this is a reflective but pessimistic satire on those who take themselves too seriously and, when things go wrong, blame Fortune; J. laughs at them, and at himself, and contents himself with a more modest aim. Courtney (446ff.) says that the composition is based on a mixture of scorn, cynicism and melancholy, and has both a negative and (at the end) a positive side; but this is a weak poem, less successful in the whole than in parts, because of holes in J.'s arguments due to the rhetorical method. Tengström (48ff.) thinks that J. sees himself as a teacher-satirist, instructing us about what we should pray for in order to be happy (so we can enter on the road to virtue), and he does this because he views Roman society as bad because of declining morality, despite Hadrian's claim to have brought back the Golden Age to Rome. Bellandi (66ff.) also considers X to be genuinely didactic, J. seeing it as his duty to show how misguided are common notions of blessings and to point out true blessings. For Rudd (35f.), J. has two roles – the upright moral commentator, who reacts to the social and ethical realities; and the cynical wit, who normally supports that reaction but sometimes undermines it; and in 10 the stance is that of a disenchanted observer reflecting on man's futile and misguided aspirations, with witty corrections offered at several points. Viansino (371) highlights the iconoclastic nature of the satire, pointing out that it amounts to a smashing of the ideology that guided Roman society (the wish for and admiration of military glory etc.). According to Fishelov, a sardonic and playfully pessimistic J. shows a distrustful and scornful attitude towards any positive or comforting ideals. Rudd and Barr (xxivf.) speak of a mood that approaches the familiarity of Horace, a harsh, sardonic laughter, a broadening of scope beyond Rome and a convincingly positive ring to the conclusion. In the view of Campana (13ff.), although J.'s earlier indignation is still in evidence here, he adopts a rational stance; he has discovered that vice is everywhere and things are just as bad outside of Rome, but he is less angry about vice now, and he continues to attach importance to virtue, but now as a way to the peaceful life. Braund (2004, 23, 364f.) opines that the poem is a didactic sermon reminiscent of Horace and that J. espouses a new cheerfulness, while exposing the confusion in our prayers and at the end gently mocking the entire process of prayer. Miller (305f.) claims that the poem's power lies in its vividly sketched vignettes and that it seems to promise philosophical repose (with the world laughed at with pity, not raked with the lash), but the vignettes offer more than enough material to feed the sadistic pleasure associated with satire's lacerating attacks, and the joys of vicariously participating in the grotesque degradation of others have not been banished, but provided with a more philosophical frame. For Plaza (251f.), this is a satire in which a reasonable attitude is evinced, but which is itself ironic and ambiguous, and in which the philosophical content of the poem is potentially demolished. Keane (2006, 98f.) maintains that J.'s moral theme is ambition, and that he warns the ambitious to beware of punishment from extralegal sources; in this world, the potential of language to function as a weapon analogous to nails, fists and sticks is realized. Hooley (123f.) writes that this is the closest that J. gets to his popular image as a grave and moral satirist, but this is not a philosophical meditation and there is no philosophical coherence in it (it is just a series of negative examples). In the opinion of Jones (122), *Satire* 10 presents a straightforward case which seems incontrovertible: prayers may result in disaster, so pray, if you pray for anything, not for uncertain goods, but for that which will enable you to bear whatever Fortune brings you – a sound mind and healthy body; the treatment may be leavened with frivolity, but it is difficult to see how the core argument can be deflected. Uden (146ff.) sees the poem as an attack on the efflorescence of Greek Cynicism in contemporary Rome. Keane (2015, 117ff.) discerns an invitation throughout 10 to look critically at the mocking attitude to life of J.'s caricature of Democritus. What I offer below is, of course, just one more reading of a long, dense and rather slippery piece of writing. I view X as containing various serious attempts to make us think amid all the humour, wit and irony, but others would see much more frivolity and misrule here, with J. playing the role of a silly and irresponsible mocker and an anarchic jokester.

This is a poem of different layers, in which Juvenal is doing several things at once. Previous critics have tended to be narrowly prescriptive and to identify one programmatic thrust and one or two main subjects, reducing *Satire* 10 to didactic moralizing or a rhetorical exercise (and so on), and claiming that it is about, say, the dangers of ambition and the tragedy of human hopes. This study will not play up one or two aspects to the exclusion of the many others present, but will try to do justice to the wide array of aims, levels, techniques and effects in this highly complex piece of writing.

One obviously important aspect is the novelty, which makes for liveliness, variety and interest. There is much here that had not appeared so far in the satirist's *œuvre*, so much that Ribbeck actually thought that the poem was not written by Juvenal at all.[3] The mood has changed from the anger and indignation of books I and II[4] and from the predominant irony in Book III.[5] In 10 we find a greater calm than was evident in the first two books and (although Juvenal had shown some pessimism earlier) an intense and all-pervasive pessimism, a great gloom, mixed with mockery (harsh laughter passim) and some pathos (most notably the pity for Nestor and Priam at 246ff. and 258ff.).[6] The global viewpoint is new too, as from his opening words our poet goes beyond Rome to satirize the world.[7] Scholars have also pointed to the innovation in the positive, constructive recommendations at 356ff.[8] and (in line with the extensive influence of philosophical ideas in this poem) the explicit use of figures from philosophy.[9] I would add that this is the first time in his writing that Juvenal attacks political power, eloquence and military glory as pointless and dangerous and things to which people should not aspire (thereby striking at the very fabric of Roman society).[10]

A useful way of dealing with the other important aspects of 10 is provided by Rudd's formulation of the satirist functioning within a triangle whose apices are entertainment, attack and preaching.[11] All three of those elements are very much in evidence and are of decided significance in this poem.

The entertainment here takes various forms. The absurd and the grotesque[12] are common, and there is lots of (especially dark) humour, wit and irony (much of it not noted hitherto). I also wonder if the relentlessly black picture of Rome and the world is not deliberately over the top, aiming at a comic Grand Guignol effect: in youth, people are raped, sold off by their parents or flogged, violated and killed for adultery, etc.; in their prime they are robbed, poisoned, deposed, defeated catastrophically, etc.; in old age they are ape-like, disgusting, extensively diseased, senile, slaughtered ignominiously, etc. (the thought would appear to be: life's a bitch, and then you die). There is intellectual entertainment too. So there are striking and moving passages of narrative (for example, the downfall of Sejanus at 56ff. and the death of Priam at 258ff.). And Juvenal's poetic skill is everywhere on display and often quite dazzling – not just the vividness and the epigrams that have come in for comment[13] but also diction, sound, rhythm, style, imagery, allusion and so on. The following chapters will look at *Satire* X as poetry and will show that as well as being a thought-provoking satirist, Juvenal is a very adroit and sophisticated poet.[14]

As for attack, to an extent the topic of prayer is a peg on which to hang criticism, another way for Juvenal to put his criticism across. There is further onslaught on Rome and on Roman sacred cows here, but now he opens things up and satirizes the aspirations, values, assumptions and achievements not just of Rome but of all humanity. Much rhetorical skill is evinced, in powerful invective that has consistent and often subtle point and bite, as I hope to show. There is also universality in all this. For readers in the western world there is contemporary relevance in this picture of a mass of unreflecting fools in pursuit of trivial and, even to them, harmful objects, because ours too is a society with unreflecting and programmed cravings for things like wealth, beauty and power.

The issue of pessimism is important in this connection. Juvenal does not say that all prayers are ill-judged, just the common ones made without any proviso or hedging (like: give me a long *and happy* life) by thoughtless people which he mentions in this piece. It is true that such petitions can turn out badly. But with a very bleak outlook he depicts only the negative outcome and intimates that such an outcome is the general rule and that the objects prayed for are generally futile or harmful.[15] However, a general rule is not proved by Juvenal's exemplification (a few developed examples and several other brief ones). There are obvious objections that can be made to his claims: political power does not always lead to trouble and death for the politician; lots of eloquent men are not killed because of their eloquence; generals fight for more than glory, and often do good for their country; many find old age enjoyable, or at least cope well enough with its discomforts (many more objections and difficulties with logic will be covered as we reach the sections in the following chapters). In addition, the vision of human life in 10 is unrelievedly dark: in a cruel and brutish world, full of danger, injustice and suffering, mortals are feeble fools whose transient achievements amount to little. Many would not accept this as a balanced view of Rome at that time, still less of the whole world; and, of course, Juvenal had not visited everywhere, so that his overall picture and sweeping generalizations (at 1–4, 112f. and 141f.) are highly dubious. Clearly the attitude and picture presented in 10 are skewed, and the argumentation is flawed. Equally clearly, this is due to pessimism (whether real or assumed).[16]

Poets (like Ezra Pound) are perfectly capable of a blinkered and excessively negative vision, and it is possible that (the ageing) Juvenal in real life grew into a pessimist because of his nature and/or circumstances.[17] However, Juvenal was an intelligent man, trained in rhetoric (but not dominated by its techniques to the extent of ignoring logic and content), and he would surely have been aware of the many glaring distortions and imperfections in his criticism and could surely have made a stronger and tighter case.[18] So what we have here is probably a pessimistic *persona* (a mask assumed by the satirist).[19] This would give the satire more depth and complexity, making it also into an attack on pessimists like the speaker and their dismal world view, and exposing them to ridicule. Juvenal might also be inviting us to reflect on writers (possibly his models Horace and Persius in particular!) who lay down the law for their readers and tell them what to think; perhaps we should ask ourselves who are they to do that, what makes them so superior and are they reliable and clear-thinking themselves. This explanation gives the piece a broader satirical thrust and makes it accomplished rather than flawed in this area too (like so many others). Then again can we be sure that Juvenal is entirely or consistently sincere?[20] Could he be satirizing himself as a moralist?[21] Do we have here a tension between two voices – the serious (moralistic) one and the mocking one?[22] His humour may be viewed as having a subversive aspect, blurring the message and creating ambivalence.[23]

Finally, there is the element of preaching. Even if the poet subverts this to some degree by means of a *persona*, on one level the poem is a vigorous didactic sermon, with overt preaching in its conclusion (and before that clear implications that one should not make the common misguided prayers that Juvenal mentions).[24] One may object to some of the criticisms, but the rejection of the pursuit of great wealth is certainly worth contemplating, and many would find the attributes listed at 356ff. to be helpful in dealing with life and its vicissitudes.

Critics have wondered if the satirist is really attempting to persuade his readers. Whether he is genuinely trying to win us over to certain attitudes or not, at the very least he can teach us to think. The poem does not let us relax but keeps us on our toes, analysing his points, accepting some, but coming up with objections to others. It must have been controversial in its day, and should make us take a second look at the ambitions and value scheme in our own culture. It makes us contemplate a variety of subjects in a variety of areas. And it raises some major questions. Does prayer achieve anything? Are there gods and, if so, are they malevolent (as at 7f. and 111) and/or benevolent (as at 347ff.)? Is religion necessary or useful? Is there any point in trying to accomplish something in life, when you will soon be dead, and it won't amount to much in the big scheme of things anyway? And so on, and so forth. For me there is a real intellectual challenge here, and real intellectual excitement.

Notes

1   This seems to me the most obvious and effective breakdown of the poem, but there is some disagreement over the length of the introduction. On the structure see Ebel, 14ff., 22ff.; Tengström, 3ff.; Courtney, 447f.; Campana, 47ff.

2   See e.g. the index in Winkler (2001), 482f.

3   Serafini (386ff.) lists several themes and attitudes in 10 that are found in Juvenal's earlier work, as does Campana (32ff.).

4   See e.g. Braund (1996b), 17ff.

5   See esp. Braund (1988).

6   See esp. Courtney (446) for the blend. On the mood see also Highet (1954), 122; Serafini, 389ff.; Anderson, 287ff.; Ebel, 6; Ramage-Sigsbee-Fredericks, 156; Bellandi, 66; Braund (1988), 184, 197; Rudd and Barr, xxiv. The combination of sadness and ridicule is in line with the references to Heraclitus and Democritus at 28ff., and the humour does provide some relief from all the grimness.

7   See Highet (1954), 122; Serafini, 389; Anderson, 287f.; Bellandi, 66f.

8   See Ebel, 6; Rudd and Barr, xxiv.

9   See Braund (1988), 184.

10   He did censure the abuse of power in *Satire* 4, but here the critique is quite different and goes much further.

11   See Rudd, 1. On the attack and preaching aspects see Keane, 42ff., 105ff.

12   On the grotesque in Juvenal, see Miller; Braund and Raschke in Plaza (2009), 327ff. and 506ff.

13   E.g. Highet (1954), 129; Ferguson, 276.

14   The entertainment alone should be enough to refute the superficial and lazy criticism that sees 10 as a dull and inept school exercise. For this view, see Friedländer, 451ff.; Marmorale, 109ff.; Serafini, 385f.; Viansino, 369. Of course, my comments on sound effects are purely subjective and should be treated as such.

15   See esp. 6, 7f., 8f., 12, 108ff., 187. The idea is reinforced as the poem progresses by the repetition of the drawbacks of such prayers (often caught vividly and densely packed) and powerful examples of damage caused by them.

16   Several scholars have remarked upon (but not probed) the distortion, flaws in argumentation and pessimism. See Duff, 327; Highet (1954), 125; Serafini, 389ff.; Ferguson, 276f.; Courtney, 453.

17   See Serafini, 391ff.; Lindo; Courtney, 446.

18   This holds true even when one allows for the fact that rhetorical practice played up aspects that suited its case and played down or omitted those that did not. Courtney (453f.) thinks that the defects are just due to a poorly judged rhetorical method of proof by examples. But Juvenal is not some hack declaimer or trained automaton giving a speech here; he has produced a poem which he knows people will read, reread and ponder at their leisure. As he has obviously lavished a lot of thought on features such as sound, style, expression and so on, it seems most unlikely that he would not do the same with logic and argumentation.

19   There has been reaction recently against the *persona* theory, which has been embraced uncritically in some cases, but it still seems to me the best explanation here. See Green, xxvii ff.; Iddeng (2000 and 2005); Keane (2006), 13ff.

20   For questioning of the long tradition that sees J. in 10 as a grave and moral critic see Hooley, 123f.

21   See Rimell in Freudenburg (2005), 81ff.

22   See Rudd, 35f.; Nadeau, 11ff.

23   See in particular Plaza (2006).

24   On the preaching see esp. Bellandi, 66ff.; Tengström, 48ff.

CHAPTER TWO

Sources

Such a long and complex poem was subject to many influences both major and minor. Some of these are now lost to us, while others are hard to determine exactly. This chapter will handle the major sources that can be discerned (minor ones will be covered in subsequent chapters, as allusion to other authors occurs in the text).

It seems reasonable to assume that Juvenal's own experiences shaped his writing, although we cannot know the extent to which that happened. It also seems feasible that he drew largely on historical narratives which we no longer have (for example, Tacitus's account of the fall of Sejanus).[1] Slightly less nebulous is his very probable debt to rhetoric for various tools in the presentation of his case.[2] He follows the common rhetorical practice of proving a point by means of *exempla* (historical and mythological examples), and all of the historical *exempla* in 10 – except for Silius – are found in the declamations, although specific reminiscences have not been established.[3] It is also possible that *Satire* 10 was structured along the lines of a speech in the *genus deliberativum* (deliberative oratory), with *exordium, narratio, peroratio* (introduction, narration of the case, peroration) and so on, as has been claimed.[4] Scholars have suggested that at 56ff.[5] Juvenal may be looking to the *locus de fortuna* (the topos of the precarious nature of human existence due to fortune).[6] It has also been pointed out that here he employs the rhetorical techniques of *praeteritio* (drawing attention to something by pretending to pass it by), gradation, antithesis and dilemma;[7] one could add to these the presence in X of rhetorical questions, exclamations, hyperbole, anaphora, epigrammatic *sententiae* and apostrophe, which were also common in declamation. However, all of those techniques were frequent in poetry as well (as was the use of *exempla*).[8]

We are on somewhat firmer ground with philosophy. Certainly Juvenal was no philosopher himself and this piece is not a consistent philosophical meditation,[9] but it is clear that philosophy had some influence on the satirist's overall attitude (which is calmer than before, and mocking) and on his analysis of prayer, criticism and recommendations at the end. The philosophical aspect makes for a reflective air, and readers may well feel invited to philosophize themselves.[10] In addition, our eclectic author presents ideas held by various schools of thought, and this is all part of the poem's rich intellectual blend, of the cerebral excitement and challenge (and he could even be trying to provoke devotees of one particular sect by means of an admixture of ideas taken from others as food for thought). Unfortunately, there are also difficulties here. Several of the ideas found in *Satire* 10 were common to various philosophers (as will become evident below), and there is also an overlap with rhetoric and moralizing literature,[11] so that it is often impossible to establish if Juvenal is following any one predecessor in particular; all we can do then is note potential influences on him.

There is a clear Socratic element in X. To begin with possible debts, Courtney points to the discussion of prayer in Plato's *Alcibiades II*, where we find several notions enunciated by Socrates which are also present in Juvenal (1ff. and 346ff.), especially the error of asking for great evils in the belief that they are blessings, while the gods grant the petition (138b); people requesting something bad under the impression that it is good (141a); men praying for monarchy or generalship or other things which bring them harm and then retracting their entreaties (142c, 148b); and the need to lift the mist that envelops the soul, so that one can discern good and bad (150d).[12] Courtney also points to Xenophon's *Memorabilia* 1.3.2 (when he prayed, Socrates asked simply for good things because the gods know best what is good, whereas appealing for riches or sovereignty is risky; compare Juv. 12ff., 346ff.) and 4.2.34f. (where Socrates says that beauty, strength, wealth and glory are questionable blessings, because lots of attractive people are ruined by admirers, the strong are led to attempt tasks beyond them, many rich men fall victim to conspiracies and many people suffer great harm as a result of glory and political power; compare Juv. 10f., 12ff., 56ff., 133ff., 289ff.).

A direct and unmistakable source of Socratic thought for Juvenal was provided by Valerius Maximus 7.2 ext. 1a. The impact of Valerius seems certain, as within that quite short passage there are so many points in common (ideas, arguments, advice, words, a consistently critical attitude to human prayer as something misguided and the demolition in succession of several entreaties cited as examples).[13] Valerius says:[14]

> *Socrates, humanae sapientiae quasi quoddam terrestre oraculum, nihil ultra petendum a dis immortalibus arbitrabatur quam ut bona tribuerent, quia ii demum scirent quid unicuique esset utile* [cf. Juv. 347f.], *nos autem*

plerumque id votis expeteremus quod non impetrasse melius foret [cf. Juv. 5f.]: *etenim densissimis tenebris involuta mortalium mens* [cf. Juv. 4], *in quam late patentem errorem* [cf. Juv. 4] *caecas precationes tuas spargis! divitias appetis, quae multis exitio fuerent* [cf. Juv. 12ff.]; *honores concupiscis, qui complures pessum dederunt* [cf. Juv. 56ff.], *regna tecum ipsa volvis, quorum exitus saepenumero miserabiles cernuntur; splendidis coniugiis inicis manus: at haec ut aliquando illustrant, ita nonnumquam funditus domos evertunt* [cf. Juv. 7, 350ff.]. *desine igitur stulta futuris malorum tuorum causis quasi felicissimis rebus inhiare, teque totam caelestium arbitrio permitte* [cf. Juv. 347f.], *quia qui tribuere bona ex facili solent, etiam eligere aptissime possunt* [cf. Juv. 349].

Socrates (like some sort of oracle of human wisdom on earth) believed that we should request nothing more from the immortal gods than that *they* should give us blessings, because only they know what is expedient for each one of us [cf. Juv. 347f.], while we generally seek in our prayers something which is better not granted [cf. Juv. 5f.]. For, your mortal mind enveloped in densest darkness [cf. Juv. 4], you scatter your blind prayers over such an extensive area of error [cf. Juv. 4]! You strive after wealth, which has proved destructive to many [cf. Juv. 12ff.]; you long for high political positions, which have ruined quite a few [cf. Juv. 56ff.]; you picture in your mind kingdoms, whose outcome is often seen to be dismal; you grasp after splendid marriages, but although they occasionally add lustre, they sometimes wreck houses completely [cf. Juv. 7, 350ff.]. So stop foolishly coveting things that will cause you trouble as though they represented the greatest good fortune, and entrust yourself entirely to the judgement of the gods [cf. Juv. 347f.], because those who are accustomed to bestowing blessings with ease can also select them with the most appropriateness [cf. Juv. 349].

However, Valerius Maximus is just a starting point for Juvenal, who allows himself a lot more space and so can be much more expansive. He adds to the number of misguided prayers; he really fills out the demolition of such petitions by including more detail and criticism, and adding *exempla*; and he achieves more impact (so he presents the negative effect of requests for riches (12ff.) and political power (56ff.) with powerful and vivid imagery and narrative). He also goes further (in his conclusion at 346ff.) in specifying what true blessings are, poking fun at the whole process of prayer; claiming that the gods are unnecessary (as you can acquire the same blessings by your own efforts); and even calling into question the very concept of divinity. There is variation in tone too, which is much darker in Juvenal thanks to the mockery and extensive pessimism. And with regard to expressions in common (*est utile, error, evertere domos, permittere* and *aptissimus*), Juvenal really makes something of *evertere domos* ('wrecked houses') at 7f.: transferring the phrase to a new context, he broadens the scope beyond trouble sometimes caused by marriages, to suggest much more widespread devastation; he also conjures up a grimly absurd picture of people actually imploring the gods to destroy their homes; and neatly and pointedly, his word order depicts the petitioners (*optantibus ipsis*) as encompassed by destruction (*evertere domos totas*) and destroying deities (*di faciles*).

Another obvious influence is Democritus.[15] Juvenal actually cites him at 28ff., approving of his laughter at humanity, and shows similar ridicule himself throughout his poem.[16] The satirist also demonstrates a greater calm than was evident earlier in his *œuvre* and at 363f. depicts a tranquil life as the goal, all of which fits with Democritus's view that mental tranquillity (on which he wrote a treatise) was the greatest good.[17] There are specific ideas in common too: in surviving fragments,[18] Democritus says that it was men who formed an image of fortune (cf. Juv. 365f.), and that people do not need to pray to the gods for health when they can acquire it for themselves (cf. Juv. 363), and he shows contempt for fortune (cf. Juv. 52f., 365f.).[19]

Epicureanism could have a bearing on *Satire X* too.[20] The Epicureans also aimed at a tranquil life; and they believed that it could only be acquired through virtue (cf. Juv. 363f.). They also attacked unnatural and unnecessary desires, such as those for wealth, political power and military glory (cf. Juv. 12ff., 56ff., 133ff., 360ff.), and rejected Chance as a god or controlling element (cf. Juv. 365f.). Juvenal's famous *mens sana in corpore sano* ('a healthy mind in a healthy body') at 356 fits with Epicurus's definition of happiness, and in line 357 the satirist recommends an Epicurean freedom from the fear of death.

Scholars have also seen possible debt to Stoic philosophers, especially Seneca.[21] Most notably, the Stoics thought (like Socrates) that one should just ask the gods for blessings (cf. Juv. 347f.) and championed *autarkeia* or self-sufficiency (cf. Juv. 363). Seneca felt that men don't distinguish between good and bad things, often wishing for the latter under the misapprehension that they are the former (cf. Juv. 2ff.); scorned prayers for wealth, which could cause one's death (cf. Juv. 23ff.); divided wishes into the useless (*supervacua*) and harmful (cf. Juv. 54); rejected petitions for longevity and good looks (cf. Juv. 188ff. and 289ff.); recommended a healthy mind and a healthy body (cf. Juv. 356); believed that fortune should be shunned (cf. Juv. 365f.); and employed as *exempla* Sejanus, Crassus, Pompey, Caesar, Cicero and Hannibal (cf. Juv. 58ff., 108f., 114ff., 147ff.).

There is a particular piece of writing by a famous satirist with Stoic leanings (Persius's second *Satire*) which critics have long pointed to as a source for Juvenal 10. That satire is a sermon on prayer. In it Persius contrasts good prayers (made openly for worthwhile things from a heart that is pure, just and honourable) with bad ones (furtive and disreputable requests made with a hypocritical show of piety, and foolish petitions that are unrealistic and are thwarted by the petitioner's own conduct). The poet warns that impious appeals will be punished, and it is no use trying to bribe the gods to grant them under the misapprehension that they are mercenary like us. He criticizes the attitude to prayer of Romans in various walks of life (especially the Roman élite), and he also preaches, showing us how we can make good entreaties that will be granted no matter how humble the offering that accompanies them.

One would naturally expect Juvenal to be aware of that poem by his satiric predecessor, just as he was acquainted with other compositions by Persius,[22] and this assumption is confirmed by extensive parallels. Both Persius 2 and Juvenal 10 are satires devoted entirely to the topic of prayer, which are highly critical of contemporary society in respect of prayer. Many of the specific petitions are common. It has already been noted that both poets cover requests for beauty, wealth and long life.[23] I would add that Persius, like Juvenal, also covers appeals for *mens bona* ('good sense', 8; cf. Juv. 356), *fama* ('fame', 8; cf. Juv. 114) and high position (36f.; cf. Juv. 57ff.). In particular, at 31ff. Persius (like Juvenal at 289ff.) dilates on misguided prayer for a child by a foolish doting woman – compare *matertera* ('aunt') in Persius 31 to *mater* ('mother') in Juvenal 290 – including a wish for good looks for the infant (37f.), the notion of the boy when grown up being desired by royalty (37; cf. Juv. 306ff.) and the use of *rapio* of the ravishment of a handsome youth by a female (37f.; cf. Juv. 332). Persius also shares various themes with our author – most notably, murmured petitions (*murmurat*, 6, 9; *murmure*, Juv. 289f.), riches inviting murder (12f., Juv. 26f.), the deflation of offerings to the gods as a *quid pro quo* (29f., Juv. 354f.) and wealthy Roman properties (36, Juv. 16f.).

Juvenal obviously found food for thought in Persius 2; but equally obvious is his independence. He decided to write a quite different poem on the same topic and to approach it from a new direction and highlight new elements (complementing and, I think, competing with Persius's second satire).

Scholars have observed that Juvenal drops the detail of hypocrisy,[24] adds prayers for political power, eloquence and military glory,[25] and, more broadly, opts for a much more expansive piece (Persius 2 is only 75 lines long) and alters the angle of presentation to go beyond his model (being concerned not with the morality of petitions or the disposition of the petitioner but with the negative consequences of their fulfilment).[26] But the variation is more ample and significant than that. Juvenal also drops *inter alia* contrast between prayers, immoral requests and the corruption of religion by avarice (to keep a tight focus on the disastrous outcome of successful appeals). He also adds vivid *exempla*, extended narrative and a pervasive pessimism, making his poem arresting and grim. And his expansiveness facilitates more detailed treatment and a quite remorseless impact for his (more hard-hitting and mocking)[27] criticism. So too, while Persius is concerned with just the Roman scene, Juvenal broadens the vision and casts a jaundiced eye over the world in general and all humanity's aspirations and achievements; where Persius attacks bad requests but encourages proper entreaties to god, our poet subverts the very concepts of prayer and divinity. All in all, Juvenal has produced a more sombre, powerful and provocative satire.

There is another piece (Horace *Odes* 1.31) which will have been in Juvenal's mind, and several similarities between the two poems have been noted.[28] In connection with the dedication in Rome of a temple to Apollo by Augustus in 28 BC, Horace wrote:[29]

> *Quid dedicatum poscit Apollinem*
> *vates? quid orat de patera novum*
> *fundens liquorem? non opimae*
> *Sardiniae segetes feraces,*
>
> *non aestuosae grata Calabriae*   5
> *armenta, non aurum aut ebur Indicum,*
> *non rura quae Liris quieta*
> *mordet aqua taciturnus amnis.*
>
> *premant Calenam falce quibus dedit*
> *fortuna vitem, dives et aureis*   10
> *mercator exsiccet culullis*
> *vina Syra reparata merce,*
>
> *dis carus ipsis, quippe ter et quater*
> *anno revisens aequor Atlanticum*
> *impune. me pascunt olivae,*   15
> *me cichorea levesque malvae.*
>
> *frui paratis et valido mihi,*
> *Latoe, dones, et, precor, integra*
> *cum mente, nec turpem senectam*
> *degere nec cithara carentem.*   20

What does the bard ask of Apollo, whose temple is now dedicated? What does he pray for as he pours new wine from the wine bowl? Not for the bumper crops of fertile Sardinia, not for the lovely herds of sweltering Calabria, not for Indian gold or ivory, not for an estate which the silent river Liris nibbles with its quiet waters. Let those to whom Fortune has granted it prune Calenian vines with their knives; let the prosperous trader drain from golden drinking cups wine bought with Syrian merchandise, dear as he must be to the very gods, since three or four times a year he sails again on the Atlantic Ocean unscathed. As for me, I eat easily digestible olives, chicory and mallows. Son of Latona, grant that I enjoy what is at hand together with good health and, I pray, an unimpaired mind, and have an old age that is not repulsive and not lacking the lyre.

Here Horace (like Juvenal) raises the basic question of what should be prayed for, and in answering that question draws on philosophical ideas[30] and adopts the priamel form (whereby one leads up to the main point by listing inferior options), rejecting a series of bad prayers (that many people would make) for some good prayers (which he personally sanctions). As in Juvenal, the request for riches is repudiated (and the danger attendant on wealth is touched on), while appeals for health and a sound mind are endorsed (cf. Juv. 12ff., 356). There are common details too – Fortune's influence (to which indifference is shown), expensive wine in golden drinking cups and repulsive old age (cf. Juv. 52f. and 365f., 26f., 190ff.). There seems to be a verbal reminiscence as well: similar to Horace's *dis carus ipsis* ('dear to the very gods') is Juvenal's *carior est illis homo quam sibi* ('man is dearer to them [i.e. the *di* ('gods') of 349] than he is to himself') in line 350.[31]

There is a thoughtful and combative engagement with this source too. The *Ode* is a gentle, genial and rather slight lyric poem, which essentially amounts to a rejection of wealth and the desire for it in favour of a simpler life of modest means and quiet contentment. By way of contrast, Juvenal 10 is a satire which has a dissimilar tone and impact (bleaker, harder and controversial) and a wider scope (going beyond the personal to attack several aspects of Roman society, and broadening out to embrace all the world); it is also a much longer composition, whose length creates space for investigation and criticism (as Juvenal pursues the negative results of bad prayer rather than simply rebuffing it). Our poet also repudiates the request for riches, but more forcefully, on the grounds that wealth is usually dangerous (a drawback caught more fully and vividly at 12ff., and with a sinister twist to the detail of costly wine in golden goblets at 26f.). He criticizes several other appeals as well, for quite different reasons. Of the acceptable prayers in Horace, Juvenal ignores the enjoyment of what is at hand and the continuation of the poetic impulse in old age, specifically spurning old age as something desirable at 188ff. (while really developing the brief mention of its repulsiveness in the *Ode*), and embraces only physical and mental health (with a more elegant expression in line 356 than is found in the text of the famously elegant lyric poet); he also adds several more permissible entreaties of his own. More than that, where Horace actually prayed to Apollo for things in 1.31, at 346ff. Juvenal pokes fun at the procedure of prayer, recommends not requesting things from deities but leaving them to bestow blessings on us,[32] states that the gods are actually unnecessary for the acquisition of those blessings and then raises doubts about the divinity of a goddess (Fortuna). Clearly Juvenal goes much deeper into the whole issue of prayer than his source did. There could even be implicit taunting of Horace here for being rather superficial, conventional and complacent.[33] At any rate, after reading *Satire* X one goes back to *Odes* 1.31 with a sharper and more critical gaze.

From the above it should be clear that in X Juvenal makes use of various sources and employs commonplaces, but also that he adapts as well as adopting and generally aims to make something new and distinctively his own out of the material that he takes over. That same process is evident in other Juvenalian poems (most notably in 3, 5 and 6).

Notes

1   See also Highet (1954), 276; Ferguson, 255. On the possible influence of history see Tengström, 46ff.

2   On rhetoric in Juvenal generally see de Decker; Schmitz; Braund in Plaza (2009), 450ff.

3   See de Decker, 109; Courtney, 452. Most of these examples also occur in Seneca (see below).

4   See Tengström, 8ff.; Ferguson, 276. I am not convinced by their proposal of a digression at 28ff. (see the next chapter). And the composition can also be classified as an extended priamel. See Courtney, 447f.

5   For text and translation of Juvenal 10 see the following chapters.

6   See de Decker, 41ff.; Highet (1954), 276.

7   See de Decker, 113, 115, 120, 124f.

8   See, for example, Propertius 1.2.15ff.; Ovid *AA* 1.283ff.

9   See Highet (1949); Romano, 47f.; Courtney, 16, 451; Mayer in Freudenburg (2005), 148, 157f. By way of contrast, Uden (146ff.) sees a consistent Cynic voice in this poem, but fails to convince me.

10   See Viansino, 371. Juvenal follows the common Roman practice (found, for example, in Cicero and Seneca) of picking and choosing theories and ideas that best suit one's case, and readers might feel encouraged to select themselves from Juvenal's philosophical points and develop some of them further.

11   For instance, many of Juvenal's historical *exempla* occur in Seneca (see below) and are also found in declamations (see n. 3), and the pursuit of wealth (cf. Juv. 12ff.) was rejected by Seneca (*Epist.* 119.6) and the Cynics (Highet [1949], 265) and also by various poets (e.g. Horace *Epode* 1.23ff.; Tibullus 1.1.1ff.). See Bellandi, 68ff.; Campana, 44.

12   Courtney, 448f.

13   For most of the parallels, see Gauger, 67; Courtney, 449.

14   The text used is that of Shackleton Bailey.

15   See Courtney, 449f.

16   At 28ff. he also voices approval of the philosopher Heraclitus's tears over men's behaviour, and there are passages in the satire (esp. 246ff. and 258ff.) that evince a pathos consonant with that.

17   See Cicero *Fin.* 5.23, 87; Seneca *Tranq. Animi* 2.3. See also Anderson, 340ff. and Viansino, 369.

18   See B119, B176, B234 (cited in Courtney, 450); Juv. 10.52f.

19   Juvenal's knowledge of Democritus may have come (at least in part) from Seneca. In his *Tranq. Animi* (at 2.3), Seneca translated Democritus's *euthymia* as *tranquillitas* (cf. Juvenal's *tranquillae … vitae* at 364); at 13.1, he wrote that when Democritus said that if a man wanted to live tranquilly he should not engage in many public or private affairs, Democritus was referring to useless affairs (*supervacua*, the word used by Juvenal at 10.54); and at 15.2 he made the contrast between the laughing Democritus and the weeping Heraclitus and advised imitating the former (cf. Juv. 28ff.).

20   See Highet (1949), 266f.; Romano, 48; Ferguson, 245, 275, 276.

21   See Highet (1949), 260; Dick; Ebel, 13f.; Ferguson, 254f.; Courtney, 450f.; Viansino, 371; Ramelli, 2214, 2226, 2228f., 2498f., 2503, 2505.

22   See, for example, Scivoletto; Reckford, 161ff.

23   Highet (1954), 276; Scivoletto. 63; Ferguson, 255; Campana, 38.

24   Fishelov, 374.

25   Highet (1954), 276.

26   For example Nisbet in Sullivan, 49ff.; Coffey, 104.

27   There is comic absurdity at Persius 2.41ff. (where people ask for a healthy body while over-eating, and ruin themselves financially with expensive offerings to bribe the gods into making them wealthy), but the humour in *Satire* X is harsher and much more frequent.

28   See especially Gauger, 73 n. 147; Courtney, 451f.; Fishelov, 372f.

29   The text used is the *Oxford Classical Text* of Wickham, but in line 18 I accept Lambinus's *et* instead of *at*. On the emendation see Nisbet and Hubbard, 357f.

30   See Nisbet and Hubbard, 348, 356, 357.

31   It is just possible that in his initial two lines Horace's *quid poscit* ('what does he ask') is taken up by 10.354 in *ut poscas aliquid* ('so you may ask for something') and that his *quid orat* ('what does he pray for') is recalled by *orandum est* ('one should pray for') in 10.356.

32   Juvenal cheekily employs Horace's own *dis carus ipsis* in 350 while correcting him.

33   Horace's poem, with its allusion to Augustus's dedication of the temple to Apollo, is also cosily implicated in the Roman power structure that Juvenal calls into question at 33ff. and 56ff.

CHAPTER THREE

Introduction (1–55)

Juvenal seizes our attention at the start of the introduction and holds it. He achieves bleak impact (and sets up the prevailing dark mood of the poem) by opening with a picture of a world of blind fools who bring danger and destruction on themselves. Further striking images (and *exempla*) follow, and there are lively progressions, as J. veers off unexpectedly in new directions (suggesting an active mind busily probing and ranging about as it grapples with the topic of prayer). There are other methods of involving readers as well (such as not spelling out the point, and posing rhetorical questions). The humour, wit and irony (sometimes at J.'s own expense) are engaging too, as is the new Juvenal whom we encounter here (an intensely pessimistic and harshly mocking satirist with a global view, critical of Rome and all humanity). Hand in hand with that pessimism there is exaggeration and generalization and cynicism, but we also find common sense, intelligence and perceptiveness in this introduction, so that we are kept on our toes evaluating the poet's remarks (accepting, half-accepting or rejecting his points). We are left wondering how sincere and serious our author is, and how reliable. He also gets us thinking by raising some big issues. Is wealth worth pursuing? Is human life comic or tragic or tragicomic? Is the mocking approach to the world as something absurd usefully liberating? Is laughing in the face of adversity the right attitude? In addition, his stance towards things generally esteemed by the Romans (wealth, status and display) is irreverent and unconventional. All of that comes together to form a stimulating and provocative mixture.

All of it also fits very well with what will follow in the remainder of X, so that lines 1–55 perform their introductory function effectively, on top of announcing the poem's main theme (prayer) and main thesis (humans pray for the superfluous, the meaningless and the pernicious). There are lots of other elements that usher in the rest of the poem too. This is an appropriately long introduction for a long satire. The debt to philosophy, the grotesquerie, the deflation (of human hopes and accomplishments, and of the apparently impressive figure of the praetor at 36ff.), the intertextuality and the poetic skill (in connection with sound, rhythm, diction and style) all look forward to the main body of *Satire* 10. And there is a foretaste of the lengthy onslaughts with *exempla* on various objects of prayer in the extended criticism of riches, rank and authority at 12f. and 35ff., while J.'s rejections of eloquence (9f.) and power (35ff.) are taken up and developed at 56ff. and 114ff.

The introduction is also well organized. Throughout the progression of thought is logical, if at times unpredictable (see the detailed discussion below). After his preamble at 1–6 on how blind, irrational and misguided most mortals are, J. moves on to these failings' effect on prayer, and develops two aspects at length. In lines 7–27 he covers 'blessings' often prayed for (especially wealth, at 12ff.) which turn out to be destructive, while making his condemnation of them clear. At 28–53 he progresses to seemingly desirable things which are excessive and pointless (the trappings of wealth, status and power), while voicing support for the philosopher Democritus, who would have mocked them. Then in line 54 he refers to prayers for objects which are *supervacua* (= 'excessive' and 'pointless')[1] and *perniciosa* (= 'destructive'). So, overall, there is a chiasmus. There is also ring structure, as the end of this section recalls the opening with its foolish mortals in line 50 (cf. 1ff.), misplaced anxiety in line 51 (cf. 4), divinities in lines 52 and 55 (cf. 2 and 8), *perniciosa petuntur* ('destructive things are prayed for') in line 54 (cf. *nocitura petuntur* ['things that will do harm are prayed for'] in line 8; and destruction at 7ff.), the pair of rhetorical questions at 54f. (cf. 4–6) and prayer in line 55 (cf. 7).[2]

After that general preface and overview, we can now move on to the Latin text[3] and translation, and then progress to more detailed discussion.

> Omnibus in terris, quae sunt a Gadibus usque
> Auroram et Gangen, pauci dinoscere possunt
> vera bona atque illis multum diversa, remota
> erroris nebula. quid enim ratione timemus
> aut cupimus? quid tam dextro pede concipis, ut te   5
> conatus non paeniteat votique peracti?
> evertere domos totas optantibus ipsis
> di faciles. nocitura toga, nocitura petuntur
> militia; torrens dicendi copia multis
> et sua mortifera est facundia; viribus ille   10
> confisus periit admirandisque lacertis,
> sed plures nimia congesta pecunia cura

strangulat et cuncta exuperans patrimonia census
quanto delphinis ballaena Britannica maior.
temporibus diris igitur iussuque Neronis   15
Longinum et magnos Senecae praedivitis hortos
clausit et egregias Lateranorum obsidet aedes
tota cohors: rarus venit in cenacula miles.
pauca licet portes argenti vascula puri
nocte iter ingressus, gladium contumque timebis   20
et mota ad lunam trepidabis harundinis umbra:
cantabit vacuus coram latrone viator.
prima fere vota et cunctis notissima templis
divitiae, crescant ut opes, ut maxima toto
nostra sit arca foro. sed nulla aconita bibuntur   25
fictilibus: tunc illa time cum pocula sumes
gemmata et lato Setinum ardebit in auro.
iamne igitur laudas quod de sapientibus alter
ridebat, quotiens de limine moverat unum
protuleratque pedem, flebat contrarius auctor?   30
sed facilis cuivis rigidi censura cachinni:
mirandum est unde ille oculis suffecerit umor.
perpetuo risu pulmonem agitare solebat
Democritus, quamquam non essent urbibus illis
praetextae, trabeae, fasces, lectica, tribunal.   35
quid si vidisset praetorem curribus altis
extantem et medii sublimem pulvere circi
in tunica Iovis et pictae Sarrana ferentem
ex umeris aulaea togae magnaeque coronae
tantum orbem, quanto cervix non sufficit ulla?   40
quippe tenet sudans hanc publicus et, sibi consul
ne placeat, curru servus portatur eodem.
da nunc et volucrem, sceptro quae surgit eburno,
illinc cornicines, hinc praecedentia longi
agminis officia et niveos ad frena Quirites,   45
defossa in loculos quos sportula fecit amicos.
tum quoque materiam risus invenit ad omnis
occursus hominum, cuius prudentia monstrat
summos posse viros et magna exempla daturos
vervecum in patria crassoque sub aere nasci.   50
ridebat curas nec non et gaudia vulgi,
interdum et lacrimas, cum Fortunae ipse minaci
mandaret laqueum mediumque ostenderet unguem.

ergo supervacua aut quae perniciosa petuntur?
propter quae fas est genua incerare deorum?   55

The following is a fairly literal translation:[4]

In all the lands which exist from Cadiz as far as
Dawn and the Ganges few people can distinguish
genuine blessings and things very different from them, with the fog
of error removed. For what do we fear or desire
according to reason? What project do you undertake
    so auspiciously   5
that you do not regret the enterprise and the accomplishment of
your desire?
The compliant gods have ruined whole households since the heads
    of them
requested it. In peacetime things that will do harm, in war things
    that will do
harm are prayed for; for many, a torrential abundance of speech and
    their own
eloquence are fatal; another met his death from putting   10
his trust in his strength and admirable muscles,
but more are smothered by money heaped up with too much
care and wealth overtopping all other fortunes
by as much as the British whale is bigger than dolphins.
Therefore during the time of terror and on the orders of Nero   15
a whole cohort blockaded Longinus and the large gardens of
outstandingly rich Seneca and besieged the splendid house of
the Laterani: seldom does a soldier enter a garret.
Although you carry a few small vessels of unembossed silver
when you set out on a journey at night, you'll fear swords
    and lances,   20
and when a reed's shadow moves in the moonlight you'll panic;
an empty-handed traveller will sing when face to face with a robber.
Almost always the number one prayer, very well known in all
    temples, is for
riches, that our wealth should grow, that our strongbox should be
the biggest in the whole forum. But no aconite is drunk from   25
earthenware; fear that when you pick up goblets that are
jewelled, and Setian wine glows in a broad gold cup.
So then after all this surely you approve of the fact that one of
    the wise men

used to laugh whenever he stirred or put a single foot out
from his threshold, while the opposite authority used to cry?   30
But the assessment of a stern guffaw is easy for anyone;
what is amazing is where all the tears came from for the eyes
    [of Heraclitus].
Democritus was in the habit of shaking his sides with
    permanent laughter
even though cities of those days did not have
the *toga praetexta, trabea, fasces,* litter and platform.   35
What if he'd seen the praetor conspicuous on the lofty
chariot and high up in the dust in the middle of the circus
in the tunic of Jupiter and carrying on his shoulders the purple
hangings of the embroidered toga and so great a circle
of a large crown that no neck is strong enough for it?   40
For a public slave holds it, sweating, and so that the 'consul'
does not think highly of himself, rides in the same chariot.
Add now also the bird that stands high on the ivory sceptre,
on this side trumpeters, on that side the escort in a long
line going in front and at the bridles snowy-white citizens   45
whom the handout buried in their cashboxes has made
    into 'friends'.
Even then Democritus found material for laughter in every
encounter with humans. His wisdom shows that
first-rate men who will set great examples can
be born in a country of wethers and in a thick climate.   50
He used to laugh at the worries and also the delights of the
    general public
and sometimes at their tears, while he himself used to tell
    threatening Fortune
to go hang herself and showed her his middle finger.
So then what pointless and excessive or destructive things are
    prayed for?
For what is it right to cover with wax the knees of the gods?   55

The very first sentence is meant to catch our attention. It has an immense
geographical range from furthest west to furthest east, and a predominantly
spondaic rhythm (with a solemn and mournful effect). The plain diction
in lines 1–3 (with simple, short words) creates directness and makes the
subsequent metaphor in *erroris nebula* ('fog of error'; 4) stand out by way
of contrast (the enjambment and emphatic placement of those two words
at the start of the line and end of the sentence also highlight them). The

phrase conjures up a striking picture of the whole earth covered in fog (apart from just a few clear patches) and its various peoples stumbling around, unable to see clearly, losing their way, uncertain, ignorant of problems and dangers, making mistakes and hurting and even killing themselves; to add to the impact, *erroris* has connotations of wandering, perplexity, going astray and derangement.[5] That initial sentence is also combative, problematical and pessimistic. It contains a sweeping assertion: in *all* the lands (*omnibus* gets stress from its position) *from east to west* only a *few* can distinguish between genuine blessings and things *very different* from them. So J. is depicting a whole world of really obtuse morons (when he could not possibly know about the perceptiveness of such a vast mass of humanity). There is subversive irony here in J. being clearly in error when he is criticizing human error (such hyperbole, rebounding on the speaker, is also evident in VI). There is winning wit too in J. himself exemplifying the error that he claims is so prevalent among mortals. There also seems to be a small joke in the allusion to *Aurora* in line 2 (not strictly necessary on top of the reference to the Ganges, and so probably included to facilitate such play). In the context of lacking perception about blessings, it is easy enough to think of the story of that goddess asking Zeus to bestow immortality on her beloved Tithonus (which proved to be a curse because she forgot to ask for perpetual youth to go with it),[6] and so one infers that even divinities can make silly mistakes over blessings and even the goddess of bright dawn was in a fog of error.

J. tries to keep our attention in lines 4–6 by means of two rhetorical questions with insistent repetition of *quid* ('what'). He thereby buttonholes us, establishes a link with us (by inducing us to respond)[7] and also makes us ponder. Clearly the implied answers to the queries are that none or very few of our fears and desires are based on reason, and that there are no or very few projects where we do not regret their realization and the whole idea in the first place. But, just as clearly, if we reflect for a moment (as we are invited to do), we can see that there is pessimistic exaggeration in such answers; and, amusingly, J. himself later undermines his standpoint here by presenting horrors of old age that can be reasonably feared (190ff.), rational prayers (354ff.) and a project that would not cause regret (363f.). In the almost epigrammatical question at 4f. (reflecting the very real importance of fear and desire in our prayers) with the first person plural J. includes himself among the misguided, disarmingly, and wittily (after his error at 1–4, and while being not strictly rational himself here). That 'we' reinforces the link with readers, and the 'you' at 5f. also builds intimacy with them and involves them. In addition, the progression from third person to first, and then to second over lines 1–6, subtly strengthens the notion of really widespread error (i.e. almost everybody is mistaken, including me and all of you readers).

At 7–9 bleak paradox and black humour now come to the fore, as J. stresses human silliness by means of a quick flurry of injurious prayers, with mock-solemn spondees in line 7 giving way to light-hearted, eager dactyls. At 7f. the destruction of whole households (rather than the odd individual) constitutes a powerful example of mortal folly and the deleterious effects of ill-judged petitions. *Optantibus ipsis* ('since the heads of them requested this'), with *ipsis* ('heads') in emphatic position, brings to mind a grimly absurd picture of people actually begging the gods to ruin their households. In the Latin word order, *di faciles* ('the compliant gods') is left to the end of the sentence for comic impact (these gods have a cruel sense of humour, it seems), and there may well be ironical play on the sense 'favourable, propitious' for *facilis*.[8] At 8f., to reinforce the point of 7f., J. strongly highlights the stupidity and damage of prayers (the forceful repetition of *nocitura* ('things that will do harm'), and the noteworthy homoeoteleuton) and asserts that such appeals are made constantly. There is also a joke there: in war it is natural to pray for things that will harm (the enemy), but here people are praying in war for things that will harm themselves.

At 9ff. with a lively change of tack J. suddenly moves on to examples of things commonly prayed for which, according to him, turn out to be not blessings but deadly. In 9–10, the twofold expression of eloquence showcases this apparent boon, but in the Latin word order *mortifera* ('fatal') is placed between *torrens dicendi copia* ('torrential abundance of speech') and *facundia* ('eloquence'), so that death is pointedly at the heart of all the facundity. That doublet also makes for a divertingly apt fulness in describing the abundance of speech, and there may well be a pawky touch in the mention of plentiful words at the start of a very long satire.[9] The torrent of speech here produces an arresting and grotesque image of the man's own words pouring out of his mouth and forming a powerful, rushing river (cf. e.g. Horace *Sat.* 1.4.11) that carries him off, helpless and drowning in his own verbiage. *Multis* ('for many') is stressed by its position, but one can reasonably object that a facility with words may get one into trouble if one speaks out, but does not destroy everybody or even most people. Our gloomy poet's case is still weaker when at 10f. he moves from mental to physical excellence, and tries to undermine that too, but cites only one person as an example. Here commentators see reference to Milo of Croton, a famous sixth-century athlete who came across an oak tree split with wedges and tried to pull it apart with his bare hands, with the result that the wedges dropped out and his hands got trapped, so that he could not defend himself when wolves attacked him.[10] J. conjures up the type of big strong man that many would like to be and cuts him down to size by giving him brief coverage, not even mentioning Milo's name and alluding to such a foolish and horrible end. This apparently worthwhile quality is also highlighted by means of twofold expression – and by the bulky and spondaic *admirandisque lacertis* ('admirable muscles') – but deflated by the little word *periit* (= 'met his death') in the centre of all the might, confidence and admiration (death being our inescapable weakness no matter how strong we are) and by the ironical tinge to *admirandis* (as he died, his muscles in fact were not all that 'admirable').[11]

In line 12, J. progresses to another 'blessing' (wealth, which at 12–14 and 24f. is excessive as well as pernicious), and with enlivening unpredictability he devotes a lot more verses to this one (12–27). Because so many people want riches, this topic merits extended treatment early on in the poem,[12] and J. mounts a strong, fourfold attack on it (at 12–14, 15–18, 19–22 and 23–7;[13] it is also entertaining to see our poet going on at length about the many problems caused by wealth; cf. the tirades about the numerous rivals at 1.95ff. and 3.69ff.). As a counterweight to that onslaught we should bear in mind that although wealth can rebound and attract predators, lots of prosperous people are happy, contented and safe.

J. begins 12–14 with powerful imagery, effective connotations and scornful sound effects (frequency of *p*, *c* and *b*).[14] 'Money heaped up with too much care' in line 12 implies excessive concern with acquiring cash and excessive pains in piling up coins – *cura* ('care') purposively embraces 'anxiety', 'carefulness' 'devotion of attention' and 'eagerness'.[15] But no matter how careful one is, a pile that is too high will topple over. So here one visualizes a great heap of coins collapsing on top of the rich man and smothering him; and, as *strangulo* ('smother') is also used of obstructions of the throat, we are probably meant to think of them being drawn into his mouth as he tries desperately to breathe. Such a horrific demise makes J.'s point (about riches being fatal) memorably, and also contains black humour (all that effort simply brings about the man's death, which serves the greedy wretch right). That seems to me the most obvious explanation, but it has also been suggested that *pecunia strangulat* means that the money 'causes to be strangled' or that there is allusion to Midas choking on the gold he created himself;[16] and it is even possible that the (surreal) idea is that the cash has a life of its own and decides to smother and/or strangle men. This all results in an intriguing richness. Again this lone term (the stark *strangulat*) has impact in the midst of many other words (here employed to denote lots of money). In line 13, the heap is taken up by *exuperans* ('overtopping') and developed into something staggering (intimating immense greed) by means of the outdoing of all other fortunes and the whale comparison, which implies a massive, towering pile of money, to which are attached the associations of Britain (that fabulous land of savages and freaks) and of the singular, strange, dangerous and monstrous whale.[17]

At 15–18, J. moves on to concrete *exempla* to back up his point, citing a full three notable cases (which do have impact, but do not prove that wealth is fatal always or most of the time). He mentions three famous and distinguished men who were very rich – Cassius Longinus, Seneca the Younger and Plautius Lateranus. They are linked in that they were all implicated in Piso's conspiracy against Nero (in 65 AD), but J. implies – with *igitur* ('therefore'), *magnos* ('large'), *praedivitis* ('outstandingly rich') and *egregias* ('splendid') – that Nero's attack on them was motivated by a desire for their wealth as well as or instead of their participation in a plot against him. Seneca was forced to commit suicide, Lateranus was executed and, according to Suetonius *Nero* 37, Longinus was put to death (in other accounts he was banished and eventually recalled, but in view of the thrust of 12–14, our poet will be following the Suetonian version).[18] As well as showing that having lots of money is fatally risky, these examples suggest that renown, eminence and service to the state are no protection for the wealthy, and that no matter how rich you are or how high you rise there will always be a predator stronger than you. Line 15 is filled with menace: *temporibus diris* ('the time of terror') has ominous associations (it occurs elsewhere only at Cicero *Div.* 1.18, of the start of Cicero's consulship, a period marked by dire omens of impending slaughter, and at J. 4.80, of the reign of terror of the dreadful Domitian), while *iussuque Neronis* ('and on the orders of Nero') sets before us the power of that monstrous emperor. At 16f. the adjectives *magnos* ('large'), *praedivitis* ('outstandingly rich') and *egregias* ('splendid') show the surface appeal of wealth, but also make clear its drawbacks (all it does here is attract the attention of the deadly Nero!). So too the impressively stylish *magnos Senecae praedivitis hortos* ('large gardens of outstandingly rich Seneca') – with its chiastic arrangement of cases and balanced ordering of adjectives and nouns, and assonance – is deflated by the immediately succeeding *clausit* ('blockaded'), and the fine-sounding *egregias Lateranorum … aedes* ('splendid house of the Laterani') is undercut by the intrusive *obsidet* ('blockaded'). Those two verbs bring out the grotesque situation of a siege by Roman soldiers not of an enemy city but of Roman citizens within Rome (such is the dangerously warping effect of cash), and *tota cohors* ('a whole cohort') (stressed by its position) means that escape is impossible. The epigram in line 18 conjures up a comic picture of troops looting attics – with pointed juxtaposition of *cenacula* ('garret') and *miles* ('a soldier') – and stands out thanks to the concision and contrast (between the safety of the poor and the vulnerability of the opulent, the garret and the preceding properties, and the single soldier and the whole cohort).

At 19ff. J. suddenly switches from the very rich and their difficulties to a level of wealth and problems more familiar to most readers' experience, getting extra impact by presenting something much closer to home, and advancing the idea that even moderate prosperity has serious drawbacks. By way of reinforcement he again links affluence with danger (and again dwells on the troubles of the man with property, briefly contrasting him with the pauper), but this time he strengthens his attack by adding the anxiety that possessions engender. In line 19 the notion of middling wealth is expressed by the emphatic placement of *pauca* ('a few') and *puri* ('unembossed'), by the diminutive *vascula* ('small vessels') and by the specification of silver rather than gold. At 20f. the concomitant peril and worry are brought out by the vivid vignette with its two verbs of fearing and two weapons to be feared (the menacingly juxtaposed *gladium contumque* ['swords and lances']), while the direct address really involves us by putting us right into that frightening scenario. One can easily infer that only a fool would expose himself to all that by praying for money. Something else that might put one off making such a request is the depiction of the reader as an undignified figure of fun when in possession of the bit of silver – in such a state of funk that even the shadow of a reed inspires terror – and *harundinis umbra* ('a reed's shadow') is deliberately delayed to the end of line 21 to underscore the absurd emptiness of the fear. There is another discouraging effect in line 19: *argenti vascula puri* ('small vessels of unembossed silver') figured at *Satire* 9.141 among the immodest desires of the repellent Naevolus,[19] so that the phrase here has a distasteful aura in general and associations of unreasonable aspiration in particular. In line 22 J. rounds off this quatrain too with a memorable *sententia* (cf. line 18). Brevity, end-stopping and sound (alliteration of *c* and *v*, assonance of *a*) draw attention to this epigram, which has added force in context: the blithe indifference of the pauper here (with *cantabit* ['will sing'] stressed by its position), when there actually is a mugger (underlined by the juxtaposition of *latrone* ['robber'] and *viator* ['traveller']), contrasts markedly with the fear and panic at 19–21, when there was only the shadow of a reed. In addition to the rather diverting picture of the insouciant wayfarer singing in the brigand's face (*vacuus* will mean 'free from anxieties' as well as 'empty-handed'),[20] there is irony in poverty being an asset (because the poor man is safe from attack).[21] Pointedly, the reader is no longer addressed in line 22 (the unworried traveller is someone else, not the reader). However, again there seems to be overstatement here (of the pauper's carefree state of mind), especially as there must be a danger of being roughed up during a search and being beaten up by a frustrated bandit.

The progression to prayer in line 23 is unexpected and lively, but it highlights the relevance of J.'s previous remarks to his main theme, and leads us back (at 24f.) to vast wealth (as at 12–14) and (at 25–7) to its perniciousness (as at 12–14), so that there is ring composition within this subsection. A whole line (23) on the frequency of a particular prayer (with the visual and aural effect of people urgently entreating in all the temples) provides a build-up by intriguing us as to the object of the petitions. The solution – the request is for *divitiae* ('riches') – leaps out as the first word in line 24, and then is repeated at 24f., with emphasis in the placement of *crescant* ('should grow') and *toto* ('whole') and in the juxtaposition of *maxima* ('biggest') and *toto*. The vigorous asyndeton, the dwelling, the increasingly demanding nature of the requests (for wealth; for more wealth; for the biggest strongbox in the centre for business and banking at Rome) and the tricolon crescendo, which puts the stress on the third and most covetous member, suggest the eager insistence of petitioners, their fixation with cash and their ever-mounting greed for it. All that seems decidedly misplaced after the preceding lines, and is immediately deflated by what follows too, with a sandwiching effect intended to make such requests appear ridiculous.[22]

J. may want us to bear in mind when we read lines 24–5 that *arca* ('strongbox') can also mean 'coffin'. At any rate, he definitely links riches with death for a third time at 25–7. Also, by way of reinforcement, in those verses he works in yet another quotable epigram (25f.), repeats the connection of affluence with anxiety – with *time* ('fear') in line 26 deliberately echoing *timebis* ('you'll fear') in line 20 – and again puts the reader in the hot seat by means of direct address. At 25f., *fictilibus* ('earthenware') is emphasized by its position as J. sets up an effective contrast between earthenware cups free from poisonous aconite and the much more expensive cups that do contain poison in line 26f. (a potent symbol of wealth and its inherent, lurking danger). Elsewhere earthenware was championed because of its use by (simple, pious) early Romans;[23] with a wry satirical twist, here in J.'s Rome it is superior not on moral grounds but for reasons of self-preservation. At 26f., J. moves on to the poisoned goblets and lingers longer on them to bring out the peril in verses that are both grim and blackly humorous. He presents a picture of great opulence in line 27 with expensive wine and wine cups – *gemmata* ('jewelled') and *auro* ('gold cup') encompass the hexameter – and spotlights the enticing glitter by means of *gemmata* and *auro* and *ardebit* ('glows'),[24] but this is all rather sinister, because it may well be a deceptive glitter and the costly wine in its sumptuous goblet – *Setinum* ('Setian wine') suggestively enclosed by *lato … auro* ('a broad gold cup') – is probably deadly. Adding to the bleakness here is the apposite echo (in thought and diction) of Seneca *Thyestes* 452f. – *tutusque mensa capitur angusta scyphus; / venenum in auro bibitur* ('a goblet is picked up in safety at a humble table; / poison is drunk in a gold cup') – because the reminiscence brings to mind the awful consequences for Thyestes, the speaker of those lines, of succumbing to a desire for wealth (and as a result his sons are killed, cooked and served up to him as a meal), and for Seneca, the writer of those lines, of having so much money.[25] There is also mockery and irony. All the luxury (which means that your prayers for great riches have been answered) may well turn out to be a literally poisoned chalice and is undermined in advance by *tunc illa time* ('fear that'). Agonizingly, this threat will operate at a time when you should be relaxed and enjoying yourself, and one of the great pleasures of being rich will be ruined, and you will face a cruel dilemma (to drink or not to drink the fine wine). So too the breadth of the gold cup means that more poison can be included, and the spondees and long vowels in line 27 have a spurious air of sadness. Here J. has in effect reduced the prayer for affluence to a prayer for worry and probable death!

Arrestingly at 28ff. J. veers right away from wealth and prayers, and moves from fools to sages and from fear to laughter. But the lines are logically integrated: as *igitur* ('so then') shows, J. is picking up directly the humorous (see 28f.) and grim (see 30) aspects of his preceding remarks and saying that, given all that, you have to approve of the attitudes of the two philosophers he mentions. Engagingly, in this subsection (28–53) the relevance of what J. says is not overtly enunciated, and readers are left to think and work out the point for themselves. What J. is in fact doing here is picking up from 9–27 and presenting at 35ff. things that many people aspire to (cf. 51) and pray for (cf. 54) and intimating that these too are misguided prayers (at 28ff. and 47ff. he is expressing support for philosophers who would have found such desires and their realization tragic or – in particular – risible). The thrust is not made crystal clear until line 54, where we see with *ergo* ('so then') that J. has been talking about things that are prayed for (*petuntur*), and that those things are *supervacua* ('pointless' and 'excessive'),[26] while the prayers before 28–53 were *perniciosa* ('destructive').

At 28ff. J. cites not just one but two respected Greek philosophers of the fifth and early fourth centuries BC (Democritus, who was moved to laughter by the spectacle of human life,[27] and Heraclitus, who was moved to tears by it) as sages who would have been critical of aspirations for the elements featured at 35ff., and he fosters approval of them from the start by means of *iamne ... laudas* ('surely you approve') and *sapientibus* ('wise men') in line 28 and *auctor* ('authority') in 30. (Should we automatically accept this commendation of these thinkers, especially in the mouth of one who earlier produced criticism of the Greeks?) In the allusions to the philosophers' responses at 28–33 (laughter, tears, laughter, tears, laughter) there is a notion of life as essentially tragicomic, and J. favours laughter by alluding to it most often and placing it first and last; he also spotlights it in line 31 – the placement of *cachinni* ('guffaw'), the novel expressions *censura cachinni* ('assessment of a guffaw') and *rigidi ... cachinni* ('stern guffaw'), and the (harsh and cackling) frequency of *c* – and keeps Democritus in our thoughts at 34ff. and 47ff. with the same effect (although lines 30 and 32 do mean that there is also much to sadden). This reflects J.'s own attitude in *Satire* 10 (our existence as represented there is a tragicomedy, and ridicule prevails over pathos) and encourages us to look for humour amid all the bleak gloom in the rest of the poem. There is a wittily appropriate pawkiness in the hyperbole in connection with Democritus: at 28f. he always laughs as soon as he places just one foot outside, and in line 33 he is permanently convulsed by mirth, with *perpetuo* ('permanent') and *solebat* ('was in the habit of') framing the line in prominent positions.[28] There is also in line 33 a suitably droll reminiscence of Ovid's recommendation concerning girls who want to attract men at *Ars Amatoria* 3.285, the only other surviving instance of *perpetuo risu* ('permanent laughter'): *nec sua perpetuo contendant ilia risu* ('they should not strain their sides with permanent laughter'). The echo of that light-hearted and mocking didactic poem comes with apt associations here. In addition, what Ovid specifically advised girls against ever doing was done continually by Democritus (who could not help himself, because everything was so comical). J. is thus changing Ovid right around, and the implication would appear to be that suppression of giggles may be appropriate for the trivial and closed world of the elegiac love affair, but the opposite holds true for the larger world of human life in general, as is proved by the great sage Democritus. So J. mischievously tops the expert on love with a more impressive expert, and inverts and twits a poet who loved to invert and twit others himself.[29]

In line 35 J. lists as things that Democritus would have found ludicrous the *toga praetexta* (a toga bordered with a purple stripe that was worn by the higher magistrates), the *trabea* (a short purple garment worn by equestrians on state occasions and by priests), the *fasces* (bundles of rods carried before the highest officials as a sign of their authority), litters (used by women of rank and by wealthy and fashionable men) and the platform where the more important magistrates sat and pronounced judgement. With punchy asyndeton J. packs into a single line a full five symbols of high and highly prized attainment, irreverently and unconventionally dismissing all those quintessentially Roman elements as risible. The (rather questionable) reduction of status, power and wealth to mere objects, presented baldly in a context of ridicule, is intended to deflate and provoke (in themselves, do clothes and a colour amount to anything; aren't bundles of sticks inherently grotesque; isn't it silly to be carried around (rather than walking) and to sit high up on show?). To bring out the emptiness further, there is mock grandeur in the sonority (the spondees and assonance) and the showy elegance of the ordering (two trisyllabic doublets frame the disyllabic *fasces*, and the first pair are clothes, while the second pair are forms of physical elevation). Then again, aren't appearances actually important to many people, rightly or wrongly?

At 36ff. J. narrows the focus to a single feature, which he develops at some length, expanding on the disrespectful jeering as he moves on to (in his eyes) still more laughable forms of transportation, elevation, clothing and symbols. The reference is to the *pompa circensis*, the procession preceding the games in the Circus Maximus, which was led by the presiding magistrate, riding in a chariot and dressed like a general at a triumph. Again J. is challenging his readers. The procession as he depicts it is absurdly bizarre, and we are, I think, meant to wonder if anyone who is actually impressed by such a hollow show (and has aspirations of his own in that direction) is not also absurd. Moreover, as becomes obvious in line 54, J. also views this whole business as not just ridiculous but also excessive (brought out by the length of the description as well as by the details) and pointless (he notably supplies no justification for it and leaves us to wonder why on earth all this pomp, which involves the aping of a general celebrating a major victory over Rome's enemies, is necessary to start off mere games).[30]

J. is facetious and mock solemn from the start. There is a grave spondaic rhythm in lines 36 and 37, and *currus altus* ('lofty chariot') in 36 is high style.[31] There may well be sport with other senses of *altus*, so that even the chariot is 'proud' and/or 'elevated'.[32] In line 37 *sublimem* ('high up'), which seems redundant, or *excessive*, after *altis* 'lofty', probably also embraces 'with lofty ambitions' and/or 'heroic' and/or 'eminent';[33] it is undercut by the immediately succeeding *pulvere* (mundane and sordid 'dust', which would be churned up and coat those in the procession). At 38f. J. moves on to the tunic embroidered with palms (*tunica Iovis*) and the purple toga embroidered with gold (the *toga picta*) which were kept in Jupiter's temple on the Capitol and were brought out for the occasion. Wearing two very ornate garments at once is meant to seem overdone, and the *toga picta* in particular receives an expression which is suitably bulky and bloated, and whose novelty[34] makes for an apt singularity and mock elevation. *Aulaea* ('hangings') conveys the idea of massive, heavy material hanging in great folds: its original sense is 'curtains' (a praetor dressed in curtains is freakish), and it was employed especially of curtains in the theatre (suggesting theatrical performance and sham here).[35] J. chooses *ferentem* ('carrying', rather than 'wearing') to denote the weight of the toga, and quite possibly plays on the 'endure' sense of the verb (because bearing such a heavy burden is a sore trial). At 39f. he progresses to the large crown of gold, which he gives an even lengthier description, so that it forms the third part of a tricolon crescendo of dwarfing ornamentation – at 38–40 the praetor only figures in *ferentem ex umeris* ('carrying on his shoulders') and is swamped by all the words for finery. The assonance (of *ae*) in line 39 and the spondees in line 40 add to the mockery. The crown's size is brought out by the dedication of a line and a half to it, by the emphatic placement of *magnae* ('large') and *tantum* ('so great'), and by the hyperbole in line 40. Ludicrously, at 41f. the diadem is too heavy to be worn and must be held over the praetor's head (by a slave, who is also there to remind the praetor that he is a mere mortal and should not get above himself); more than that, the crown is so weighty that holding it makes the slave sweat. The collocation of elaborately costumed praetor and sweaty slave in the same chariot is meant to seem queer and to undercut[36] (and in the Latin word order the public slave enfolds the magistrate, making it still easier to imagine the former's sweat dripping on to the latter). Given the grotesquerie of the *pompa circensis* as J. presents it, the very idea of the presiding magistrate thinking highly of himself is a sardonic joke. If *consul* is the correct reading in line 41,[37] most probably J. there increases the humour, by employing the word to represent the praetor's point of view and to show the way in which he *is* in fact getting above himself (thinking of himself as a higher official), so that the purpose clause ('so that …') is undermined and the slave's admonition becomes another absurdly superfluous and pointless element of the preposterous proceedings. In line 43, as if there wasn't enough costly elaboration already, J. includes the ivory sceptre with the top in the form of an eagle that was part of the paraphernalia. Again there is a specious air of solemnity, in the spondees, picking up from those in line 42, and in the lofty *sceptro … eburno* ('ivory sceptre').[38] In addition, instead of saying that the eagle is carved, J. uses *surgit* ('stands high') and, as that verb can also mean 'rise', he may well be trying to paint a surreal picture of the bird soaring up and away (to escape all the nonsense?).

At 44–6, to broaden his attack, he moves on to and duly subverts other members of the parade. A weighty five-word hexameter with a grave rhythm, 44 is an 'impressive' line to usher in further 'impressive' elements – the musicians blaring away, and the long train of the praetor's clients dressed in clean white togas (until the dust gets to them). At 44–5, the vacuous show is described with a showy arrangement of words: the balance and rhyme in *illinc … hinc* ('on this side … on that side'); the parallel order of epithets and nouns together with a chiasmus of cases in *praecedentia longi / agminis officia* ('the escort in a long line going in front'); the juxtaposition of *frena* ('bridles') and *Quirites* ('citizens'). In line 45 *niveus* ('snowy-white') is largely poetic[39] and is rarely used to mean 'clothed in white',[40] while *Quirites* is the formal term for citizens and *nivei Quirites* ('snowy-white citizens') is unique, so that there is a surface grandeur to the phrase. However, the adjective has connotations of coldness (cf. 46) and (ironically) purity, and in the same line *ad frena* ('at the bridles') hints at the Romans themselves being bridled.[41] There is further undercutting in line 46, where J. tacks on a whole hexameter to expose how fake the escort is by bringing it down to the sordid level of money – the diminutives *loculos* ('cashboxes') and *sportula* ('handout') help cut the attendants down to size. According to our cynical satirist, the great man has to buy his friends and to pay them to support him thus, while they are swayed entirely by mercenary motives (rather than by affection or respect). Furthermore, *defossa* ('buried') implies avarice and miserliness, while *amicos* ('friends') is heavily ironical, and there is the pointed internal rhyme in *loculos* and *amicos* (which links friendship with cash aurally). This is all meant to reflect badly on the magistrate and his train and to undermine the whole procession and anyone who is taken in by all the display. This comprehensive debunking is left uppermost in our thoughts when J. suddenly switches away from the *pompa circensis* in line 47.

At 47–53 J. achieves a neat ring structure by recalling 28ff. He returns to Democritus and his constant mirth (47f.; cf. 29f. and 33) and wisdom (48; cf. 28), and he repeats the key motifs of laughter (*risus* 47, *ridebat* 51; cf. *ridebat* 29) and tears (52; cf. 30 and 32). He praises Democritus too (cf. 28) in line 48 and especially 49, a ringing line which gives prominence to *summos* ('first-rate') and aligns him with other great intellectuals from his home town of Abdera.[42] That strong commendation also reinforces support for this philosopher who would have scoffed at prayers for the things mentioned at 35ff. And this wise man and genuinely fine role model is intended to make the praetor seem even more silly and negligible in retrospect (so J. claims at 47f. that Democritus found all aspects of life risible even in his day, i.e. before modern 'advances' like that magistrate's parade).

In line 50 our poet refers to the common notions that generally the inhabitants of Abdera were stupid[43] and that a thick atmosphere had a deleterious effect on the intellect. He tries thereby to ensure that Democritus stands out and appears even more impressive. He also works in some more wittily apt humour in connection with this philosopher: although *vervecum* ('wethers') stands for 'morons', the expression brings to mind a quaint image of a country of castrated sheep under a brooding atmosphere and produces paradoxes (how can humans be born in a land of sheep, and how can wethers father anything?). There is also some intertextual entertainment here. Several scholars have seen allusion to Horace *Epistles* 2.1.244 – *Boeotum in crasso iurares aere natum* ('you would swear that he had been born in Boeotia's thick climate') – and the echo does seem definite (the combination of *nascor* and *aere crasso* occurs elsewhere only in that verse of Horace, and *aere natum* appears at the end of the hexameter like J.'s *aere nasci*). Horace was talking about Alexander the Great, and his point was that he was so undiscriminating when it came to poetry (being pleased by the adulatory epic of the worthless Choerilus) that you would swear that he was a fool; in other words, someone who could be viewed as a first-rate man who set a great example (*Satire* 10.49) was so misguided that it seemed as if he had been born in a thick climate. With a diverting twist in his line J. comes out with somebody far from misguided who proves that first-rate men who set a great example actually *are* born in a thick climate.

At 51–3 J. is not just filling out the picture of Democritus's all-embracing laughter and continuing his support for him (as a man of independence and spirit, with an appealing common touch, who smiled in the face of adversity); he is also starting to link closely with the main body of his poem (56ff.). He subtly undermines in advance (by means of the wise philosopher's scorn) the preoccupations behind most people's prayers, which generally revolve around our *curae* (translated above as 'worries', but the word here will also mean 'devotion of attention', 'eagerness' and 'tasks'),[44] things that give us pleasure and cause us misery, and our reactions to misfortune. As part of his bleak world vision J. puts the stress on the negative side in the largely spondaic 51f. ('delights' are engulfed by 'worries' and 'tears' and 'threatening Fortune'), which also leads directly into the grim vignettes and pessimism at 56ff. There is a foreshadowing admixture of mockery and levity as well: *ridebat* ('used to laugh') is highlighted by its position and its plurality of objects; Democritus jeers at Fortune twice over, comically telling a goddess (and one who is therefore immortal) to hang herself and making an obscene gesture at her;[45] and in *mandaret laqueum* (literally: 'he used to assign a noose to threatening Fortune') there is sport with the verb's sense of committing someone or something to the care of a divinity.[46]

With the text accepted here,[47] as well as looking backwards (clarifying the point of 35ff.), lines 54–5 also look forwards, leading directly into the rest of the *Satire* by effectively announcing that J. will consider first (at 56ff.) the things that people do pray for but should not – *supervacua* (= 'pointless' and 'excessive') and *perniciosa* (= 'destructive') adumbrate the thrust of the attack on them – and then (at 346ff.) the things that we can pray for (and this promise of a constructive aspect tends to militate against an alienating effect for all the destructive criticism at 56ff., and encourages us to read on in the midst of it, and facilitates teasing via extensive retardation). These two engaging questions (with insistent alliteration of *q* and *p*) also contain a mixture of gloom and derision that suits well what follows. In line 54 there is grievous futility and destruction, but also dark humour in the juxtaposition *perniciosa petuntur* ('destructive things are prayed for') (as cretins actually ask for their own downfall). In line 55 the reference is to the practice of fastening votive offerings to divine statues with wax,[48] but the expression suggests the whimsical idea of the statues or (more likely, because still funnier) the gods themselves with wax all over their knees. Poking fun at even reasonable prayers like this (as well as being in the spirit of Democritus) fits with the attitude to such entreaties at 346ff.

Notes

1   For these senses of the word see *OLD* s.v. 1 and 2. Both are felt in the introduction and later in the poem (see 26n.).

2   Scholarly disagreement over the exact length of the introduction has a bearing on structure. See esp. Tengström, 3ff.; Campana, 48ff. It has been maintained that the introduction is formed by the first 11 lines, or the first 14, or the first 22; that there is a digression at 28ff.; and that 54f. are not part of the introduction and stand on their own (or should be deleted). It seems to me most obvious and natural to count as introduction everything that precedes the main body of the satire (= 56ff., lines which are set off as something distinct, with a series of sections that each treat in detail one particular prayer, prior to the conclusion); and, it should now be evident that lines 1–55 cohere well as a unit. I fail to see any manifest break at line 12 (where J. is just continuing with another example of something superficially attractive which is in fact fatal), at line 15 (where he moves on to examples to back up his point about riches being very dangerous) or at line 23 (where by talking about prayers for money he is highlighting the relevance to his main theme of the previous remarks on wealth, and is in fact ensuring ring composition within the subsection [12–27]: see the discussion of those lines later in this chapter). Nor do 12ff., 15ff. or 23ff. form a clear and coordinated section on their own, certainly not one on a par with those at 56ff.; and to posit a digression (especially when 28ff. are smoothly integrated: see the comments on that later in this chapter) smacks of desperation (or woolly thinking). Lines 54–5 are tied in to 1–53 by means of *ergo* ('so then') in line 54 and by the chiasmus and ring. They do not merit deletion: apart from being unobjectionable in themselves, they perform important structural functions (in the patterning just mentioned, and as the useful pivot described at the end of this chapter).

3   The text of Housman is employed. In this and the following chapters after the preface I provide text and translation of the section under consideration, so readers can go through the whole passage with the overview in mind and get the big picture. For the more detailed comment that follows, readers should refer back to the Latin or the English version sentence by sentence.

4   The translation here has no pretence to literary merit and is purely functional, intended to convey the basic sense of the Latin (as I see it) in order to facilitate appreciation for those with little or no Latin.

5   See *OLD* s.v. 1, 2, 3, 4.

6   See for example *Homeric Hymn* 5.218ff.

7 See Courtney, 37.

8 See *TLL* VI.1.62.22ff.; *OLD* s.v. 9b.

9 Such fulness of expression and in particular the phrase *copia dicendi* (*TLL* IV.903.48ff.) were common in Cicero (who was put to death because of his eloquence), so there might be a Ciceronian allusion here, prefiguring 114ff. For the river of words, Martin Winkler compares Manilius 2.8ff.

10 See esp. Mayor, ad loc.

11 See Ebel, ad loc.

12 It may seem surprising that Juvenal does not devote a whole section in the main part of X to the desire for riches, but he does give it a priority here that reflects its importance, and he does assail it with vigour. In addition, this theme is picked up in *Satires* 11 and 12, where it is developed at greater length and in greater detail than would be possible in a single section of this poem.

13 See Campana, 90.

14 See Ferguson, ad loc.

15 See *OLD* s.v. 1, 2, 3, 6.

16 See Ferguson, ad loc; Courtney, ad loc. Martin Winkler suggests to me that there may also be allusion to the fate of Crassus (molten gold poured into the mouth of his severed head at Cassius Dio 40.27).

17 On whales and Britain see Mayor, ad loc; Campana, ad loc. See also Pliny *N.H.* 9.4, 8; Tacitus *Ann.* 2.24.

18 See Mayor for references, and for the particularly unpleasant deaths of Seneca and Lateranus, which J. may well be hoping his readers will recall.

19 See Ferguson, 253; Courtney, 444.

20 See Ferguson, ad loc. See also *OLD* s.v. 12b.

21 See Romano, 159.

22 There is also subtle wit in putting *prima* ('number one') as the first word in line 23, in using a tricolon crescendo to depict increasing demand for riches and in making the member of the tricolon that contains *maxima* ('biggest') the longest of the three.

23 See, for example, my commentary on Tibullus 1.1.39–40.

24 *Ardebit* will certainly be part of the brilliance and so mean 'glow, sparkle', but there will also be play of the word's sense 'burn' (of the consuming effect of poison). The word could even mean that the wine 'is eager' (to kill). It is also possible that the wine 'is fiery' (i.e. strong). See Ferguson; Campana; *TLL* II.485.20ff., 487.39ff., 46ff.; *OLD* s.v. 3, 4, 6.

25 At the same time, J. tops Seneca with the specification of the poison (the insidious aconite had ominous associations, with Cerberus, Medea, Hecate and Prometheus's blood: see Mayor on 1.158; *TLL* I.419.80ff.) and with the expansion of the affluence in the more menacing line 27.

26 The excessiveness at 35ff. is immediately apparent, while the pointlessness can be seen there after a moment's reflection. Both aspects are very much in evidence at 56ff.

27   The laughter is hearty – *cachinnus* ('guffaw') in line 31 is used of a boisterous laugh; see also 33f. – but not inane and unreflecting, as *rigidi* ('stern') and *censura* ('assessment') in 31 make clear. See Plaza (2006), 36f.

28   There is similar exaggeration over Heraclitus's tears lines in 30 and 32. J. may well have taken from Seneca the contrast between the two wise men, the depiction of them laughing/crying when they went out and the championing of laughter over tears as a reaction (see Anderson, 340ff.; Campana). If this was the case, and J.'s readers saw it, our poet would thus have further philosophical support for his stance (as well as capping Seneca by means of the hyperbole). See further Romano, 158f.

29   On J.'s deflation of love elegy, see Jones, 127ff.

30   For this attitude, see 11.193ff. and Seneca *Controv.* I proem. 24.

31   Elsewhere, the phrase occurs at Manil. 1.363; Ovid *Met.* 2.105, 12.128; Sil. It. 17.487; Stat. *Theb.* 3.292, 430, 12.641.

32   See *OLD* s.v. 12, 13.

33   See *OLD* s.v. 7a, 7b, 8.

34   *Sarrana aulaea* ('purple hangings') and *aulaea togae* ('hangings of the toga') are unique. For elevation achieved via unusual language, see my commentary on Tibullus 2.1.5–6.

35   See Schmitz, 27f.

36   See Maier, 49f.

37   Many scholars have been perplexed by the praetor suddenly becoming a consul here (see esp. Campana). Some have emended the text, but no fully convincing conjecture has been offered yet, and in any case the mss reading does make good sense. In defence of *consul* it has been suggested that J. is moving from the praetor's procession to a triumph by a consul in line 41, but (as Courtney points out) *quippe* 'for' in 41 makes such a change most unlikely. Campana opines that *consul* may be used ironically, because the praetor in all his pomp seemed like a consul (comparing 11.194, where the praetor is likened to a triumphing general). More probable and more pointed is the explanation that he seemed like a consul *to himself* and that *consul* represents *his* point of view. This would be an engaging and bold form of expression (i.e. typically Juvenalian) and a neat and economical way of saying that the praetor *is* thinking highly of himself because he equates himself with the more important magistrate. I can find no exact parallel for such a use of *consul*, but there are enough analogies to make it feasible. There is similar looseness in the application of the word to consuls elect at Cicero *Phil.* 13.16. For a person's inflated viewpoint concerning himself, see Petronius *Sat.* 77, where Trimalchio describes himself as an *amicus* ('friend') (when he does not even know some of his guests and is exploited and despised by others) and as a *rex* ('king'). For the appellation in inverted commas as it were ('consul'), cf. *amicus* ('friend') in line 46 and at 5.173, and *bellus* ('smart') at Catullus 24.8. With a similar usurpation of titles, *coniunx* ('spouse') was employed of people who were only would-be or intending spouses (Catull. 64.123, 182; Ovid *Her.* 9.118; Virgil *Aen.* 3.331 and 9.138); *gener* is found of a 'son-in-law' to be (*Aen.* 2.344); and *domina* of one whom the reader would like to become his 'mistress' (Ovid *AA* 1.139, 421, 488, 504).

38 Elsewhere the phrase appears at Hom. Lat. *Ilias* 140; Ovid *Met.* 1.178, 7.103.

39 See Campana.

40 Elsewhere only at Calpurnius *Ecl.* 7.29.

41 See Ferguson, ad loc.; Tengström, 44.

42 Writers of philosophy, history and poetry (see Mayor in particular). Note also the sly point in *magna exempla daturos* (= setting a great example for J. and his readers).

43 Mayor (83) cites several ancient jokes about Abderites (e.g. having heard that leeks and onions produce wind, a citizen of Abdera on a ship caught in a storm hung a bag of them on the stern; and another one tried to hang himself, but the rope broke and he fell and cut himself, so he went to a doctor and got patched up, and then hanged himself again).

44 See *OLD* s.v. 1, 3, 6, 9.

45 On this gesture see esp. Mayor. In view of the general influence of Persius 2 on *Satire* 10, it is quite possible that J. consciously took the detail of the middle finger from 2.33. If so, it has been deftly transferred from something used seriously to ward off the evil eye by a foolish woman concerned about misfortune to something employed frivolously to show contempt by a sage completely unconcerned about misfortune.

46 See Ebel, 53. See also *TLL* VIII.263.3ff. and *OLD* s.v. *mando* 4a. On the attitude of Democritus and J. to Fortune, see Plaza (2006), 125f.

47 On the textual problems at 54f. see esp. Highet (1954), 278; Ebel; Tengström, 19ff.; Campana. Both line 54 on its own and lines 54 and 55 together have been deleted, unreasonably (see 2n.). The mss offer *ergo supervacua aut perniciosa petuntur* for 54. It has been argued that the final *a* in *supervacua* should be lengthened (in hiatus), but this does not seem tolerable (and the emendation *supervacuo* does not improve matters). It is most probable that a monosyllabic word dropped out after *supervacua*. Various supplements have been proposed. Of the most commonly accepted is Buecheler's *quae* (together with his punctuation of lines 54 and 55 as a pair of questions). This is palaeographically plausible (see Housman, ad loc.) and provides good sense, neat balance and a clear signpost for the rest of the poem, although certainty is not possible. At any rate, *supervacua* and *perniciosa petuntur* seem secure whatever supplement is accepted, so overall my interpretation is not seriously affected.

48 And/or perhaps the placing of wax tablets containing prayers on the knees of the statues, although the evidence for such a custom is problematical (see Mayor; Courtney; Campana).

CHAPTER FOUR

Power (56–113)

Here begins the main part of X, as J. picks up line 54 and begins to provide the 'proof' that humans pray for things that are *supervacua* ('pointless' and 'excessive') and *perniciosa* ('destructive'). In this section, he highlights the latter element in petitions for power; but, as he nowhere allows that *potentia* ('power') serves any useful purpose, they are also intended to seem meaningless, and the notion of excess comes out too, at 90ff., 104f. and 110. To smooth the transition, the gloomy and derisive mood of the questions at 54f. continues here, and some motifs from the introduction are taken up – destructiveness in line 54 (cf. *praecipitat* ['brings down'] in line 56, *mergit* ['overwhelms'] in line 57 and the demolition at 58ff.), statues in line 55 (cf. 58ff.) and the chariot in lines 36 and 42 (cf. 59f.). J. has already handled *potentia* and a potentate at 34ff. by way of a preliminary skirmish, and here he returns to them, treating them at greater length, and presenting a new (more ominous) take, as this time he adds and stresses invective (on top of mockery) and the pernicious aspect of power.

The satirist here mounts his attack in a long, densely packed and consistently pointed section, which makes effective use of *enargeia* (vividness), telling details (e.g. at 62–4), epigrams (at 81, 96f. and 112f.) and suggestive imagery (especially in lines 82 and 105–7). This is a wide-ranging assault on *potentia* from its highest to its lowest form, in the past and present, throughout the world (and in heaven and the Underworld), and various criticisms of it are made (it is limited, paltry, vulnerable, ephemeral and in particular it brings problems, degradation and death for its holder and those connected to him), while its possessors are shown as unattractive, and its trappings and perks are undermined.

With regard to structure, there is an artful progression: at 56ff. J. begins by observing that eminence is harmful for some (evident in the downfall of the unnamed *quosdam* ['some people']); at 61ff. he puts across the idea that it was really harmful for one person (seen in the downfall and death of the named and famous Sejanus); then at 108ff. he intimates that it is really harmful for countless people all over the world and always has been (evinced by the downfall and terrible deaths of named and famous Romans and very many others). At the core of the section the main thrust comes via Sejanus (a good example to support J.'s case, presented forcefully); on either side of him, by way of reinforcement, there are groups of other grandees who form a frame at lines 56–60[1] and 108–13; and the ring is strengthened by echoes of theme (downfall) and words (*magnus* in lines 56 and 111; *descendo* in 58 and 113; *caedo/caedes* in 60 and 112).

Again there is problematizing, and readers have to be on the alert, as among various palpable hits on J.'s target there is also cynicism, pessimism, dubious generalization and a largely one-sided point of view. So J. does not actually say that *potentia* is always bad, but he is dismissive of it at the lower levels, and presents it as almost always entailing trouble and death for humans at the higher level (97f., 108ff.). And he strongly plays up the negative side, putting it across to us strongly and repeatedly, while downplaying and subverting the positive aspects of predominance. As ever, it is important for readers not to let themselves be swept along by J.'s words but to question and reflect on them (and my interpretation of them).

Our poet's critical attitude to power and politicians will strike a chord with many readers today, and his challenging treatment of this topic should get us thinking. We may counter his vision and object that *potentia* can be used selflessly for the general good, but how often *is* this the case? And what does it actually consist of and amount to? How stable is it? Is it really something impressive? And what does wielding it actually achieve in the long run and in the grand scheme of things? These are big questions, to which, stimulatingly, the satirist provides only partial answers. The Latin text is as follows:

> *quosdam praecipitat subiecta potentia magnae*
> *invidiae, mergit longa atque insignis honorum*
> *pagina. descendunt statuae restemque secuntur,*
> *ipsas deinde rotas bigarum inpacta securis*
> *caedit et inmeritis franguntur crura caballis.*   60
> *iam strident ignes, iam follibus atque caminis*
> *ardet adoratum populo caput et crepat ingens*
> *Seianus, deinde ex facie toto orbe secunda*
> *fiunt urceoli, pelves, sartago, matellae.*
> *pone domi laurus, duc in Capitolia magnum*   65
> *cretatumque bovem: Seianus ducitur unco*

spectandus, gaudent omnes. 'quae labra, quis illi
vultus erat! numquam, si quid mihi credis, amavi
hunc hominem. sed quo cecidit sub crimine? quisnam
delator quibus indicibus, quo teste probavit?'   70
'nil horum; verbosa et grandis epistula venit
a Capreis'. 'bene habet, nil plus interrogo'. sed quid
turba Remi? sequitur fortunam ut semper et odit
damnatos. idem populus, si Nortia Tusco
favisset, si oppressa foret secura senectus   75
principis, hac ipsa Seianum diceret hora
Augustum. iam pridem, ex quo suffragia nulli
vendimus, effudit curas; nam qui dabat olim
imperium, fasces, legiones, omnia, nunc se
continet atque duas tantum res anxius optat,   80
panem et circenses. 'perituros audio multos'.
'nil dubium, magna est fornacula'. 'pallidulus mi
Bruttidius meus ad Martis fuit obvius aram;
quam timeo, victus ne poenas exigat Aiax
ut male defensus. curramus praecipites et,   85
dum iacet in ripa, calcemus Caesaris hostem.
sed videant servi, ne quis neget et pavidum in ius
cervice obstricta dominum trahat'. hi sermones
tunc de Seiano, secreta haec murmura vulgi.
visne salutari sicut Seianus, habere   90
tantundem atque illi summas donare curules,
illum exercitibus praeponere, tutor haberi
principis angusta Caprearum in rupe sedentis
cum grege Chaldaeo? vis certe pila, cohortes,
egregios equites et castra domestica; quidni   95
haec cupias? et qui nolunt occidere quemquam
posse volunt. sed quae praeclara et prospera tanti,
ut rebus laetis par sit mensura malorum?
huius qui trahitur praetextam sumere mavis
an Fidenarum Gabiorumque esse potestas   100
et de mensura ius dicere, vasa minora
frangere pannosus vacuis aedilis Ulubris?
ergo, quid optandum foret, ignorasse fateris
Seianum; nam, qui nimios optabat honores
et nimias poscebat opes, numerosa parabat   105
excelsae turris tabulata, unde altior esset
casus et inpulsae praeceps inmane ruinae.

quid Crassos, quid Pompeios evertit et illum,
ad sua qui domitos deduxit flagra Quirites?
summus nempe locus nulla non arte petitus   110
magnaque numinibus vota exaudita malignis.
ad generum Cereris sine caede ac vulnere pauci
descendunt reges et sicca morte tyranni.

Power exposed to great envy brings down some people,
a long and distinguished record of honours overwhelms
them. The statues come down, and follow the rope,
then an axe dashed against them splits open the very wheels
of chariots, and the legs of undeserving nags are smashed.   60
Now the fires are hissing, now thanks to the bellows and furnaces
the head that was worshipped by the people glows and great
Sejanus crackles; then from the face that was number two in the
     whole world
are made little jugs, basins, frying pans, chamber pots.
Place laurel on your house, drag up to the Capitol a large bull   65
whitened with chalk: Sejanus is being dragged along by a hook,
worth looking at, all rejoice. 'What lips, what a face
he had. I never liked this fellow, if you believe me
at all. But on what charge was he convicted, which
informer by means of which betrayers, which witness(es)
     proved his case?'   70
'None of that. A wordy and lengthy letter came from
Capri'. 'Fine. No more questions'. But what of
Remus's mob? They follow fortune, as always, and hate
the condemned. The same people, if Nortia had favoured the
Etruscan, if the aged emperor had been overpowered   75
off his guard, at this very hour would be calling Sejanus
emperor. Long ago, ever since we stopped selling our votes
to anyone, they discarded their responsibilities; for those who once
bestowed power, *fasces*, legions, everything now restrain
themselves and anxiously pray for only two things –   80
bread and races. 'I hear many will die'.
'No doubt; the oven is large'. 'My Bruttidius was
rather pale when he met me by the altar of Mars.
How I fear that the "defeated Ajax" may exact punishment
for having been poorly defended. Let's run headlong and,   85
while he lies on the bank, let's trample Caesar's enemy.
But let the slaves see, so that none of them can deny it and drag

his frightened master to court with a rope around his neck!'
   These were the
remarks about Sejanus then, these were the secret whispers of the
   common people.
Do you want to be called on like Sejanus, to have as much
   as him   90
and to give one man the highest curule offices,
to put another in charge of armies, to be regarded as the guardian
of the emperor who is sitting on a narrow crag on Capri
with his flock of Chaldaeans? Certainly you want the javelins,
   cohorts,
splendid cavalry and a personal camp; why shouldn't you   95
desire them? Even those who don't want to kill anyone
want to be able to. But what prestige and prosperity are worth
   so much
that you are willing to have trouble in equal measure to success?
Do you prefer to take up the *toga praetexta* of this man who is
   dragged along
or to be the man in power at Fidenae or Gabii, and to   100
lay down the law about measurements, to smash vessels that are
too small as a raggedy *aedile* in empty Ulubrae?
So you admit that Sejanus did not know what
to pray for. For he who prayed for excessive honours
and demanded excessive power was building up many storeys   105
of a lofty tower, so that from it there would be a fall from
higher up and a terrible sheer drop of the toppled debris.
What brought down the Crassi, what the Pompeii and the man
who tamed the Romans and brought them under his lash?
Why clearly the top position sought by every trick in the book   110
and prayers for greatness heeded by malignant deities.
Few are the kings who go down to Ceres's son-in-law without
   slaughter
and wounds, few the tyrants who go down due to a bloodless death.

Aptly enough, there is no quiet start to this section. The poet immediately
involves us with quite graphic and violent aperture (although worse follows,
so this is part of the careful gradation) and a considered and vigorous attack
on two superficially appealing aspects of dominance – external trappings
(plaques and statues) and adulation.

Helpfully, in line 56 *potentia* ('power') soon makes it clear which
particular prayer is being dealt with here, but the undermining begins even

before we reach the word *potentia*. The deleterious effect of political power is foregrounded by *praecipitat* (second in the sentence), a pregnant term (combining the meanings 'hurls down', 'causes to fall to death', 'reduces in rank' and 'brings to ruin')[2] which involves disturbing personification (Power turns on the men and gives them a push, presumably from a height, as at 104ff.). *Subiecta* also precedes *potentia* in the text. The primary meaning of *subiecta* is 'exposed to', but J. will be playing on the sense 'having an inferior status' to intimate that even power itself is subject to something[3] – so too it is *invidia* ('envy'), not *potentia*, that gets the epithet *magnus* ('great'). *Potentia* is immediately succeeded by *magnae* and *invidiae* (both stressed by their positions), as J. specifies what he sees as an inevitable drawback (but whether or not there is great envy surely depends on the extent, nature and circumstances of another's power). As well as ensuring that the lone *potentia* is swamped by negative aspects like this, J. is careful to open with a picture of power ended (not held or enjoyed, which might make it seem attractive to readers). He reinforces the impact in the rest of his opening sentence at 57f. There the (exaggerated and grotesque) picture is probably that of massive plaques[4] (of bronze or marble, containing lists of the men's distinctions, attached to their statues) falling on top of the men, rendering the powerful totally powerless and crushing them. All their achievements lead only to death, and their own plaques kill them! The emphatically sited *mergit* deflates beforehand the long and distinguished record of honours and combines various senses ('overwhelms', 'plunges in ruin', 'buries' and 'covers over'),[5] to convey the notion of complete destruction. Here, as often below, eminence ends in diminution and death, so that praying for it is meant to seem pointless.

In the next sentence, *descendunt* ('come down') is the last in a series of a full three foregrounded main verbs denoting a fall from power and presented with an asyndeton that is punchy and suggests the speed of events. In *restemque secuntur* ('and follow the rope'), J. increases the damage and disrespect, with the statues dragged through the streets, and is very probably playing on the man of power (via the statue that represents him) no longer commanding but 'following' (and following a *rope* at that!). In *descendunt … secuntur*, attention is drawn to this meaningful vignette of statues toppled and dragged off via chiasmus (of verbs and nouns), juxtaposition (of statues and the rope attached to them – *statuae restemque*), isocolon, alliteration and assonance. At 59f. (and presumably in 58 too, as we suddenly realize),[6] pointedly, J. will have in mind images of men celebrating triumphs, and the fall from such a high point of attainment and honour brings out well how hollow and vulnerable are the trappings of even very great power. The hissing sigmatism and clattering consonants in line 58 continue in 59–60, adding to the graphic effect.[7] The total destruction conveyed by means of the three violent verbs at 59f. and the attack on the chariot and horses (as well as the representation of the man himself) demonstrate the extent of the *invidia* ('envy') and the frailty of such seemingly impressive symbols of might. There may well be a wry twist in line 59, with one sign of *potentia* employed against another (axes were carried in front of the highest Roman magistrates to denote their authority). In line 60 the colloquial *caballis* ('nags'), highlighted by its position and conjunction with the poetic word *immeritis* ('undeserving'),[8] diminishes the team of horses and so too the human driving them.[9] Some quirky humour also undercuts them (and him): *immeritis* suggests that representations of animals could somehow deserve such treatment and that, quite illogically, the poor horses are being subjected to a common form of punishment[10] for what the man did, while J.'s expression in line 60, by not specifying statues, conjures up a picture of real horses having their legs broken.

At 61ff. our poet now concentrates on one statue[11] and one particular man, stepping up from people who celebrated triumphs to one of the greatest potentates in Rome, as is suddenly and startlingly revealed in line 63 with the deliberately delayed *Seianus* (stressed by its position at the end of its clause and the start of the line). During the reign of Tiberius, Sejanus built up immense influence as the commander of the Praetorian Guard, and he virtually ran Rome and the empire after Tiberius retired to Capri, until his downfall and execution in 31 AD, on account of his aspirations for supreme power (according to the ancient accounts). He is a good example to support J.'s case, because after achieving so much he famously fell so far, supposedly due to his ambition for still more *potentia* (although one can reasonably protest that not all magnates are bad and suffer a decline like him). The satirist presents a selective, impressionistic sketch of the fall, omitting the background and build-up to it (so that it has dramatic suddenness) and distorting the chronological order of events for negative effect (he foregrounds the destruction of the statue and maltreatment of the corpse, mentioning only later the letter from Tiberius which brought it about). He zooms in on supposedly representative Romans and achieves an unsettling immediacy by means of direct speech that shows adulation turned to vilification. Also functional is the closure, because the final picture of Sejanus (at 86–9) is of his body being trampled, a concretization of his decline with strong visual appeal (like the melted head at 61ff.). At the same time, in the lines on Sejanus we should also see satire on those writers, like Tacitus and Pliny, who criticized the past with a ready indignation.[12]

At lines 61–4 J. again opens with a vision of potency finished, showing us first a demeaned Sejanus – his statue being melted down, not the man himself (who has already been toppled and killed: see 65ff.) – and again he employs quite violent main verbs (for the purpose noted above). He also highlights three times the great might which Sejanus had attained and carefully undermines it each time. Line 61, with its dramatic and significant repetition of *iam* ('now'), is dominated by (hissing) fire, bellows and furnaces, to bring out the idea of determined and total demolition (reinforced by the intensity of the fire evident in the glowing and crackling in line 62, with onomatopoeia in the sputtering consonants). In 62 *adoratum* ('worshipped') refers to the divine honours paid to Sejanus,[13] while the juxtaposed *ardet* ('glows') shows that not even his statue was immortal (so his 'divinity' was only a temporary, false one). *Ingens* ('great') means primarily 'large' (of the statue) but also suggests 'powerful', 'proud, heroic', 'haughty' and 'intimi-dating'[14] (of the man), and it too is subverted in advance by a juxtaposed verb. Once more, because the satirist does not specify a statue, there is some freakish and debunking humour: the expression briefly brings to mind a picture of Sejanus's actual head on fire and the man himself crackling (rather than speaking with authority, issuing orders, etc.). At 63f. Sejanus is built up for a third time – in the grandiose second half of line 63, where *facies* ('face') is well chosen, as we tend to view the face as being largely the essence of a person – only to be pulled down, by the list in line 64 (with hard-hitting asyndeton) of the utensils into which the impressive visage is transformed. In line 64 J. conveys extensive degradation by including so many (mundane, trivial and little) items, by grouping together four nouns confined to prose and lowly poetic genres, by starting with the diminutive *urceoli* ('little jugs') – offsetting *ingens* ('great') in line 62 – and by ending with the supreme indignity of *matellae* ('chamber pots'). So too the representation of the man who was in command of so many people and who was worshipped in all seriousness is now made into things that serve people and are comically urinated on,[15] while the line with the asyndetic list recalls line 35 and offers an effective contrast with it.

At 65f. the narrative is interrupted abruptly by a couple of imperatives which enjoin open rejoicing over the demise of Sejanus for all to see, especially the agents of Tiberius: at 65ff., and also at 81ff., the emperor is a sinister figure in the background who diminishes Sejanus's power and functions as an off-putting representative of power himself. The outer doors of houses were decorated with laurel on happy occasions, and the bull is to be offered publicly at Jupiter's temple on the Capitoline Hill in thanksgiving for the emperor's safety. To underline the loyalty to Tiberius, the bull will be large (i.e. costly) and all-white (to ensure ritual correctness); but here too there is sham and hollow show, as chalk is to be used to cover any dark spots.[16] Unfortunately, in connection with the imperatives, there is uncertainty over the speaker and the addressee. The ancient scholiast thought that lines 65–7 are supposed to have been spoken by one Roman to another at the time of Sejanus's collapse, and some modern critics agree. However, it would be much more functional if these words were addressed by J. to his readers (compare 329ff.), with an arresting turn that puts us right there in Rome at the time of the end of Sejanus and gets us involved in events, trying to save our own skins in case we are reported to the authorities for lack of enthusiasm (prior to overhearing comments by others there at 67ff.).

In any case, in the second half of line 66 we move from maltreatment of Sejanus's statues to maltreatment of his corpse, at a very grim moment (after execution, the bodies of criminals were dragged by a hook under the chin to the Gemonian Steps and left there to be abused for three days before being thrown into the Tiber). This is our first view of the actual man himself, and he is dead and damaged, completely diminished and impotent.[17] There is reinforcement and progression here, as what happens to the corpse is more personal and even worse than what happened to the images (according to ancient belief, his ghost would bear the physical disfigurement for all eternity).[18] There are also reversals which bring out the extent of his decline: instead of killing others, he has been killed; he is now a sight to see in his death and disgrace rather than as a great man; and he inspires joy (in place of adulation and fear). In line 67 (with its grave spondees), *spectandus* ('worth looking at') is given prominence by its position and intimates not only that Sejanus is a spectacle but also that he is worth scrutinizing[19] (as one who gives an important lesson about *potentia*). *Omnes* ('all') is also stressed by placement, and here there is not just joy for public consumption but people will be genuinely happy to see one of the high and mighty fallen, especially a malignant grandee like Sejanus (the fragile and dubious nature of popular backing further detracts from his supremacy).

At the end of line 67 there is a sudden switch to direct speech, resulting in a vividness and immediacy that really make the (eloquent) fall of Sejanus come alive for readers.[20] Those harsh words (uttered while the corpse is actually being dragged along) begin with low abuse of Sejanus's appearance (as being haughty and/or ugly), which contrasts strongly with *adoratum populo caput* ('the head that was worshipped by the people') in line 62, and which is expressed with animated and forceful repetition, asyndeton and alliteration (the latter continues down to line 70). Then, to reinforce the present distaste, comes a careful denial of past affection, in which the verb *amavi* ('liked') will embrace 'felt affection for' and 'esteemed, supported'[21] to extend the renunciation, and *hominem* ('fellow') has a contemptuous nuance.[22] Whether the denial is genuine or not, the speaker is keen not to be seen as an adherent of Sejanus, and the comically jittery *si quid mihi credis* ('if you believe me at all') betrays his unease. In either case, this all subverts the positions of power that Sejanus had and the speaker himself now enjoys (he is in the ascendant at present, but clearly feels at risk, prior to the purge of Sejanus's family and supporters). At 69f. there is perturbation in the flurry of questions with asyndeton, assonance and clattering consonants. All this has its bleakly amusing side, because the presumption of due legal process is completely wrong,[23] and because there is a rebound in the notion of Sejanus himself being a victim of the informers whom he encouraged and in him actually suffering the same death without a trial to which he had subjected others. More seriously, the collocation of informer, betrayers and witness(es) underscores the fact that even Sejanus's extreme *potentia* was vulnerable (to such people); and the automatic assumption that a *delator* ('informer') is at work amounts to criticism of the dark days of the reign of Tiberius (whose authority was bolstered by so many of these dubious characters).

Lines 71f. look to the long and ambiguous letter from the emperor read out in the senate, which contained some censure of Sejanus and the instruction that he should be kept under guard, and which was interpreted to mean that he should be imprisoned and executed (and so he promptly was). Here we see how tenuous his sway was (just an epistle from Tiberius with no specific directive ensures his demise). There is also a negative take on the emperor as a wielder of power: the wording *venit / a Capreis* ('came from Capri') – rather than something like 'was sent by Tiberius' – represents him as an ominous unseen force, and the reference to Capri reminds us of the cruelty and perversion in which he was reputed to have indulged there; his use of his authority here to bring about Sejanus's death is malevolent and corrupt; and he has created such a climate of fear that people are afraid to refuse what seems to be his wish for murder and to question or criticize it afterwards. Were J.'s readers meant to read between the lines here and see relevance in the sketch of Tiberius to the contemporary imperial set-up? In line 71 – with its curt *nihil horum* ('None of that') and grave rhythm – there is pawkiness in the expression: the allusion to the letter is aptly vague and unspecific, and *verbosa* ('wordy') and *grandis* ('lengthy') are suitably long-winded; the latter adjective also probably has in addition to its primary meaning the senses 'powerful', 'of consequence' and 'illustrious',[24] to form a wry contrast with Sejanus's current state as a result of the epistle. In line 72 the speaker shows a quick and craven acceptance of extraordinary goings-on, and there is marked irony in *bene habet* ('Fine') (of the killing of a high-ranking Roman citizen without trial on the basis of an obscure letter with no actual charge or command to execute sent by a renowned pervert in semi-retirement) and in *nil plus interrogo* ('No more questions') (when he should be asking many more – what Sejanus did to justify his death, how Tiberius could secure it in this way, etc., etc.). Campana also points out that the common use of the verb *interrogo*, of judicial questioning and examination, underlines the illegality of the proceedings here.

At the end of line 72 J. breaks in again, with an engaging question about the plebs of Rome, which suddenly reveals that the speakers in the previous verses were Romans of some standing. In line 73, *turba Remi* ('Remus's mob'), which is unique (and so takes the attention), implies antithesis between the old Romans and their degenerate descendants,[25] and also disparagingly links the plebeians with a loser (someone who, like them, had shared power but forfeited it).[26] Some may feel that the prejudice and snobbery here undermine J.'s stance, and he may well have wanted them to feel that. The contemptuous tone of that phrase is complemented by their behaviour in the following verses. At 73f. they are misguided enough to follow fortune (contrast 52f. and 365f.) and promptly replace veneration with hatred, so that the affection, esteem and support of such people (a superficially attractive perk of authority) seem hollow and worthless (a point reinforced below). Gloomy spondees predominate at 74–8; and at the start of line 74 *damnatos* ('the condemned'), in emphatic position, is well chosen: in view of Sejanus's situation, the verb cannot have its common sense of formally 'condemn' in a court (so that the absence of legality is again raised) but must mean 'find fault with' and/or 'discredit' and/or 'doom' (to death).[27] At 74f. J. refers to Nortia, an Etruscan goddess of fortune who had a temple at Volsinii (Sejanus's birthplace in Etruria). There is a sardonic touch in this deity spurning a man from her own land who was a well-known worshipper of fortune[28] and in the Latin word order (which puts the Etruscan in close contact with non-favouring Nortia). We also see that Sejanus's *potentia* was restricted (he was inferior to this divinity, as well as to Tiberius) and dependent on mere chance, while *Tusco* ('the Etruscan') brings up the theme of transience again briefly and obliquely (the Etruscans had been dominant before the rise of Rome). In the rest of the sentence of lines 74–7 the mob is again presented as contemptible, with *Augustum* ('emperor') deliberately delayed to spotlight their fickleness. We are also shown (amid rather sinister sigmatism) that even the power of the *princeps* is ephemeral and frail, in view of his old age (which prompts us to think of a basic limitation to power – its possessors grow old, and feeble, assailable, and then die), and raises of the possibility of assassination and the allusion to his actual death subsequently: *oppressa* ('overpowered') often means 'smothered',[29] as Tiberius later was). So too *secura* ('off his guard') brings out another off-putting drawback – the dangers of relaxing when prominent.[30]

At 77–81 J. continues his assault on the plebs, and displays in their case too the transitory nature of *potentia*, conveying again the extent of the fall from eminence, by depicting them as now frivolous, irresponsible and insignificant (there are problems here: if the plebeians were as impotent as our negative poet claims, by disparaging them he is here presenting to the reader not power but its *absence* as something unappealing; and it can be objected that in imperial times they did have some influence in connection with the acquisition and retention of high position).[31] At 77f. the wry (and emphatically sited) *vendimus* ('selling') instead of *damus* ('giving')[32] contains further digs at *potentia*: in the republican period, the people abused their position for money, and politicians relied on bribery for theirs. In line 78, the pregnant *curas* (translated as 'responsibilities' but also meaning 'serious attention', 'devotion of attention', 'concern' and 'zeal')[33] criticizes the mob strongly by intimating that they are not interested in affairs of state at all. In line 79, with vigorous asyndeton and fulness of expression, the satirist brings out the great power which the people once possessed and whose loss, amazingly, does not bother them (and the asyndetic list including the *fasces* recalls line 35, so that there is further undermining in the suggestion that even the administrative and military authority that they conferred had its laughable side). J. goes on to claim that in place of what they had, all they want now is food and entertainment, which was provided by the emperor,[34] so that they are manipulated and there has been a total reversal of power. *Se continet* ('restrain themselves') is sarcastic (as they are actually *under* control), and *anxius* ('anxiously') sneers at their desperation for trivia (instead of anxiety for Rome and the empire) amid clear contempt for their selfishness and foolishness. The whole sentence builds to the artfully delayed *panem et circenses* ('bread and races') in line 81 (referring to the free distribution of corn at Rome and the chariot races in the Circus Maximus). The long syllables are mock-solemn, and both words are stressed by their position, highlighting the mean items that the people desire (as yet another prayer is demolished). There is effective antithesis between the two things they now want to be given (conveyed with brevity) and all the (more imposing) things that they used to give others (occupying most of line 79). This reveals their degeneration in general and their present impotence in particular, and also the despicable poverty of their aspirations: what they crave is the most basic subsistence (the bread here may be intended as a spin on early Roman simplicity) and a low level of entertainment[35] (at which they are passive, in contrast to the activity of all the bestowing at 78f.). *Panem et circenses* has force and has proved to be very quotable, but there is problematizing once more. There is pessimistically sweeping generalization and over-simplification here: this cannot have held true of all the Roman commons, as at least some of them would have felt strong desire for food other than bread, and for other types of shows (gladiatorial etc.), and for other things as well (wine, sex, etc.). In fact, the other prayers assigned to people in the rest of this poem contradict the claim of just two cravings made here.[36]

In the middle of line 81 there is an arresting lurch (in a short, shocking sentence that stands out in opposition to the much longer one at 77–81) from the mundane, peaceful and relaxed *panem et circenses* (where bread ensures the continuation of life) to extraordinary and terrifying massacre. The impact is heightened by the juxtaposition of *circenses* ('races') and *perituros* ('will die'), by the emphatic positioning of *perituros* and *multos* ('many') and by the unexpected and unannounced return to direct speech. At first readers may think that these are still the words of the poet, and even when one works out that he is now again quoting Romans at the time of Sejanus's downfall, one is left wondering (until line 89) who exactly these speakers are. All of this fits with the confusion of the moment in Rome. In the response in line 82, J. jokes about this with *nil dubium* ('no doubt'), when in fact there is lots of doubt (e.g. about who is speaking, and to whom, and who will die). There is also realism here, in the (panicky) immediate acceptance of a (typically vague and fearful) rumour despite the absence of any source or basis for it, and in the building on it (going one better) with *magna est fornacula* ('the oven is large').[37] It seems likely that *fornacula* denotes an oven (as used to bake bread) rather than a furnace (to work metal etc.),[38] because there would then be a sardonic twist to *panem* ('bread') in line 81 (like the one to the *circenses* in the humans' headlong gallop before an audience at 85ff.). But whatever the precise sense of *fornacula*, there is a singular and horrifying image here, which recalls (and outdoes) the bronze bull in which the barbarous tyrant Phalaris reportedly burned alive one man at a time.[39] It suggests inhumanly cruel killing and conjures up a picture of agony and death *en masse* with no chance of escape or survival (and writhing, blackening, dripping, screaming figures). The allusion at 81f. is to the large number of Sejanus's friends, family and supporters executed by Tiberius, and this image strengthens J.'s satirical points here, implying that power can lead not just to death but a terrible death for many people connected with the magnate, and bringing out the dreadfulness of Tiberius's abuse of his position (and so also making the potentate and *potentia* seem repellent).

With the remark about Bruttidius at 82f. the (very apt) unsettling confusion continues. Although Bruttidius is presumably someone who is now pale with fear because he had been or could be seen as having been to some extent an adherent of Sejanus, we cannot tell exactly who he is,[40] what precisely is his relationship to the speaker, what the tone of the comment is (e.g. concern? schadenfreude?) or why Bruttidius and the speaker were near the altar of Mars (in the Campus Martius). There are ominous associations (and probably grim humour) in that setting for their encounter: Mars was a god of violence, slaughter and vengeance, while an altar connotes sacrifice to a greater being of constrained and helpless victims, and *pallidulus* ('rather pale') may play on the whiteness of the sacrificial animal (mentioned at 65f.) as well as hinting at the pallor of death. At 84f. the speaker fears that Tiberius may feel that he was not properly protected against Sejanus's machinations and punish those who failed to defend him. He likens the emperor to Ajax, who lost the contest for the arms of Achilles (to be awarded after his death to the bravest of the Greeks at Troy), and subsequently wanted revenge and (driven mad by Minerva) massacred sheep/cattle under the impression that they were Greek leaders, and then committed suicide. The basic idea is that Tiberius may similarly kill in a vengeful spirit.[41] The oblique allusion to the emperor will be due to a cautiousness natural in such a situation on the part of the intimidated speaker,[42] who will certainly be intending a positive comparison of Tiberius to a major hero. However, comically, he seems quite unaware that he could get himself into serious trouble by pairing the *princeps* with a murderous madman (the interlocutor could well inform on him). And, at another level, the satirist is exploiting that negative aspect, summoning up a picture of Tiberius (like Ajax) on a demented rampage of revenge slaughtering innocent victims, and with heavy irony equating the sinister pervert of Capri (cf. 93f.) with an illustrious and revered character of epic and tragedy who was a figure of real pathos. In this way the supreme representative of power in the contemporary world is made to appear still more repulsive. And our poet extends the attack on *potentia* by alluding to the (diminishing) defeat and downfall of one of the major leaders of the past, whose power proved to be transitory and inferior to that of another (Minerva).

The unpleasantly menacing influence of Tiberius is also intimated by the realistically panicked reaction at 85f. (where the speaker fears that the absence of a show of hostility to Sejanus may be observed and reported). There may well be a disdainful nuance to *praecipites*: the primary meaning is 'headlong' but J. quite possibly has an eye to the 'impetuous, acting precipitately' sense of the word.[43] So too in line 86 *iacet* will embrace 'lies', 'lies helpless', 'is brought low' and 'lies in death',[44] to put across the comprehensiveness of Sejanus's decline. That notion is also conveyed by the nasty and violent *calcemus Caesaris hostem* ('let's trample Caesar's enemy') with its onomatopoeia and animated frequency of *c* and *s*. There is dark humour in the sight of what the ambitious Sejanus actually achieved in the long run (his own death and degradation) and in the inversions (instead of being the emperor's helper and partner,[45] he is now his enemy; so far from being worshipped by the people (62), he is physically and verbally abused; and instead of being the second most influential man in the world (63), he is totally impotent).

At the same time, J. is also critical of the speaker there: the verb *calco*, which was used (especially in epic) of trampling enemies underfoot in the press of battle,[46] highlights how cowardly and unheroic this action is (done in a non-military context to an already dead person exposed on the bank of the Tiber). The injunction at 87f. (with its forceful alliteration) comes as an unexpected and amusing addition, representing a sly afterthought and humiliating reversal of 'not in front of the servants'.[47] It makes the point that *potentia* is fragile not only at the highest level but all the way down to ordinary Roman citizens (in relation to their slaves), and the dragging of the man with the rope around his neck forms a clear link with the treatment of Sejanus's statue in line 58. In addition, the actual possession of power is given a negative spin again: the inversion here whereby masters are so afraid of their slaves (who could lay information about their owners in cases of treason) shows the grim panic brought about by the emperor and his practice of encouraging informers, while the idea of despised slaves having power like this would be appalling to the poet's readers. At the end of line 88 and in 89 there is an arresting suddenness as J. breaks in again to round off this sketch of the fall of Sejanus (with gloomy gravity in the rhythm). Here he finally reveals that the speakers at 81ff. were plebeians (picking up naturally from 72ff., as members of Remus's mob). Assigning such remarks to the common people (after their superiors held forth at 67–72) makes for a broader picture, extending the revilement of the potentate Sejanus (in marked opposition to line 62), increasing the spread of the repellent terror inspired by the powerful Tiberius (so too fear accounts for the secrecy here) and bringing out further the impotence of the Romans (in particular, the people, who had so much authority at 78f., are now reduced to secret whispers, as well as being under the thumb of the lowest of the low (their slaves), so that we can see how transient *potentia* is and how completely it can disappear).[48]

It is only after the downfall of Sejanus has been depicted vividly, at length and in detail that J. enlarges on his massive influence; soon (at 98ff.) he again accents the drawbacks of such eminence and dwells on them, so that lines 90–7 are swamped and subverted by a critical frame. There is also debunking within these lines themselves (where J. goes on and on to bring out a desire for inordinate power). In line 90, with an abrupt switch, he buttonholes his readers and puts them potentially in the position of Sejanus, a position which can hardly seem alluring after the foregoing (and the hissing sigmatism in the line and mock-solemn spondees are also off putting). The reference at the start of 90 is to the first of several more perks, the *salutatio* (the morning visit to show respect and curry favour), and Sejanus had throngs of such visitors,[49] but all this attention is offset by the very different treatment meted out to Sejanus in the preceding verses. So too at 90–1, *habere / tantundem* ('to have as much as him') is on the surface positive (alluding to wealth, authority, etc.), but in the context created by our satirist one cannot help thinking of other things that he also had (wounds, notoriety, etc.). Later in line 91, J. moves on to the top offices (consulship and praetorship) which Sejanus bestowed on people, but their worth has already been called into question at 35ff. And those powerful positions and the military command in line 92 are devalued by being shown as dependent not on personal qualities but on the whims of another (who was moved by family connections, courting and bribery,[50] and who has been presented as an unimposing figure, with frail *potentia* of his own). At 92f. there is irony in the man who assigns armies ultimately being unable to defend himself against his enemies; *tutor...* / *principis* ('the guardian of the emperor') has been counteracted in advance by *Caesaris hostem* 'Caesar's enemy' in line 86; and the mention of Capri brings to mind the letter from that island which ended Sejanus's domination (and life).

Tiberius is also diminished at 92–4. His presence on Capri (while allowing Sejanus to run the empire) is given no motivation, and so seems irrational and strange; and a feeling of revulsion would also be created easily in ancient readers familiar with the stories of his depravity and savagery on the island (and it would appear that the supreme possessor of *potentia*, who would know all about it, and to whom therefore the reader should pay close attention, was so unimpressed by it that he relinquished it almost entirely and removed himself from the centre of power!). *Tutor* (translated as 'guardian') will mean both 'protector' (ironically) and 'legal guardian' (as if Tiberius were a child or lunatic, unable to look after his own affairs, let alone govern an empire).[51] In line 93 there is an unflattering picture of the lord of the world perched on a crag on a small island (in residence high up on Capri) in a bizarre self-imposed exile to a place that is made to seem cramped and unpleasant, while *sedentis* will combine 'sitting', 'being inactive' and (with irony again) 'sitting in an official capacity'.[52] Style and sound also play their part here. In addition to the paradoxical juxtaposition of *principis* ('emperor') and *angusta* ('narrow'),[53] *principis* and *sedentis* ('sitting') are placed at either end of line 93, so that Tiberius ominously engulfs Capri (mentioned in the middle of the line), but it is only a little isle rather than Rome that he engulfs now. There is a piquant elegance too: the framing, assonance, rhyme between first and last words and patterning of cases and of singulars and plurals mean that this is an attractive verse about an unattractive person and (according to J.) place. The mention of the Chaldaeans (astrologers) in line 94 fills out the picture and adds to the disparagement. The odd image of just Tiberius and the astrologers on a narrow crag out at sea represents him as really withdrawn and superstitious (surrounded and influenced by a gang of despicable charlatans).[54] As several scholars have noted, *grege* ('flock') shows that J. is connecting *Caprearum* ('Capri') with *caper* ('goat') and depicting Tiberius as a goatherd surrounded by his animals. This amounts to a comically grotesque variant on the pastoral idyll, and several derogatory connotations of (smelly, lustful, bleating, non-human) goats are thus attached to the people with whom the *princeps* saw fit to surround himself.

In the second half of line 94 J. brings us right back to Sejanus and alludes to his very powerful position as commander of the Praetorian Guard, whose units he brought together into one camp in Rome under his personal control.[55] Here J. puts his readers on the spot by means of the pushy *vis certe* ('certainly you want')[56] and the list of four items, with punchy alliteration and asyndeton, and with the enticing epithets *egregios* ('splendid') and *domestica* ('personal'), to stress the magnitude of the military capability on show. Many (especially militaristic Romans) would find all this tempting; but some (I myself, for example) would not, and would question the cynicism about human nature here, as they find that (provocatively and engagingly) it is extending to them personally in a decidedly uncomfortable way. At 95–7 J. is even more pushy (and provocative), by means of the brisk and direct *quidni / haec cupias?* ('why shouldn't you desire them?') and the subsequent epigram, with *posse volunt* ('want to be able to') artfully delayed and stressed by position) and *praeclara* ('prestige') plus *prospera* ('prosperity') accented by alliteration – all this prior to the pay-off in line 98. There is some truth in the epigram, but really it amounts to a misanthropic generalization. It reduces power to killing and low human urges, and it reminds us that Sejanus was a murderer (of many people and of innocent victims, according to the ancient sources), so that again the grandee appears in an unattractive light (and there is an implication that you too could be a murderous monster!). The pay-off is also open to objections. There is certainly impact in line 98: there J. has a full line to put across the drawbacks (with gloomy spondees, forceful alliteration and emphatic siting of *malorum* ('trouble'), whose meanings also include 'hardships', 'misfortunes', 'damages', 'injuries' and 'evils');[57] and the blunt equation of success with trouble means that all the positives at 90ff. are suddenly turned into negatives, and we can now see a sardonic undercurrent to *quidni / haec cupias?* at 95–6. But again there are problems with the logic. Some people *are* prepared to put up with trouble if it means that they have predominance and prosperity;[58] and there is a purely selfish outlook here (concern with one's own interests is all that is envisaged) which J. cynically and cheekily assumes is shared by all his readers (but there are those who are prepared to suffer themselves if they can use their authority to do good for others). And in any case, there is patent pessimism in the implication that trouble, and equal trouble, attends on success.

J. reinforces line 98 with the grim detail of the manhandling of the body in line 99, carefully presenting Sejanus at this particular moment as the representative of power, and giving a dark spin to his ability to kill others (which has resulted in his own death here). Sejanus's *potentia* is denoted by *praetextam* ('the *toga praetexta*'),[59] with which *trahitur* ('is dragged along') is eloquently juxtaposed. To make great authority seem still more unappealing and dangerous, the expression in line 99[60] summons up a grotesque and repulsive picture of stripping Sejanus's corpse (a wry twist on the epic despoliation of a fallen hero) and putting on his (very significantly soiled, ripped and bloody) *toga praetexta*, which would be a dangerously misguided thing to do at the point when his body is being subjected to violence.

At 100–2 the satirist moves on to the lowly authority (with jurisdiction over weights and measures specified by way of example) of magistrates in three small towns near Rome which had become depopulated and unimportant. He further attacks massive *potentia* such as Sejanus had by making this alternative seem superior through extensive antithesis. There is contrast in lines 100 and 102 between these deserted towns and Rome (with its fickle and hate-filled mob and all the people there assaulting the magnate), and between *esse* ('to be') and the non-existence of Sejanus in line 100, and between the power that the official has and the complete powerlessness of Sejanus in line 99. Pronouncing on *mensura* ('measurements') in line 101 appears more desirable than having the *mensura* ('equal measure') of trouble in line 98; and the ability to lay down the law for others (*ius dicere*) tops the denial of the legal process for the great man at 69ff. So too at 101f. smashing (*frangere*) vessels is better than having your statue smashed (*franguntur*, 60) and turned into vessels (64), and the *aedile*'s clothes are raggedy due to poverty rather than through being roughly handled. However, at the same time, these verses poke fun at the provincial officials and undercut their position. J.'s point would appear to be that this low-level *potentia* is preferable, but is not really worth having (so that all power, from very high to very low forms, should come across as unattractive to a greater or lesser degree). Although some may protest that with this twofold attitude to the minor functionaries the poet is trying to have his cake and eat it, and that his neglect of all *potentia* between the two extremes is questionable, nevertheless the deflation is adroitly managed. In line 100 the deliberately delayed *potestas* ('the man in power') is subverted in advance by the mention of (inconsequential) Fidenae and Gabii; and there is mock-solemnity in the bulky polysyllabic block formed by the juxtaposition of those two names in the genitive (which means that those tiny, uninfluential towns dominate the line!). The mention of Fidenae and Gabii here, and of Ulubrae at the end of line 102, ensures that there is a frame of insignificance for the magistrate and his activities,[61] which are themselves presented as trivial and mundane – so *ius dicere* ('lay down the law') is counteracted by the humble *mensura* and *vasa minora* ('vessels that are too small') which encompass it, and *pannosus ... aedilis* ('raggedy *aedile*') is a striking collocation that makes the official seem seedy and contemptible. Thanks to the exaggeration in *vacuis* ('empty'), J. gives us a bizarre and absurd picture of the *aedile* (with jurisdiction over nobody) as a lone, tattered and irrational figure in a ghost town, pointlessly pronouncing on measures (when there are no shopkeepers or shoppers) and smashing vessels (which will never be used). This is a good image of isolation, futility and meaningless power. There is also undermining in a clear allusion to Persius. At 1.129f. among the despicable people he did not want reading his satire, Persius mentions one who had been in charge of a small town: *sese aliquem credens Italo quod honore supinus / fregerit heminas Arreti aedilis iniquas* ('thinking he is someone because, haughty with provincial dignity, he smashed short measures as *aedile* at Arezzo'). The reminiscence comes with negative associations (an aura of rejection and contemptuous sneering and the concept of the *aedile* as a groundlessly pompous nobody) which attach to J.'s magistrate also.[62]

At 103f. J. nudges us into going along with his dismissal of the *puissant* Sejanus by means of the logical *ergo* ('so'), which seems reasonable after line 99 especially, and the emphatically placed *fateris* ('you admit' = you *do* admit rather than you would or might admit), and he adds immediate support for that point of view at 104–7 (where he looks back to 101f.: better to pronounce on measurements and smash vessels that are too small than to lack all measurement like Sejanus here and go for excess and be smashed yourself). J. satirizes the great man as ignorant in line 103 and as a self-destructive fool at 104ff. (where we can clearly see that his prayers were excessive and pointless and also deleterious). There is (deterring) unbalanced intemperance at 104–5: pregnant diction gets across the vast extent of Sejanus's cravings: *honores* ('honours') also means 'esteem', 'privileges' and 'political offices', while *opes* ('power') also has the senses 'military strength', 'dominion', 'resources' and 'wealth';[63] and the iteration of *nimius* ('excessive') and the extensive repetition of sounds (*nimi-*; *-bat*; *-es*) suggest Sejanus going on and on with relentless insistence and obsessiveness. In the light of 97f. in particular, lines 104–5 make for an uncomfortable suspicion of impending disaster, which is confirmed with an effective aural touch at the end of 105, where *optABAT* ('prayed for') and *posceBAT* ('demanded') are picked up and corrected by *parABAT* ('was building up'), which intimates that all he achieved with his prayers and demands was to set up the doomed structure that led to his own downfall. The black humour of this is increased at 106f., where J. presents the inevitable result of his actions as a purpose clause (and so he appears as a perverse lunatic who deliberately aimed at his own demise)[64] and accentuates the catastrophic crash that he brought about for himself in line 107 by means of chiasmus, ringing sound, grave spondees and an extensive collocation of words, of which *praeceps* ('sheer drop') draws attention because it is rarely used as a noun with the sense of 'drop, descent'[65] and *immanis* ('terrible') blends the meanings 'savage', 'frightful' and 'immense').[66]

The image of the lone soaring tower (an odd and striking picture) is effective in itself. The building's height denotes Sejanus's eminence (and excess), but the more it rises, the more unstable and vulnerable it is, as would be obvious to anyone in his right mind. However, Sejanus, with his comically blind greed and ambition, goes on and on adding storeys, a demented one-man construction team, working away remorselessly up on top. Once the fall of the tower starts it cannot be halted, and its great height means that there is no chance of survival for him; the tower (= his lofty position) will inevitably be completely wrecked and many others will be crushed too (cf. 81ff.). The effectiveness is increased by reminiscence of an episode in Virgil's *Aeneid*.[67] During the fall of Troy, Aeneas and some other Trojans dislodged a tower on the roof of Priam's palace and sent it crashing down; it killed many of the Greeks who were attacking the king's residence, but more came up in their place and the assault continued. Aeneas describes the incident at 2.460ff.:

> *turrim in praecipiti stantem summisque sub astra*
> *eductam tectis, unde omnis Troia videri*
> *et Danaum solitae naves et Achaica castra*
> *adgressi ferro circum, qua summa labantis*
> *iuncturas tabulata dabant, convellimus altis*
> *sedibus impulimusque; ea lapsa repente ruinam*
> *cum sonitu trahit et Danaum super agmina late*
> *incidit.*

a tower standing over a sheer drop and rising towards the stars from the rooftop (from which we used to look out over all Troy and the Greek fleet and camp) we attacked with iron bars all around, where the upper storeys offered weak joints, and we wrenched it from its high bed and toppled it; suddenly collapsing, it dragged down its debris with a crash and fell on top of the Greek ranks far and wide.

The Virgilian allusion gives Sejanus's tower an aura of futility, suggestively linking it with an edifice which is at first sight impressive but inherently weak. There is also a pronounced mock-heroic element, and much irony and antithesis, all of which reflect badly on Sejanus. He is put on a par with (revered, moral, high-born, brave, etc.) Aeneas. The absurd downfall of the foolish Sejanus during a sordid power play in vile Rome is equated with a sensible and noble exploit in heroic combat during the tragic end of the great city of Troy. Aeneas was trying to protect his ruler (unlike the would-be usurper), and had men to help him (whereas Sejanus is so self-destructive that he topples the structure all on his own), and Aeneas killed only the enemy (while Sejanus, in bringing down his tower, destroyed himself and many of his relatives and adherents). All of this produces a marked climax to the passage on Sejanus.

At 108f. J. moves on to further examples by way of buttressing, and broadens the scope to include the republic as well as the empire. He is referring in particular to Crassus, Pompey and Julius Caesar, who banded together to form the first triumvirate and control Rome in 60 BC; *Crassos* ('the Crassi') and *Pompeios* ('the Pompeii'), to get a wide sweep, will denote primarily men like Crassus and Pompey, but may also include the sons of those two. Suiting J.'s case, all three triumvirs were very powerful (especially Caesar, who later became dictator) but lost even their extreme *potentia*, and died violent and horrible deaths, called to mind by *evertit* ('brought down'): Crassus, after being defeated with vast slaughter by the Parthians at Carrhae in 53 BC, was killed and had his head and a hand cut off and sent to the Parthian king; Pompey, after being beaten by Caesar at the battle of Pharsalus in 48 BC, was murdered and beheaded in front of his wife while trying to land in Egypt; and Caesar was assassinated in 44 BC under a hail of blows, receiving 23 wounds (one in the groin) from supposed friends and associates at the foot of a statue of Pompey.[68] With a witty touch J. produces a tricolon crescendo in which increasing space is assigned to Pompey (whose life and power lasted longer than Crassus's) and especially to Caesar (who lived longer and became more powerful than the other two). In line 108 (with its grave rhythm and forceful repetition, alliteration and homoeoteleuton) *evertit* (translated as 'brought down') picks up the collapsing tower image of 106f. and means 'overturn' (calling up a quaint picture of a whole series of people crashing to earth); the sense of (political) 'ruin' is also to the point; and the verb was frequently employed in a military context with the meaning 'destroy, overthrow'[69] (here it is pawkily applied to generals who used to destroy and overthrow others). In the variously functional periphrasis in line 109 there is further assault on the potentate. Caesar is shown in a distinctly unfavourable light, taming human beings (as if they were beasts) and using the whip on people; one flogged animals and slaves,[70] but not Roman citizens – hence the outraged juxtaposition of *flagra* ('lash') and *Quirites* ('the Romans'). This dominance has been already countered by *evertit* in line 108. There is play with the military usage of *domo* (= 'subjugate': here Caesar is subjugating Romans instead of foreign enemies) and *deduco* (= 'lead': here he is leading not troops but civilians, and leading them to the whip).[71] And there is mockery: the treatment of fellow citizens that J. assigns to Caesar is stupid and just asking for it; and if he really did tame the Romans, one wonders how a group of them got up the courage to attack him.

At 110f. J. provides a sharp answer to his insistent rhetorical question of 108f. with vigorous expression, in *nempe* ('why clearly'), the alliteration and repeated -*us* in line 110, and derisive irony in ambitious men pulling out all the stops (again the excess) to ensure their own ruin, and in their seriously misguided prayers, which are heeded by the gods. J. subtly strengthens his point in 110 by echoing Seneca, someone who suffered a calamitous decline himself (retirement from public life and enforced suicide) because of the high position he sought (and attained, under Nero). The phrase *nulla non arte petitus* ('sought by every trick in the book') occurs elsewhere only at Seneca *Epistle* 95.3, where in a facetious preamble to a long letter to Lucilius on a topic on which he had solicited instruction, Seneca says that it might make him one of those who regret having their wish granted and bringing a burden on themselves, so he might class himself among unfortunates such as those *quos honores nulla non arte ... petiti discruciant* ('whom honours sought by every trick in the book torment'). J. also gains impact by changing the tone to something much grimmer and the vision to something much darker – the deadly *evertit* instead of *discruciant* ('torment'). In line 111, *magna* ('for greatness')[72] probably makes a pointed nod to Pompeius Magnus, the doomed 'Pompey the Great' alluded to in 108. The word is in tension with *malignis* ('malignant') at the other end of the line, suggesting a wry contrast between men's aspirations and their realization.[73] *Magna* is also undercut by the juxtaposed *numinibus* ('deities'): even supreme human potentates are inferior to the gods. And the gods themselves (who represent potentates at the very highest level) are here depicted as unappealing, in an unsettling picture of malevolent and unnamed divinities (an ominous force in the background) just waiting for fools to pray for greatness so they can grant their prayers and bring about their destruction with their cruel sense of humour (cf. 7f.). *Malignis* is left to the end of the verse to provide a sting in the tail, with bitter joking in the attitude ascribed to heaven and in the application of this adjective – rather than *benignus* ('benign') – to deities who grant a request.

Ending the section with the end of *potentia* and of life, and achieving a strong climax – by means of a truly bleak vision, the memorable epigram, the vehement alliteration and assonance in line 112, and in 113 the sombre spondees and eloquent juxtaposition of *descendunt* ('go down') and *reges* ('kings') and of *morte* ('death') and *tyranni* ('tyrants') – J. strengthens his case still further in the final two lines. He broadens the scope by moving out beyond Rome and – via *paucis* 'a few' placed at the end of line 112 for stress – making us think of countless rulers throughout the world throughout all history (although we may wonder how the satirist can speak with authority about such a vast compass). He reinforces the violent ends of the triumvirs with many more such deaths for other potentates, dwelling on carnage, with *sicca morte* ('bloodless death', literally 'dry death') in 113 bringing to mind deaths wet with blood, and conjuring up for our final picture of men in power an endless series of figures now dead and impotent, variously wounded and bloody (and so permanently deformed) and making their way through the murk down to Hades, where they will become feeble subjects of Dis for the rest of eternity. J.'s point is that the *potentia* of all these men, no matter how great, is temporary and ultimately brings them only an awful demise; and in any case, it is not that great (the people who kill them prove to be more *puissant*, and again there is mention of deities who are still more *puissant*). It will not be by chance that our poet concludes this section with Dis: the reader may pray to the gods for power, but here is a much more relevant divinity – the one we all end up with, under his thumb, forever. But, to round out his attack on power, J. leaves us to infer that even divine sway is limited. The rather flippant periphrasis for Dis reduces him somewhat, by describing him as a mere son-in-law (rather than something majestic like the lord of the Underworld) and reminding us of the setback he suffered due to Ceres after he abducted her daughter Persephone to be his wife and queen (in response to Ceres's complaints, Jupiter made Dis return her to her mother for six months out of every year).[74] The only parallel for *gener Cereris* ('Ceres's son-in-law') is found at Ovid *Metamorphoses* 5.415: *non potes invitae Cereris gener esse* ('you cannot be Ceres's son-in-law against her will'). Those words were spoken by the nymph Cyane, who tried in vain to stop Dis carrying off Persephone (so that minor goddess was powerless); and even mighty Ceres, although unwilling, had to bow to the will of Jupiter and fate, and recognize the marriage of Persephone to Dis,[75] so that her authority too was circumscribed.

Ben Jonson (1572–1637) presents Sejanus's end with an eye to J. 10.58ff. in Act V of his play *Sejanus His Fall*. It is interesting to see how Jonson expands upon and otherwise alters his model, topping him over individual details and actually achieving an even grimmer overall impact.[76]

Notes

1   Some – e.g. Serafini, 177; Campana, 131 – think that lines 56–60 also refer to Sejanus, but (apart from the neat and functional structural patterning) J. would have made his case stronger by including other characters in this passage. Also, he has the plural *quosdam* 'some people' at the start of line 56 and does not even allude to Sejanus until line 62 (and there is no particular reason why, on a first reading, one would think of him specifically at 56–60, while a progression to him at 61ff. works well).

2   See *TLL* X.2.465.75ff., 467.63ff.; *OLD* s.v. 1a, 1b, 4a, 4b.

3   See *OLD* s.v. *subiectus* 5; Ferguson (who describes *subiecta potentia* as almost an oxymoron).

4   See esp. Mayor; Ebel; Campana. *Pagina* could also refer to a page of the consular *Fasti*, but that would not be massive or crushing, and the plaque ties in neatly with the closely succeeding *statuae* ('statues') in line 58.

5   See *OLD* s.v. 5a, 7, 10a, 10b. Some (e.g. Mayor; Campana) think that *mergit* means 'shipwrecks' or 'drowns', but this does not fit with the main image as I see it.

6   It is just possible that J. is thinking of statues of men on their own in line 58 and of separate equestrian statues at 59f.

7   Scott (23) cites 58ff. as an example of *enargeia* (rhetorical vividness).

8   See Ebel.

9   Some see a touch of (Heraclitean) pathos in *caballis*. See Courtney; Rudd and Courtney.

10   Cf. e.g. *TLL* IV.2.1249.61ff. for legs broken by way of punishment.

11   The singular nouns in lines 62–3 focus on a single image of Sejanus, even if we are to deduce that this process was repeated in the case of many other statues of him.

12   Cf. Freudenburg (2001), 209ff.

13   See Mayor; Courtney.

14   See *TLL* VIII.1.1537.38ff., 1540.23ff.; *OLD* s.v. 1, 4, 5a, 5; Campana (on *ingens* used in epic of heroes).

15   It is possible that J. is here alluding obliquely and giving a dexterous twist to his own 1.131, where he says that it is permissible to urinate (and more) on the actual statue at Rome of another despised 'great man'.

16   Courtney remarks: 'This passage may have the satiric point that a pure white victim would be more expensive, and it would be an insult to the emperor to offer any less'. Schmitz (73f.) suggests that *cretatum* ('whitened with chalk') is an ironical variant on *auratum* ('gilded') (it was common practice to gild the horns of sacrificial animals).

17   Courtney points out that the use of the same verb, *duco* ('drag'), of Sejanus and the bull reduces him to the level of a sacrificial animal.

18   See my note on Tibullus 1.10.37–8.

19   See *OLD* s.v. *specto* 6.

20   It is far from certain who the speakers are at 67–88, and which particular groups of words are to be assigned to individuals there. See esp. Duchesne; Ebel, 75ff.; Campana, 139f. The uncertainty may well be deliberate, to get the reader's attention, and to match and suggest the chaos and confusion of the actual events depicted. The following interpretation of this vexed issue seems to me the likeliest. Lines 72f., where J. moves on to talk about plebeians, make it clear that 67–72 are supposed to represent words spoken by Romans socially superior to them (cf. Duff), and an exchange between two persons there seems most obvious and natural. At 72–81 the tone, expression and satirical thrust suggest strongly that the verses should be ascribed to the poet himself (rather than to men caught up in the alarming disturbances at the fall of Sejanus). At 81–8 there is more direct quotation of Romans, and 88f. inform us that the speakers were plebeians this time. This exchange coheres well as one between two men (matching the probable duologue at 67–72). However, quotations from three different characters here would give a broader picture, and, although I have accepted Housman's punctuation, which assigns all of 82–8 (*pallidulus … trahat* = in my translation 'My Bruttidius … his neck') to one speaker, another person or persons may break in at line 84 and/or 85 – *curramus* ('Let's run') – and/or at 87.

21   See *TLL* I.1952.76ff.; *OLD* s.v. 5, 7.

22   See *TLL* VI.3.2882.13ff.; *OLD* s.v. 3b.

23   The main meaning of *cado* is 'be convicted' (in line with the judicial terminology elsewhere at 69f., and to bring out the absence of a formal trial), but the senses 'be killed' and 'be ruined' also come across strongly (*OLD* s.v. 9, 11a, 11b).

24   See *TLL* VII.2.2186.50ff.; *OLD* s.v. 5.

25   See Ebel. Cf. especially Catullus 58.6.

26   There are similarities to Sejanus too in Remus's fall from joint eminence and death (cf. Ferguson; Campana).

27   See *TLL* V.1.17.28ff., 18.39ff.; *OLD* s.v. 3, 5.

28   See Tengström, 21f.

29   Possible senses for *oppressa* are 'caught unawares', 'killed' and 'smothered'. See *OLD* s.v. 2, 7; *TLL* IX.2.791.26ff.

30   With Duff, I take *secura* ('off his guard') to be part of the hypothesis. Some (e.g. Courtney) believe that the word refers to the actual situation of Tiberius being generally incautious with Sejanus alone, but he was clearly not incautious with him at this point (hence the end of Sejanus).

31   Cf. e.g. Suet. *Calig.* 14; *Nero* 45; Tac. *Ann.* 14.7; *Hist.* 3.85.

32   Cf. Duff; Romano, 161.

33   See *OLD* s.v. 2, 3, 5, 6, 9.

34   See e.g. Campana, 151; Mayor.

35   Compare the disdainful attitude to the races at 11.193ff.

36   Contrast Fronto *Princ. Hist.* p. 210 (Naber), who talks more moderately of the plebs being controlled by means of two things *in particular*: the supply of corn and *shows*.

37   *Magna* ('large') cancels the diminutive *fornacula* ('oven'). This is a lifelike colloquialism (see Courtney), but may well represent another little joke (linguistic play) by the poet.

38   For the 'oven' sense see *TLL* VI.1.1118.8f., 18f., 1119.43ff. and cf. also Ovid *Fasti* 2.525f. Certainly J. will not be thinking of the melting down of statues in furnaces (as some imagine): a progression here from many people dying to images of them being destroyed does not seem obvious, and one wonders who all these people are who have statues of themselves, which Tiberius wants eradicated.

39   Cf. e.g. Pindar *Pythian* 1.95f.; Diod. Sic. 9.18f.

40   The reference may be to Bruttidius Niger, with *pallidulus* representing sport with *niger* ('black'), as Ferguson suggests, but, even if it is, his specific connection with Sejanus remains unclear. See Mayor; Courtney; Griffith, 78ff.; Campana.

41   The interpretation of 84f. is much disputed, and various emendations have been proposed, but Housman's text does provide good sense with this explanation. Tiberius is the obvious candidate for someone who inspires fear at this point, who could be identified with the famous chieftain of noble birth (cf. 4.65) and who could see himself as poorly defended and take revenge. *Victus* ('defeated') applies not to Tiberius but to Ajax (specifying this particular point in his career, and distinguishing him clearly from the other hero of that name), and *ut male defensus* ('for having been poorly defended') refers not to Ajax but to Tiberius (who could easily take such a viewpoint: cf. Suet. *Tib.* 65 for claims that he needed to be protected). Other interpretations with different candidates for Ajax are in general strained, contrived and often highly speculative. See esp. Ebel; Courtney; Griffiths, 78ff.; Campana; Hendry, 260f. The theory that the speaker is claiming ironically that Bruttidius is being punished by Ajax for a bad speech defending him in a mock-debate is effectively countered by Friedländer, Duff and Courtney (and this would also be a very odd claim to make in the midst of such disturbing circumstances). Some maintain that Ajax represents Sejanus, but in view of his death Sejanus cannot reasonably take revenge on anyone. It has also been suggested that the speaker is saying 'some Ajax (i.e. someone involved in the fall of Sejanus) may denounce us for abandoning him', but it would not be at all easy for readers to grasp this, and there appears to be no good reason for calling such a person an Ajax. Others opine that Ajax stands for Bruttidius, either intending to commit suicide like Ajax and thus get revenge (this bizarre notion is adequately refuted by Campana) or (Campana's own idea) pale at the prospect of ending up like Sejanus, and likely to avenge himself on the political colleagues who have abandoned him by informing on them at his imminent trial, if he is defeated there like Ajax (but such a point is certainly not readily apparent, and one has to read in a great deal).

42   See Courtney.

43   See *OLD* s.v. 3.

44   See *OLD* s.v. 1, 3, 5, 6.

45   Cf. Tac. *Ann.* 4.2, 4.7; Vell. Pat. 2.127.3.

46   *TLL* III.136.75ff.

47   See Jenkyns, 170.

48   In line 89, *volgi* could mean 'crowd' (rather than 'common people') and denote the general throng in the vicinity of Sejanus's corpse, but the word would then be rather colourless and lack all this point.

49   See Mayor; Campana.

50   See Mayor.

51   On the legal position see Mayor.

52   See *OLD* s.v. 1, 3, 7.

53   Cf. Schmitz, 70. Some mss have *augusta* ('majestic'), but that reading possesses much less point. However, there could be a pun in *angusta* on *augusta* (note *principis* and *Augustum* at the start of lines 76 and 77).

54   For J.'s attitude to the Chaldaeans see 6.553ff.

55   As the first two and the final item on the list at 94f. concern Sejanus's Praetorians, it is clear that *egregios equites* (translated as 'splendid cavalry') in line 95 will also have such a connection. The Praetorian Guard had cavalry, and it seems natural and obvious to me that J. would have them in mind here (with *egregios* accenting for the reader the attraction of having such a force under one's control). Also possible is Courtney's suggestion that J. is thinking of those illustrious equestrians who possessed the senatorial census and were selected by the emperor to enter a career as *procurator Augusti*, and who might have performed part of their military service as tribunes in the Guard (but these men are not elsewhere called *egregii*, and the reference to killing at 96f. makes me think of mounted soldiers rather than members of the equestrian order).

56   *Certe* could mean 'at any rate', but that sense would be less pressing.

57   *OLD* s.v. *malum* 1, 2, 5a, 5b, 7.

58   E.g. Agrippina at Tac. *Ann.* 14.9.

59   He had been granted this as an honour in 20 AD and was also entitled to wear it as consul in 31 AD at the time of his death.

60   Possible senses for *sumere* (translated as 'take up') are 'put on' and 'take possession of'.

61   The places are also examples of the ephemeral nature of influence (see Mayor on line 100).

62   Typically, J. tops his model, with *pannosus* ('raggedy') and *vacuis* ('empty'), which suggests a much stranger scene, and indulges in a bit of literary fun (J.'s reader could become the kind of man that Persius did not want for his reader).

63   See *OLD* s.v. *honor* 1, 2, 4, 5 and *ops* 1a, 1c, 2, 3, 4.

64   On the construction see Courtney and cf. line 167. The implication that he could have had no other purpose conveys the essential pointlessness of the exercise.

65   See *TLL* X.2.418.31ff.

66   *OLD* s.v. 1, 2, 3.

67   Several scholars suggest Virgilian influence here, and numerous similarities in language and situation make it clear that there is conscious echoing. Note also that Troy is another instance of the transience of dominion.

68   Cf. e.g. Plutarch *Crassus* 26ff.; *Pompey* 78ff.; *Caesar* 66.

69   See *TLL* V.2.1027.51ff., 1030.23ff., 1031.26ff.; *OLD* s.v. 3, 4, 5.

70   For *flagrum* so used, see *TLL* VI.1.848.49ff., 84ff.

71   For these senses for the verbs see *TLL* V.1.274.63ff., 1946.45ff.; *OLD* s.v. *domo* 2 and *deduco* 1.

72   There may also be connotations of intensity and arrogance (see *OLD* s.v. 9, 15).

73   See Campana.

74   See Ovid *Met.* 5.544ff. The echo of *gener Cereris* (see below in the main text) shows that J. is looking to this account.

75   See Ovid *Met.* 5.533ff.

76   For a text of the fifth act see Winkler (2001), 34ff.

CHAPTER FIVE

Eloquence (114–32)

J. now moves on to the petition for *eloquium* ('eloquence'). The switch is sudden and unannounced, thus securing the reader's attention. But it is not jarring, because the poet is just moving on to another object of prayer (one which has already been touched on at 9f.), and because there are several links with the preceding lines – eloquence is a form of power (128); Cicero in line 114 recalls the other politicians of his day at 108f.; the desire for pre-eminence at 114f. mirrors that in 110; prayer and divinities figure at 115f., as they did at 111f.; and death at 118f. takes up 112f.

There is a lot in the way of enlivening variety. In particular, this is a much shorter section than the previous one, with two *exempla* this time (one of them not Roman), and they (though handled much more briefly) dominate the whole passage. The attack now shifts to a corner stone of the Roman educational system (oratory), and the tone becomes sadder. The investigation of the topic is not full, probing and wide-ranging (as it was at 56–113), and the critical position adopted here is a lot more questionable and weak.

J. is picking up his claim at 9f., that many have died as a result of their facundity, and here with his two examples (Cicero and Demosthenes) he allows for no other outcome. The main thrust is that eloquence leads to death (and a horrible death at that: see 120 and 126f.), and so its harmful aspect is emphasized. But he does not allow that the two orators accomplished anything significant through their speeches, so that pointlessness is implied also. One wonders how such a well-educated and eloquent a person as J. can reasonably be so damning.

There is force in J.'s presentation. His first *exemplum* (Cicero) is a Roman one, which would have had impact on readers of his day, and he reinforces that with a non-Roman one. Death is put across strongly at 118f., is then immediately succeeded by the sensational 120, and for stress features again at 123 and 126f. The satirist also attacks *eloquium* by deglamourizing its exemplars and trying to make them seem positively unattractive, implying that Cicero was a pompous, posturing fool, and presenting Demosthenes as a pathetic figure and (at the end, in emphatic position) with more bigotry showing him in an inglorious light by highlighting his father's (supposed) trade as a blacksmith. J. carefully downplays and subverts the fame, admiration and influence that great oratorical ability can win (at 114, 125 and 127f.), and what we should go away with uppermost in our thoughts is, in Cicero's case, his awful mutilation and ridiculous verse and, in Demosthenes's, the filthy smithy of his background. So too the structure is neat (after the first two sentences, concerned with both orators, at 120ff. each man is allocated just over six lines) but above all pointed: the section opens with a schoolboy praying for eloquence and ends with a schoolboy being sent to acquire it by his ambitious father, so that these (to the poet) misguided aspirations form a frame, and in between comes the grim demise that is presented as their ultimate result.

J. does write with power here, and does have a few valid points. His stance will have been controversial and challenging in his day (given the importance attached to education and public speaking), and his remarks should make us think too (e.g. is it worth getting mixed up in politics, especially in view of the unreliability of one's fellow citizens; is renown desirable; is a humble, low-key life preferable to a high-profile one?). However, the cynicism and distortion are pervasive and really blatant, and the flaws in the argumentation are glaring. Cicero and Demosthenes may have been splendid speakers who were killed as a result of their ability, but J. presents a highly selective and overly negative sketch of them. As well as undercutting their rhetorical pre-eminence, he passes over their many achievements, does not even countenance that they may have done some good for their cities and taken satisfaction from it, and ignores the fact that the (undying) fame which they acquired by means of their orations was actually a form of immortality, which in ancient thought offset death and so was highly prized (something to which the satirist himself contributes here!). A brief and superficial examination of only two *exempla* in a short passage does not make for a strong case, especially when they are restricted to political speeches, totally disregarding forensic and epideictic oratory. Very obviously, *eloquium* does not lead inevitably to death, as it appears to do in this section. And, of course, it can be employed circumspectly (not, as here, offending people in power), and it can also be used to bamboozle (as in J.'s own *Satire* 4) or win over such people. In addition, many would object that a person *should* (like Demosthenes and Cicero) speak out to the best of his or her ability in support of what they see as an important and noble cause, even if it endangers their life. There are also further (minor)

problems with J.'s assertions, which are handled below. All of this means
that at 114–32 the pessimism really comes into the spotlight and the satire
is very much concerned with that. It also leaves one wondering how serious
J. is in saying all this and if he genuinely imagined that he might win over
readers like this.

> *eloquium ac famam Demosthenis aut Ciceronis*
> *incipit optare et totis quinquatribus optat*   115
> *quisquis adhuc uno parcam colit asse Minervam,*
> *quem sequitur custos angustae vernula capsae.*
> *eloquio sed uterque perit orator, utrumque*
> *largus et exundans leto dedit ingenii fons.*
> *ingenio manus est et cervix caesa, nec umquam*   120
> *sanguine causidici maduerunt rostra pusilli.*
> *'o fortunatam natam me consule Romam':*
> *Antoni gladios potuit contemnere si sic*
> *omnia dixisset. ridenda poemata malo*
> *quam te, conspicuae divina Philippica famae,*   125
> *volveris a prima quae proxima. saevus et illum*
> *exitus eripuit, quem mirabantur Athenae*
> *torrentem et pleni moderantem frena theatri.*
> *dis ille adversis genitus fatoque sinistro,*
> *quem pater ardentis massae fuligine lippus*   130
> *a carbone et forcipibus gladiosque paranti*
> *incude et luteo Volcano ad rhetora misit.*

The eloquence and fame of Demosthenes or Cicero –
that's what he begins to pray for and prays for during the entire
   Quinquatrus,   115
anyone who still worships stingy Minerva with a single *as*,
whom a young slave escorts as guardian of his small case of books.
But each orator died because of eloquence, a great stream
of talent in flood sent each to his death.
Talent had its hands and neck severed, and the rostrum   120
has never been drenched with the blood of an insignificant
   advocate.
'O how fortunate the Roman state, born in my consulate!' –
he could have disregarded the swords of Antony, if everything
   he said
had been like this. I prefer the laughable poem

to you, divine Philippic of remarkable fame,   125
the one unrolled next after the first. A savage end also
snatched away the man at whom Athens marvelled
as he flowed headlong and controlled the reins of the packed
    theatre.
He was born with the gods hostile to him and with fate baleful,
the boy whom his father, blear-eyed from the soot of the glowing ore,
    130
sent away from the charcoal and tongs and sword-producing
    anvil
and grimy Vulcan to the teacher of rhetoric.

In line 114 the first word – *eloquium* ('the eloquence') – clarifies from the start the prayer that this section will cover. The surface appeal and impressiveness of supreme oratorical skill are well conveyed in that line, which is taken up by eloquence, fame and the two great (polysyllabic) names, with an elegant balance in the doublets (of accusative nouns and genitive names), and with *eloquium* and *Ciceronis* framing the verse in emphatic positions; line 115 reinforces all of this with its solemn spondees and the earnestness of the petitions. However, the prayer is not just for facundity but for the exceptional gifts and renown of Demosthenes or Cicero (generally held to be the best and most famous orators of Greece and Rome), and the petitioner repeats his request over and over again[1] throughout the full five days of the Quinquatrus (a school holiday and festival of Minerva, from 19 to 23 March, especially observed by teachers and pupils, when prayers were made to her),[2] so that we are given a rather quaint picture of a suppliant who is excessive (*supervacuus*) and obsessive in his ambition. (Or do you think that this is a rather noble aspiration, as boys can wish for worse things?) He is also represented as sadly misguided, as he begs for a rhetorical skilfulness which, from the Juvenalian point of view, will prove fatal to him. In addition, *famam* ('fame') in line 114 has a subtle point. The (quite calculating) petitioner wants not just oratorical ability but also the concomitant 'benefit' of renown, but he is not as calculating as he should be, since the fame of Demosthenes and Cicero is double-edged: as 118ff. intimate, they are also well known for their deaths (so that he is praying for that too, according to our author); and, thanks in part to J.'s mockery of his poetry at 122ff., Cicero is famous for being ridiculous as well (just like the one who makes such a prayer). There is also irony in urgently appealing to a celebrated protectress (of heroes like Odysseus and Hercules, and of cities like Athens) for something that will bring destruction on oneself, and in directing such a stupid appeal (as J. sees it) to the goddess of wisdom.

The attractive and imposing façade of supreme oratorical ability built up at 114f. is undermined by the sudden revelation at 116f. that the person craving it is a mere schoolboy (and restricting the request to such a suppliant in this section implies – erroneously – that nobody else would be so ill-advised as to make it). Assigning this prayer to a boy is intended to make it seem childish and naive, and J. carefully brings out how young (and therefore immature and inexperienced) he is in line 116 (where he makes an offering of a tiny coin to Minerva, because as a lad he cannot as yet give her any more, in return for which he wants eloquence)[3] and in line 117, where as a minor he needs a guard,[4] and his *capsa* ('case of books') is small (so he has not acquired enlightenment from wide reading), and the juxtaposed *vernula* (a little, i.e. young, slave) adds to the diminishment. There are further digs. In line 116 I have translated *parcam* as 'stingy', which implies with wry humour that the goddess is chary in dispensing wisdom to the silly youngster – a cynic might feel that he is unlikely to get much from her for a paltry *as*,[5] or she may be grudging as a general rule and just another (cf. 111) malign deity. The adjective could also mean 'restrained, moderate' (in contrast to her worshipper with his disproportionate requests and admiration of Demosthenes and Cicero).[6] And the poet may well be playing on a quite different sense for *parcam colit ... Minervam*, suggesting that the boy 'develops his paltry intelligence' by means of the *as*.[7] There is also a barb in *custos* ('guardian') in line 117: if the pupil becomes a second Demosthenes or Cicero he will require much more than one young slave in the way of guards, and he will need people to protect his person rather than his case of books. Lines 116f. amount to a vigorous put down, but a thoughtful reader might object that J. is rather quick to write off the schoolboy and wonder if there is anything wrong in wanting to do well at school and striving for intellectual excellence, especially as facundity is not always lethal.

After four lines on the youth's ardent wish, *eloquio* in 118 (in the same place in the line as the wished-for *eloquium* in 114) ushers in a balancing four lines on the disastrous results of eloquence, to put across what the petitioner is actually asking for (according to J.). The allusion is to the demise of Demosthenes (who was condemned to death for opposing the power of Macedon and poisoned himself in 322 BC) and Cicero (who, after verbally attacking Antony, was proscribed and executed in 43 BC). There is dark wit at 118f.: by stating twice that their skill was fatal, J. is employing a doublet (over two lines) in connection with the death of this pair; and he is using typical oratorical devices (the doublet with amplification, saying the same thing twice, and anaphora of *eloquium*, *uterque* and, at 119f., *ingenium*) against oratory. There is also emphasis, in the brief and bald statement in 118, with juxtaposition of death and oratory in *perit orator* ('orator died'), immediately reinforced by a suggestive metaphor at 118f., for the reader to ponder. There J. takes the image of the stream of intellect, skill, etc.[8] and gives it a grim twist. The talent of the two speakers is so great (excessive) that it becomes a force for harm and is a powerful flood they can't control and which takes over, sweeping them off, submerging and drowning them – a particularly unpleasant and frightening way to die. To increase the bleak impact, the liquid imagery has a grisly connection with the poison swallowed by Demosthenes and with Cicero's bloody end (see 120f.); the jerky rhythm at the close of 119 puts the stress on *fons* ('stream') and conjures up a flood suddenly falling on the two speakers; there is solemnity in *leto dedit* ('sent to his death'), which was an old Roman formula;[9] and the placement of that phrase in the middle of the line surrounded by *largus et exundans ... ingenii fons* ('a great stream of talent in flood') sets death at the heart of eloquence (all of this on top of the inherent pathos in the demise of these two superlative orators).

There is intensification in the still darker 120f., which refer to Cicero's head and hands (or a hand) being cut off after he was murdered and affixed to the speakers' platform in the forum. In line 120 J. holds out the prospect of mutilation on top of death, a grotesque and horrific end, and one which would have been especially appalling to his ancient readers, because ghosts were supposed to show the wounds that killed them,[10] so that the disfigurement would continue for all time in the Underworld. In *manus est et cervix caesa* ('had its hands and neck severed') there is curtness and bluntness, and gruesome onomatopoeia as well (the frequency of *e, s, x* and *c* makes for a gurgling, splashing, hacking effect). And if, as seems probable and as I have translated, *ingenio* ('talent') is a dative (of disadvantage or possession),[11] the expression is also striking, with a surreal picture of personified talent so maimed.[12] That is followed by all the blood soaking the rostrum, as J. makes the point that the heads of other fine orators who were executed had been fixed up there as well[13] and invites us to imagine a series of bleeding heads, intimating that you too could end up like this (not revered but attacked, and reduced to silence and impotence), if you become successful and important rather than being just a humble pleader. As well as vividness there is economy in the allusion at 120f.: the rostrum is the place where men show their eloquence and also where, as a result of it, their severed body parts are shown, in a different (ghastly) type of display (and the drenching blood here picks up the great stream of talent at 118f., to strengthen this clear link between facundity and a negative outcome).

In line 122 the satirist quotes a line of Cicero's poetry that was notorious in antiquity[14] (carefully selected, because not all of his verse was this bad). As consul in 63 BC Cicero put down an attempted coup by Catiline, and subsequently wrote an epic (*De Consulatu Suo*) of three books celebrating that feat, from which this verse is taken. To broaden the onslaught on Cicero and make that representative of *eloquium* seem more unattractive, J. now employs ridicule and effectively lets the orator condemn himself with his own words (introduced abruptly so as to draw attention to them). This absurd, self-glorifying line is the very opposite of eloquence. It is pompous (note the spondees) and fatuous in respect of both sound (there is excess in the jingling *fortunatam natam ... Romam*) and thought (presumably the idea is that he saved Rome from death and brought about a rebirth, but he describes Rome as not reborn but born in his consulate, which is ludicrous, as the city was founded long before). Context increases the humour: after the preceding seriousness and sadness, there is bathos here; and (in between references to his execution) one who will soon experience misfortune and death talks glibly of good fortune and birth, claiming to have brought to birth the state whose agents will kill him (= parricide?).

There is a pointed progression in line 123 as J. moves from quotation of Cicero's inept and harmless poetry to allusion to his skilful and harmful prose, suggesting that if all his output had been as ineloquent as the verse just cited he would not have antagonized Antony and been proscribed. In line 123 J. is looking to Cicero *Philippic* 2.118 (invective directed at Antony): *contempsi Catilinae gladios, non pertimescam tuos* ('I disregarded the swords of Catiline, I will not dread yours'). The satirist is poking fun at the (in his view) empty and foolish bravado on Cicero's part, which was just asking for it (as eloquence ran away with him [cf. 118f.], and proved to be excessive, pointless and pernicious): he could claim to have disregarded Catiline's swords, but would not be able to disregard[15] Antony's, when they were used on him (and in fact he *should* have dreaded them, as they not only killed but also mutilated him). There is also mockery in *si sic* at the end of 123, which parodies the jingle in 122,[16] and hissing sigmatism in *si sic / ... dixisset*.

At 124–6, J. concludes his remarks on Cicero with an arresting touch – an extraordinary inversion of normal literary values in the preference of Cicero's risible epic over the second *Philippic* (the most famous of his 14 celebrated speeches attacking Antony).[17] This is an especially surprising claim for a poet to make, and it strongly puts across the idea that a real way with words is not a desirable thing, as it is better to be laughed at for poor poetry than to be executed and maimed for superb oratory (but at the same time, one can't help wondering if J. *really* prefers the poem to the speech, so that his stance here is called into question).[18] J. brings out the paradox in several ways. *Ridenda* ('laughable') and *malo* ('I prefer') are stressed by their position. He diminishes Cicero's verse by using *poemata* ('poem'), which is largely prosaic,[19] and which, as a Graecism, has a contemptuous nuance (as so often in J.). As part of his general critique and assimilation of the epic genre,[20] he minimizes Cicero's poem by referring to it in just two (dismissive) words, in contrast to all the (often grand) ones applied to the oration. In addition to its textual prominence, in line 125 the second *Philippic* receives an honorary address in a euphonious line and is surrounded by laudatory terms (with juxtaposition of *conspicuae* and *divina*) in a chiastic arrangement of accusatives and genitives and a parallel ordering of adjectives and nouns, while in line 126 there is the grandiose periphrasis (= 'second') with alliteration and assonance of the long a sound.[21] All of this does build up the speech but, in view of the deflating start of the sentence in line 125 and the fact that the *Philippic* brought about Cicero's end, there is also mock-solemnity here, as J. with apposite verbal excess parodies Cicero's own high-flown wordiness with and in particular reflects and mocks the awe that many (like the schoolboy and no doubt many of J's own readers) feel for that oration. On top of this, there is a subtle dig in *divina* ('divine'). The primary senses here are 'superlative' and 'divinely inspired',[22] and *divinus* was often applied to speeches by Cicero,[23] but J. is turning the orator's own term against him here, because in this context one readily thinks of the freedom from death of actual divinity that the author of the *Philippic* did not enjoy. In addition, *famae* ('fame') recalls the *famam* which was prayed for in line 114 with a considered echo (the speech did win him the great fame that the schoolboy prays for, but, of course, it also resulted in his assassination).

At the end of line 126 J. moves on to Demosthenes and tries to make this exemplar of *eloquium* seem unattractive too. At 126f. he puts his demise on a par with Cicero's by means of *et* ('also'), encompasses him with cruel death – in the word order *illum* ('the man') is surrounded by *saevus* ('savage') and *exitus* ('end') – emphasizes *saevus* by putting it first, employs the violent verb *eripuit* ('snatched away') and uses vigorous alliteration of *e* to drive his point home (but again there is problematizing which subverts J.'s case: *eripuit* and *saevus* seem rather exaggerated, as Demosthenes's death was voluntary (suicide when cornered by the Macedonians in Thrace), was reportedly brave and noble, and may well have saved him from savagery, such as the treatment which the orator Hypereides is said to have endured at Macedonian hands when he had his tongue cut out before he was finished off).[24] After sniping at Demosthenes there, and just prior to the additional undermining at 129ff., J. highlights the speaker's great skill at 127f. (again carefully assigning supreme eloquence to the role model so that he can make it seem undesirable). In 127 *mirabantur* is a strong verb with two senses ('marvelled at' and 'admired') and actually goes beyond mere fame, while *Athenae* ('Athens') does stand for (all) the Athenians but also suggests that his expertise was such that the city itself wondered at him. However, given the start of the sentence, we are probably intended to recall that the Athenians may have admired and marvelled at him, but they did not try to save him when a Macedonian army approached Athens in his final days (in fact he had to flee to Thrace, and the Athenians condemned him to death).[25] The same kind of building up with subtle deflation is also in operation in 128. With *torrentem* ('as he flowed headlong') J. conjures up a powerful mass of fluent words. But the image of the torrent (recalling 9f. and 119 with their negative associations) also implies excess, lack of control, senselessness and destructiveness, with the orator rushing headlong to his own death, and as a torrent bringing destruction on himself rather than others. There is a similar sardonic touch in *moderantem frena* ('controlled the reins'), which represents Demosthenes as completely in control of his audience, while unable to control his own mouth (death snatching him away at 126f. also offsets his mastery here). So too the reference to the packed theatre (i.e. the theatre of Dionysus at Athens, which was sometimes used for meetings of the assembly of the people in Demosthenes's day) means that the Athenians flocked in large numbers to hear him speak, but also insinuates likeness to an actor (considered disreputable in Rome) putting on a performance, and has connotations of tragedy (with its standard character flaw and reversal of fortune) apt for this Juvenalian creation and also suggestions of comedy (in line with Democritean mockery).

In 129 a full line brings out how unlucky the possessor of eloquence was: in the word order, *ille* ('he') and *genitus* ('was born') are enfolded and swamped by *dis … adversis* ('with the gods hostile') and *fatoque sinistro* ('and with fate baleful'); there are gloomy spondees and reiteration of long -*is* and -*o*); and the bestowing of such (fatal) facundity is represented (twice) as being due to hostility of supernatural powers (who also diminish the human Demosthenes). As well as arousing sympathy for their victim, J. stresses the malevolence of the beings to whom we direct appeals, disparaging the recipients and granters of our entreaties for a third time (cf. 7f. and 111) as part of his onslaught on the whole process of prayer from various angles. Lines 130–2 also try to cut down the illustrious Greek man to size, by dwelling on his lowly origins and stressing how mundane[26] and unpleasant was his father's trade as a blacksmith (our poet follows the tradition that he was a working man, but he was also said (correctly, it seems) to have been a gentleman and a wealthy factory owner, so for informed readers there is a problem over his status here, as there is over the detail of him sending Demosthenes to the teacher of rhetoric, since he died when the boy was only seven years old and too young for such instruction).[27] At the same time, J. invites us to conclude that Demosthenes would have been better off following the profession of a smith (Demosthenes as a grubby labourer!), and the more he goes on about how dull and disagreeable this trade is, the more oratory (to which it is preferable) is depreciated. We are left to infer that humble toil out of the public eye is better than the glory of 128f.; that the din of the forge beats the noise of speeches; and that being bleary-eyed (and dirty) may be an occupational hazard for the blacksmith, but is nothing like as bad as dying for eloquence! In fact, there is a primarily tragic irony in Demosthenes leaving an occupation that produced lethal weapons (swords) to be used on others (like Cicero) for one that would prove lethal for its own practitioner, and in his father thinking that he was helping the boy by getting him away from the forge into a good education but actually sending him to his death.[28] Finally, line 132 contains a novel and engaging phrase – *luteo Volcano* ('grimy Vulcan'). Although there is clearly metonymy here, the expression does momentarily summon up a bizarre and comical picture of a mucky god at work in the smithy of Demosthenes's father (further deflating divinity). What the words actually mean is 'grimy fire', which is something of a paradox (this workplace is so filthy that even the flames are dirty!).[29]

The first English version of *Satire* 10 to be published (in 1617) was by William Barksted. It is an adaptation that adds a huge amount of material to the original. See Winkler (2001, 44f.) for his passage on eloquence. J.'s sharpness and bite become even clearer when the Latin is set beside Barksted, who turns it into a much more diffuse attack and presents a gentler and feebler satirist.

Notes

1   In line 115 the repetition of *opto* ('pray for') brings out the iteration, and the frequency of *t, p, c* and *q* suggests to me the pattering of restated entreaties.

2   See Ovid *Fasti* 3.815f.; Mayor; Courtney.

3   For the *as* as an offering to Minerva rather than the schoolmaster's fee, see Duff; Courtney; Campana.

4   School began before dawn, and in the dangerous unlit streets of Rome a child had to have an escort (see Campana).

5   See Courtney.

6   Less pointed but also possible are the senses 'thrifty' (i.e. the goddess makes do with the schoolboy's small offering) and 'economical' (a transferred epithet, which really belongs to *asse* ['as']).

7   For this explanation of the words, see Edgeworth, 187. Edgeworth thinks that the boy is cultivating his paltry talent as a speaker with the offering. On the various meanings for *parcus* here see *OLD* s.v. 1, 2, 3.

8   For which see e.g. Ebel; Campana.

9   See Campana; Schmitz, 205.

10   See my commentary on Tibullus 1.10.37–8.

11   *Ingenio* might be an ablative, and the Latin could mean 'because of talent, hands and a neck were severed', but this has a lot less punch.

12   J. may also be playing (with black humour) on the senses of 'intellect' and 'genius' in *ingenium* (in connection with someone so unintelligent as to bring about his own destruction by enraging Antony).

13   On the practice see Mayor; Ebel; Campana.

14   See Mayor. On J.'s general attitude to Cicero see Winkler (1988).

15   There may also be sport with the 'avoid' sense of *contemnere*. See *TLL* IV.636.68ff.

16   See Lelièvre, 242.

17   These were named after the *Philippics* of Demosthenes, which were aimed at Philip of Macedon, and they represent another link between the Greek and Roman orators in this section, smoothing the transition to Demosthenes at line 126. On the connections between the pair see Campana's note on lines 114–32.

18   Duff opines that J.'s position here is also shaky in the light of 8.83f., where he had said that one should not put mere survival ahead of honour.

19   See Urech, 216f.; Campana.

20   On which see Jones, 95ff.; Connors in Freudenburg (2005), 123ff.

21   See Scott, 25; Winkler (1988), 86.

22   See *TLL* V.1.1619.81ff., 1624.34ff.; *OLD* s.v. 3b, 4b.

23   See Ebel.

24   See e.g. Plutarch *Dem.* 28ff.; Lucian (?) *Demosthenis Encomium* 43ff.

25   Plutarch *Dem.* 28.

26   So J. introduces words common in prose and lowly poetic genres: *fuligo* ('soot'), *lippus* ('blear-eyed'), *carbo* ('charcoal') and *luteus* ('grimy').

27   See Mayor; Courtney.

28   Schmitz thinks that *ad rhetora misit* ('sent to the teacher of rhetoric') plays on the phrase *ad mortem mittere* ('to send to death'). See Schmitz, 206. It is also possible that as well as referring to the actual effect of all the soot and smoke, *lippus* ('blear-eyed') hints at the father not being clear-sighted in dispatching his son (for *lippus* used figuratively like this cf. e.g. Horace *Sat.* 1.3.25).

29   Some think that *Volcanus* here stands for 'metal-working', but they can cite no parallel for such a meaning (whereas *Volcanus* = 'fire' is well established), and it deprives the phrase of its colour.

CHAPTER SIX

Military Glory (133–87)

With another abrupt new tack, J. moves on to a different topic of prayer. As part of the jolting effect there is contrast with 130ff., as we are taken from the forge to the battlefield, from peaceful activity to war, from productivity to destruction and from whole objects to smashed ones. However, there are also some links, to ensure that the progression is not too violent: the list of odds and ends at 133ff. parallels that at 131f.; the weapons in line 134 pick up the sword in 131; the chariot yoke at 135 recalls the reins at 128; and the petition for glory in this section has a counterpart in that for fame in the previous one (114ff.).

For variety, this time J. piles up the critical points in a much longer section and a much more comprehensive assault on the object of entreaty. Here there are three *exempla* (Hannibal, Alexander and Xerxes) rather than two. In contrast to Cicero, none of the examples is Roman; in opposition to Demosthenes, his Macedonian enemy is cited; and Xerxes and especially Hannibal receive more development than the two orators did, so that in this case barbarians predominate. In addition, in this passage there is extended narrative, greater structural complexity (see below) and much more humour and mockery (touches of pathos only at lines 136, 165, 172f. and 185f.).

This is a vigorous and entertaining treatment (J. obviously saw ridicule as an effective way of dealing with the three commanders). The diction is often arresting, and the narrative engages in various ways. In this dense and extensive attack on military glory itself and those who seek at and acquire it, J. is consistently cutting and relentlessly deflating, and his *exempla* have quite a wide geographical and chronological range. In line with his overall thesis, he portrays the desire for *gloria* as destructive (to others this time), excessive (in the cases of Hannibal and Alexander) and pointless (nobody actually achieves anything substantial here). In his introduction (133–46) he puts across his main points – that glory in the form of a trophy and triumphal arch is paltry, grotesque and absurd, and in the form of an inscription is transitory, while longing for it (137–42) is hybristic, stupid, mad, destructive and futile. At 147ff. J. supports and develops his case by showing all those key points in operation in connection with Hannibal, Alexander and Xerxes. With a careful selection of events he plays down their accomplishments and offsets them with drawbacks in their careers, and he also highlights the men's unappealing aspects, attaches derogatory associations to them and constantly pokes fun at them, so that those who sought and won *gloria* (Hannibal and Alexander) or just sought it (Xerxes) will come across as no kind of figure for emulation.

The structure is neat and functional. The introduction (133–46) opens and closes with fracture and futility, so that there is a gloomy and subversive frame. J. undermines two concrete forms of martial glory at 133ff. (the trophy and the arch), to make those who crave it seem foolish and crazy at 137ff., and then (at 143ff.) he bolsters the notion of them as foolish and crazy by undermining another concrete form of *gloria* (the inscription). Having intimated that attempts to secure such negligible things are misguided, J. goes on at 147ff. to illustrate just how misguided it is by means of three ambitious leaders. Of these our poet craftily begins with the (to Roman readers) least sympathetic exemplar of glory, and dwells on his inglorious end; then by way of reinforcement he presents an Alexander who is decidedly dissatisfied with his exploits, and he concludes strongly with Xerxes and his disastrous effort to win renown. The more negative passages on Hannibal and Xerxes bracket the lines on Alexander, and are linked by means of length, repetition of *qualis* (157, 179, 185), a successful advance followed by a reverse and thousands of corpses (165, 185f.). Suggestively, death occurs near the end of each *exemplum* (163ff., 172f., 185f.), as it did at the close of the introduction (144ff.). Within the section as a whole, the final line is not part of the Xerxes narrative but a general comment by the satirist and so provides a conclusion to balance the introduction. Lines 185f. also recall the opening, by means of death on a massive scale (compare the destruction at 133ff.), the ship (cf. 135) and the barbarian commander (cf. line 138) bringing catastrophe on his countrymen through his ambition (cf. 142f.).

Whether or not one admires and aspires to military glory is a subjective matter, but many people do not. J.'s verses would appeal to all those who hate war, and they will feel that he makes good points (e.g. that such *gloria* is trivial, and its pursuit is often excessive and destructive). But even people who would agree with J.'s overall thrust, if they are being honest and analytical, should see that his handling of the topic is one-sided and logically flawed, in line with an excessively pessimistic *persona*. For example, he allows for no positive aspects at all; but in their quest for glory, as a side effect or as part of their motivation, men can do good for their country (helping to make or keep it safe, prosperous and powerful) and they can oppose and wipe out evil (like the Nazis). His implications are open to objections too: *gloria* is not always transitory, and inscriptions and other (e.g. literary) forms of it do survive; those who prize it are not all insane, idiotic or hybristic, and they don't all end up badly. Only three *exempla* do not prove J.'s case, especially when there is obvious distortion in their presentation. He cynically writes off the great generals Hannibal and Alexander, blatantly condensing their careers and minimizing their accomplishments (while citing them as examples of glorious commanders!), and intimates questionably that their downfall and death cancelled out what they had achieved earlier. With Xerxes he focuses solely on the invasion of Greece (ignoring his successes elsewhere in crushing revolts in Egypt and Babylon), and in connection with that campaign he does not even mention the victory at Thermopylae, the capture of Athens and the submission of other Greek states. And the Persian has to be included as one who wanted (rather than acquired) martial renown, but this is pure speculation on the poet's part (and it does not allow for other obvious objectives, like getting revenge for Marathon, extending the empire and ending interference by mainland Greeks in Persian affairs). Is J. deliberately subverting and satirizing himself as a critic?

The stance adopted here would have been controversial then, given Rome's militaristic culture, and it should give us pause for thought today too, when large parts of the world are devastated by war, and western civilization is racked by ambition and cravings (cf. 140ff.). It is tempting to reflect in a modern context. Is martial glory worth pursuing as something fine and noble in itself (or is it touted by military authorities and politicians as a means of manipulation)? Does it provide acceptable grounds for fighting and killing one's fellow man? Does others' estimation of you really matter (when it is debatable how well they know you, how valid their value system is, etc.)? Do the trappings of fame have any actual substance or importance?

> *bellorum exuviae, truncis adfixa tropaeis*
> *lorica et fracta de casside buccula pendens*
> *et curtum temone iugum victaeque triremis*   135
> *aplustre et summo tristis captivos in arcu*
> *humanis maiora bonis creduntur. ad hoc se*
> *Romanus Graiusque et barbarus induperator*
> *erexit, causas discriminis atque laboris*
> *inde habuit: tanto maior famae sitis est quam*   140
> *virtutis. quis enim virtutem amplectitur ipsam,*
> *praemia si tollas? patriam tamen obruit olim*

gloria paucorum et laudis titulique cupido
haesuri saxis cinerum custodibus, ad quae
discutienda valent sterilis mala robora fici,   145
quandoquidem data sunt ipsis quoque fata sepulcris.
expende Hannibalem: quot libras in duce summo
invenies? hic est, quem non capit Africa Mauro
percussa oceano Niloque admota tepenti
rursus ad Aethiopum populos aliosque elephantos.   150
additur imperiis Hispania, Pyrenaeum
transilit. opposuit natura Alpemque nivemque:
diducit scopulos et montem rumpit aceto.
iam tenet Italiam, tamen ultra pergere tendit.
'acti' inquit 'nihil est, nisi Poeno milite portas   155
frangimus et media vexillum pono Subura'.
o qualis facies et quali digna tabella,
cum Gaetula ducem portaret belua luscum!
exitus ergo quis est? o gloria! vincitur idem
nempe et in exilium praeceps fugit atque ibi magnus   160
mirandusque cliens sedet ad praetoria regis,
donec Bithyno libeat vigilare tyranno.
finem animae, quae res humanas miscuit olim,
non gladii, non saxa dabunt nec tela, sed ille
Cannarum vindex et tanti sanguinis ultor   165
anulus. i, demens, et saevas curre per Alpes
ut pueris placeas et declamatio fias.
unus Pellaeo iuveni non sufficit orbis,
aestuat infelix angusto limite mundi
ut Gyarae clausus scopulis parvaque Seripho;   170
cum tamen a figulis munitam intraverit urbem,
sarcophago contentus erit. mors sola fatetur
quantula sint hominum corpuscula. creditur olim
velificatus Athos et quidquid Graecia mendax
audet in historia; constratum classibus isdem   175
suppositumque rotis solidum mare credimus, altos
defecisse amnes epotaque flumina Medo
prandente et madidis cantat quae Sostratus alis;
ille tamen qualis rediit Salamine relicta,
in Corum atque Eurum solitus saevire flagellis   180
barbarus Aeolio numquam hoc in carcere passos,
ipsum conpedibus qui vinxerit Ennosigaeum
(mitius id sane. quid? non et stigmate dignum

credidit? huic quisquam vellet servire deorum?) –
sed qualis rediit? nempe una nave, cruentis   185
fluctibus ac tarda per densa cadavera prora.
has totiens optata exegit gloria poenas.

Spoils of wars (a breastplate attached to a lopped
trophy and a cheek-piece hanging from a smashed helmet
and a chariot's yoke shorn of its pole and a defeated trireme's   135
stern ornament) and a dejected captive on top of an arch
are believed to be more than human blessings. It's for this
that the Roman, Greek and barbarian *generalissimo*
spurs himself on, he has his incentive for danger and hard work
in this: so much greater is the thirst for glory   140
than for manliness. (For who embraces manliness for its own sake,
if you remove the rewards?) Yet at times their own fatherlands are
    overwhelmed
by the ambition of a few and their lust for renown and an inscription
that will be attached to the stones that guard their ashes, stones
    which the
harmful strength of a barren fig tree has the power to shatter,   145
since tombs themselves too have been assigned their own doom.
Weigh Hannibal: how many pounds will you find in that
first-rate general? This is the man who was not contained by Africa
(pounded by the Moorish Ocean and stretching to the warm Nile
and down to the peoples of Ethiopia and their different
    elephants).   150
Spain is added to his empire, he leaps over the
Pyrénées. Nature has put in his way both the Alps and snow:
he splits the rocks and cleaves the mountain with sour wine.
Already he holds Italy, but he aims to advance further.
He says: 'Nothing has been achieved, unless I shatter their city
    gates with my   155
Carthaginian soldiers and plant my standard in the middle of
    the Subura'.
Oh, what a sight, what a painting it would make,
when the Gaetulian beast carried the one-eyed general!
So how did it end? What glory! The same man is defeated
of course, and flees headlong into exile, and, a mighty   160
and marvellous client, sits there at the king's palace,
until it pleases the Bithynian tyrant to be awake.
The end for the soul that once convulsed the world will come

not from swords, not from rocks nor from javelins, but from
    that famous
punisher of Cannae and avenger of so much bloodshed –   165
a ring. Go on, you maniac, and race through the savage Alps,
in order to appeal to schoolboys and become a speech in
    the schools!
One earth is not enough for the young man from Pella,
the poor man seethes because of the narrow limits of the world,
as if confined on the rocks of Gyara or tiny Seriphos;   170
but when he has entered the city fortified by potters,
he'll be content with a sarcophagus. Death alone shows
how tiny are humans' puny bodies. People sometimes believe
that Athos took sail and whatever else lying Greece
dares to say in its histories; we believe the sea was covered   175
by the same fleet and placed solid under wheels, that deep
rivers ran out and watercourses were drained by the Mede
while breakfasting and whatever Sostratus sings with
    dripping armpits;
but in what a state did he return after abandoning Salamis,
the barbarian who was in the habit of savagely flogging
    Corus and   180
Eurus (though they had never suffered this in Aeolus's prison),
who had bound with shackles the Earth-shaker himself?
(That was really rather merciful. Why? Didn't he believe him worthy
of branding too? Which of the gods would have been willing to be
    his slave?)
But in what state did he return? Of course, on a lone ship   185
amid bloody waves, his prow moving slowly through crowded
    corpses.
Such is the punishment that prayers for glory have so often exacted.

From the very beginning (133–7) J. invests military glory with associations of the *perniciosum* and the *supervacuum*: the smashing of equipment
involves (harmful) destructiveness and renders it useless (= pointless),
while the estimation in line 137 is represented as excessive. At 133–6, with
a provocative and problematical start, J. is referring to a simple form of
trophy erected at the site of a victory on land or near the site of a successful
naval battle (branches were lopped off a tree and the conquered enemy's
gear was attached to it), and he is trying to subvert this concrete form of
glory by reducing it to its physical components, intimating that to aspire
to this is to aspire to something paltry and grotesque. Some readers would

laud a hard-headed detachment here,[1] while others would object that this is a blinkered viewpoint and the trophy amounted to much more than mere objects, and in fact constituted a venerable symbol and celebration of success. Similarly controversial is J.'s minimizing of the triumphal arch in line 136.

The imposing opening *bellorum exuviae* ('spoils of wars' – wars in the plural, and spoils of war rather than just battle) – seems intended to conjure up an enticing and pointedly illusory picture of masses of booty (precious and magnificent items taken from the enemy during a series of campaigns), a picture which is promptly punctured by the following words, where we suddenly realize that *exuviae* in fact denotes arms and decorations which are taken from the foe in battle,[2] and which are damaged (and so worthless). In what is quite a long sentence with cumulative impact and mock-solemn spondees (especially in 136), J. presents an odd and rather comical jumble of bits and pieces (the stern ornament in particular is a jarring addition). He stresses their broken state – *truncis* ('lopped'), *fracta* ('shattered') and *curtum* ('shorn') undercut in advance the nouns with which they agree) – and also in passing brings out – and by means of *victae* ('defeated') – the dangers of war (would you risk your life for *this*?), as well as building up an atmosphere of vulnerability and transience (cf. 144ff.).

In line 133, by describing the trophy itself (rather than the tree) as 'lopped', J. diminishes it and represents it as disfigured and itself subject to violence (compare the tomb in line 146). The phrase *truncis ... tropaeis* ('a lopped trophy') is found elsewhere only at Ovid *Epistulae ex Ponto* 3.4.103ff. There Ovid is predicting a triumph for Tiberius, to be celebrated reverentially in his poetry, and imagines the emperor decked out for the parade (obviously in the hope of winning him over, so that he will review the decree of exile for the poet):

> *scuta sed et galeae gemmis radientur et auro,*
> *stentque super vinctos trunca tropaea viros:*
> *oppida turritis cingantur eburnea muris,*
> *fictaque res vero more putetur agi.*

> but let his shield and helmet glitter with jewels and gold,
>   and let lopped trophies stand over the fettered captives;
> let cities depicted in ivory be ringed with turreted walls,
>   and let that fiction be taken for the truth.

J. has taken the phrase over from Ovid to exploit its context of illusion (at 105f.) and its aura of futile and misguided respect (Ovid did not win recall from Tiberius). The satirist also makes his own lines seem even more bleak by way of contrast, as he replaces the Ovidian splendour with junk, and in particular substitutes the smashed arms (including a helmet) for Ovid's intact and costly shield and helmet.

In line 136, J. tries to deflate another concrete instance of *gloria*. He dismisses the large triumphal arch in less than a line, and reduces all its sculptural decoration to a single figure, high up (and so hard to see and be impressed by). In fact, the expression briefly calls up a subversively surreal picture of a lone (living) prisoner moping on top of a bare arch. So too *tristis captivos* ('a dejected captive') might well arouse some pity,[3] and touches on misery and loss of liberty as further drawbacks of militarism. There is undermining on the intertextual level too. The only other place where *tristis* is applied to a captive is Ovid *Amores* 1.7.39 – *ante eat effuso tristis captiva capillo* ('let her walk in front, a dejected captive with loosened hair') – where a sole prisoner is also used to poke fun at martial renown. Ovid had struck his girlfriend, and at 35ff. sarcastically told himself to celebrate a proud triumph for this 'victory', driving a chariot in a triumphal procession, with a retinue praising the brave hero's conquest of a girl, who was to precede him (as prisoners of war did in the parade). There are various demeaning and fitting associations: the phrase comes from a frivolous poem in a lowly genre and has a rather sordid background; it is redolent of mockery of things military; and it has connotations of hollow magnificence and show and of irony and exaggeration (cf. J.'s 137).

The pay-off to the first sentence comes at line 137, where *creduntur* ('are believed to be') is deliberately left to the end (accentuating mere belief as opposed to actuality), and where *humanis maiora bonis* ('more than human blessings') after the foregoing is meant to look ridiculous and crazy (like the attitude of the generals in the next sentence). The hyperbole here is to bring out how ludicrous such veneration is; it also hints at something which is developed later in the *exempla* – hybris (and 142ff. could be seen as a form of nemesis). There is a tart corrective at 143ff., where we are shown the mortality of people who win such supposedly superhuman *gloria*; and *bona* ('blessings') here pointedly directs us back to *bona* in line 3 (where J. contrasted real blessings with things very different from them). At the same time, the reference to divinity undercuts by reminding us of human inferiority and shortcomings.

The following sentence (with more mock-solemn spondees) scoffs at soldiers of the highest rank who pursue such 'rewards', encouraging a critical frame of mind towards commanders prior to the onslaught on particular examples of them at 147ff. In 137 the curt, reductive and contemptuous singular *hoc* ('this')[4] – compare the elided *inde* ('in this'), stressed by position, in 140 – punctuates in advance the sonorous 138, a line (with an impressive geographical sweep) that is filled with generals and contains in emphatic position the bulky and lofty *induperator* ('generalissimo').[5] Because that word is uncommon, one is reminded of the only other use of it (also quasi-grave) in J., at 4.29, where it is applied to the sinister and despised Domitian, in connection with his extravagant banquets. The redeployment of the noun here means that it suggests excess, and it also has an aura of dangerous and deadly absurdity, which fits with 142ff. below – in *Satire* 4, Domitian, who killed so many in his reign of terror (37, 84f., 95f., 151f.), calls a meeting of his Privy Council to discuss how best to cook a large fish. Line 138, with its repetition of *-us* as generals of nation after nation are mentioned, means that the stupidity spreads out from Rome wider and wider to embrace the whole world (cf. 1ff.), and also that the Romans in their risible ambition are no better than Greeks and barbarians.[6] In line 139, J. works in further allusion to drawbacks to the quest for *gloria*, with *discriminis* ('danger', referring to the perils of war again for emphasis) and *laboris* ('hard work'), which economically combines 'toil', 'industry', 'a task', 'hardship' and 'physical pain';[7] and, a consideration that makes the quester seem still more unattractive, he brings all this down on not just himself but many others too – his officers and troops and (142) his own countrymen, as well as his opponents. In 140, *famae* ('glory') aptly comes before *virtutis* ('manliness') and is juxtaposed with *sitis* ('thirst'), while *virtutis* does not even appear in the same line as *sitis*. The metaphor denotes a strong desire that a man really wants and needs to satisfy, and also has an ironical aspect – one normally thirsts for something that brings pleasure and relaxation (wine) or preserves life (water), but this *sitis* involves misery, toil and death. *Famae sitis* ('thirst for glory') recalls Silius Italicus 3.578,[8] where Jupiter describes the early Roman as being *famae sitiens* ('thirsty for glory'). There, after Hannibal has encamped in the Alps prior to swooping down to ravage Italy, Jupiter says that the Romans of the present (unlike their ancestors) have become inactive, so he will test their manhood in a great conflict that will cost intense effort. That context means that *famae sitis* here has dismal associations of danger, hardship and terrible war, as Silius's phrase is given a negative, mock-heroic spin.

The rhetorical question in the epigrammatical 141f. is engaging but also problematical (the clear but highly dubious implication is that nobody embraces manliness[9] for its own sake). Here J. writes off the petitioner's role model as not interested in manliness *per se* but (stupidly, madly) only concerned with the 'rewards' (*praemia*, stressed by placement at the start of the line), which are sandwiched between and swamped by the derogatory pictures of them at 133ff. and 144ff. There is also sardonic humour. On top of the basic joke of a man embracing (or not embracing) manliness, J. is

exploiting the fact that *virtus* ('manliness') is a feminine noun. By person-
ifying *virtus* here he is depicting it not as a goddess (as *virtus* was often
viewed)[10] but as an unattractive, lonely and rejected female (ugly, ageing,
old, etc.), who has to pay men to get them to embrace her (i.e. to have sex
with her).[11] This represents the ambitious military man as a gigolo (a cold,
calculating, hypocritical, despicable and inglorious male prostitute) and the
acquisition of glory as a sordid, demeaning and inglorious transaction.

In line 142 the potential figure for emulation appears in an even worse
light, as his thirst for fame is shown as selfish, unpatriotic and massively
harmful. In this vigorously alliterative line, *obruit* (turned into a passive
in my translation, 'are overwhelmed') has several senses – 'bury', 'crush'
(e.g. under missiles), 'overwhelm' (an enemy) and 'bury in obscurity'.[12] This
brings out the notion of total destruction, and also has implications about
the ambition and lust in line 143 (the subjects of the verb in the Latin),
which are so huge as to bury and crush a whole country, which overwhelm
ambitious people's own fatherlands rather than the enemy, and which do
broader and long-lasting damage (by consigning to oblivion). The verb also
sets up some ironical rebounds at 144ff., where these characters themselves
are destroyed (as are their tombs) and are buried in graves and obscurity.
In 143, *paucorum* ('a few') will refer to a few men (e.g. officers, politicians)
in cahoots with the commander, working in concert for their own selfish
ends in an unattractively sinister and dangerous cabal.[13] J. thus depicts once
again the spreading of stupidity, and strengthens his attack by increasing
the number of instances of desire for glory wreaking great harm (it is not
just lone generals who do damage because of this but other people too). The
(excessive) extent of the ambition of the few is brought out in line 143 by the
threefold expression of it – with stress in the placement of *gloria* ('ambition')
and the juxtaposition of *laudis* ('renown') and *tituli* ('inscription') – and
by the fact that it occupies the whole line. *Cupido* ('lust') may well have
unpleasant sexual connotations (especially after the 'embrace' in line 141).
The progression to death at 143f. diminishes the reader's potential role model
by showing him as mere ashes (cf. 143f.) and foolishly (cf. 146) concerned
with the inscription on his sepulchre. But one can reasonably object that the
short, lone *laudis* ('renown') in 143 minimizes what he would desire and enjoy
in life (military glory would go hand in hand with power, prosperity and so
on), as J. hastens to dwell on the man's death and subvert his posthumous
fame; and in any case, many tombs and epitaphs do survive, and lots of
people win immortal fame by other means (such as mention of them in
literature). In 143–4 (with its contemptuous frequency of *s, x, c* and *q*) there
is the joke of the military man ending up with stones (rather than troops)
as his guard (and they are ineffectual at guarding – see 144f.); and in *haesuri*

('that will be attached') there will be ironical play on the verb's senses of being permanent and persisting in memory.[14]

At 145f. this cutting sentence ends with a grim picture and, as the fig tree will not propagate, it too will eventually die (like the man and his grave), so that there is a strong sense of transience, annihilation and oblivion. There is a strong sense of futility too: the ambitious ruin their fatherland (and endure all the toil and danger mentioned above) in their craving for *gloria*, but in the long run (when their tomb and inscription are obliterated) they end up being forgotten totally and permanently (the exact opposite of fame). There is also ironical reversal in the fig tree and the smashed monument taking up the trophy tree, smashed equipment and the arch at the start of the section (this is how all the glory ends up, a sardonically apt fate). In line 145 the fact that the fig tree manages to split open the sepulchre means that the latter has already been neglected (so the celebrity was not long-lived). Deflatingly for the man who wanted to be special, in contrast to (say) an impressive oak or a sombre cypress, this was a commonplace tree – and *ficus* ('fig tree') was a largely prosaic word[15] – while the destruction of tombs by it was a common occurrence.[16] This particular tree had demeaning associations too (the Latin word also designated the anus, piles and a sore on the genitalia).[17] Sterility is appropriate in connection with someone engaged in the sterile pursuit of *gloria* which, like the fig tree here, does not extend its existence. The pregnant *mala* (translated as 'harmful', it also embraces 'unpleasant', 'evil' and 'hostile')[18] increases the bleakness. In addition, it is the *ficus* that is strong and powerful now (rather than the human), and, as *discutio* ('shatter'), *valeo* ('has the power') and *robur* ('strength') were used in connection with warfare,[19] there is a facetious suggestion that the ambitious man (via his monument) is encountering a superior military force, in the form of a tree (the dactyls fit with the levity). In line 146, to round off the subsection, J. produces a memorable epigram that contains a macabre jest, with lilting, light-hearted dactyls, and mock-solemnity in the elevated *quandoquidem* ('since') and *data sunt … fata* ('have been assigned their own doom').[20] At the same time, although the tone is primarily mocking, there is an admixture of (Heraclitean) pathos, and the final two words – *fata* ('doom') and *sepulcris* ('tombs') – make for a dismal conclusion.

With a startling turn (but a logical enough progression from the ashes and death of ambitious men), in line 147 J. moves on to his first historical example: Hannibal, a brilliant general of the African city of Carthage (Rome's great rival), who crossed the Pyrénées and the Alps in 218 BC and invaded Italy, ravaging it for 16 years before returning to Africa to oppose Roman forces which had landed there, and being decisively defeated at the battle of Zama in 202 BC (which put an end to the Second Punic War). J.

picks up the mournful theme of little remaining from a great man in the form of his ashes[21] and gives it a novel and humorously bizarre twist by means of the detail of weighing. Initially he conjures up a surreal image of the man Hannibal on scales, and even when we realize that he means just Hannibal's remains, a comical picture is summoned up of the reader solemnly holding up a balance with a grisly little mound of ashes in one pan and carefully working out the weight, quite unnecessarily (we know they won't weigh much), not to say impossibly (as they have long since been lost).[22] J. is trying to cut the Carthaginian down to size from the start (and subvert his exploits in advance at 151ff.) by means of the levity at his expense and the depiction of him as already dead and reduced from a first-rate commander to a small and paltry pile of dust.[23] However, the logic here is debatable. Much more survives of a grand man than his physical remains: things like his achievements and fame live on (and J. is here himself helping to immortalize Hannibal). And if the idea is that his accomplishments ultimately amount to nothing because he ends up as something insignificant, the same applies to all of us, so why should any of us try to accomplish anything (e.g. by writing satire)?

The poet's sniping continues at 148–50. By dwelling on the vast extent of Africa, while touching on its boundaries in the west (the Atlantic off the coast of Mauretania), the east (Egypt) and the south-east (Ethiopia), J. leaves us to infer that the man who is not content with all this is absurd, guilty of hybris and insane.[24] He also brings out at length the foreignness of this representative of soldierly renown, and relies on the negative associations in his poetry so far (and elsewhere in Latin literature) of Moors, Egyptians and Ethiopians[25] attaching to Hannibal here. Similarly, the mention of the Ethiopians and their different elephants[26] reminds us that there were elephants in all of Africa, not just Ethiopia, so that he is encompassed by these (ugly, stinking, grotesque, savage, monstrous) beasts.[27] So too *Nilus tepens* ('the warm Nile') has a debasing and unpleasant aura as a result of its two prior occurrences: at Propertius 2.33.3f. (*atque utinam pereant, Nilo quae sacra tepente / misit matronis Inachis Ausoniis*, 'a curse on the rites which the daughter of Inachus sent from the warm Nile to the matrons of Italy'), a frustrated lover complains about a hated alien import – the ten days of sexual abstinence imposed on his mistress by the dismal rites of Isis; at Seneca *Oedipus* 606, repulsiveness, horror and death are to the fore, as the throngs of ghosts summoned up from Hades by Tiresias are compared to the flocks of birds that migrate from chill Strymon to the warm Nile. There is mock-solemnity as well: in connection with (to him) barbaric Africa, J. employs in *percussa Oceano* ('pounded by Ocean') a kind of expression that was common in poetry, especially its higher genres, and the archaism *rursus*

('back', i.e. southwards, 'down to'),[28] while repeating the (grave) long *o* and
-*os* sounds throughout 148–50. On top of that, there is deflating humour.
After 147f. it is not hard to take a small mental step and see here the grim
joke that huge Africa could not contain Hannibal when he was alive but a
tiny urn does when he is dead. There also seems to be frivolous verbal play:
capit in line 148 must mean 'contain', but in connection with a general the
'capture' sense is readily felt; *percussa* ('pounded') is an apt word for the
homeland of this warrior, as the verb often means 'beat', 'strike' and 'kill';[29]
and in *admota* ('stretching to') there is probably sport with the military
usage of *admoveo*.[30]

Lines 151–3, while assigning exploits to J's exemplar of *gloria*, also have
pejorative nuances: excessive ambition and greed are implied by the fact that
Hannibal is not content with all Africa (this exaggeration of Carthaginian
power there is suggested at 148–50) or all Spain, but still goes on; and the
drive and determination shown here are those of a major enemy of Rome,
on his way to Italy. In addition, these successes make the fall at 159ff. seem
all the greater, and are meant to increase the puncturing effect of 164–6,
where the man who overcame massive opponents (the Pyrénées, the snowy
Alps, Nature itself) is finished off by a tiny ring. At 151f. there is menacing
rapidity thanks to the dactyls, asyndeton, brevity and skimming of detail.
Within three words Hannibal is out of Africa and in possession of Spain
(he was made commander of the Carthaginian troops there in 221 BC and
consolidated the conquests of his predecessors Hamilcar and Hasdrubal).
Within two words he has crossed the Pyrénées. The bulky *Pyrenaeum* ('the
Pyrénées') slows the rhythm with its long syllables and intimates a large
barrier, only to be succeeded by the brief, dactylic and vigorous *transilit*
('he leaps over'), rendered doubly emphatic by its position. The verb denotes
(rather impudent and contemptuous) speed, and brings before our eyes a
comically quaint image of the Carthaginian vaulting over the mountains; it
was also used of overstepping bounds and so hints at hybris (an idea which
is developed in the following verses).[31] At 152f. J. dwells at greater length
on the larger barrier of the Alps (building it up by means of alliteration,
assonance, the epic -*que* ... -*que* ('both ... and') and Nature's role) and
makes Hannibal take longer to get over that range (that he does manage
to surmount it is even more disquieting). There may well be flippant play
on the military use of *oppono* ('put in the way'),[32] representing Nature
as an opposing general whom Hannibal defeats. Certainly to go against
Nature was stupid (because traditionally Nature was very powerful and in
the long run could not be beaten)[33] and in this case hybristic (Cicero at *De
Provinciis Consularibus* 34 claims that Nature, with the favour of heaven,
protected Italy by means of the Alps, and in Silius Italicus 3.500ff. Hannibal's

troops move slowly towards the Alps because they think they are marching in defiance of Nature and in opposition to the gods). There is also subtle foreshadowing of a comedown for the Carthaginian here. The language of 152f. recalls Lucan 2.619f. at several points – *hinc illinc montes scopulosae rupis aperto / opposuit natura mari* ('on this side and that Nature has put in the way of the open sea mountainous masses of rocky cliff') – which comes from Lucan's description of the harbour at Brundisium, where another great general (Julius Caesar) failed to pen in and capture Pompey despite his great efforts (Lucan 2.660ff.). In line 153, after all the opposition put together in the previous verse, Hannibal masters Nature with alarming ease in just two words – *diducit scopulos* ('he splits the rocks'). At the top of the Alps he reportedly constructed a road down the mountain for his army by building huge bonfires to heat the rock till it glowed, pouring the soldiers' sour wine over it to make it brittle and then smashing it with iron tools.[34] J. reduces this series of procedures to the sour wine alone, leaving it to the end of the line for impact, and presenting the freakish and ludicrous notion of wine on its own splintering rock. His expression also suggests a whole mountain splitting apart when some liquid is poured upon it.[35] As part of the debunking facetiousness J. has fun here with the cleaving process, using two words for rock and separating (or splitting) them by means of *et* ('and').

In the first half of line 154 there is again an off-putting rapidity as Hannibal (thanks to extensive ellipse) suddenly holds Italy, within three short, dactylic words (*iam tenet Italiam*, highlighted by means of the tricolon crescendo). The allusion is to the situation after his crushing victory at the battle of Cannae in 216 BC, which left him in control of most (but not all) of Italy.[36] The exaggeration depicts him as a remorseless foe and a crazy and greedy fool who is never satisfied when he goes further (to Rome!) in the second half of the line. There may well be some dark wit there too: the primary reference is to his march on Rome, but he also advances further later on, when he goes to Bithynia in exile (160ff.). Campana sees a reminiscence of Lucan 1.191, *quo tenditis ultra?* ('to where are you marching on?') spoken by the sorrowing personification of Italy to Caesar and his army as they are about to cross the Rubicon and invade Italy. An echo of that seems very probable in view of the links in language and context (the words are used with a similarly disapproving tone of another mighty commander, who had just crossed the Alps quickly (1.183), and who was intent on fighting and taking Rome), and it would contribute to the antipathy by importing from Lucan the details of the distress of Italy and a fierce and unstoppable general (1.205ff.) proceeding to bring suffering, death and destruction to Roman citizens (and likening the Carthaginian to Caesar also exploits the critical picture of the latter at 108f. above).

At 155f., Hannibal's determination and the vivid sketch of the longed-for capture of Rome show the representative of *gloria* in the most unappealing light so far for J.'s original readers. Significantly, the words are given to the Carthaginian himself, who speaks nowhere else and so draws attention to what he has to say, as he comically condemns himself out of his own mouth. Coming right after the preceding feats, his speech evinces an extreme and unbalanced dissatisfaction, ambition and hostility. It also intimates the ultimate futility of his glorious exploits (certainly in his own eyes, as he did not take Rome; and this might well incline others to conclude that in the long run he didn't really accomplish anything). The quotation assigned to Hannibal makes fun of him too. The stern, martial tone, with forceful alliteration in line 155 and emphatic placement of *frangimus* ('I shatter') in 156, is kept up right until the unexpected final word, where the general wants to plant his standard not on one of the celebrated hills of Rome but in the demeaning Subura (the noisy, dirty and crowded red-light district). Perhaps we are to infer that the foreigner doesn't know what he is talking about and in aiming for the Subura is showing risible ignorance. Then again, perhaps he does know what he is talking about and is eager to get into the night life there with its drinking and sex! In either case, we are left with the bizarre image of a lone Carthaginian standard set up in this seedy area (quite possibly with partying going on around it).

There are some effective allusions at 155f. too. Many scholars have noted the similarity in language to Lucan 2.657 (of Julius Caesar at Brundisium again) – *nil actum credens, cum quid superesset agendum* ('thinking that nothing had been achieved, while anything still remained to be achieved'); and, in addition to the diction, there too a great general only deems that he has achieved something with a demanding proviso, and presses on although he already possesses all Italy (2.659f.). J. thereby denigrates Hannibal, equating him with Lucan's dispiriting and deadly Caesar, and bringing in associations of failure (Pompey himself escaped from Caesar at Brundisium) and inferiority (by way of contrast, Caesar did actually capture the city of Brundisium, and went on to take Rome). At the same time, J. seems to have in mind Livy 22.51.2 where, after the battle of Cannae, a Carthaginian (the cavalry commander Maharbal) talks of what had been accomplished and pictures the Carthaginians ensconced victoriously inside Rome, saying to Hannibal *ut quid hac pugna sit actum scias, die quinto ... victor in Capitolio epulaberis* ('so that you may realize what has been achieved by this battle, in five days ... you will banquet as victor on the Capitoline Hill'). J. turns 'what has been achieved' to 'nothing has been achieved', and also undercuts by changing the triumphant feast up on the venerable Capitol to the planting of the standard down in the low-lying and low-life Subura (and readers should recall that in Livy, Hannibal took a day to think over the march on Rome recommended by Maharbal, thus losing his chance to seize the city). Finally, *media … Subura* ('in the middle of the Subura') recalls the earlier instance of that phrase (in the same position in the hexameter) in J. (at 5.106, of the foul Tiber fish that feeds on the Subura's sewage) and so has a degrading aspect.

At 157f. J. jumps back in time to 217 BC and refers to the long, hard march (lasting four days and three nights though country flooded by the River Arno) made by Hannibal on the sole surviving elephant after the battle of Trebia in 218, during which he was deprived of the sight of one eye due to an infection and lost many men and animals (all of which brings up the pernicious element in the desire for martial glory). Initially the sentence seems approbatory (with apparently weighty spondees and celebratory anaphora in line 157), but then comes 158 – in particular its final two words, *belua* ('beast') and *luscum* ('one-eyed') – making for a sting in the tail again, and showing that the rhythm (in lines 157 and 158) is in fact mock-solemn (as well as fitting with slow movement). There we see the mighty leader decidedly diminished: he is disfigured (*luscus*, a down-to-earth word,[37] is emphasized by its place in the line, and perhaps hints at a lack of mental perception); and he is mounted on the only elephant he has left out of his squadron of 37, a grotesque form of transport for a supreme commander (which puts him now in direct contact with this repellent creature), but also an apt one – it too is unsightly and African; note also the pointed juxtapositions of *Gaetula* ('Gaetulian') and *ducem* ('general') and of *belua* and *luscum*. J. designates Hannibal's conveyance by means of a 'poetic' and highly pejorative periphrasis: there are connotations of savagery in *Gaetula* and of monstrosity, abnormality, strangeness and stupidity in *belua*.[38] With a blackly comic touch there is elegance in line 158 to convey and point up the ugliness: in this variant on the Golden Line there is chiasmus (of adjectives and nouns), balance (of nominatives and accusatives, with a trisyllable preceding a disyllable each time) and assonance of *u*, involving rhyme between first and last words.[39] The vignette at 157f. also builds effective antithesis, as J. moves on from successes to (greater and greater) setbacks: right after 155–6 we now see the general himself damaged rather than inflicting damage, and ensconced on an elephant (not in Rome); so too, rather than advancing further under his own steam he is carried, and after his rapid acquisition of Spain and crossing of the Pyrénées and Alps, his progress is slowed here, as nature causes him real problems; and *ducem … luscum* ('the one-eyed general') is a distinct deflation from *duce summo* ('first-rate general') in line 147. In addition, the notion of the painting in 157 (in marked contrast to equestrian statues of Roman emperors and victorious generals) reduces Hannibal to a wall decoration in someone's house (to be goggled at and derided by his enemies for many years), tamed, domesticated and living on in this unflattering pose (rather than thanks to undying renown).[40]

With an engaging rhetorical question, a sarcastic exclamation and an abrupt lurch forward in time, in line 159 J. draws attention to the Carthaginian's defeat at Zama in 202 BC. To lessen his impressiveness, our poet refers to this decisive reverse without having mentioned a single one of Hannibal's victories (and of his military successes only Cannae is included, later, and then briefly, and in a deflating context, at line 165). The ironical *o gloria* ('what glory!') is meant to deny him any such thing (as J. progresses to the inglorious end of his career) and is tartly juxtaposed with *vincitur* ('is defeated'). So too, Hannibal is beaten in just two words, *vincitur idem* ('this same man is defeated'), and the swiftness of his decline is also conveyed by the bustling dactyls, alliteration and assonance in line 159 (continued in 160), offsetting the celerity of his earlier successes, and signifying that glory is transitory.

Readers who know their history will find fault with not just the ellipse of Carthaginian victories but also the distortion at lines 160–2. To lessen Hannibal's standing still further, the condensation and the inclusion of *praeceps* ('headlong') in 160 suggest an immediate flight into exile after the loss at Zama, but in fact when the war was over Hannibal stayed on in Carthage for several years, working in government, until he left in 196/195 BC for fear of being handed over to Rome. He went first to Antiochus of Syria, and then ended up in the court of Prusias I, King of Bithynia, about 190 BC, where he eventually committed suicide some time between 183 and 181 BC, after the Romans had demanded his surrender and the king would not protect him. In addition, there is no evidence elsewhere for the picture J. paints in 161f. of Hannibal as a humiliated dependant in Bithynia, and actually he held a position of authority there, training the king's troops and commanding them in battle.[41]

In line 160 there is a wry twist to all the speed at 151ff., as Hannibal now speeds off in flight to exile. At 160f. there is a very good reason for the collocation *magnus mirandusque* ('mighty and marvellous') – *magnus* combines 'great in reputation or authority', 'great in achievement' and 'proud',[42] and both epithets are stressed by placement, alliteration and assonance). This represents a common view of the Carthaginian, one which the reader might well share, and that is why J. attacks it extensively with a flurry of put-downs, which give the collocation an ironical and sneering flavour, and make *mirandus* double-edged (he is also an amazing client because of the great fall from eminence, and he was amazingly idiotic and mad to bring about his own downfall like this). The first put-down is the juxtaposed *cliens* ('client'), which immediately takes Hannibal down a peg by intimating very low status and contains the cruel mockery of Rome's supreme enemy reduced to the position of the Roman client. Next comes *sedet* ('sits', in the posture of a suppliant): the man whom all Africa could not contain (148ff.) is thus contained in Prusias's palace, and all his restless and rapid onward progress (151ff.) is halted there (in Bithynia, as a client!); and probably the satirist is also exploiting the verb's senses of 'is inactive' and 'remains encamped'[43] (the leader who wanted to smash down gates and set up camp in Rome as victor is here inert and camps in Bithynia as a subservient exile). *Praetoria* will mean primarily 'palace' here, and so visually Hannibal is dwarfed by the large edifice; the noun can also mean 'general's HQ' (a sense easily felt in this Hannibalic context), so there may be a notion of Hannibal not inside his own headquarters and in charge but sitting in attendance at the HQ of another. Carefully placed at the end of line 161, *regis* ('king') accentuates the inferiority of the position as client. That effect is reinforced in the next line by *tyranno* ('tyrant'), also stressed by its placement, which adds the connotations of oppressiveness and cruelty.[44] *Bithyno* ('Bithynian') means that Hannibal is not just a dependant but the dependant of a petty oriental king (rather than being in control of Spain and Italy). In line 162 the Carthaginian is depicted as paying the client's morning call on his patron, which flippantly locates a Roman practice in Bithynia and activates thoughts of the discomfort, maltreatment and humiliation endured during such a *salutatio* earlier in J.'s *Satires*.[45] And Hannibal is made to wait at the pleasure of Prusias (a much lesser man), who arrogantly and slightingly takes his time before deciding that he is fully awake and ready to receive. In another telling snapshot (cf. 157f.), all the years with King Prusias are contracted into one moment of supreme ignominy, as J. freezes Hannibal in a deferential posture, waiting for his lord and master to deign to stir (at which point he will have to jump up and pay his respects). There is also bleak irony here in Hannibal being subservient to the very man who will himself be subservient to the Romans, and encompass his client's death[46] (as 163ff. remind us).

According to J., with all his efforts and ambition, in the long run what Hannibal actually achieved in his life was clientship in exile; and then (163ff.) he died. So too there is a tricolon crescendo in reversals at 159–62 (defeat; exile; the morning visit), with the stress on the most degrading part; and then J. devotes still more lines to his decease (163–6), so that there is a tetracolon crescendo, with even greater emphasis on Hannibal's (as J. presents it) laughable end (when his house in Bithynia was completely surrounded by troops and there was no escape, he took poison which, as one tradition has it, he carried around with him in a ring). For gloomy impact, from the rapidity J. moves on directly from the picture in 161f. to Hannibal's death, and the future tense in *dabunt* (translated as 'will come') means that he keeps Hannibal in that humble sitting pose with only an ignominious demise ahead of him. (Then again, it might be objected that he chose a quick death at his own hand, which was better than being publicly paraded and humiliated in Rome and then put to death there by his enemy.)

In line 163, after the frivolous touch of putting *finem* ('the end') as first word in the line, the satirist with weighty spondees (and with questionable exaggeration) builds up the height from which the general fell (*olim* ['once'] in emphatic position underscores the demeaning decline), and at the same time shows the exemplar of *gloria* in a very unappealing light (causing untold havoc, suffering and death, as a scourge of all humanity). In line 164, with forceful repetition and alliteration (and the more he goes on here, the greater the deflation in 166), J. underlines the fact that this military man did not pass away in a military fashion: he did not meet his end in action on the battlefield like a soldier or a mythological hero – *saxa* ('rocks') could refer to slingers' missiles or the boulders hurled by warriors in epic[47] – and in particular, when hemmed in by troops at his home, he did not go out fighting and taking some of them with him (noticeably, he is not depicted as actually in combat at any point in this whole subsection). In line 165, as part of the build-up, J. mention's Hannibal's greatest victory over the Romans (at Cannae in 216 BC) and expands on the theme of vengeance in a line of great gravity – in addition to the thought there is a spondaic rhythm and unique, and thus lofty, diction in *Cannarum vindex* ('punisher of Cannae') and *sanguinis ultor* ('avenger of bloodshed').[48] Everything in this sentence has been leading to the pay-off at the start of line 166 in *anulus* ('a ring'), a short, dactylic word, doubly emphatic by position, denoting such a small thing to kill a great man, and seeming even smaller next to all the blood in line 165, the rocks and other weapons in 164 and the whole world in 163. The expression (whereby the ring, rather than the poison in it, kills) results in the inherently ridiculous and mocking notions of death by ring and a ring as an avenger. In addition to the wry inversion of Hannibal as the avenger of Virgil's Dido and of the Carthaginian defeat in the First Punic War,[49] J. will be alluding to the story of the rings of the Roman dead at Cannae being sent back to Carthage by the general as proof of his crushing victory, and with a darkly comic spin presenting this symbol of his most glorious success as the implement of his inglorious death.

All of this is meant to ensure that there is nothing imposing or dignified in Hannibal's demise, which is made into a joke. This is part of the attempt in the second half of this subsection to turn someone who the reader might see as a figure for emulation into a person very definitely not to be emulated. That process is continued in the next sentence, where arrestingly J. suddenly addresses Hannibal and comes out with the derisive *i, demens* ('go on, you maniac'). Allusion adds to the facetiousness, as there is a droll transfer to Hannibal invading Italy of that phrase, which is found elsewhere only in Silius Italicus 10.62 (*sneering* advice to a Roman to flee the Carthaginian at Cannae) and 11.96 (a *dismissive* injunction to go over to Hannibal made by a Roman to an Italian). At the end of the subsection, for impact, with *demens* J. voices openly the earlier implication that the general was unbalanced, and then goes on to bring out his madness by means of the notion of rapid progress – *curre* ('race') activates a quaint picture of him sprinting through the awful Alps while the unexpected and unique epithet *saevas* ('savage') for the mountains underscores danger and hardship – with the sole intention of becoming an attractive rhetorical exercise for schoolboys (the ironical purpose clause is redolent of risible futility). With *pueris placeas* ('appeal to schoolboys') there is an image of Romans finding the (sorely diminished) commander now pleasing (as an exciting topic) rather than terrifying (as a real threat), and the idea is that only (naive, inexperienced, silly) boys with romantic notions of war and glory would find Hannibal and his activities attractive (rather than crazy). To underline that idea, there is very probably an echo of Petronius *Sat.* 4.3 – *nihil esse magnificum quod pueris placet* ('there is nothing fine that appeals to schoolboys') – on the lack of taste of immature and unformed boys when it comes to oratory.[50] In *declamatio fias* ('become a speech in the schools') there is final and total diminution.[51] At the start of the subsection, Hannibal was just light ashes, but here he is weightless and insubstantial hot air, and even more negligible as an artificial and pointless speech by an incompetent child.[52] This would appear to be all that he has achieved after his death (reinforcing the dour notion of what he achieved in his life at 160ff.) and, as J. puts it across here (also inaccurately), this seems to be the only form of immortality for Hannibal. This vigorous and memorable conclusion (with forceful alliteration and false gravity in the rhythm) is addressed to Hannibal but also speaks to the reader: he too would be mad to go through labours and peril in pursuit of *gloria*, and at best he too would just end up as adolescent declamation.

Keeping us on our toes, in line 168 J. abruptly moves on to the famous Greek general and king Alexander the Great, who was born at Pella (in Macedon) in 356 BC and died in Babylon in 323 BC, after conquering Greece and Asia as far as India. The poet passes over him quickly, ignoring his numerous accomplishments, while concentrating instead on his (to J.) misguided ambition and his paltriness, in a diminishing tricolon (168–70; 171–2; 172–3) which represents Alexander too as a figure not fit for emulation. J. implicitly (only implicitly) allows that he won glory (at 168f.), but he shows it as bringing Alexander no peace in his life and his quest for it as proving pointless (because checked by death).

The onslaught begins at once. In line 168 J. likens Alexander to the undermined Hannibal in that he cannot be contained. In fact, even worse than the Carthaginian, he cannot be contained by the entire world – *orbis* ('earth') is left to the end for effect – something which depicts Alexander (for our first impressions) as even more insanely acquisitive and hybristic. So too the periphrasis (bringing up the theme of transience again) reminds us that he had a short life, and that he came from a town which in J.'s day was just a small provincial backwater.[53] There is also levity to cut Alexander down to size: amid mock-solemn spondees (continued in line 169) there is the joke of the king being enclosed in the word order by *unus ... orbis* (the 'one earth' by which he does not want to be confined) and the amusing cheek of the small-town boy not content with the whole wide world.[54] J. also attaches to him a phrase from Lucan with uncomplimentary associations – *non sufficit orbis* ('earth is not enough'), which before here occurs only in Lucan, at 5.356 (applied to mutineers, who are portrayed as greedy and despicable villains) and 10.456 (of the ambitious Julius Caesar, brought down a peg, when trapped and afraid in Ptolemy's palace). However, there is also gross hyperbole here, which calls into question from the start J.'s presentation of Alexander: despite his eagerness to push on and on, and despite his vast conquests, the king did not subdue or even reach all parts of the earth (for instance, India was left alone, and he did not go near most of Europe); and rather than feeling that one world was not enough for him, he is said to have lamented the fact that he had not reduced all of this world.[55]

Our first view of Alexander here shows him not winning glory by fighting or conquering but unenviably dissatisfied. The next two lines take this further, by portraying him as positively chafing and by increasing his bizarre sense of confinement. In line 169 *aestuat* ('seethes') denotes his emotional disturbance, but the verb is often applied to water in violent movement,[56] so that J. is flippantly comparing him to a confined and seething sea when it is water (the encircling Ocean) that confines him and makes him seethe (and the sea is unreasoning). As *aestuare* can also mean 'be hot', there may well be macabre sport with the fever from which he suffered at the end of his life. *Infelix* (translated as 'the poor man') is a challenging and disparaging adjective for the highly successful leader. It is double-edged: it means 'unhappy' (because hemmed in) and also 'unfortunate' (because of his demented ambition etc.), applied ironically to a foolish, misguided person.[57] The paradoxical *angusto limite mundi* ('because of the narrow limits of the world'), with *mundi* delayed for impact, represents the ludicrously skewed point of view of the Greek, and contains a grim joke (he did get beyond the limits of this world when he died and went to another *mundus* – the Underworld).[58] In line 170 the satirist mentions two small islands in the

Cyclades which were used as places of exile for criminals and others who offended the emperor, and which were notoriously harsh and uncomfortable spots.[59] Continuing his ascription of a distorted vision to Alexander, J. intimates that to him the earth (like the islands) seemed a negligible land mass surrounded by water and a cramping, hateful jail, and that Alexander (like someone banished) saw himself as a prisoner and miserably fretted and longed to escape confinement – *scopulis* ('rocks') and *parva* ('tiny') bring out the discomfort and constriction. Again there is frivolity at the expense of the *exemplum*: in addition to the incongruous image of Alexander exiled, there are Greek rather than Italian islands for the Greek general; these are small places for Alexander the Great; in the word order, *clausus* ('confined') is surrounded by rocky Gyara and tiny Seriphos; and there is probably play on *clausus*'s senses of 'bury' (of one who will soon die) and 'blockade' (in connection with a soldier).[60] There is also a subtly demeaning aspect: Alexander is likened to an inferior and helpless exile/criminal in an unimpressive setting; and in particular *parva Seriphos* ('tiny Seriphos') only occurs elsewhere in J.'s 6.564 (with reference to a despicable and villainous astrologer) and Ovid *Metamorphoses* 5.242 (*vis-à-vis* the immoral and foolish King Polydectes, who shortly afterwards was easily killed by Perseus).

To downgrade the king, of all the territory ruled by Alexander in his vast empire and of all the cities entered by him in his extensive march, in line 171 J. mentions only the place of his death (and going there was rather silly, as he had been warned away from Babylon by seers).[61] Our poet also employs a jocular and depreciatory periphrasis (a parody of poetic erudition)[62] to refer to the city, which was famous for its massive walls of baked brick, which had been constructed by its legendary Queen Semiramis. The twist in J.'s introduction of potters creates pawky paradox (how could such craftsmen protect a town?), underlined by the juxtaposition of the prosaic *figulis* ('potters') and the imposing *munitam* ('fortified'); and it elicits a fantastic picture of great squadrons of these workmen toiling away to make preposterous and useless walls (consisting of masses of pots joined together?). This is intended to render Babylon a grotesque place to die and thus deny Alexander's end any impressiveness or dignity. There is also the joke of the man for whom the world was too small ending up confined by potters' walls, and then in line 172 by an even more constricting coffin within them. Placed at the start of the verse for emphasis, *sarcophago* ('sarcophagus') (a Greek term for a Greek) is a big word to cut down to size Alexander the Great, and its literal sense ('flesh-eating')[63] is a reminder of human frailty and transience (reinforced in the next sentence). There is sneering irony in the notion of the king being content with his coffin, which sports with his motionless embalmed body giving an appearance of being peaceful and at ease after all the restlessness, and which seems to imply that this crazy fool could only achieve contentment when no longer alive (and lusting for glory). In addition, J. is probably playing on the fact that *contentus* could also be the perfect participle passive of *contineo* meaning 'confined', 'controlled' and 'enclosed'.[64]

After that final picture of Alexander the Great as a corpse, the subsection ends at 172f. with him almost totally elided (figuring only obliquely, in an allusion to his inglorious littleness) and with death (superior to such mere mortals) dominant. A memorable epigram accents our insignificance by means of two diminutives – *quantula* ('how tiny') and *corpuscula* ('puny bodies') – which are largely prosaic and down to earth,[65] and are highlighted by placement and rhyme, and which form part of a predominantly dactylic sequence of little sounds.[66] It is true that many people (especially grand men) seem small in death, and J. will also be exploiting the unflattering tradition that the king was of less than average height.[67]

At line 173 (rather startlingly within the line) J. suddenly progresses to the invasion of Greece in 480 BC by the large army of Xerxes I (who ruled Persia from 486 to 465 BC). There is a complex start to this subsection, with various things going on at once, as the satirist (rather questionably) tries to have his cake and eat it. J. allows that Xerxes might have done the things mentioned at 174–8, and might have had huge forces (especially because this makes his defeat by mere lying Greeks all the more shameful). But he also casts doubt on all this, by means of *creditur olim* ('people sometimes believe'),[68] with *olim* stressed by its position, plus the emphatically placed and juxtaposed *mendax* ('lying') and *audet* ('dares to say'), and J. thereby undercuts Xerxes's accomplishments there. Furthermore, those carefully selected 'achievements' are trivial and hardly very glorious in themselves (not military victories), and are described in such a way as to make them seem absurd and bizarre (prior to being decidedly offset at 179ff.). At the same time, the sweeping generalization in line 174 (all Greeks are liars) invites charges of pessimism and exaggeration, and so undermines the position taken here.

The debunking of Xerxes begins in line 174. Mount Athos stands on the tip of a promontory in the northern Aegean, where a Persian fleet (belonging to his father Darius) had been wrecked by a gale while trying to round it a few years earlier. Therefore, to avoid that happening again, Xerxes dug a canal across the promontory before his invasion. J. pokes fun at this feat by means of his expression. The verb *velificare* was normally intransitive and meant 'to sail', so at first sight, *velificatus Athos* suggests a sailing mountain! In fact, the verb here is transitive and has the unique sense 'sail through', but even so we are presented with the most peculiar image of ships sailing through a mountain (rather than the promontory).

In line 175, *audet* (literally 'dares', i.e. dares to say) contains a barb at the Persian king's expense, representing Greeks rather than him as the daring ones. There is a barb in the ambiguous *historia* too: I have opted for the sense 'histories', but the noun can also denote a story, specifically a lying tale.[69] There is disagreement over the reference in the rest of line 175, but most probably J. has in mind Herodotus 7.45, where Xerxes sees the whole Hellespont covered by his ships.[70] There is an obvious dig here in bringing out the massiveness of the naval forces, because despite this advantage the Persians were beaten at sea (at Salamis, in 480). Moreover, the context of the Herodotean allusion tells against the fleet's impressive appearance: at 7.46, Xerxes weeps at the sight of his ships, mindful of the shortness of human life and the fact that none of his men would be alive one hundred years on. There seems to be pert play in *constratum* ('covered'): the verb can also mean 'calm, make smooth',[71] and rough seas were responsible for substantial losses of Persian vessels. Some critics have suspected *isdem* ('the same') and see it as unclear and pointless, but it does work well. It will signify the same ships that sailed through Athos, but it also invites us to think of other things *vis-à-vis* the same fleet and the sea, and I find it easy enough to make the connection that the sea also damaged large numbers of the same fleet in storms, and the sea was the stage for the major defeat of the same fleet at Salamis.

Line 176 is concerned with the two boat-bridges constructed over the Hellespont to transport the Persian army from Asia to Europe, for which vessels were anchored side by side and lashed together, and were paved over by planks placed on cables and covered with brushwood and soil. After turning a mountain into a sea (so his ships could sail through it) Xerxes here turns the sea into land (so his chariots can ride over it), acts which were viewed as contrary to nature.[72] J.'s strange and whimsical expression subverts this feat of engineering and calls into doubt Greek accounts of it: instead of saying a solid bridge was placed on the Hellespont, he describes the liquid sea itself as made solid by Xerxes, and he also summons up a truly surreal picture of sea taken and set under (disembodied) wheels.

At the end of line 176, J. incorporates more levity in connection with the king, in the form of a tease in *credimus* ('we believe'). Initially we think (*we believe*) that he is moving on to something that he does credit as true, but as the sentence progresses we come to realize that *credimus* is heavily tinged with irony (people may generally believe this stuff, but J. has serious reservations). J. goes beyond Herodotus,[73] who said that there were so many Persians that they drank dry the smaller rivers (but not the major ones). Our jokey and hyperbolical satirist depicts even great ones – *altos* ('deep') highlighted at the end of 176 – failing and whole watercourses being thoroughly drained;[74]

in line 177 the two verbs and two plural nouns denoting rivers intimate enormous imbibing by a massive army descending thirstily on stream after stream; with *Medo* ('the Mede', in fact a singular for plural) J. momentarily conjures up an individual Persian doing all the drinking; and the carefully delayed *prandente* ('while breakfasting', emphatically at the start of line 178) represents this extensive consumption of liquid as taking place during the (traditionally light) morning/midday meal.[75] All of this is meant to make the Greek claims about the rivers seem ludicrous, and the repetition of the detail of drinking and the allusion to various waterways look like a dig at Greeks going on and on about all the streams that ran dry.[76] There is also a grisly twist to the water here keeping the Persians alive, at 185f., where the sea is filled with Persian dead. So too it is all very well for the king's men to drink water, sail on it through a canal, cover it with their ships and bridge it, but it would be better if they could win a victory on it.

In the rest of line 178 there is another humorous take on the liquid motif with *madidis* ('dripping'). Sostratus would appear to be a poet who wrote about Xerxes's invasion,[77] and J. is surely punning on the name – made up of the Greek *sōs* ('safe, intact') and *stratos* ('a military force' – by including it immediately before the very damaging defeat of Xerxes's fleet off the island of Salamis near Athens (480 BC) in line 179. The phrase *madidis ... alis* clearly undercuts Sostratus (and also the deeds of Xerxes celebrated by him), but its precise meaning is not certain. In my translation I have opted for 'dripping armpits', the most derogatory sense, with its combination of ridicule and disgust: the notion will be that during a performance of his verse, Sostratus is so carried away, and perhaps also so anxious that he might not be believed, that his body temperature rises and he sweats. But *alis* can mean 'wings' as well as 'armpits', and there may well be a playful *double entendre* here. In this case, the image would be that of the poet taking wing, and because his wings are wet (and thus heavy) Sostratus is unable to get off the ground and soar;[78] if J. had in mind a specific source of moisture, Sostratus may be sweating again or have turned to wine for inspiration and splashed his wings with it.[79] There is also some effective intertextuality. Many critics have pointed to the similarity to Ovid *Metamorphoses* 1.264 (the only other prior occurrence of *madidis alis*): *madidis Notus evolat alis* ('the South Wind flies forth with dripping wings'), where the Wind, his terrible face shrouded in darkness, flies out from Aeolus's cave as part of Jupiter's plan to destroy the wicked human race in a great deluge. In our poet's echo of that, with the 'wings' sense for *alis*, the human Sostratus seems even more risible and negligible beside the dread South Wind (who *is* flying) and his wings (wet with stormy rain) and his (momentous) activity, while the 'armpits' meaning for *alis* (which is perfectly possible in the new context) represents an even more amusing and demeaning twist. The Ovidian reference is also a tart reminder of what really impressive verse is like, and the parody of that line of serious poetry, turning it into something comical, is wickedly apt for a figure of fun, a comically bad poet who makes a hash of serious poetry. In addition, the associations of massive destruction with a watery connection as divine punishment and the allusion to a wind leaving Aeolus's cave fit neatly with Salamis, the winds and Aeolus in the following verses.

After the advance of the Persian host at 174–8, one might have expected something on their victory at Thermopylae and their capture of Athens, but in line 179 J. jumps forward to the major reverse at Salamis that sent Xerxes home. With his tunnel vision he also has nothing to say about the large land forces that remained in Greece under the Persian general Mardonius. Instead, in his first mention of the king himself, while dwelling in a full line, J. catches Xerxes (not even dignified with a name here or elsewhere in this subsection) at a very unappealing point, freezing him in inglorious flight after inglorious defeat. The question posed in 179 is an engaging one. Teasingly, and to provide a build-up, J. holds back the answer until as late as 185f., while arousing expectations of a really bad state for Xerxes as nemesis for the hybris that is put into the spotlight in the interim.

According to Herodotus (7.35), when an initial pair of boat-bridges over the Hellespont were destroyed by a storm, Xerxes on that (sole) occasion had the sea lashed. At 180f. J. has something similar, but significantly different, as the king whips winds (the north-west and the south-east winds), and whips them repeatedly (details not found elsewhere). Whether J. is exaggerating Herodotus or passing on now lost material from another source (or sources), the effect on his depiction of the Persian is the same. In a powerful collocation, word after word makes this seeker after *gloria* look far from admirable. He is brutal (brought out by 'barbarian' plus 'savagely'). He is also stupid, crazed and absurd: we are invited to envisage his men flogging thin air (and the whistling sigmatism in line 180 makes for vividness!), and we are left to wonder how one lashes a wind and how one would know that one is hitting it; the habitual flogging would come about because the gales were not brought to heel,[80] hardly surprising, as this is a perfectly pointless thing to do (but evidently the royal megalomaniac somehow never managed to grasp this). Hybris is also in evidence. J. specifies particular winds by name because Corus and Eurus were regarded as gods, but are here treated as slaves by Xerxes. The disciplinary action against them has a subtler (literary) aspect too. There is a cluster of details that call to mind the tempest at Virgil *Aeneid* 1.52ff., where gales rushed from their master Aeolus's cave, called a *carcer* ('prison', cf. 181), and fell upon Aeneas's fleet, causing major upheaval, until Neptune (cf. 182) reprimanded Eurus and

Zephyrus for causing the storm (cf.180). Neptune's chastisement of Eurus and Zephyrus there was purely verbal (a superior ticking off, with a threat of harsher punishment later), whereas here the mortal Xerxes's chastisement of and contempt for Eurus and Corus exceed those of a major god, and he actually inflicts (savage) punishment. Hand in hand with that, J. is having fun with Virgil's reference to Aeolus's cave as a prison with chains,[81] taking it further (inmates of a jail might well be flogged) and prompting a fleeting image of Aeolus actually wielding a whip. This also brings out the human Xerxes's arrogance, by depicting him as not just usurping the role of the divine Aeolus but actually going beyond that strict and imperious master. The epic reminiscence also points up the futility of Xerxes's conduct, because it reminds us of how Aeolus did handle the winds in his cavern – really controlling and calming them,[82] in contrast to the Persian's repeated botched attempts to do so.

The treatment of gods as slaves continues in line 182 (where J. now definitely starts to accept Greek stories about the invasion without question, because it suits his purpose). According to Herodotus,[83] after the destruction of the first boat-bridges, Xerxes also had fetters thrown into the Hellespont. Line 182 is J.'s mocking way of referring to what the king intended to do (chain the god of the sea, to punish him as an unruly slave) but, of course, could not actually do (as the shackles just sank and could not touch Neptune).[84] But by portraying Xerxes as actually fettering the deity, J. presents an arresting and disturbing picture, one that makes the Persian seem even more idiotic and insane, and even more above himself. The juxtapositions of *vinxerat* and *Ennosigaeum* ('had bound', 'the Earth-shaker') and *ipsum* and *conpedibus* ('himself', 'with shackles') spotlight the hybris. J. draws attention to the god's power, producing in an uncommon five-word hexameter an unusual five-syllable ending by placing in emphatic position *Ennosigaeum*, an impressively bulky epicism (first here in surviving Latin), which indicates his dominion over land (as the cause of earthquakes) as well as the sea; and in the word order that great divinity (*ipsum ... Ennosigaeum*) ominously enfolds the enchaining mortal, dwarfing him, and bringing out how puny and ridiculously misguided he is. Moreover, the Homeric *Ennosigaeus* brings to mind the Poseidon of the *Iliad* and *Odyssey*, a god who had Greek sympathies,[85] and an angry and vengeful figure who pursued Odysseus relentlessly for offending him, so that Xerxes seems to be really asking for it.

At 183f. (where I have opted for what I see as the most pointed text and punctuation),[86] the reference is to the story that after the loss of the boat-bridges, Xerxes also sent men to brand the water (in this way too punishing Poseidon like a slave who had misbehaved). J. shows an inconsistency which is amusing and also militates against his reliability.

After questioning details found in Herodotus, and satirizing others for their credulity, J. now accepts as fact an item about which there is some doubt in the Greek sources (Herodotus reports it as just a rumour).[87] He embraces it because it is a supreme and climactic example of preposterous insanity (how does one brand water, let alone a god?); and there is witty play in applying the verb *credo* ('believe') to Xerxes here, when like him, the satirist himself is expressing belief in something dubious. Adding to the humour is the little joke in *stigmate* ('branding', a Greek term for the Greek *Ennosigaeus*), and the irony in *mitius* (I translate the word as 'rather merciful', but 'tolerable', 'gentle' and 'civilized' are also possible senses[88] and would extend the irony), and the spin in the use of *mitis* (often employed of divinities),[89] which suggests that the mortal is behaving like a merciful god, to a god.

The question in line 184 (with mock gravity in the rhythm) gains force from the placement of *huic* (referring to the king) as first word and *deorum* ('the gods') as last, and from the juxtaposition of *servire* ('to be his slave') with *deorum* – all of which brings out the mad unreality of the Persian's assumption of mastery. *Vellet* ('would have been willing') is a reminder of Xerxes's inferiority: the decision about servility was down to the deity, not the human, so the actions in the preceding verses are meaningless and mere show. The question brings to mind kings for whom gods did consent to function in a servile capacity. Apollo served the silly and short-sighted Admetus, who encompassed the death of his own dear wife by allowing her to die in his place and then bitterly regretted it, while Laomedon foolishly and impiously refused to pay Neptune and Apollo for their services and thus brought disaster on his country (a flood and sea monster sent by Neptune, and a deadly plague caused by Apollo).[90] There are obvious parallels with Xerxes, and he does not manage to measure up even to these brainless monarchs (as he did not have a divinity for a slave).

In line 185 J. returns to the question posed in 179, repeating it insistently and raising our expectations further, before finally providing a memorable answer. There is provocative pawkiness in the use of the affirmative *nempe* ('of course') to introduce the unparalleled and highly improbable picture of Xerxes returning home in flight on a single ship right after the defeat at Salamis and sailing through the corpses of Persians just killed in that battle. According to Herodotus and other reliable authors, a few days after the engagement the king went off to Boeotia by land with his large army, pausing there for Mardonius to select his best troops, and only after that retreated (overland) to Persia; and there is no reason why Xerxes would abandon the protection of his soldiers and go by sea, sailing off on just one ship when a number of them had survived, and putting his life at risk in this way at a time when the Greek fleet was rampant.[91] Such a farfetched claim after J.'s earlier criticism of lying Greek historians and the credulity of people who believe in them is entertainingly outrageous, while also further undermining his reliability.

Even if flawed, it is a powerful, cinematic image that the satirist provides – the isolated ship in a sea of blood and corpses moving slowly because there are so many dead to thrust through. The impact is increased by the tricolon crescendo (in ablative phrases) whose subjects become increasingly bleak (lone ship; bloody waves; prow moving slowly through crowded corpses) and by grimly graphic touches (the juxtapositions *nave-cruentis* ('ship', 'bloody') and *cadavera-prora* ('corpses', 'prow'); the slowness in several spondees and the long *a* sounds; and in line 186 the frequency of *t, c, d* and *p*, which suggests to me the noise of bodies bumping against the prow). The direct progression from Xerxes's arrogance towards the god of the sea at 182–4 to the sea filled with his dead men here makes it clear that this is nemesis, and a reminder of who the master is in reality, as he is himself punished for punishing Neptune. Numerous humiliating reversals of elements at the start of this subsection also diminish the king and spotlight his fall: in place of his successful advance, he is now retreating in defeat; instead of sailing through Athos, he is sailing through his own dead; his huge fleet is reduced to one vessel; the waves that were covered by his ships (and boat-bridges) are now covered by dead bodies; instead of masses of live soldiers there are masses of their corpses; and instead of drinking rivers dry, they have poured their blood into the sea. This is our final (and most unappealing) view of Xerxes, and it is a vivid and chilling snapshot of him in inglorious flight, which brings right before our eyes what the quest for *gloria* brought him (and his troops) and foregrounds the themes of destruction and futility. There is some pathos here, but above all there is black humour in the come-uppance (the moron was asking for it, and here he duly gets it, really gets it).

Line 187 suddenly spreads out from Xerxes and broadens the picture, concluding the section with a daunting statement of the frequency of the deleterious effect of petitions for military glory. In this full, end-stopped, largely spondaic line of summary (which also subtly reminds us that there are more powerful (and more glorious) figures set above us, no matter what we achieve), *has ... poenas* ('such is the punishment') forms a frame, ominously enfolding the prayers for glory (*optata ... gloria*), and *gloria* and *poenas* are eloquently juxtaposed, while the last word of the whole section is *poenas*. There is also a sardonic flavour: the idea is that in the light of the foregoing arguments and *exempla* (and right after 185f.), one would have to be a fool to ask for martial *gloria* (in effect praying for something like a nightmarish voyage through a sea of bodies); and *totiens* ('so often') conjures up a whole host of fools down the ages actually making the entreaty and bringing catastrophe down on themselves as a result. The implication in *exegit ... poenas* ('the punishment ... exacted') is that such a request merits chastisement, and this would most obviously be because it is hybristic (cf. 137 and the overreaching arrogance shown by Hannibal, Alexander and Xerxes above). This amounts to a final bit of problematizing, since it is debatable that very many of those who pursue and have pursued martial glory are guilty of hybris and J. has no way of corroborating such a sweeping claim.[92]

In 1748 Samuel Johnson completed the most famous reworking of X – *The Vanity of Human Wishes.* In it he omitted and expanded as he saw fit, substituted contemporary parallels and gave the poem something of a Christian flavour. It is instructive to compare his lines on military glory (for which see Winkler, 2001, 225ff.). His criticism of Xerxes is stronger; but generally he tones down the attack, going for something calmer and less negative, and producing a mood of quiet and thoughtful melancholy rather than savage mockery and pessimism. This is a different approach, which should appeal more to those readers who find J. too hard and dark. Then again, some might say that Johnson's is a Juvenal for bed-wetters.

Notes

1   For example, Jenkyns writes: 'with remorseless accuracy he sees through the fog of convention to what is truly there' (209).

2   For *exuviae*, denoting valuable spoil in general and specifically armour taken in battle, see *TLL* V.2.2131.17ff. and 2130.75ff.

3   See for example, Jenkyns writes: 'The note of harsh pity for the captive is just right; terse and unsentimental' (209).

4   The jerky rhythm in the three monosyllables at the end of the line (on which see Ferguson and Campana) brings the reader up short and attracts attention.

5   See *TLL* VII.1.554.5ff. for the word's elevation. It is unusual for a hexameter to end with a word of five syllables (see Campana), and this rarity also puts stress on *induperator.*

6   *Barbarus* means 'foreign' (i.e. not Roman or Greek) but will also embrace 'uncivilized' and 'savage', to depreciate the *generalissimo* (see *OLD* s.v. 1, 2, 3; *TLL* II.1735.69ff., 1739.6ff.).

7   *OLD* s.v. 1, 2, 3a, 6a, 6b.

8   See Urech, 245.

9   In this martial context, *virtus* must denote 'the qualities typical of a true man, manly spirit, resolution, valour, steadfastness or sim.' (*OLD* s.v. 1).

10   See *OLD* s.v. 4.

11   For *praemium* of a payment or inducement for service see *OLD* s.v. 1, and for

amplector with reference to copulation see *TLL* I.1990.33ff.; Adams, 181f. This type of woman figures below at 319ff.

12   See *TLL* IX.2.151.64ff.; *OLD* s.v. 2, 3b, 4, 9a.

13   Many critics take *paucorum* to denote a few generals over the course of history, but with such a reference – on top of *olim* ('at times') in line 142 – J. would be saying that this destruction of countries happens only very occasionally, which would seriously weaken his case, and which is not on all fours with the breadth of his claims in lines 138 and 141f.

14   See *OLD* s.v. 7; *TLL* VI.3.2494.7ff., 2498.80ff.

15   See Urech, 245.

16   See Mayor; Campana.

17   Adams, 15 n. 1, 113.

18   See *OLD* s.v. 1, 3, 4, 5.

19   For *discutio*, see e.g. Caes. *BC* 2.9, *Bell. Alex.* 46.2; Livy 21.12.2; Virg. *Aen.* 9.810, Val. Max. 3.2.23b; Sen. *Contr. exc.* 5.5; Amm. 25.1.3. On *valeo* see *OLD* s.v. 5. On *robur* see *OLD* s.v. 6.

20   On the diction see Urech, 245; Ebel; Campana.

21   E.g. Achilles at Prop. 2.9.13f., Ovid *Met.* 12.615f. and Hercules at Sen. (?) *HO* 1762f.

22   This may also be a mock-heroic variant on Zeus weighing heroes' fates with his balance at Hom. *Il.* 8.69ff. and 22.208ff.

23   Which appears all the smaller beside the vastness of Africa at 148ff., as Campana points out.

24   Campana suggests that with *hic est* ('this is the man'), J. may be deliberately echoing a formula common in funerary inscriptions. If so, there are suitable connotations of death here, and this would be a dismissive epitaph for the Carthaginian commander. On Hannibal as anti-hero see Stocks.

25   On Moors see 5.53f., 6.337 (and cf. e.g. Hor. *Odes* 3.10.18; Calp. *Ecl.* 4.40). On Egyptians see 1.26 (and Courtney, ad loc.), 130, 4.31ff., 6.83f., 489, 526ff., 9.22 (and cf. also *Satire* 15; Hor. *Epod.* 9.13ff.; *Odes* 1.37.9f. (and Nisbet and Hubbard, ad loc.); Virg. *Aen.* 8.698; Prop. 3.11.39ff.; Sen. *Dial.* 9.9.8; [Sen.] *Oct.* 521; Lucan 8.542ff., 10.63ff.). On Ethiopians see 2.23, 6.600, 8.33 (and cf. also *OLD* s.v. *Aethiops* 2; L & S s.v. *Aethiops* I B 2; Snowden, 179; Beardsley, 119f.).

26   Housman has *aliosque elephantos*, which I accept, but the text and interpretation of line 150 are uncertain. On the controversy see esp. the summaries in Tengström, 28ff.; Ronnick (1992); Campana. There seems to me to be no case for deletion and no need for emendation. Of the mss readings, *altosque* ('and the tall [elephants]' strikes me as redundant and lacking in pertinence (it could be a deliberate 'correction' because *aliosque* was not understood, or be due simply to misreading or a slip of the pen, with confusion of *i* and *t*). The other mss reading (also supported by Priscian *GLK* ii.217) is *aliosque*, which gives good sense and has real point if taken to mean 'and the other [elephants]', i.e. the Ethiopian elephants, not the African (or specifically Mauretanian) ones – hence my translation 'and

their different elephants' (*alius* instead of *alter* to signify one of a pair was common and appears elsewhere in J.; see Campana). Pliny *N.H.* 8.32 talks of three types of elephants – African (beyond the deserts of Sidra and in Mauretania), Ethiopian and Indian. Contrary to some scholars, after line 148 I find it easy enough to make a small logical supplement and understand *aliosque* to mean other than those found in the place that J. has just mentioned. Significantly, with this explanation, *aliosque* contributes to J.'s undermining of Hannibal here by highlighting the fact that in his own Africa too there are elephants, as well as on his borders.

27   Compare the attitude to the creatures at 12.103ff. Hannibal, of course, used them in fighting and rode on one (see 158).

28   See Urech, 247f.

29   *OLD* s.v. *percutio* 1, 2, 3.

30   For which see *TLL* I.771.76ff., 773.17ff., 774.19ff.; *OLD* s.v. 1b, 3.

31   See *OLD* s.v. 5. Courtney and Campana both note the hybris in these lines.

32   See *OLD* s.v. 5a, b, c.

33   See Mayor on 10.303; Otto s.v. *natura*. Hannibal later lost an eye because of the weather and the air of the marshes of the Arno (see 158; Livy 22.2.10f.), which could be viewed as nemesis.

34   See Mayor; Ferguson; Livy 21.37.2 (and Walsh, ad loc.).

35   *Rumpo* often means 'cleave', and (for comic effect) that sense will be prominent here, but 'break through' is also feasible (see *OLD* s.v. 1, 3).

36   See Livy 22.54.10; Polybius 3.118.2.

37   It is found in prose and the lower genres of poetry. See Urech, 251.

38   See Pease on Virg. *Aen.* 4.40 and *OLD* s.v. *belua* 2 and 3.

39   Cf. Campana, ad loc.; Plaza (2006), 313f.

40   Note also that in *facies* ('sight') in line 157 there may be malicious play on the senses 'face' and 'good looks'.

41   Cf. e.g. Nepos *Hannibal* 11f.; Justin. *Epitome* 32.4.

42   See *OLD* s.v. 12, 13, 15.

43   See *OLD* s.v. 4 and 7. Cf. Campana.

44   *OLD* s.v. 3.

45   Cf. 1.95ff., 5.19ff., 76ff.

46   See e.g. Nepos *Hann.* 12; Livy 39.51; Justin. *Epitome* 32.4.

47   E.g. Turnus at Virg. *Aen.* 12.896ff.

48   Cf. also Urech, 253.

49   See Campana.

50   The phrase *pueris placere* also appears at Martial 14.129.2, but without the rhetorical context, and with the addition of *militibusque* (a colour appeals to boys and soldiers).

51   Cf. Miller, ad loc.; Romano, 164.

52   For the use of Hannibal as a topic in schools (e.g. for speeches advising him on whether or not he should attack Rome after Cannae), see Mayor and cf. esp.

7.160ff. On the frequently low level of attainment of young pupils in such exercises, cf. e.g. 7.150ff.; Tac. *Dial.* 35.4.

53   Courtney cites Sen. *Epist.* 119.8, which refers to Alexander as coming from an unknown corner of the world.

54   Cf. Duff and Rudd and Barr's note.

55   See Val. Max. 8.14 ext. 2; Plut. *Mor.* 466D; Aelian *Var. Hist.* 4.29.

56   *TLL* I.1113.43ff.

57   *OLD* s.v. 3b.

58   For *mundus* of Hades see *TLL* VIII.1638.31ff.

59   See esp. Mayor; Campana.

60   See *OLD* s.v. 6, 7a.

61   See Mayor.

62   See Courtney.

63   Cf. Pliny *N.H.* 2.211.

64   See *OLD* s.v. 6, 7, 8.

65   Cf. Urech, 256f.

66   Cf. Jenkyns, 212.

67   See e.g. Curtius 3.12.16f., 6.5.29; Diod. Sic. 17.66.3.

68   The most likely sense for *olim* is 'sometimes' (which increases the doubt about veracity). Others translate: 'it has long been believed that …' or 'it is believed that once …', but such meanings for *olim* here seem rather pointless and redundant.

69   Campana notes this ambiguity, citing *TLL* VI.3.2834.32.

70   For *consterno*, used of ships so numerous that they hide large stretches of water, see Courtney; and for *mare* ('sea') applied to the Hellespont cf. e.g. Ovid *Her.* 18.108. Some scholars think that J. is alluding here to the boat-bridges over the Hellespont, and that *consterno* could denote such paving over of the water (cf. Campana). However, I can see no particular reason for referring to these bridges in line 175 as well as 176, and the notion here of ships paving over the sea would detract from the deliberate oddness of 176, while a reference to Herodotus and the vastness of the fleet facilitates additional sniping at the king.

71   *TLL* IV.509.19ff.

72   See Campana.

73   7.21, 196.

74   For *epoto* = 'drink up' see *TLL* V.2.698.36ff.

75   Cf. Courtney.

76   Cf. e.g. Herod. 7.21, 43, 58, 108, 187, 196.

77   His exact identity remains unknown. For various candidates proposed by scholars, see Campana.

78   For the image see Nisbet and Hubbard's introduction to Horace *Odes* 2.20. For the soaring bard cf. e.g. Horace *Odes* 4.2.25ff. For damp wings preventing flight cf. e.g. Ovid *AA* 1.233f.

79   See *OLD* s.v. *madidus* 2b, 6, and s.v. *madeo* 2b.

80   Storms (caused by winds) destroyed the boat-bridges at the start and end of the expedition and twice damaged the Persian fleet severely.

81   *Aen.* 1.54. For the jesting cf. *Sat.* 5.100f.

82   See *Aen.* 1.54, 57.

83   7.35, 8.109.

84   Cf. Seneca *Dial.* 2.4.2.

85   See e.g. *Il.* 13.43f., 59ff., 14.139ff., 151f.

86   *Quid* ('what?') is Weber's emendation for the manuscripts' *quod* ('that'). Housman accepts *quod* and punctuates as follows: *mitius id sane quod non et stigmate dignum / credidit: huic quisquam vellet servire deorum?* ('It was really rather merciful that he didn't believe him worthy of branding too: which of the gods would have been willing to be his slave?'). This is not nonsensical (there would be sarcasm), but *quid* is more condemnatory than *quod*. There *were* stories that Xerxes branded the Hellespont, and surely J. would want to include such an act as a further example of the king's hybris (leading directly into the nemesis at sea in 185f.) and as a climax in grotesque absurdity. I do not see much point in mentioning the branding only to exclude it, or the logic in moving from a denial of maltreatment of the god to the following question ('Which of the gods would have been willing to be his slave?'). The corruption of *quid* to *quod* (especially before *non*) seems easy enough.

87   Herod. 7.35. Plutarch *Mor.* 455D believes the tale.

88   *OLD* s.v. 4, 5, 6a, 6d.

89   *TLL* VIII.1152.73ff.

90   See e.g. Eur. *Alcestis*; Apollod. *Bibl.* 1.9.15, 2.5.9.

91   Cf. e.g. Aesch. *Persae* 480; Herod. 8.92, 113ff. Other writers mention a lone ship (see Mayor; Campana) but do not have Xerxes using it to sail away immediately through Persian dead.

92   There may be a reminiscence here of Petronius *Sat.* 120.66 – *has gloria reddit honores* ('such is the honour that glory gives as a repayment') – where there is a similar brief summing up after lines on the downfall of a trio of generals (Crassus, Pompey and Caesar). If there is a deliberate echo, J.'s allusion would bring in three additional (and Roman) examples to reinforce his case against *gloria*.

CHAPTER SEVEN

Longevity (188–288)

The sudden direct quotation of the supplication in line 188 seizes the attention and immediately alerts us to this section's topic. J. progresses easily enough from the request for glory backfiring in 187 to another request backfiring here – with a verbal link in *optata* ('prayers') in 187 and *optas* ('you pray') in 189 – and from the mass of corpses (186) to the mass of evils (190f.) attendant on both misguided entreaties. Jupiter's appearance in line 188 picks up the gods from 180–4 too. But there are also lively contrasts – between death (185f.) and long life, between the red of the waves at 185f. and the pallor of the face in 189, and between Persians at sea and Romans on land.

The military aspect of the *exempla* at 246ff. draws together this section and the previous one, but there are major differences as well, because at this point in X there is a definite danger of monotony. This is a much longer section (almost twice as long) and it contains many more *exempla*, of which, for a change, four are mythological and two are Roman. There is much more pathos here too, especially in connection with Nestor (246ff.) and Priam (258ff.). In addition, this is the first time in the poem that J. engages combatively with an extended episode in a predecessor, when at 258ff. he emends and 'improves on' Virgil's account of the death of Priam in *Aeneid* 2. Also new in this satire is the sordidness – in the ugliness at 191ff., the feebleness at 229ff. and especially the sexual material at 204ff., 223f. and 238f.

But the biggest difference is that J.'s basic point in this section is indisputably sound. If you live for a long time, you are necessarily elderly for a long time; and normally advanced old age (line 190) does sooner or later involve the drawbacks mentioned by our poet, and the longer you survive the more likely you are to experience many or even all of them (J. does allow that they are not all inevitable at 204f. and 240). Of course, the satirist gives his usual deeply negative and one-sided picture, totally ignoring the positive aspects (for instance, old age can be a peaceful and contented time, and some people stay active, alert and healthy until the very end),[1] and we can reject individual points (see below), but he does present what are undeniably real prospects for the very old. And J. presents them with great power. Exploiting the fears we all have of old age and which we generally push to one side, he shoves the drawbacks right in our faces, catching them with bluntness and vividness, and with perceptive and telling details. In a broad onslaught he covers the deterioration of physical appearance (191–202), reduction of pleasure (203–16), diseases and their effects (217–32), loss of wits due to dementia (232–9) and loss of relatives through bereavement (240–5). He thus handles physical problems at length (191–232), and then adds as extra blows mental impairment (232–9) and emotional damage (240–5), the three groups forming a tricolon diminuendo that fits depressingly well with the shrinking of the old man's world at 232–9 and 240–5. Then at 246ff. he varies and strengthens his attack by means of striking and wide-ranging *exempla* to provide graphic vignettes of the disadvantages of longevity. Four of them (at 246–72) are connected with the Trojan War, and there Nestor and Priam are placed first and last for stress and are developed at length, as the saddest, and the strongest support for J.'s case. Another four examples (at 273–88) are historical, and there the foreigners Mithridates and Croesus are touched upon briefly, while the more pertinent Romans Marius and Pompey are given greater prominence via position and the number of lines devoted to them. Overall there is cumulative impact in the relentless succession of gloomy and bleak elements. There is also lots of black humour to get to us. As our poet lists the horrors of old age with apparent glee, running on and on in a way that mischievously matches the garrulity of the elderly,[2] there is wit in producing a long section on the prayer for a long life and the long old age that goes with it. The more he goes on, and the darker the vision he creates, the more absurd and crazy he makes the request for longevity seem, as it entails all this. And there is a comic Grand Guignol effect, as in the course of this section one puts together all the satirist's points and builds a picture of the *senex* (old man) as ugly, trembling, bald, toothless, deaf, impotent, demented etc. etc., a totally debilitated dotard whose relatives drop dead in droves all around him. But is it possible that the poet also intends this over the top frivolity to sabotage the overall seriousness of his stance? Readers may also find themselves induced to stiffen their resistance to being battered into submission by a lengthy (overlong?) series of pictures and arguments.

Due to the baby boomers, this section has decided relevance today. Different people will respond to it in different ways, and their age will probably have a bearing on their reaction. As I write this, I am 62. As ever, I find that Juvenal's words stimulate me, but this time, for me, they don't raise issues as much as make me face up to the future (and old age is also ahead of younger readers, if more distantly). One could just go into a massive depression, but it is also possible to make profitable use of these lines, resolving to appreciate properly the present, enjoy life while one can, toughen up mentally for what probably lies ahead and so on. In this way, something positive can come out of all the negativity and Roman satire can improve the lives of its audience.

> 'da spatium vitae, multos da, Iuppiter, annos'.
> hoc recto voltu, solum hoc et pallidus optas.
> sed quam continuis et quantis longa senectus   190
> plena malis! deformem et taetrum ante omnia vultum
> dissimilemque sui, deformem pro cute pellem
> pendentisque genas et talis aspice rugas
> quales, umbriferos ubi pandit Thabraca saltus,
> in vetula scalpit iam mater simia bucca.   195
> plurima sunt iuvenum discrimina, pulchrior ille
> hoc atque ille alio, multum hic robustior illo:
> una senum facies, cum voce trementia membra
> et iam leve caput madidique infantia nasi;
> frangendus misero gingiva panis inermi.   200
> usque adeo gravis uxori natisque sibique
> ut captatori moveat fastidia Cosso.
> non eadem vini atque cibi torpente palato
> gaudia. nam coitus iam longa oblivio, vel si
> coneris, iacet exiguus cum ramice nervus   205
> et, quamvis tota palpetur nocte, iacebit.
> anne aliquid sperare potest haec inguinis aegri
> canities? quid quod merito suspecta libido est
> quae venerem adfectat sine viribus? aspice partis
> nunc damnum alterius. nam quae cantante voluptas,   210
> sit licet eximius, citharoedo sive Seleuco
> et quibus aurata mos est fulgere lacerna?
> quid refert, magni sedeat qua parte theatri
> qui vix cornicines exaudiet atque tubarum
> concentus? clamore opus est ut sentiat auris   215
> quem dicat venisse puer, quot nuntiet horas.
> praeterea minimus gelido iam in corpore sanguis
> febre calet sola, circumsilit agmine facto
> morborum omne genus, quorum si nomina quaeras,
> promptius expediam quot amaverit Oppia moechos,   220

quot Themison aegros autumno occiderit uno,
quot Basilus socios, quot circumscripserit Hirrus
pupillos, quot longa viros exorbeat uno
Maura die, quot discipulos inclinet Hamillus;
percurram citius quot villas possideat nunc   225
quo tondente gravis iuveni mihi barba sonabat.
ille umero, hic lumbis, hic coxa debilis; ambos
perdidit ille oculos et luscis invidet, huius
pallida labra cibum accipiunt digitis alienis,
ipse ad conspectum cenae diducere rictum   230
suetus hiat tantum ceu pullus hirundinis, ad quem
ore volat pleno mater ieiuna. sed omni
membrorum damno maior dementia, quae nec
nomina servorum nec vultum agnoscit amici
cum quo praeterita cenavit nocte, nec illos   235
quos genuit, quos eduxit. nam codice saevo
heredes vetat esse suos, bona tota feruntur
ad Phialen; tantum artificis valet halitus oris
quod steterat multis in carcere fornicis annis.
ut vigeant sensus animi, ducenda tamen sunt   240
funera natorum, rogus aspiciendus amatae
coniugis et fratris plenaeque sororibus urnae.
haec data poena diu viventibus, ut renovata
semper clade domus multis in luctibus inque
perpetuo maerore et nigra veste senescant.   245
rex Pylius, magno si quicquam credis Homero,
exemplum vitae fuit a cornice secundae.
felix nimirum, qui tot per saecula mortem
distulit atque suos iam dextra conputat annos,
quique novum totiens mustum bibit. oro parumper   250
attendas quantum de legibus ipse queratur
fatorum et nimio de stamine, cum videt acris
Antilochi barbam ardentem, cum quaerit ab omni,
quisquis adest, socio cur haec in tempora duret,
quod facinus dignum tam longo admiserit aevo.   255
haec eadem Peleus, raptum cum luget Achillem,
atque alius, cui fas Ithacum lugere natantem.
incolumi Troia Priamus venisset ad umbras
Assaraci magnis sollemnibus Hectore funus
portante ac reliquis fratrum cervicibus inter   260
Iliadum lacrimas, ut primos edere planctus

Cassandra inciperet scissaque Polyxena palla,
si foret extinctus diverso tempore, quo non
coeperat audaces Paris aedificare carinas.
longa dies igitur quid contulit? omnia vidit   265
eversa et flammis Asiam ferroque cadentem.
tunc miles tremulus posita tulit arma tiara
et ruit ante aram summi Iovis ut vetulus bos,
qui domini cultris tenue et miserabile collum
praebet ab ingrato iam fastiditus aratro.   270
exitus ille utcumque hominis, sed torva canino
latravit rictu quae post hunc vixerat uxor.
festino ad nostros et regem transeo Ponti
et Croesum, quem vox iusti facunda Solonis
respicere ad longae iussit spatia ultima vitae.   275
exilium et carcer Minturnarumque paludes
et mendicatus victa Carthagine panis
hinc causas habuere: quid illo cive tulisset
natura in terris, quid Roma beatius umquam,
si circumducto captivorum agmine et omni   280
bellorum pompa animam exhalasset opimam,
cum de Teutonico vellet descendere curru?
provida Pompeio dederat Campania febres
optandas, sed multae urbes et publica vota
vicerunt; igitur Fortuna ipsius et urbis   285
servatum victo caput abstulit. hoc cruciatu
Lentulus, hac poena caruit, ceciditque Cethegus
integer et iacuit Catilina cadavere toto.

'Grant a long period of life, grant many years, Jupiter!'
You pray for this, only this, with a face not distorted, and also
    when pale.
But how many and how incessant are the evils with which a
    lengthy old   190
age is filled! First of all, take a look at the face, ugly and horrible
and unlike itself, ugly hide in place of skin
and sagging jowls and wrinkles like those that,
where Thabraca spreads out her shady woods,
a mother ape has long been scratching on her aged cheeks.   195
The differences between young men are very many: A is more
    handsome
than B, and C is than D; E is much stronger than F;

the appearance of old men is one and the same – limbs and voice
    trembling,
a head now smooth and the childishness of a dripping nose;
the wretch has to break up bread with his unarmed gums.   200
He is so offensive to his wife and his children and himself
that he disgusts the will-hunter Cossus.
There is not the same pleasure in wine and food, as the sense
    of taste
is dulled. Again, intercourse has by now long been forgotten, or,
should you try, your little penis with its varicocele lies there   205
and, despite being stroked all night long, will lie there.
Can this sickly, white-haired phallus really hope for
anything? What about the fact that lust which strives after sex
without strength is quite rightly suspect? Now look at the loss
of another part of the body. For what pleasure is there in
    a singer,   210
even if he is outstanding, or in Seleucus the lyre player
or in those whose custom it is to dazzle in golden cloaks?
What does it matter in which part of the big theatre he sits,
as he will scarcely hear horn players and trumpets playing
together? The slave boy has to shout so his ear can hear   215
whose arrival he is announcing, what time he says it is.
In addition, the very little blood in his now cold body
is warmed up by fever alone, all types of diseases leap around him
in a horde; and, if you asked their names, I could more
easily recount how many adulterers Oppia has made love to,   220
how many sick people in one autumn Themison killed,
how many partners Basilus defrauded, how many wards
Hirrus defrauded, how many men tall Maura gulps down
in one day, how many pupils Hamillus bends over;
I could more readily run through how many country houses
    are now   225
owned by the man who used to shave off my youthful beard
    with a rasp.
One man is ailing in the shoulder, another in the groin, another
    in the hip; this
one has lost both eyes and envies the one-eyed; that one's
pale lips take in food from the hands of another person;
the very man who was accustomed to open his jaws wide at
    the sight   230
of dinner now just gapes like a swallow's chick when its fasting

mother flies to it with a mouth full of food. But worse than
any physical impairment is dementia, which does not
recognize the names of slaves nor the face of a friend
with whom it dined the previous night, nor the children   235
whom it fathered, whom it reared. For in a savage will
it prohibits its family from being its heirs, all its goods are
bestowed on Phiale – so powerful is the breath of her
    skilled mouth,
which for many years had stood for sale in a brothel's cell.
Even if the mental faculties are intact, still one has to lead the   240
funeral processions of children, has to gaze on the pyres of one's
beloved wife and brother and on urns full of sisters.
This is the penalty assigned to long-livers – calamity for their
    house is
constantly renewed and they grow old amid much lamentation,
in perpetual mourning and dressed in black.   245
The king of Pylos, if you believe great Homer at all,
was an example of survival second only to the crow.
He was without doubt a lucky man, putting off death for so many
generations and now counting his years on his right hand
and drinking the new wine so often. I pray that you
    pay attention   250
for a moment to how much this very man complains about fate's
laws and his overlong thread of life, when he sees the beard
of spirited Antilochus burning, when he asks every comrade
present why he survives to this moment in time,
what crime he has committed worthy of such a long lifespan.   255
Peleus makes the same complaint, when he mourns his lost
    Achilles,
as does the other one, for whom it is natural to mourn the
    shipwrecked Ithacan.
Priam would have gone to the shade of Assaracus while Troy was
still standing, with grand ceremonial, his corpse carried
    by Hector
and the necks of his remaining brothers, amid the   260
tears of the women of Troy, as Cassandra and Polyxena
with torn cloak began to utter the cries of lamentation,
if he had died at a different time, when Paris had not
begun to construct his bold ships.
So what did length of time bring him? He saw all   265
overthrown and Asia collapsing through fire and sword.

Then, a trembling soldier, he removed his crown, took up arms
and fell before the altar of highest Jupiter, like an old ox
which presents its pitiful thin neck to its master's
knife, now disdained by the ungrateful plough.   270
His end at any rate was a human being's, but the wife who lived
on after him opened her canine jaws and barked fiercely.
I hasten on to our own people and pass over the king of Pontus
and Croesus, whom the eloquent voice of just Solon
told to take into account the final stretch of a long life.   275
Exile and prison and Minturnine marshes
and the begging of bread in conquered Carthage
were caused by this; what could nature ever have produced
    on this
earth, what could Rome have produced, more fortunate
    than him,
if, after the line of captives and the whole parade of war   280
had been led around, he had breathed out his triumphal soul
when on the point of getting down from the Teutonic chariot?
Provident Campania had given Pompey the fever that he
    should have
prayed for, but the public petitions of many cities
won out. Therefore his own Fortune and that of Rome took away
    the head   285
which had been saved after he was conquered. Lentulus avoided
this agony, this punishment, and Cethegus died
unmutilated, and Catiline lay dead with his corpse intact.

At 188f., with its engaging and combative second person in *optas* ('you pray'), the solemn spondees, the doublets, the verbal iteration and the address to the highest god bring out the extent of the petitioner's urgency and desire for a long life – only to bring misery on himself (according to J.) with his own insistence. The bleak humour is underlined by ominous echoes in line 189 of the closely preceding 187 on the awful outcome of entreaties to heaven – the repeated prayers call to mind *totiens* ('so often'), and *optas* ('you pray') picks up *optata* ('prayers').

There is probably an intertextual aspect to line 188. Although *da … da* ('grant … grant') does appear in several other authors,[3] there are two passages in particular which may well have been in J.'s thoughts here. At lines 45–6 of Persius 2 (J.'s satirical model for X) the poet also addresses someone and attributes to him a request – *da fortunare Penatis, / da pecus et gregibus fetum* ('grant prosperity to my house, grant me herds and young for my flocks') – for wealth directed to Mercury by a man who ruins himself by making expensive offerings in support of his entreaty. An allusion to this by J. would mean that there are fitting associations of a misguided prayer by a foolish person; and, with a twist, where the petition in Persius cannot be fulfilled, J. in the following lines would be homing in at length on the dreadful consequences if it is granted. In addition, the repetition of *da* in an address to Jupiter in particular occurs elsewhere only at Seneca (?) *Hercules Oetaeus* 87 (in Hercules's prayer for deification): *da, da tuendos, Iuppiter, saltem deos* ('grant, grant me at least to protect the gods, Jupiter'). A reference to this would bring connotations of pain and distress involved in the success of a request (later in the play, Hercules achieves divine status by having his mortal part burnt away on the pyre on Oeta) and would have a mock-heroic flavour (the ordinary reader, wanting a long life, is compared to Hercules, who wants a really long life).

The exact sense of line 189 is much disputed,[4] and it seems to me likely that the expression is deliberately ambiguous (to involve us, to make for comprehensiveness and to facilitate much play). Interpretation is complicated because there are various feasible senses for *recto voltu* (which I have translated as 'with a face not distorted') and several possible reasons for the pallor later in the line, and we cannot tell if *pallidus* ('when pale') produces contrast (as in most explanations) or reinforcement (the petitioner could be preoccupied and so have a set face and be pallid with anxious longing, or he may be looking the god full in the face, pale with nervous desire). *Rectus* could mean 'not distorted' (i.e. young, in contrast to the distortion of sagging jaws and pendulous cheeks in old age; or not distorted by misery, worry, fear, etc.), or 'upright, erect' (because feeling confident, or as a sign of youth, health and strength), or 'facing squarely' (confronting the god's statue and looking him full in the face) or 'set' (i.e. preoccupied; or the reference may be to the set face of self-assurance and a clear conscience). There is lots of scope in these senses for irony and for pointed change subsequently. The pallor could be due to sickness, old age, worry, unhappiness, a bad conscience, apprehension and anxious desire. It is easy enough to see a tart implication that the man *should* go pale when making such a disastrous plea, and will be *really* pale if it comes to fruition. Finally, I also suspect a barb in *solum hoc* ('only this'): it is stupid to ask for just longevity and not longevity plus something else (health, happiness, etc.).

In the next sentence (at 190f.), J. talks sense (a long life must entail a long old age, something which petitioners might well overlook), and he underscores the drawbacks of that corollary while picking up the prayer in line 188 and presenting a grimly amusing rebound: *spatium vitae* ('a long period of life') results in *longa senectus* ('a lengthy old age') and, according to J., *multos annos* ('many years') result in many, many *mala* ('evils'). The expression of the disadvantages is powerful: there are exclamations, grave spondees, forceful alliteration, emphasis by run-over and placement in line 191 for *plena* ('filled') and *malis* ('evils'), a word order that encompasses *longa senectus* ('a lengthy old age') with words describing the horrors filling it, and also pregnant diction – possible senses for *continuis* ('incessant') are 'lasting', 'constantly recurring' and 'uninterrupted'; *quantis* ('how many') will mean both 'how many' and 'how great'; and *malis* ('evils') embraces 'hardships', 'misfortunes' and 'diseases'.[5] At the same time, J. overstates his case, allowing for no exceptions at all and maintaining that *senectus* is *filled* with *numerous* and *incessant* evils.

That sentence acts as a signpost, ushering in the list of specific drawbacks of old age that follows, where J. does make good points, but is again guilty of distortion (so, for a start, it is not true that all aged faces are ugly and horrible: there are, for example, apple-cheeked and twinkle-eyed grannies who have an attractiveness of their own). At line 191 J. begins his list. He devotes lines 191–202 to physical appearance. His first example, the effect of ageing on the face (*vultum*, stressed by its position), is well aimed. Although some might view the state of their features as the least of the burdens of advanced years, many people are (and were) sensitive about their looks,[6] feeling that the face is important (as being very much representative of the person, and containing clear and immediate indications of age). So our poet puts the face first, and dwells on it, in quite a long sentence with cumulative impact, telling epithets and nouns, lots of emphatic placement, mournful spondees at 191–3 and vigorous alliteration at 192f., while implying with *ante omnia* ('first of all') that there is still more to follow. There is a nasty backfire in the prayer made *recto voltu* in line 189 resulting in the *vultus* ('face') here (whatever the primary sense of *recto* there, and in particular with the meaning 'not distorted'). To characterize the face, J. foregrounds *deformem* ('ugly', but 'degrading, shameful' is probably intended too),[7] then reinforces it with the strong word *taeter* ('horrible', i.e. physically offensive, foul), and adds *dissimilemque sui* ('and unlike itself') as the final member of the triad, which hits home because it is often shocking to see how much people's faces change in old age. There is mockery and flippant paradox in *dissimilemque sui*: the meaning is that the face no longer retains the appearance it long had; but, of course, even when aged, it *is* still the same face and so does look like itself, like the new self that it has now acquired. The notion of the old not seeming like themselves is taken further in the following words where, by means of the hide and jowls and ape comparison, the elderly are put on a par with animals rather than humans; and, as beasts were traditionally unreasoning,[8] this would be a cruelly apt fate for someone who made the unreasoning prayer for longevity.

In line 192, repetition stresses *deformem* ('ugly') and pointedly takes up the repetitions of *da* ('grant') and *hoc* ('this') at 188f. to underline the idea that the prayer is in fact one for ugliness. *Deformem* there introduces another forceful triad (more explicit this time), in which J. develops the comic rebound again, by adding to *dissimilemque sui* and so intimating that a request for many years gives rise to many instances of ugliness. *Pellem* ('hide'), artfully juxtaposed with *cute* ('skin'), suggests something unattractive, coarse, hard, mottled, smelly and not human. In line 193, *aspice* (which appears in line 191 of my translation as 'take a look at') draws us in by inviting us to picture the face; there is probably also rather sharp play on the verb's sense of 'consider, think about',[9] with J. urging readers to use their brains (and the more the poet goes on here, the more stupid anyone who prays for all this is meant to seem).

At 194f. J. expands on the wrinkles that so many people hate,[10] and builds on the animality motif, here specifying a very pertinent animal (*senectus* can make humans seem simian), and one with lots of associations to attach to the old man. As well as being ugly, alien, despised, stinking, babbling and monstrous,[11] apes were viewed as ridiculous parodies of humanity.[12] Motherhood adds to the grotesqueness, with the beast's pendulous breasts[13] suggesting the sagging chest of the *senex*, and it may well hint at a loss of sexual identity (cf. 205f. below). The creature is also depicted as harming itself (appropriately enough, in connection with one who makes the self-harming prayer for longevity), and the grooves on its face are conspicuous and irreversible. No reason is given for the scratching, and it has been going on for quite some time – long enough to leave furrows; and the likeliest sense for *iam* ('long')[14] reinforces this notion – so that it all seems rather manic. As the ape is old, this recalls in particular the unreasoning and obsessive behaviour of many patients suffering from senile dementia and Alzheimer's disease (repetitive scratching and plucking at skin on the face and elsewhere),[15] which, in view of his acquaintance with dementia (see 232ff.), J. could easily have observed. If this is the idea, there is the black joke of an ape suffering from dementia, and there is aptness in connection with the *senex* who, according to J. (232ff.), suffers from it himself.

Line 194 increases the effectiveness of the comparison in various ways. Thabraca was a town on the coast of Numidia, so the creature is cut off from civilization (cf. the old man at 210ff.), and the other negative connotations of Africa[16] are exploited too. That line also has visual impact. It builds up a picture of extensive darkness, and so adds a touch of gloom. In particular, black was linked with ill omens, and also with death, mourning and the Underworld;[17] *umbra* can mean 'ghost', and another sense for *umbrifer* is 'ghost-conveying',[18] while trees often figure in descriptions of Hades.[19] As a result, line 194 has a rather unsettling undertone, with a hint of death that is fitting for someone whose family die on him (240ff.) and who is nearing the end of life himself. That line also depicts a single (contemptible) ape swamped and dwarfed by broad forests – a powerful image of insignificance and (cf. 210ff.) isolation. Line 194 is poetic and elaborate as well: *umbriferos* ('shady') is rare and mainly poetic; the learned and exotic *Thabraca* occurs seldom in extant literature; there is alliteration and assonance, and a pair of adjectives separated from a pair of nouns by a verb, in an arrangement like that of the Golden Line. All of this means that the sudden descent in line 195 comes across very strongly as we are taken on to the ludicrous beast, with *simia* ('ape') and *bucca* ('cheeks'), words confined to prose and the lower genres of verse, left until the very end for maximum bathetic punch.[20] Finally, among the extant examples of *umbrifer* there is only one other phrase that is close to J.'s *umbriferos ... saltus* ('shady woods'), and that is the *nemus umbriferum* ('shady grove') in Hades at Virgil *Aeneid* 6.473. There, after rejecting Aeneas's attempts to apologize for leaving her, the soul of Dido, queen of Carthage (and Thabraca is not far from Carthage), flees into the shady grove back to her husband Sychaeus. So there are further suggestions of death and the Underworld, and there is also a sardonic spin, as we find in place of the beautiful, tragic heroine rejoining her loving spouse in a very sad episode of the epic, an ugly and absurd female ape on its own manically scratching its cheeks in a mocking aside in a satire.

At 196ff. J. builds on the loss of looks and adds loss of individuality. Lines 196–7 look both backwards and forwards.[21] The progression there to handsome young humans makes the ugly, ape-like old man of the preceding verses seem even more repulsive. More significantly, the mention of the youths here enhances the force of what follows at 198ff. To play up the lack of variety in the appearance of the elderly, a full two lines on the differences of young men, together with *plurima* ('very many', which may mean 'very great' too) and *multum* ('much'), both stressed by placement, and several pronouns differentiating them (translated as A, B, C, D, E and F), heighten the impact of the bleak brevity in *una senum facies* ('the appearance of old men is one and the same') in line 198, where *una* (emphatic by position) confronts *plurima* ('very many') in 196, and the singular *una ... facies* is opposed to the plural *plurima ... discrimina* ('differences ... very many'), and the lone *senum* for all the undifferentiated oldsters is set against the sundry pronouns distinguishing the young. Lines 196–7 also bring to mind a picture of a series of good-looking and robust youths – and *multum ... robustior* ('much stronger') implies great sturdiness – as a foil to the unattractiveness (198ff.) and frailty (200) of the elderly, which seem even worse by way of contrast. There is an intertextual thrust as well. Several critics have noted the obvious similarity to Ovid *Amores* 2.10.7 (of two equally beautiful girls loved by the poet at the same time): *pulchrior hac illa est, haec est quoque pulchrior illa* ('A is prettier than B; B is also prettier than A'). The allusion comes with an appropriate aura of beauty and appeal (Ovid dilated on these aspects at 4–8) and variety (in the style and expression of charms in the miniature *tour de force* at 5–8), which reinforces the contrast with 198ff. In addition, the fleeting evocation of the wit and humour in Ovid's poem throws into relief the ensuing gloom in J.

Of course, it is simply not true that all old men look alike. There is also exaggeration in the following list of further physical flaws, because the elderly do not all suffer from all these complaints. However, our poet is as forceful as ever. The allusion to trembling limbs[22] and voice in line 198 represents a significant addition. The voice is a telling detail, as another strong indicator of personality, and the allusion adds breadth by appending to visual disgust the aural element, the quavering wickedly brought out by the rhythm and repetition of -*um*, *me*-, *e* and *a* in this line. The voice is in grotesque collaboration with the body, and *membra* ('limbs', a general term, rather than just 'hands', and in the plural) suggests a blackly comic picture (of a whole lot of shaking going on) and opens up the attack in connection with physical appearance (making the entire body, not just the face, risible and repellent). Moreover, the limbs and voice are flanked by facial features (three at 192–5 and three at 199–200) and, further out, by revulsion at 191f. and 201f., so that there is a pawky incongruity in such attractive and controlled patterning in J.'s description of ugliness and lack of control (the quivering limbs here and the runny nose in the next line).

In line 199 J. goes back to the visage, and the unexpectedness of that return and the specification of still more facial damage highlight further that important feature. The baldness should really get to readers, as it does change the appearance drastically, in a way that many people dislike.[23] Here *iam* ('now') points to the degeneration, and the *senex* is completely bald (without even a few white hairs) and thus displays even more of his hide-like skin. Later in this verse, the phrase *infantia nasi* ('childishness of a nose') is unique (and so attracts attention to this defect) and rather comical, while the form of expression (in place of 'the wet nose of a child') gives prominence to the off-putting childishness. Primarily the (demeaning, revolting) idea is of an old man's nose dripping with mucus like that of an infant; but the notion of second childhood is evoked too,[24] and babies are helpless, inarticulate, witless and often irritating (e.g. when they scream) and repugnant (due to uncontrolled evacuation from diverse orifices, etc.). The addition of the wet nose of an infant to the wrinkles of an aged mother ape also makes the *senex* a ludicrous hybrid, a combination of child and mother, young and old, human and monkey, male and female.

On top of all that comes the complete toothlessness in line 200. This should really hit home, and its force is increased by the cruel humour in *inermi* ('unarmed') (deliberately left until the end of the verse), which represents a new and striking application of the adjective, with connotations of defence-lessness and vulnerability. Apart from the sardonic twist to line 81, bread makes for a boring and not very nutritional diet (which would weaken the *senex* and make him prone to illness), all the pleasure of chewy and crunchy food lost. As the satirist represents the situation here, it would also appear that nobody is cutting up solid food for the old man or giving him tasty soft food, that he is just presented with bread and left to fend for himself. This implies that he is being neglected, and that nobody cares about his happiness or health, most obviously (cf. 201f.) because he is so repulsive. The adjective *misero* (translated as 'the wretch') fits with this idea, primarily depicting the *senex* as 'contemptible' (although 'wretched in health' and even, with a touch of pathos, 'pitiful' may also be felt).[25] In addition, the spondees and the frequency of *m* and *n* suggest the slow mumbling of food and so enable us to hear the repellent process of eating without teeth.

At 201f. J. moves back out from specifics to general remarks on disgust, reinforcing 191f., and also expressing the abhorrence here more strongly to get real punch. The first half of line 201 is taken up with words denoting the intensity of the revulsion – and in *gravis* ('offensive') there may well be ironical play on the adjective's sense of 'venerable, respected')[26] – while the rest of the line dilates on persons feeling revulsion (with conspicuous collocation and isocolon). First come close relatives, which means that the old man must be revolting in the extreme and elaborates on the implication in line 200 of a hurtful lack of love and affection, while building up the sense of isolation. Then (intentionally held back until the end of the verse) we learn that the man is also obnoxious to himself. So he is not in his dotage and blissfully unaware of his effect on people, but still has some wits left; and offending himself is actually worse than offending others and would make for an abject misery. Still greater disgust follows in the darkly comic climax at line 202. Will-hunters courted rich old persons in the hope of being named in their wills and were calculating and hardened types, but even one of them (who would have a strong stomach and want to see the *senex* in a bad way because that would mean that he would inherit soon) is repelled at the sight of this wreck of a man. The jibe is given a full line to itself, and the rather odd expression that runs together the nauseated parties (so offensive to X, Y and Z as to disgust Cossus)[27] helps focus attention on the will-hunter. Lines 201–2 play on the fact that many of us are concerned about what others think. And there is a bleak implication in the attitude of the people here, together with bitter mockery. Those who should love the old man or at least show him affection feel only revulsion, so it does not matter how good a husband or father you have been, or what you have achieved in life that you might have taken pride in, or how much money you have – when you reach this state, all that counts for nothing, and all you amount to is something absolutely repulsive. And if you are moronic enough to pray for longevity, you may well bring this on yourself.

At 203–16 J. progresses to loss of enjoyment – *gaudia* ('pleasure') in 204, stressed by the run-over and its position in the line announces the new topic – which represents a further blow, as there is no real joy to offset the misery of 200–2. In case you connect a long life with happiness, J. writes off what are the major pleasures for most of us (alcohol, food, sex and entertainment). It is true that many (but not all) find their sense of taste impaired in old age, and this deprivation is depressing, but again there is worse to come. In 203f. we find just the first member of a tricolon crescendo (taste; sex; entertainment) with an increasingly dispiriting effect: there is diminished but still wholesome enjoyment here; at 204–9 there is only dubious and demeaning sexual gratification as a possibility; and at 209–16 there is no delight at all.

With the abrupt progression to sexual intercourse in line 204, J. moves on to what many would regard as a more serious loss, and starts to dwell on it at much greater length, depicting via oblivion and impotence a total absence of pleasure (rather than just a reduction of it) and also humiliation before a partner (in contrast to the private and personal dulling of taste). J. achieves a stronger impact by raising the theme of geriatric sex, which was thought to be unsuitable, disgraceful and ridiculous,[28] but again his scenario is open to objections – not all old men are impotent (or have a varicocele), and in any case many people's interest in sex declines in old age, so they are not bothered by its lack and even welcome it.[29] The idea of somebody having forgotten about coitus for a long time (an extreme instance of the forgetfulness of the old!) implies a total disconnection and builds up a picture of *many* completely sexless years ahead, an awful prospect for male readers (but then again, if the *senex* can't remember intercourse, he won't miss it). Next comes a bleak joke, as J. addresses the reader directly[30] and involves him with a derisive and unsparing vignette: if you have not forgotten copulation, it is in fact worse, because you want it but are not up to the task. So *coneris* ('should you try') denotes only an attempt, and is immediately followed by failure in *iacet* ('lies there', which also embraces 'lies ill', 'lies helpless', 'lies dead', 'is overthrown' and 'is inactive', and plays ironically on the sense 'has sexual intercourse').[31] All this is meant to be doubly disheartening: there is sexual frustration, and there is also mortification (in the loss of manhood, status and respect).[32] Most of line 205 is devoted to the limp penis (with a collocation of negative aspects), so that we are invited to contemplate that (synecdochic) image of uselessness, unmanliness, degeneration and degradation; and J. just had to add the varicocele, an enlarged condition of the spermatic veins (the only swelling in that groin!) which is abnormal, ugly, painful (after prolonged sitting), embarrassing and depressing.

Line 206 keeps the focus on the phallus – *iaceo* ('lie there') repeated for emphasis and left until the end of the verse – and makes the picture more unpleasant, adding fingers caressing the flaccid and deformed organ. This last also increases the frustration, as stroking for hour after hour after hour achieves nothing, reinforced by the rhythm: the penis is as torpid as the spondees,[33] which also fit with a long, slow night. The line adds to the mortification too, as the partner now plays a role[34] and, in the course of a whole night's futile efforts to rouse him, would inevitably become bored, tired, irritated and contemptuous. There is also a very funny echo of some solemn words of Virgil in this low context.[35] Many scholars have noted the obvious similarities in expression and situation to *Aeneid* 6.617f., where the Sibyl, telling Aeneas of the great sinners in Tartarus, mentions Theseus rooted to a throne: *sedet aeternumque sedebit / infelix Theseus* ('Theseus sits there dejected and will sit there for all eternity'). There is the basic joke of the small, impotent, old and ugly penis equated to the large, virile, young and handsome hero. In addition, Theseus was punished for trying to abduct Persephone, so the attempt at coitus by the organ can be seen as a similar sexual act of presumption and stupidity, doomed to failure and a permanent punishment. Like Theseus on his throne, the tormented phallus cannot rise (and in fact lying amounts to greater diminution than sitting), and its former feats are now beyond it and count for nothing. Finally, because the words in Virgil that are taken up by our satirist were spoken by the Sibyl, we have the whimsy of Juvenal as the Sibyl, that wise and knowledgeable prophetess, who was also very old (when J. is mocking those of advanced years) and a highly respectable virgin (when our man is talking dirty).

The lively question at 207f. goes beyond the single attempt at intercourse in 205f. to intimate that there is no hope of it *ever*, with the emphatically placed *aegri* ('sickly') and *canities* ('white-haired') reinforcing the hopelessness. There is humour in the personification of the penis[36] as an old man. So too a hopeful phallus is a comical concept in itself, and there is frivolous play here on the idea that it cannot hope for anything (a euphemism for sex),[37] being impotent, and it cannot hope for anything (at all), being a phallus. There is harsher derision in *aegri*, which will not simply mean 'sick' (because of the varicocele) but also 'weary', 'weak' and 'distressed'.[38]

The *senex* depicted by J. is not up to full intercourse, if he has not forgotten all about it, but it might be claimed that he would still be capable of some other erotic activity, so J. proceeds to undermine such an idea at 208f. *Venerem ... sine viribus* ('sex without strength'), which would cover receiving or giving oral stimulation, and also penetration by another, is the only sex that J.'s frail old man could manage, so J. is attacking even that pleasure as something dubious and repugnant. With *merito suspecta* ('quite rightly suspect') by way of reinforcement, he adds his own support to the general Roman view of such conduct as unmanly and disgraceful;[39] and one should bear in mind that J.'s *senex* has no teeth and a runny nose, so the idea of his participation in such acts (especially oral sex) is particularly unpleasant. Also significant is the presence of *adfectat* ('strives after', i.e. tries to achieve, rather than actually achieving), which conveys the idea that the old man is so feeble and/or revolting that he may not even succeed in securing 'sex without strength'. The possibility of failure is highlighted by a reminiscence of Virgil's *Georgics*, as J. transfers a phrase from serious didactic to a frivolous and disgusting new context. Several critics have pointed to *Georgics* 3.95ff., on an old stallion whose procreative powers have waned and whose attempts at mating are futile, like a fire *sine viribus* ('without strength') in straw/stubble. The hybrid nature of the *senex* is thus extended, as he is now linked with a horse; and a useless old horse at that, which Virgil says should be locked up without pity. All of this amounts to quite a strong onslaught on the only sexual gratification possibly open (according to our poet). However, despite general disapproval, some people (i.e. the practitioners who are attacked in Roman literature) were clearly happy enough having such sex and, if that is all that is left for you, you might well be resigned to it[40] (and what you do in the privacy of your own bedroom need not become public knowledge).

Towards the end of line 209 J. moves on to the loss of hearing, ushering it in by means of a little tease which increases the surprise of such a progression and so draws attention to it. As we are still in the middle of a line and have just had nearly six verses on sex, and as *pars* ('part of the body') was often used of the sexual parts,[41] readers are encouraged to assume that J. is continuing with the erotic subject matter here[42] and is now considering the anus. An unreflecting, knee-jerk reaction would be that auditory problems are not as bad as amatory ones. However, in connection with the love life of J.'s old man there was a possibility of some (guilty) gratification (and he might have forgotten totally about intercourse and not miss it at all). But when it comes to hearing, our satirist depicts a (definitely felt) complete absence of pleasure. So too at 211f. he highlights what the *senex* is losing (in a way that he did not with sex), and he subsequently goes beyond delight to show deafness affecting the man's whole life, while the presence of some Heraclitean pathos in this impairment heightens the impact. Of course, it can be objected that there are many other things that a person hard of hearing may enjoy, and not everybody becomes deaf or this deaf in old age.

At 210–12 J. conjures up not just lack of pleasure but also frustration, misery and envy in being unable to hear while others can. He refers to three different types of music (song, the lyre and in line 212 pipes)[43] and produces a triple emphasis on excellence to rub in the deprivation (Seleucus is unknown, but was obviously a splendid lyre player). The euphony in these lines (much assonance and alliteration, and also, in 212, internal rhyme and impressive spondees) builds up the performers and is apt for musicians, wickedly underlining the kind of sound that the old man cannot hear. In line 212 there is stress on the visual (the only aspect of the performance that the *senex* can perceive), which means that he knows that he is losing out on something special; and there is a further tease in *fulgere* ('dazzle'), which will combine the literal ('shine') and figurative ('excel, be conspicuous')[44] senses of the verb. Line 213 brings out the deprivation and isolation of the old man in the midst of a large crowd of people who can hear and are enjoying themselves, and also intimates in passing that the man's status will count for nothing (even if he can sit in the *orchestra*, as a senator, or in the fourteen rows behind that, as an equestrian,[45] it won't help him at all). The addition at 214f. accentuates the privation (and mockery), as J. presents a gradation in hearing problems (with a single singer or lyre player at 210f.; with a group of pipers in 212; with groups horns and trumpets playing together at 214f.).

There is also intensification at 215f., where deafness, operating in the private sphere too, affects more than just pleasure, interfering with the ability to function on a basic level in day-to-day life, and making for humiliation and still greater isolation. With *auris* ('ear') at the end of 215, J. pointedly zooms in on and reduces the old man to a defective ear (synecdoche again). He is now dependent on a slave and a child (beside whom he seems all the more decrepit), and one can easily imagine the servant's contempt (or at best pity) for his master, as he needs to bellow to perform the standard functions of announcing visitors and telling him the time. On every single occasion when somebody comes to see him, the *senex* would look foolish and be demeaned, as he would not be able to understand what the visitor was saying and would find conversation very difficult (and thus be denied the enjoyment of normal social intercourse). Loud declarations of the time throughout the day, and day after day, would be a constant reminder of his hearing defect (and no doubt irritate the rest of the household), and represent a sardonic twist to the prayer for lots of time in line 188. There is also derisive irony: why is the old fool bothering about what the time is when (according to J.) it doesn't really matter, as he can't socialize or enjoy himself, or easily conduct important business, and the announcements just underscore the prolongation of his misery and futility?

At line 217 J. begins a long sentence with cumulative impact as he moves on to the countless diseases attendant on old age on top of the degeneration already mentioned – and *praeterea* ('in addition') spotlights the fact that this is yet another drawback – so that the person who prays for a long life may seem even more of a fool for wishing all this on himself too. In 217 the poet puts his finger on one of the unpleasant aspects of being old (feeling the cold), but there is more than that to this full line on the diminution of heat and blood which the ancients believed was a part of ageing. To strengthen his attack, J. will have in mind the theories found in various authors that this coldness and loss of blood had an impact on both the body and the mind, causing weakness, depression, timidity, moroseness and stupidity.[46] In addition, as dead bodies were also described as bloodless and cold,[47] there is mockery (the *senex* is like a corpse) and irony (the longed-for old age is virtually death anyway, except for the fact that you are exposed to all the painful, debilitating and depressing diseases, and so would be better off actually dead).

From the nasty joke about fever at the start of line 218[48] there is a progression to the host of other ailments and even nastier humour. At 218f. there is a freakish picture of grisly figures (the personified diseases) forming a sinister retinue for the geriatric, who may be in blissful ignorance (if he cannot see them) or bemused and terrified (if he can make them out). They surround him totally[49] and are (unlike him) swift and vigorous. The fact that they are leaping around him rather than actually assaulting him implies that they are jumping for joy (at having a victim) and are toying with him, limbering up and biding their time, to attack him when they see fit and in the numbers and order that they choose, so that they have a malevolent intelligence. Their helpless prey is also massively outnumbered, and *agmen* ('horde') will mean not just a throng moving and acting together but also an army on the march or drawn up for battle (hostile, organized, impossible to resist, etc.).[50]

In line 219, with its lugubrious spondees and echoing of *-or*, prior to the rapid dactyls in 220, the satirist seems to be intimating archly that he may have got his reader worried (hence the question about the names of the ailments). In any case, he works in a bleak joke (akin to *praeteritio*) for even if the reader does not ask their names, J. still brings out for him their vast numbers, and does so in a way hard to ignore or forget. At 220–6 there is parody. The poetic topos of conveying copiousness via comparison, which is here developed at a length that recalls the epic catalogue,[51] is given a low-life and flippant spin, and also has its macabre side (the maladies connection).

Moreover, those lines attach to the diseases the sordid and menacing associations of the characters depicted there, with connotations of insatiability, murderousness, malice, mercilessness and so on. The longer the list goes on, with repeated *quot* ('how many') and vigorous asyndeton, the more it puts across the notion of massive numbers. But there is a danger of monotony, so J. enlivens it. For example, there are sleazy and salacious examples, which also satirize contemporary Rome and question the wisdom of wishing for a long life and a vulnerable old age in such a grim place with all its predators.

In line 220 Oppia (if that is the correct reading) is a serial adulteress,[52] and (like the other characters mentioned at 221–4) may be actual or imaginary. The verb *amaverit* (translated as 'has made love to') may contain sneering play on the sense 'love', but the primary meaning (making for more punch) will be 'have sex with'. There seems to be no parallel for *amo* with a female fornicator as the subject,[53] so the point would appear to be that she is so forward and lustful that she usurps the male role. The sexual activity here and at 223f. makes the impotent *senex* appear even more feeble.

In line 221 Themison is a bad doctor of Juvenal's day who amusingly bears the name of an eminent physician of the Augustan period,[54] so that *occiderit* ('killed', rather than 'healed') comes as a comical surprise after the mention of that good doctor's name. There is also black humour in the picture of this Themison as some sort of weapon of mass destruction (if he slaughtered so many in just one autumn, when fever was rife at Rome, what must the total be for his whole career?). There is a malevolently ominous touch too, because the *senex* will need a physician to treat his fever and all the other complaints, and might end up with Themison or another just as incompetent and not be healed.

At 222f. there is contemptuous frequency of *c* and *q* and a repetition of *quot* and of *-us* and *-os* endings that suits the repeated swindling. There is also intratextual sport. At 7.145ff. Basilus (as part of a pair, with Gallus) was on the side of the law, an impoverished lawyer whose activities were restricted; here with an engaging and playful twist Basilus (as part of a pair, with Hirrus) is breaking the law and prospering, and his activities are extensive.

The one day at 223f. tops the one autumn in line 221, as J. now presents the shocking and darkly comic picture of the relentlessly fellating Maura.[55] *Longa* ('tall') is barbed. Tallness, which could hint at strength and endurance too, was an attribute of heroines and goddesses,[56] so that there is great irony in attaching such an aura to such a creature. The primary meaning of *viros* is 'men', but the associations of the juxtaposed *longa* activate the sense 'warriors, heroes'[57] – of the scum she serves, the degenerate descendants of Trojans,[58] passive and dominated by a female in a far from glorious context. There may well be a further mock-heroic aspect, as the expression creates a horrific image of Maura swallowing down whole men (rather than their semen or penis), like some sort of Charybdis,[59] a devouring monster with a very powerful suck.[60] A promiscuous Maura had appeared at 6.306–8, where she and Tullia show contempt for the altar of chastity, and one of them (quite possibly Maura) sneers as she sniffs – *sorbeat* ('gulps in') – the air;[61] here, the gulping verb is given an entertainingly nasty spin. In the Latin, Maura and the depraved schoolmaster frame line 224 in emphatic positions, and both their verbs are rarely employed with a sexual sense,[62] so that attention is drawn to their nefarious conduct. With *inclinet* ('bends over', but J. probably wants us to feel the 'crush, deject' meaning[63] too), the action is frozen at the moment when the child is exposed, helpless and frightened, just prior to penetration. This is a grim picture, and one which may be intended to parallel the position of the old man about to be entered and hurt by a disease (or diseases).

At 225f. the poet alludes to 1.24f., where he complained that the man who used to shave off his youthful beard with a rasp[64] single-handedly challenges all the nobility of Rome with his wealth. This means that the man would own countless country houses, so that there is not an anticlimax here (as some critics have claimed) but simultaneously yet another indication of the huge number of ailments and a further howl of disgust at the *parvenu* barber (with an iteration suggestive of bitterness). In fact, line 226 repeats 1.25 exactly,[65] so that the allusion is unmistakable. It reminds us of the vigorous assault on Rome in the first *Satire* and so underscores the humour in somebody praying for a prolonged existence in such a corrupt hell hole. However, at the same time, this echo calls to mind J. in mid-rant as the angry satirist presenting a distorted vision of unrelieved blackness in his opening poem;[66] and this comes shortly after a reference back to VI, in which J. also ranted, going on and on in an unbalanced attack on women.[67] This should subtly remind readers to question the view here and encourage them to reflect (e.g. that not just the elderly but other people, especially the very young,[68] were also vulnerable to hosts of ailments then; that if the old man fell sick he might well die, which would be a *good* thing in J.'s scenario; and that devoting a full seven verses to the diseases could be seen as going over the top). Furthermore, as various scholars have noted, line 226 (like 1.25) contains a reminiscence of Virgil *Eclogue* 1.28 (spoken by the ageing Tityrus): *candidior postquam tondenti barba cadebat* ('after my beard was whiter, as it fell, shaved off'). But this time, interestingly, the allusion has added point, in the contrast between J.'s unfortunate *senex* stuck in an awful city and Virgil's fortunate *senex* (*Ecl.* 1.46), who at 27ff. recalls a short and profitable visit to Rome (gaining his freedom and recovering his property), while enjoying a healthy and happy life in an idyllic rural setting.

At 227–32, rather than just depicting diseases circling the old man, J. goes on to their actual attacks on the elderly and their effects, presenting a multiplicity of victims and areas affected, dwelling for impact (in an increasingly gloomy tricolon crescendo) and showing the harmfulness of the prayer for longevity. All of this should hit home, as most people of advanced age are subject to such (painful and depressing) disabilities. This is a bleak picture of debilitated *senex* after *senex*; but I suspect that there is also meant to be hard humour here, in a panorama of cripples, inviting us to wonder if we really want to live on and become part of such a freak show.

With the first three physical problems in line 227, isocolon and parallel ordering of pronouns and nouns draw attention and suggest a regular succession of sufferers, while brevity and asyndeton make for a rapid series of hammer blows. Here J. clearly has in mind again the philosopher Seneca. In *Epistle* 101.11–13 Seneca quoted with extensive disapproval some poetry by Maecenas praying to live for a long time even if it meant being disabled. The first line of Maecenas – *debilem facito manu, debilem pede coxo* ('make me ailing in the hand, ailing in the lame foot') – has much in common with our poet's line 227: there is *debilis* ('ailing') with ablatives of respect, the asyndeton, the similarity of *coxo* to J.'s *coxa* and the progression after that verse to another two disabilities (a hump and loose teeth) as in 228–32. No doubt the satirist intended his readers to recall Seneca's contemptuous description of such an existence in old age as supreme misery and a lingering death, and his strong condemnation of such a prayer as absolutely disgraceful and womanly. The three infirmities mentioned in line 227 are bad enough (impeding movement – hence the wickedly slow spondees), but next comes something worse: blindness. Here too there is a grim joke, in the apparently paradoxical envy of those with only one eye. *Luscis* ('one-eyed') also recalls *luscum* attributed to Hannibal in line 158, and raises the prospect of envying (i.e. being even worse off than) that absurd madman.

In the third member of the tricolon, J. proceeds to something still worse – the humiliating inability even to do something as basic as feeding oneself and keeping oneself alive, a supreme example of the faded powers of the *senex*, who is hardly a functioning human being any more. There is a chilling vignette in line 219, with a cinematic close-up on the lips, food and fingers, with effective juxtaposition of *labra* ('lips') and *cibum* ('food'), and with *alienis* ('of another person') deliberately left until the end of the line. The dactyls and assonance (of *a* and *i*) fit with fluttering lips, and the elision of *cibum* suggests a gulp as the morsel is sucked down.[69] *Pallida* ('pale') covers the pallor of old age, illness and anxiety, and also brings to mind the paleness of death and a ghost[70] – so the old man seems like a living corpse again. Once more the implicit point is: *this* is what you are praying for! If one looks back to 188f., one can see how *pallidus* there is turned with *pallida labra* ('pale lips') here. The lips that prayed for longevity would bring all this on themselves as a result, and from being independent and insistently demanding to be given a long life, they would be totally reliant on another and reduced to silently accepting food, which keeps the long life (which is absolutely wretched) going.

In line 230 the spondees (with their specious air of gravity), the alliteration and the internal rhyme showcase the grotesque picture of a glutton opening wide (in anticipation) at the mere sight of a dinner. This is a man who clearly loved eating and would have fallen on his food, but would get little pleasure now from being fed by another food which he could not taste properly (203f.). The phrase *diducere rictum* ('to open his jaws wide') comes from Horace *Satire* 1.10.7, where it was used of somebody guffawing as he hears the verse of a satirist (so it fits neatly with the humorous aspect in line 230). The image is also given a spin, as it is now used in connection with someone no longer able to open wide, and is transferred from a self-sufficient listener laughing at satire to a completely dependent geriatric who is an object of laughter and satire himself. *Suetus* ('was accustomed to') reflects the dispiriting inability in old age to do things (even rudimentary things) that one repeatedly did with no trouble at all when younger. A sense of decline is also present in the chick-like smaller aperture of the mouth – so *hiat* ('gapes') is shorter than *diducere rictum* – and the little amount of food taken in (in line with the slight appetite of many elderly people).

At 231f. the comparison of the old man to a baby bird slots in with the idea of a second childhood in line 199 and makes him still more of a hybrid. This dense simile may contain some pathos, but disgust, irony and harsh humour are predominant. Textual prominence is given to the mother bird, which diminishes the chick-*senex* and brings out the (vital) importance of the nurturer. Suggestively, the nestling is unable to feed itself, totally reliant on another for its survival; it is weak, small (people often shrink in old age), twittering (cf. 198), sexually inactive (cf. 204ff.), immobile (an easy target for a predator) and not human. Given the great repulsiveness of the Juvenalian *senex* (202f.), even to his own family, presumably a slave will be feeding him,[71] so there is irony in likening the servant doing his (unpleasant) duty to a loving relative carefully cherishing her charge and even stinting herself of sustenance to ensure that it gets fed. So too, unlike the old man, the chick is at the start of its life, and is not just kept alive by food but thanks to it grows stronger and develops, and will soon be able to look after itself and go out into the world, an attractive, musical and swift-moving creature. There is also an ironical aspect in the fact that the swallow was a sign of spring,[72] that period of rebirth, growth and joy. In addition to all this, there is parody of a Homeric simile (introduced by the mock-solemn *ceu*).[73] Although comparisons to birds were not uncommon in poetry, the detail of the mother denying herself nourishment in particular points clearly to Homer *Iliad* 9.323f.: 'just as a bird brings whatever mouthfuls of food she finds to her unfledged chicks, going hard on herself'. There Achilles, at a sombre point in the epic (amid desperate circumstances for the Greeks on the battlefield), likens himself fighting at Troy and winning lots of booty for Agamemnon to the bird feeding its young, as he refuses the king's offer of recompense and persists in his terrible wrath with its tragic consequences. Here the simile is transferred to a mundane and low situation in degenerate Rome, with a sardonic change in the correspondences: now the chick is equivalent to a decrepit and disgusting geriatric (rather than the vigorous and aristocratic commander-in-chief), and the mother bird stands for a slave performing a repellent task (instead of the glorious hero Achilles sacking city after city in bloody combat and heaping up splendid spoils). There are other diverting modifications (which tend to distract and so detract from the pathos). The single chick makes for closer parallelism and spotlights the isolation of the *senex*, while its gaping mouth is a graphic touch, indicative of need and vulnerability. The specification of the swallow produces a sharper picture and irony, and what the mother carries in her mouth now denotes a small rather than a large amount.

At 232–9 J. moves on to something which most people would agree is more serious than physical decline – senile dementia (which undermines a person's status and authority and strips away his identity).[74] The poet thus devotes more lines to the effects of this than he did to those of diseases. He also presents a considered gradation. He begins with loss of memory, and has gloomy spondees, insistent repetition (of the negative *nec*) and alliteration at 233–5. The dementia is described as *maior* (translated as 'worse'). The word means 'of greater consequence', but there will be sarcastic play on the senses 'great in authority', 'great in achievement' and 'confident, lofty',[75] underlining the absence of such qualities in the senile. With arresting and chilling personification, the dementia has taken over and *is* the man. Dementia not recognizing names and faces is odd, but odder (to the point of grotesquery) is dementia dining and fathering children. J. depicts both long-term and short-term memory loss, which would make for constant confusion and humiliation. The *senex* does not just forget the names of slaves but cannot recognize them when reminded of them, and as a result would come across as a ridiculous and exasperating old fool (undeserving of respect and ripe for exploitation by his slaves). Worse, he cannot even identify the face of a friend, one with whom he dined the night before. Worse still, and a sign of extreme mental impairment, he does not know his own children (and there is focus on the closeness of their relationship in line 236 thanks to the pair of verbs, the isocolon and the homoeoteleuton). At the start of that verse, *genuit* ('it fathered') and *eduxit* ('it reared') are reminders of his former vigour, diligence and authority as *paterfamilias*, and make his descent at 238f. even more sad and shocking.

In the sentence that begins at the end of line 236 with the striking and unique *codice saevo* ('in a savage will'), no change of subject is indicated, so dementia is now making a will! Here we find something beyond mere forgetfulness, another awful aspect of senility – being feeble-minded and malleable, to the extent of being manipulated by a prostitute into leaving her everything, and bequeathing nothing to one's own flesh and blood (not just sons but the whole family).[76] Now the *senex* is not just absurd but also harmful, as the satirist holds out for his readers the prospect of great damage as a result of living on and on. In addition to the financial and emotional impact on his kith and kin, the old man would end his days amid humiliation and execration, ruining his own standing in the community and his posthumous reputation by this act of stupidity and *impietas* (neglect of his duty to his family).

There is an effective slow revelation of information. First, we are told that all his goods are bestowed on someone called Phiale. We deduce that she must be his mistress, which is bad enough. But next we infer that she is an expert fellatrix. And finally we discover that she is an old whore. Much to the fore is the old man's ludicrous foolishness here (matching the foolishness of praying for a long life in the first place). He has to be a moron not to realize that she is just trying to get named in his will (does he really imagine that she fancies him and/or loves him?). An aged prostitute is unlikely to be attractive, and the breath of a fellatrix was supposed to stink,[77] but this cretin is beguiled by her. Line 239 shows that she no longer needs to work in a brothel, as she now has the old man to keep her, and her many years of service there mean that out of a whole long line of men, nobody else was stupid enough to set up a relationship with her (even when she was younger). Hand in hand with that goes a highly demeaning depiction of the old man's beloved. In contrast to the will-hunter in line 202, she is represented as so hardened and predatory that she is actually prepared to perform oral sex on the disgusting *senex*. There is dark humour in the name ascribed to her. *Phialē* is a Greek word that denoted a broad, flat bowl for drinking: as well as suggesting a tippler,[78] this is suitable nomenclature for one with a gaping mouth who takes in liquid. One of the nymphs attending Diana as Actaeon catches sight of her at Ovid *Metamorphoses* 3.172 is called Phiale. So we have here an elderly tart who sucks off an old man and who worked in the cell of a brothel given the name of a young, lovely and virginal divinity who helped a major deity bathe in a beautiful cave (and there are also connotations of a doomed male as prey). In line 238, *artificis … halitus oris* ('the breath of her skilled mouth') is unpleasantly suggestive of intimacy and geriatric sex, and conjures up Phiale breathing on parts of her ancient lover's body (especially the genitalia) and panting in simulated passion, while *artificis* will embrace 'skilled' (she is a professional), 'cunning' and (ironically) 'artistic'.[79] The whole of the climactic line 239 brings out her prolonged service as a whore in a foul brothel. *Quod* ('which') reduces her to a mouth (that is her in essence, that is all the fellatrix amounts to), and gives us a surreal picture of just a mouth standing for sale in a brothel. The use of *carcer* for a cell there rather than in a jail is unique, suggesting something dark, dirty, cramped and smelly, and possessing an aura of criminality. *Multis … annis* ('for many years') echoes the same phrase in line 188: what your many years of life get you is to become the victim of a tart who sold herself for many years. There is also a wry touch in the old preying on the old, and in the only elderly person who prospers being a repulsive ex-prostitute.

Lines 240–5 concern the pain (the emotional damage) caused to the *senex* by loved ones dying before him. The basic point is well aimed, because when people live on and on, relatives do predecease them. J. presents a depressing alternative to going gaga: full possession of the senses means only that you are in full receipt of sorrow.[80] There is obvious pathos here, but there is also savage humour: even if you don't disinherit them, your family will not inherit anyway, as they will pass away before you; if you don't lose them by forgetting them, you will lose them via their demise; if you continue to love your wife and don't drop her for a mistress (like Phiale), that is worse, because she will die on you; and while the retention of mental powers might seem a good thing at first sight, you would be better off not keeping them, since what it actually means is that you appreciate properly the upset of these deaths and experience fully the harrowing obsequies.

Lines 240–2 pack in a series of dispiriting details, intimating that you would attend funeral after funeral, and building a real sense of isolation (and loneliness often *is* a hardship of old age). There is much interweaving of words denoting last rites and relatives, with *funera* ('funeral processions') and *rogus* ('pyres') surrounding *natorum* ('children'), with *rogus* and *urnae* ('urns') embracing *coniugis*, *fratris* and *sororibus* ('wife', 'brother' and 'sisters'), and with *funera* at the start of 241 and *urnae* at the end of 242 encompassing all the family members. The deceased are all close kin (and their deaths seem sadder in their contrast to Phiale's survival). For maximum impact, children are mentioned first (their demise before their parents was not in the natural order of things and so was regarded as particularly tragic);[81] J. then proceeds to the terrible loss of a dear spouse – both *amatae* ('beloved') and *coniugis* ('wife') are stressed by placement. Finally, the ends of the brother and sisters come as further blows. J. takes us through all the obsequies (procession, cremation, urns containing ashes), catching the points when it comes home with full force that these relations really are dead. By means of insistent gerundives (translated as 'one has to ... has to ...') and asyndeton, the poet makes us actually take part in the funeral processions and gaze on the pyres (as the bodies burn) and the urns (containing the pathetically scant remains of the sisters). In line 242 the unprecedented *plenaeque sororibus urnae* ('and urns full of sisters') is blunt and graphic; and there is also macabre wit in the expression, in the word order *sororibus* ('sisters') is enclosed by the *plenae ... urnae* ('full urns'). So too there is a ghastly elegance in the interlocking chiasmi (the gerundives and nouns of *ducenda funera* and *rogus aspiciendus*, and the singulars and plurals of *natorum, coniugis, fratris* and *sororibus*, of the deceased).

J. increases the gloom at 243–5 with a further three lines which append domestic disaster and threefold allusion to mourning, which have a grave rhythm (in 244f.), and in which every word hits home. Furthermore, the verb *dare* (whose basic sense is 'to give') appears in 243 (*data*, 'assigned'), which pointedly picks up its imperative form in 188 (*da ... da*, 'grant ... grant'): the idea is that you may be given a long life, but will also be given this terrible concomitant drawback.

Our poet will be going on and on about death, catastrophe, obsequies and sorrow in this subsection to suggest how they go on and on for the old man. There is probably sombre wit in that. There is certainly a sardonic touch in the paradox of lots of life exposing one to lots of death (you may think that you will escape it by surviving for a long time, but you won't, as it will affect you constantly). Similarly, there is the notion that longevity results in unhappiness rather than happiness, and the longer you live the more miserable you are, so that a prayer for the prolongation of life is in fact a prayer for the prolongation of misery. The humour is broader than that, as the satirist here goes comically over the top. One might object that relatives do not necessarily predecease the elderly as extensively as is depicted at 240–2, but at 243–5 J. takes that a big step further and presents an absurd scenario. There is gross exaggeration in *semper* ('constantly') and *perpetuo* ('perpetual'), which are both stressed by their position, while *semper* forms a block spondee, as J. builds up a picture of the *senex* permanently at funerals and permanently in mourning, while his kinfolk die off like flies around him and his whole line disintegrates in some sort of appalling holocaust (and how huge, and how unhealthy and unlucky, must his family be to keep on dying during his lengthy old age?). There are other problems with the logic that also bring one up short: a succession of deaths may leave one in shock and numb rather than racked by grief; there are people with only a few relatives; many are not close to their kith and kin, and so are not upset by their demise; and some even feel malevolent glee at seeing them expire and outliving them.

In line 246 there is a sudden and unexplained progression to Nestor, the king of Pylos who ruled over three generations of men according to Homer,[82] and who was a vigorous fighter and wise counsellor for the Greeks in the Trojan War. In fact, the hero is cited as an old man devastated by the loss of a close relative (his son Antilochus, who was killed in the fighting at Troy), and so he illustrates the thrust of the previous subsection. But this is not made clear until 252ff. Those who are quick on the uptake would soon guess this; but other readers would not, and they would be perplexed at 246–50, where J. apparently presents Nestor as somebody *blessed* with a long life, mischievously teasing them and ensuring impact for 252ff. The point is that even a powerful, wealthy and glorious king (who had many advantages and many ways of making life pleasant which J.'s readers do not have) could not cope and was absolutely miserable, so a long life is awful for humans from the highest to the lowest, and always has been (even as long ago as during the Trojan War).

The notion of the old man as an exemplar of great bliss is totally exploded in the sentence that begins in line 250, but the process starts before that with subtle undermining which smarter readers will see. Line 246 opens with the grand *rex Pylius* ('the king of Pylos'),[83] and the mention of 'great Homer' adds to the feeling of elevation, as does the grave rhythm at 246f. But the question of whether one gives any credence at all to what the epic poet says about Nestor's age starts to undercut the (very positive) Homeric picture of Nestor which is conjured up here (prior to its total deflation at 251ff.). In line 247, on the surface, the proverbially long-lived crow is there to bring out the king's longevity. But there are disruptive negative associations: it is perhaps not very flattering to compare a glorious epic hero to a crow[84] – *cornix* ('crow') is a term of abuse at *Priapea* 57.1, and it was often considered a bird of ill omen.[85] There are also witty aspects which detract from the seriousness: the carrion crow has a connection with death that fits with Antilochus below, and its dark plumage matches funeral dress, while its garrulity suits Homer's Nestor.[86] At the start of line 248, with its seemingly solemn spondees, there is strong stress on Nestor's good fortune (the unreflecting reaction to his lengthy span of years) in *felix* ('a lucky man'), which is the first word in the line, forming a block spondee, and in the reinforcing *nimirum* ('without doubt'). But *nimirum* here, as often the case,[87] is in fact ironical. With a droll touch at 248–50 J. adds more on the king's advanced age, continuing on and on as his life went on and on, and

as the man ran on and on in his speeches in Homer. There our poet adds
three more expressions for longevity to the one found in 247. This group of
four recalls the quadruple set of deaths at 240–2 and the quartet of domestic
calamity, lamentation, mourning and funeral dress at 243–5. There is a barb
in Nestor putting off death for so many generations:[88] he postponed his
own end, but could not do the same with his son's death, and so he would
really have been lucky if he had *not* put off his own end.[89] There is also a
subversive element in the reference to him counting his years on his right
hand (the ancients reckoned ones and tens on the fingers of the left hand
and hundreds on those of the right, so that he has turned 100). *Computat
annos* ('counting his years') in line 249 calls to mind the identical phrase in
the same place in the line within a context of old age and a Greek allusion
at 6.199. There J. was criticizing an old woman for indecently employing
Greek endearments to be seductive, while all the time her face allows you
to count her years. The echo comes with associations of deflation and the
drawbacks of old age, and the expression is frivolously transferred from a
disreputable hag to a venerable Homeric hero (and one recalls again and
reflects here too on the fact that *Satire* VI was a cynical and unbalanced
rant by our author). In line 250 J. concludes rather surprisingly with Nestor
drinking new wine year after year. Ferguson sees this as a 'satirical climax',
and J. may be depicting the illustrious king as some sort of antiquated toper.
Again, there is intertextual undermining. The only parallel for this use
of *mustum* ('new wine') to denote old age occurs at Ovid *Metamorphoses*
14.146,[90] where the Sibyl (another revered ancient with a Trojan and epic
connection) says she must live on for 300 years and *ter centum musta videre*
('see the new wine 300 times', i.e. often, as in J.). There the Sibyl (somebody
who made a foolish prayer: see 14.138) is clearly unhappy with having to live
such a span, so J.'s reminiscence has undertones of the evils of longevity
and prefigures Nestor's complaint in the next line.

At 250 ff. J. openly attacks the notion of Nestor as fortunate in a lengthy
sentence that packs in a lot. So that a long life will not seem attractive, our
poet takes one of the most famous old men in antiquity and depicts him
as devastated by grief and wishing he was dead. This weak and querulous
Nestor is a far cry from the tough and vigorous warrior of the *Iliad*[91] (where
his son's death does not yet take place), to show the degeneration that results
from living on and on. To give the passage force, J. also places a strong
condemnation of longevity in the mouth of a hero who was wise, respected
and full of good advice.[92] J. goes for vividness too, using present tenses to
represent the funeral as happening now, before our very eyes (so that we
are there with Nestor), and highlighting the king's misery and confusion,
because this is the type of thing that his readers could bring on themselves.

All of this makes for impact. Then again, the whole incident is, of course, just an invention, carefully tailored by the satirist to suit his case.

The authorial intrusion – *oro* ('I pray') – in line 250 and the address to the reader in 251 have a buttonholing effect. *Oro* is pointed: this is *my* prayer – that you pay attention to Nestor (so that your prayer will not be for many years). Similarly, the ensuing allusion to fate's laws and the thread spun by the Fates, determining the length of a man's existence, implies in passing that it is futile to ask for a long life, as it all depends on destiny anyway. In 251f. the pathetic picture of Nestor is ushered in with gravity, in the rhythm and by the lofty *legibus ... / fatorum* ('fate's laws').[93] As well as indicating the king's sorrow, the twofold complaint here about a long life given by a higher power inverts the twofold prayer to a higher power for a long life in line 188. A similar pair of complaints occurs at 253–5 (and these two pairs eclipse the lone doublet in 188). In between there is a grim centrepiece, in the temporal clause at 252f., which catches the horrific and supremely sad moment when the beard ignites on the pyre and the face (youthful, handsome and so representative of the person) blackens and is destroyed for all time. Vehement alliteration, spondees and the suggestive elision of the final syllable of the consumed *barbam* ('beard') add to the effect. The pregnant *acris* (translated as 'spirited'), placed at the end of 252, accentuates the loss for Nestor (the adjective embraces 'keen', 'shrewd', 'energetic', 'enthusiastic' and 'fierce') and has graphic undertones in this fiery context (it also has the senses 'acrid' and 'bright').[94] In line 253 there is a tragic transference: *ardentem* ('burning') can also mean 'eager'[95] (and *acris* alerts us to that meaning); the only thing *ardens* about Antilochus now is his beard.

The pathos continues with the temporal clause that commences at the end of line 253, with insistent repetition of *cum* ('when'). There must have been many people at the funeral, increasing the poignancy by their presence; and the emphatically positioned *omni* would have particular power if we are meant to envisage Nestor approaching each one of them individually and asking his questions, going on and on (a pitiful development of Homer's loquacious hero), bewildered and distraught, while his beloved son's body burns in the background. The inquiries are, of course, pointless, but they are also realistic and affecting: the wise man is here so upset that he is not thinking straight; and in place of the calm elder statesman in Homer, who keeps his head when others lose theirs, and who has lots of ideas and advice for his comrades, we are shown a Nestor who is highly agitated, at a loss and takes recourse to other people. His pair of questions (with vigorous asyndeton) and in particular the notion of old age as a punishment for some crime amount to a strong condemnation of longevity put in the mouth of somebody for whom we really feel.

Many scholars have noted the similarities (in general situation and individual details) to Propertius 2.13.43ff., where because of amatory problems the elegist wishes that he had died young and not lived to endure such anguish, just as it would have been better for Nestor to die early:

> *atque utinam primis animam me ponere cunis*
>   *iussisset quaevis de Tribus una Soror!*
> *nam quo tam dubiae servetur spiritus horae?*
>   *Nestoris est visus post tria saecla cinis:*
> *cui si longaevae minuisset fata senectae*
>   *barbarus Iliacis miles in aggeribus,*
> *non ille Antilochi vidisset corpus humari,*
>   *diceret aut 'O mors, cur mihi sera venis?'*

And I wish that one of the Three Sisters [i.e. the Fates]
  had ordered me to end my life in my infant cradle.
For why should the breath of such a precarious life be prolonged?
  Three generations passed before Nestor's ashes were seen.
But if some foreign soldier at the ramparts of Troy
  had cut short his destiny of a long-lived old age,
he would not have seen the burial of Antilochus's body
  or said, 'Death, why are you late in coming to me?'

J. extends and fleshes out the vignette of the funeral, making it more vivid and emotive. He drops the mention of Nestor's death, keeping him alive and suffering, and fixes the focus on the obsequies that cause him so much agony. He adds an epithet for Antilochus, to spotlight the loss, and has the burning beard in place of the vague burial of the body. He also increases the distress of his king, expanding his plaintive question (in 251–2 and 254–5) and working in the dismal notion of longevity as punishment. There is functional topping here. J. has seized on the Propertian passage as something suitable to his purposes and used it as a starting point, building on it in order to get to us, and making his Nestor's circumstances a lot worse, because this is the prospect that he is holding out and he wants it to be daunting. And there is extra point for readers who pick up on the allusion: Propertius, when miserable in love, likened himself to his wretched Nestor, but J. is telling his reader, you will be like my much more miserable Nestor, and so will be much more miserable in old age (more so than even the morbid and mournful elegist of 2.13).

At 256f. J. quickly inserts two additional Greek examples, more kings whose royalty could not help them cope with grief when old, and again he employs the present tense for immediacy and has insistent repetition, of *lugeo* ('mourn'). Both Peleus (father of Achilles) and Laertes (father of Odysseus, the shipwrecked Ithacan) were without wives in their old age, and so were even more isolated. The word order separates Peleus from Achilles, placing between them lamentation and deprivation. The loss of the greatest Greek warrior at Troy would be particularly felt, and one is reminded in line 256 of the sad sketch of Peleus's sorrow at *Iliad* 19.323f.[96] So too line 257 calls to mind the poignant picture at several points in the *Odyssey*[97] of the years of abject misery endured by Laertes as he missed his son deeply during the two decades he was off fighting at Troy and making his way back home. However, at the same time, there is also a lighter aspect to these two verses, making for effective brief relief after the pathos of 246–55 and before the still greater pathos at 258ff. In 256 there is sport with different senses of *raptum* (translated as 'lost', and meaning literally 'snatched away'): Achilles was taken away from Peleus to Troy, and was also taken by death; and the warrior who carried off plunder, had Briseis snatched away from him and dragged along the dead Hector tied to his chariot,[98] is here himself carried away. There is more extensive levity in line 257. Most obviously, Laertes's son did not die before him, and so his complaint here about his span being too long is comically inappropriate, because thanks to it, he sees his son return alive. The primary sense of *fas* is 'natural',[99] but there is also play on the meaning 'proper, fitting': it was natural but not in fact fitting for Laertes to grieve over his long-lost son as dead, and it was *nefas* ('improper') to mourn for the living.[100] Similarly, *natantem* ('shipwrecked', but 'swimming' is also a feasible sense) underscores the fact that Laertes's grief was not fitting, because on both occasions when he was shipwrecked, Odysseus swam to safety – to the Phaeacians and to Calypso.[101] Finally, there is an amusingly off-hand vagueness in referring to Laertes by means of *alius* ('the other one'), while the employment here of the word to denote a mythological figure via learned allusion recalls the same usage at 1.10, where J. mocked a Greek hero (Jason)[102] in the course of deflating epic subject matter.

At 258ff. J. returns to pathos and to the long, detailed *exemplum*. He presents another famous miserable *senex* and another king with an epic and Trojan War connection, but he now moves from Greeks to a Trojan, and achieves intensification. To underscore the horrors that Priam endured through living so long, J. depicts him as not just bereft of close relatives like his Greek counterparts (and he lost many more sons than just one, as 259f. remind us) but also, on top of that, witnessing the demolition of Troy, being cheated of a suitable funeral and meeting a wretched end as Troy was taken by the enemy. In the long sentence at 258–64 the dwelling on destruction, death and obsequies is sombre enough in itself, but still more depressing is the fact that Priam was denied the funeral with all the ceremonial mourning due to a great king and descendant of Assaracus. And the more J. goes on, the more we see what Priam missed, so that death with proper exequies may actually seem preferable to a long life. In this sentence there is also much that makes us think of the funeral of Hector in *Iliad* 24. It too was marked by grand ceremonial. Hector carrying Priam's corpse inverts Priam carrying Hector's body in his chariot back from Achilles at 24.709 and others carrying his corpse to the pyre at 24.786. Hector's brothers officiated at his funeral (24.793), and the women of Troy wept at it (24.722ff.). Cassandra starting the lamentation here calls to mind 24.698ff., where she was the first to see Priam bringing back the ransomed corpse and the first to mourn for it, and *primos edere planctus / ... inciperet* ('began to utter the cries of lamentation') echoes similar Homeric expressions at 24.723, 747 and 761. As well as bringing with it the poignancy of Hector's obsequies, the allusion makes the point that if he had not lived so long, Priam would have had such a funeral for himself (and his soul would have had satisfaction from getting its due)[103] rather than being present at such rites for Hector (and enduring agony).

In line 258 *incolumi Troia* ('while Troy was still standing') at the start of the sentence foregrounds the annihilation of the king's beloved city. Priam going down to the shade of Assaracus (his great-uncle) must recall Aeneas's sight of Assaracus at *Aeneid* 6.649f., when he goes down to the Underworld in much happier circumstances (alive, and in command, on a glorious mission, with more glory ahead of him), and thus Priam's decline is accentuated. So too, by way of sad contrast, Assaracus was a much more fortunate and successful ruler,[104] and to meet him after losing Troy would be particularly painful for his descendant. In keeping with the solemnity of the funeral (nullified for Priam), expressions like *venisset ad umbras* ('would have gone to the shades') were common in epic,[105] and line 259 is a weighty five-word hexameter, while *funus portare* ('to carry the body') is also elevated.[106] In line 259, out of Priam's fifty sons Hector is mentioned first because he was the one most loved and most keenly missed by his father.[107] The positioning of *funus* ('corpse') next to Hector here is effective in several ways: it aptly associates that doomed hero with death; it brings out the closeness of father and son, and the physical proximity at the funeral denied to Priam; and it reminds us of the tragic inversion of the normal situation of the father dying before his offspring. In the largely spondaic line 260 there is affecting ambiguity in *reliquis* ('remaining'), which can mean both 'other' and 'surviving' (many of his sons died in Priam's last years).[108] In this verse there is also a cinematic zoom in on the necks of the other brothers, which encourages us to picture two long lines of necks, twenty-five on either side of the (huge, impressive) bier, straining under their dismal burden. Lines 261–2, as well as containing grimly graphic onomatopoeia (consonants suggestive of cries of grief and ripping) and the lofty *edere planctus* ('utter cries of lamentation'),[109] are dominated by mourning women, including two of Priam's daughters. The sketch becomes even more touching when one thinks of their deprivation, as they (like the sons) did not have the chance to pay their last respects to their beloved father and king in the state funeral they would have wanted. J. has carefully selected these two particular daughters. Cassandra was raped at the fall of Troy, and was then taken as a captive by Agamemnon to Greece, where she was promptly murdered by his wife (and she knew in advance that she would be), while Polyxena was sacrificed at the tomb of Achilles. So these two bring in a touch of horror as well as increasing the overall pathos (in addition to their sad ends, there is the emotive vignette of them duly lamenting here when they will soon die and not have a fitting funeral with proper mourning themselves). The cloak torn in grief is a clear allusion to Virgil: *scissa palla* ('with torn cloak') occurs elsewhere only at *Aeneid* 8.702, where there is also a female name before *palla* at the end of the hexameter. There Virgil describes Discord exulting at the battle of Actium with the war gods Mars and Bellona: *et scissa ... Discordia palla* ('and Discord with torn cloak'). The echo makes for solemnity and also invests Polyxena with associations of violence and death. At the same time, there may also be a reference to Euripides *Hecuba* 558f., where Polyxena tears her robe to bare her breast for the killing blow, so as to conjure up the sacrifice for us. In the mainly spondaic line 263 there is grisly play in *foret extinctus*, which I translate as 'had died' but which means literally 'had been extinguished': Priam was snuffed out as Troy famously went up in flames (cf. 266), and he, rather than the fire, was put out. *Diverso* ('different') in this verse pointedly recalls the other occurrence of that adjective in this poem – in line 3, where J. spoke about things that are very different from true blessings (like longevity). In line 265, another five-word hexameter, the idea of Priam breathing his last before Paris even began to build the ships on which he sailed off to elope with Helen easily brings to mind all the misery that ensued from that voyage down to Priam's actual death – ten long years of fighting and killing which the king lived to endure. Again, there is an intertextual aspect: *audax carina* ('bold ship'), together with mention of the ship's construction, is first found at Seneca *Medea* 607, also referring to a ship of myth (the Argo) under the command of a flawed hero (Jason), who journeyed to a foreign land and brought back from it a royal female (Medea). The reminiscence has gravity and a gloomy aura of punishment and death (at *Medea* 613ff. there is extensive expatiation on all the deadly retribution for the bold voyage).[110]

The influence of philosophy is evident here too, and several critics have pointed to verbal[111] and thematic similarities to *Tusculanae Disputationes*

1.85, where Cicero discusses the timing of Priam's death (and he goes on to talk of Pompey's end at 1.86, for which cf. 283ff. below). Cicero's argument there is that death takes us away from evil and so is not bad in itself: if Priam had perished earlier, he would have left good things, but by dying when he did he escaped the sense of the evils around him, so his death was not a bad thing. Our poet clearly has an eye to Cicero, but engages with him combatively. He agrees with his predecessor that Priam's end was terrible and that expiring sooner would have been better. He caps Cicero (and supports his own case) by making Priam's actual demise worse, in a more detailed, vivid and pathetic account at 265ff., and by bringing out more fully the blessings of passing away earlier at 258ff. But J. does not want the king's death to seem a good thing, and so does not even hint at any idea of it as an escape. Rather he presents it as a further, crowning calamity during Priam's life by alluding to the Trojan War and the loss of Hector and his other sons, where Cicero only mentions prior felicity. J. also suggests misery continuing after death, rather than being eluded thus, by conjuring up a meeting in Hades with Assaracus at 258f. and implying that Priam received no funeral, so that his soul would have to wander disconsolately for many years before being admitted to the Underworld[112] (he describes the obsequies denied to Priam, and then his death, but makes no mention of a funeral, and one would imagine that at this point it would have been impossible to hold one for him).[113] In addition, by depicting magnificent exequies at 258ff., which are not found in Cicero, J. highlights what the king missed, so that his death comes across as tragic deprivation rather than escape.

The challenging rhetorical question in line 265 ushers in a version of Priam's final moments that is obviously based on Virgil *Aeneid* 2.506ff., especially 550ff., where Achilles's son Neoptolemus butchers the king, after murdering his son Polites before his eyes:

> *hoc dicens altaria ad ipsa trementem*
> *traxit et in multo lapsantem sanguine nati,*
> *implicuitque comam laeva, dextraque coruscum*
> *extulit ac lateri capulo tenus abdidit ensem.*
> *haec finis Priami fatorum, hic exitus illum*
> *sorte tulit Troiam incensam et prolapsa videntem*
> *Pergama, tot quondam populis terrisque superbum*
> *regnatorem Asiae. iacet ingens litore truncus,*
> *avulsumque umeris caput et sine nomine corpus.*

He dragged him, trembling and slithering
in a great pool of his son's blood, right up to the altar.

He wound up Priam's hair in his left hand, and with the right
he raised his flashing sword and buried it in his side up to the hilt.
This was the close of Priam's destiny, this was the fated end
that carried him off, as he saw Troy in flames and its citadel in ruins,
this man who once was the proud ruler of so many peoples
and lands of Asia. His mighty trunk lies on the shore,
the head hacked from the shoulders, a corpse without a name.

While exploiting all the solemnity, sadness and horror of these lines, which the allusion calls to mind, the satirist also streamlines the Virgilian narrative, picking out from it just a few significant points. He also adds to the *Aeneid* passage – a suggestive simile, extra details and other epic reminiscences. In this way, on top of their emotional impact, J.'s lines have an intellectual aspect, which gives them an extra level and further interest, and which precludes mawkishness; and there is even an undercurrent of humour, as within a narrower compass J. cheekily tries to 'improve on' the account of Priam's death in *the* epic poet of Rome, and uses snippets taken from elsewhere in Virgil's own poetry to do so.

Lines 265–6 obviously pick up Priam's vision at *Aeneid* 2.555f. But for J.'s poor old monarch there is a picture of even more terrible destruction. He beholds everything overthrown, not just the citadel in ruins. Rather than Troy in flames he sees Asia collapsing through fire (although 'Asia' here stands for 'Troy', the expression creates an apocalyptic image of the whole continent ablaze). And there are two pregnant verbs to accent the devastation: *eversa* ('overthrown') combines 'overturned', 'overthrown' and 'ruined', while *cadentem* ('collapsing') embraces 'falling down', 'being overthrown' and 'perishing'.[114] J. increases the power and pathos of the vision in *Aeneid* 2 like this by actually taking over all those details and words from *Aeneid* 3.1ff.:

> *postquam res Asiae Priamique evertere gentem*
> *immeritam visum superis, ceciditque superbum*
> *Ilium et omnis humo fumat Neptunia Troia.*

After the gods decided to overthrow
the kingdom of Asia and Priam's innocent people, and proud
Ilium collapsed, and all Neptune's Troy was smoking from the
    ground up.

J. also tops the lines from *Aeneid* 2, and highlights the horror, with his word order in line 266: the lone *Asiam* ('Asia') is engulfed by the juxtaposed and dramatically alliterating *flammis* ('fire') and *ferroque* ('and sword') and, further out, by *eversa* ('overthrown') and *cadentem* ('collapsing') in emphatic position at either end of the hexameter.

In line 267 J. picks up *trementem* ('trembling') in *Aeneid* 2.550 with his *tremulus* ('trembling'), but adapts it to form a collocation with *miles* ('soldier'), which is primarily pathetic but may well also contain irony,[115] and he adds dactyls and frequency of *t* to reinforce the tremulous effect. With a meaningful juxtaposition of *arma* ('arms') and *tiara* ('crown'), J. introduces the action of the crown's removal, which is symbolic of Priam's sad loss of regal status. In such a heavily Virgilian passage it seems to me very probable that there is another reminiscence of the epic poet here. Priam's *tiara* was among the relics snatched from the burning Troy that were offered as gifts to king Latinus by the Trojan envoy Ilioneus at *Aeneid* 7.247 (the only instance of *tiara* in the poem). There Priam's city was destroyed and he was dead, so there would be gloom and foreshadowing in an echo here. With *et ruit* ('and fell') at the start of line 268, our author (unlike Virgil) actually mentions the king's collapse, inviting us to picture it. And it is a quick collapse. At *Aeneid* 2.508ff. Priam armed himself, and then was addressed by his wife, saw his son murdered before his eyes, and bravely upbraided and hurled a spear at Neoptolemus, who briefly replied and then killed the old man. J. keeps his focus on the very relevant figure of Priam, who with shocking and brutal suddenness is no sooner armed than he falls dead (two words later, with the swift dactyl *et ruit*), an even more feeble and pitiful figure. In contrast to Virgil, J. specifies whose altar it is, and his identification of highest Jupiter makes the sacrilege even more awful, and diminishes Priam, who seems still more weak and negligible beside the supreme deity.

At 268–70 J. pawkily adds to Virgil by employing a multiple correspondence simile of the type often found in epic, and one as pregnant as the best epic similes. It is primarily poignant, but there is also some hard mockery here, and it really brings out the demeaned and despised state of Priam, as more food for thought for readers (you too could live so long that you are unable to defend yourself and die an ignominious death). The aged king killed at the altar is likened to an old ox sacrificed by its master (which contrasts pointedly with the rite at 258ff.). As well as depriving the Trojan of his royal and human standing, the imagery implies that he is similarly in a poor physical state (with an old man's scrawny neck), decrepit, helpless and unthreatening, deserving of pity but scorned instead. The animal has outlived its usefulness, and its achievements are now over and count for nothing. The equivalent to its master is Neoptolemus, who is thus portrayed as a superior figure totally in control, with the power of life and death, who employs the killing weapon impassively. The presenting of the neck to the knife suggests a lack of resistance on Priam's part, perhaps even a deliberate self-sacrifice, and an absence of any desire to live on in that terrible situation. Line 270 intimates a saddening contempt for the aged ruler, but there is also some deflating mockery and quirky humour there. The personified plough does stand for the ploughman, but the novel and arresting expression depicts even the inanimate plough scorning the ox in its sorry state; and it ascribes feelings to this implement (when wood was traditionally unfeeling), which should be grateful for what the ox did in the past but rejects the animal, a snooty tool with standards not prepared to work with an inferior partner.

This is not just a dense simile but also an erudite one, and *contaminatio* (blending of models) is part of the cerebral appeal. As several scholars opine, J. may have in mind *Odyssey* 4.535 (= 11.411), where King Agamemnon, briskly murdered by Aegisthus, is likened to an ox slaughtered at its stall. If there is a deliberate Homeric echo, it would reinforce the pathos here[116] and the ease and quickness of the killing. Certainly in J.'s thoughts was a simile in Virgil applied to the priest Laocoon, who was sacrificing when two huge snakes appeared and dispatched his two sons and then Laocoon himself, when he tried to help them, weapon in hand. At *Aeneid* 2.223f. we find another well-born and armed Trojan who dies by an altar (after the demise of his offspring there) compared to a bull being sacrificed at an altar. Virgil talks of Laocoon raising cries *qualis mugitus, fugit cum saucius aram / taurus et incertam excussit cervice securim* ('like the bellowing when a wounded bull has escaped from the altar and shaken from its neck a badly aimed axe'). J.'s allusion to the death of Laocoon brings in appropriate associations of a horrific killing by an irresistible and merciless superior force. And J. also builds on his source again: more affectingly, his Trojan is equated not with a creature that is merely wounded and vigorous enough to escape, but with one that is frail and unresisting and just collapses in death at the altar. J. also adds the touching details of the ox's age and pitifully scrawny neck, and in line 270 introduces the plough and thereby an element of levity and derision not found in Virgil. At the same time, and with entertaining dexterity, at the end of line 268 our poet works in a reminiscence of *Aeneid* 5.481, another hexameter which closes abruptly with *bos* ('ox'), a rare monosyllabic hexameter ending which catches the sudden fall of the animal by means of the rhythm: *tremens procumbit humi bos* ('the ox collapses on the ground trembling'). In Virgil, Entellus has won a boxing match and to demonstrate his strength kills with one blow the ox that is his prize. As in J., there is a sudden, swift and effortless execution of a trembling victim that poses no threat by a powerful and pitiless character. In addition to its aptness, the Virgilian echo brings in the suggestion of an unnecessary killing, a murder committed for show. J. also adds *vetulus* ('old') for greater poignancy and a closer connection to his overall onslaught on old age.

The account of Priam's death in *Aeneid* 2 ends with his headless trunk, a corpse without a name, lying on the beach. J. also closes his passage with a sudden switch away from the altar in the palace and a literary 'jump-cut' (a jump to a point later in the narrative, omitting intervening events) and a grim final picture (in a little over one line) of an old member of the Trojan royal family who is mutilated and nameless. And J. picks up Virgil's *hic exitus illum / sorte tulit* ('this was the fated end that carried him off') in 2.554f. with *exitus ille* in line 271. But he adds a twist with his *exitus ille utcumque hominis* ('his end at any rate was a human being's'), as he brings in Priam's wife Hecuba, who rather than being like an animal (an ox) actually became one (after she is captured by the Greeks, the old woman is transformed into a bitch). J. also presents an even grimmer final picture for his own climax. The king suffered but at least kept his human form; his wife went through all that he did and then more – capture and enslavement for herself and dear ones, the killing of additional relatives (her grandson Astyanax, her daughter Polyxena and, in one tradition,[117] her son Polydorus) and then the awful metamorphosis as well. She also experienced a more drastic and extensive change to her body, one conducive to nightmarish horror rather than sadness, with the grotesque animality and ferocity stressed by the collocation *torva canino / latravit rictu* ('opened her canine jaws and barked fiercely'). In some versions, she lived on in misery after that.[118] J.'s introduction of Hecuba here also makes one think of her brief appearance earlier in the death scene at *Aeneid* 2.515ff. and appreciate the Juvenalian spins, which increase the bleakness. There she was with her daughters and was likened to a dove; here she is isolated and has actually turned into an animal. There she spoke gentle words to Priam, who was alive, and whom she was trying to keep alive by getting him to sanctuary; here she barks fiercely, and he has been killed. J. has also turns her remarks to her husband at 2.520–4 (*quo ruis? / ... haec ara tuebitur omnis / aut moriere simul* ('where are you rushing? ... This altar will protect us all, or you will die with us') with his *et ruit ante aram* ('and fell before the altar') in line 268, where Priam in fact dies on his own.

The unexpected switch to Hecuba after all the focus on her spouse makes for surprise, and the bald and dense brevity here (especially in contrast to the foregoing expansiveness), together with the spondees in line 272, means that these two verses on yet another suffering old person come like a sudden blow to the solar plexus. This adds force to all the negativity in connection with the king in the earlier part of this subsection, to get J.'s point across about longevity.[119] Then again, few readers are likely to suffer a fate similar to Priam's, and none will undergo an end like Hecuba's.

At 273–5 the poet employs the rhetorical device of *praeteritio*, actually mentioning some more examples while saying that he is passing over them. He covers them quite quickly because he chooses to concentrate on pertinent Roman figures at 276ff., and also to imply that they are such obvious *exempla* that he does not need to waste many words on them. In addition, *festino ad nostros* ('I hasten on to our own people') is a signpost which arouses expectation and curiosity, and J. achieves a build-up by means of retardation, not revealing who his Romans are for a while. There is also facetiousness here: in fact, he does not really hurry (he takes another two and a half lines, with slow spondees at 273f., to reach his own people), and if he had just proceeded to the Roman examples without all the talk about hastening on and passing over he *would* have got to them swiftly.

Staying with barbarians, the satirist adds two further *exempla* with no narrative for a change, moving on to more recent (historical) figures, and extending the geographical scope. Smoothly picking up Priam, Mithridates (the king of Pontus) and Croesus were also rulers who were conquered and deprived of their thrones, and they also show that even famous and impressive monarchs (never mind J.'s readers) can suffer seriously through living too long, and get no help or comfort from their great wealth and power. Mithridates VI (120–63 BC) extended his influence beyond Pontus and built up a large kingdom. He fought three wars against Rome and was one of her most formidable enemies, before being decisively defeated by Pompey. After that his son led a revolt against him, his troops deserted him and he committed suicide; and it was an agonizing death according to one tradition.[120] Croesus ruled over Lydia from about 560 to 546 BC and was renowned for his fabulous wealth, but he lost his kingdom to Persia, was very nearly burned alive on a pyre and ended up as the servant of the Persian king Cyrus and subsequently his unbalanced son Cambyses.

Croesus seems to be a barbed choice as an example for those who might pray for longevity, as he was a silly man who ignored words of wisdom. In one well-known story he entertained the Athenian statesman Solon, showed him his riches and asked him who in his opinion was the most blessed of men, expecting it to be him. Solon named others (Tellus, Cleobis and Biton) and told Croesus that a man cannot be counted blessed until he has reached the end of his span and the changes of fortune in the course of his life are taken into account. Croesus dismissed him as a fool, but his subsequent reversal proved Solon right. In these lines J. employs the famously wise statesman to support his case and so plays him up. While minimizing Croesus, he devotes most of 274f. to Solon and his advice. In the final four words of line 274 he draws attention by means of chiasmus (of nouns and adjectives) and parallelism (in the order of nominatives and genitives). He also elevates the Athenian by combining two reminiscences – *iustus Solon* ('just Solon') at Manilius 1.773 (where he heads a list of highly endowed sages possessed of mental strength and exact and weighty judgement) and *vox facunda* ('eloquent voice') at Ovid *Fasti* 4.245 (of a very learned goddess – the Muse Erato). And in line 275 there is stylistic highlighting again, of Solon's injunction, by means of chiasmus (of cases) and balanced arrangement of epithets and nouns. However, there is one major problem in all this. While remarking on Solon's fairness, J. is unfairly reporting his words and distorting them to make his point: Solon told Croesus to look to the end of a man's life, but did not specify a *long* life; and in the case of Cleobis and Biton, who were young men when they died, he was taking into account the end of short lives.[121]

At 276ff., broadening his range, J. moves from foreign kings to a member of a poor Italian family who became one of the most popular and powerful men in the Roman republic, and who also suffered a reverse through living long. Gaius Marius (approximately 157–86 BC), after being consul six times, beating the formidable Jugurtha in Africa and saving Rome from very dangerous barbarian invaders (the German Cimbri and Teutones in 102–1 BC), was driven out when his political enemy Sulla seized the city in 88 BC. Marius hid in the marshes of Minturnae (in southern Latium), but was captured and imprisoned for execution. He was almost killed, but at the last moment the executioner refused to put him to death in his prison, and Marius escaped to Carthage, where he lived as a beggar in the ruins of that city (destroyed by the Romans in 146 BC). We perceive his fall even more clearly when we recollect his earlier appearance at 8.245ff., as a man of humble origins who worked his way up and outdid aristocrats, celebrating a triumph over the Cimbri and Teutones. However, the satirist deliberately fails to mention Marius's later return to Rome, where he became consul for a seventh time and took bloody revenge with a massacre of his enemies, in a reversal of fortune which had been remarked upon by several earlier authors.[122] Cultured readers might well say to themselves that things (as depicted at 276f.) were bad for Marius, but look what he did when he got home later. As well as being aware of the facts undermining J.'s case, they might even see a ghastly humour in the subsequent inversion of each of his points at 276f.: Marius was begged to spare the lives of the citizens, demanded that they annul the sentence of banishment (and they hastened to comply), entered the conquered city of Rome, made his opponents hide and (rather than nearly killing) actually killed a large number of them, while exiling others.[123]

With a mixture of pathos and derision J. packs 276f. with adversity, presenting a series of moments that catch Marius at a very low ebb, in marked contrast to 280–2, where he is victorious, in Rome, and a revered triumphing general who has captives of his own. In line 276 the bulky and ponderous *Minturnarumque paludes* ('and Minturnine marshes') highlights this scene of ignominious hiding, capture and imprisonment. After the flurry of bald allusions there, which leave us to fill out the picture, there is impact in the more detailed snapshot in 277, a whole line on this supreme degradation, where every word counts, and there are lugubrious and weary spondees and assonance of long *a*. There is bitter irony in the conqueror of Rome's enemies ending up in the city of another enemy and inferior to that foe, and in Marius defeated rather than defeating in Africa (the scene of his victory over Jugurtha), begging rather than commanding and dictating terms, and humiliated rather than distinguishing himself. There is also a wry twist to *panem et circenses* ('bread and races') in line 81. As there, we find in 277 one of the people praying for donated bread; but Marius is in the ruins and shacks of Carthage rather than Rome, wants bread alone and has no chance of entertainment there, and is a spectacle himself[124] instead of a spectator, so that he has fallen below even the degenerate and despised plebs of 72ff.

At 278f. there is vigorous alliteration, emphatic repetition – of *quid* ('what') – and placement – of *hinc* ('by this') and *umquam* ('ever') – and a weighty rhythm (in line 279). However, for thoughtful readers all this forcefulness does not cover up the weaknesses in the satirist's argument. With *hinc causas habuere* ('were caused by this'), he means that the sufferings at 276–7 were due to living on into old age; but this is an oversimplification (there were obviously other causes too), and it was also thanks to living on that Marius got to take revenge on his opponents, reverse the humiliations inflicted on him and become consul for a seventh time. The claim that there could not have been anybody more fortunate than Marius in the whole world is absurdly sweeping, and the reference to Rome is also rather dubious, as Marius was not born in Rome but in Arpinum in Latium. The question of who could have been more fortunate than Marius makes me smile and think at once of Sulla, whose *cognomen* was Felix ('Sulla the Fortunate'), and who was the eventual victor in the power struggle between the two men. The notion that Marius would have been supremely blissful if he had died while celebrating his triumph over the Germans in 101 BC is open to question: other writers saw him as being very fortunate in view of his whole career.[125] It has in any case been sabotaged in advance by the mockery of the triumph-like ceremonial in this very poem at 36ff. and the deflation at length of military types and their achievements in the previous section at 133ff. And the poet stresses how outrageous it is for him to say all this now by directing us back to those earlier passages by means of a cluster of words at 280–2 that recall them: *agmine* ('line') and *curru* ('chariot') echo lines 36, 42 and 45; *captivorum* ('of captives') looks to *captivos* in line 136; *bellorum pompa* ('parade of war'), which would include booty, picks up *bellorum exuviae* ('spoils of war') in line 133; and the breathing out of the *animam* ('soul') calls to mind the end of the *anima* of the mad fool Hannibal at line 163. In addition, the end envisaged for Marius here is undignified (see below), and J. has already intimated at 163ff. and 171ff. that Hannibal's and Alexander's undignified demises cancelled out all their earlier accomplishments, so he can hardly maintain now that such a death for Marius would have made him exceptionally fortunate. J. is thus cheerfully undermining his own case, and in doing so he is exposing and ridiculing the distorted view of the pessimist which leads him to take up untenable positions and say silly things.

There is also yet more mockery of the military man here, reinforcing the poet's earlier onslaught on such characters. At 280–3 J. catches the culminating point of the whole triumph, when the general at the end of the parade got out of his chariot at the temple of Jupiter on the Capitoline, deposited his splendid clothing and accessories there and then sacrificed bulls. But here, grotesquely, at this particularly elated moment we see Marius (rather than the bulls) dropping dead, which ties in wickedly with the admonition to remember he was a mortal by the slave riding in the chariot with the Roman celebrating his triumph (cf. 41f.); and, whether Marius collapsed inside the vehicle or tumbled out of it, one can easily imagine the comically shocked faces of the crowd. The humour is increased by the mock-solemnity in all the spondees, the bulky and alliterating *circumducto captivorum* in line 280, the stately five-word hexameter in 281 and the lofty diction – *bellorum pompa* ('the parade of war'), *anima opima* ('triumphal soul') and *Teutonicus currus* ('Teutonic chariot') are all unique – and expressions like *animam exhalare* ('breathe out the soul') were high style.[126] In the phrase *animam … opimam*, with its droll elision of the final syllable of *animam* to suggest the cutting off of the breath, the primary sense of *opimam* is 'triumphal'; but there may well be flippant play on the meanings 'rich' and 'plump'[127] (in contrast to the poor, emaciated beggar of line 277), and in such a context it is hard not to think of the *spolia opima*, the 'rich spoils' won by a Roman general from an enemy commander in personal combat, an exceptionally distinguished trophy which Marius did not win, so that he can hardly be viewed as the luckiest of men. In line 282 I have translated *vellet* as 'on the point of',[128] but there is probably derisive sport with the sense 'wanting to' – he wished to get down, but could not actually do so, and after his splendid victories and the grand procession he could not even manage something as simple as getting out of a chariot. In the same line *Teutonico ... curru* ('Teutonic chariot') denotes the one ridden in the triumph over the Germans, but also conjures up an outlandish and crude barbarian vehicle in place of the elaborate gilded car used in the triumph.

At 283ff. J. appends the illustrious general Pompey, who fell ill with a dangerous fever in Campania (the area around Naples) in 50 BC. Cities throughout Italy prayed for his recovery, and he did survive – only to be murdered and decapitated two years later, when he landed in Egypt after his defeat in the civil war by Caesar at Pharsalus, seeking asylum. This is a sardonic subsection. There is quirky humour in the personification of Campania as prescient (able to foresee Pompey's brutal end) and provident, generously giving the man a gift, but the gift of a serious illness, although this was in fact something to be desired. *Febres* ('the fever') and *optandas* ('that he should have prayed for') are emphasized by their positions in their respective lines and are both delayed to ensure a jocular and challenging surprise effect. The phrase suggests a bizarre entreaty ('Gods, give me a fever!'). But, according to J., that was preferable to those of all the Italian cities: *optandas* and *vota* ('petitions') are in tension at either end of line 284 and set up an opposition between what should have been prayed for and the prayers that were actually made. In 284, with its mockingly mournful spondees, we see yet again misguided appeals, as all these blind, well-meaning fools in effect only help preserve Pompey for a much worse death (beheading after defeat in the civil war). The verb of conquering, *vicerunt* ('won out'), placed prominently at the start of line 285, is carefully chosen. There is a nod to the great conqueror Pompey. With *victo* ('conquered') in 286 we see that the cities' victory led on to his defeat. There is also frivolous play on the coming civil war in these towns contending with Campania and winning; and in this miniature struggle, as in the real thing later, Pompey and his supporters (both Campania and the Italian cities) lose, in the short term in the case of former, and in the long run for the latter.

To fill out the joke about the supplications for Pompey's recovery, in line 285 J. selects two particular divine powers as the ones answering them. He thereby gives a wry twist to Pompey's famous good fortune and to the Fortune of Rome, which thus itself helps ensure that the city is subjected to the tyrannical Caesar of line 109. He also arouses doubts about divinity (prior to questioning it more fully in the final section), because in saving him from fever they secured an even worse end for Pompey, and J. represents *them* as actually cutting off his head, with *caput abstulit* ('took away the head') kept back until the end of the sentence for shock value. There is pawkiness whether these divinities were equally misguided in acquiescing to the ill-advised treaties in all ignorance or were positively malicious and possessed of a cruel sense of fun (as at 7f. and 111) in granting prayers that they knew would be ultimately pernicious. This divine pair also cut down to size the mere mortal grandly styled Pompey the Great, and insinuate that even for such a powerful figure (never mind ordinary people, like most readers) living too long was a curse; although one can reasonably object that surviving for just two more years hardly equates to a long old age, for Pompey was only 58 when he died. The first four words in line 286 increase the bleakness and humour: in addition to the bald, blunt language and the powerful collocation of preservation, defeat and decapitation, there is a dreadful wit in the density, as *servatum* ('which had been saved') combines 'preserved' and 'reserved' (for mutilation),[129] *caput* means 'head' and also 'life', and *abstulit* ('took away') embraces both decapitation and the carrying off of the head, for viewing by king Ptolemy of Egypt and Pompey's enemy Caesar.[130] The final two words in 286, while extending the awful onomatopoeia (hacking *c* and *t* sounds), add a further blow, because *hoc cruciatu* ('this agony'), which covers severe physical and mental pain,[131] must mean that Pompey was still alive and conscious (a point reinforced at 286f.) when he lost his head.[132]

In the final sentence in the section the poet alludes to the Catilinarian conspiracy, an attempt to seize power in Rome which was thwarted largely thanks to the consul Cicero. Lentulus and Cethegus, henchmen of Catiline, were supposed to murder Cicero and set Rome on fire while their leader marched on the city with an army. They were arrested and put to death by strangulation in the Tullianum (Rome's underground prison) late in 63 BC, and early the next year Catiline fell in battle, fighting government forces at Pistoria. Again there is a philosophical aspect and J. engages combatively with Cicero's *Tusculan Disputations*. At 1.86 Cicero claims that by succumbing to fever in Campania at the height of his prosperity, Pompey would have left good things, but by expiring later he escaped evils (defeat in the civil war, flight from Italy, etc.), so that his death was not bad in itself and calamity was evaded by means of it. The satirist agrees that Pompey would have been better off perishing earlier, but in line with his own argument he does not want Pompey's death to seem a good thing. So there is no notion of his demise as an escape from evil, and it is presented as a crowning evil. He depicts Pompey's end as a calamity in itself, something that involved the great pain of beheading (not mentioned by Cicero), and he highlights the mutilation at lines 286–8 and deploys the very negative terms *cruciatu* ('agony') and *poena* ('punishment'). That is something worth evading, but Lentulus and Cethegus (not Pompey) are the ones who escape. In J.'s satire death is something that diminishes Pompey (see above) rather than bringing him release; and instead of being relieved of his suffering, he is relieved of his head! And the misery continues after his assassination, as line 288 brings to mind the decapitated body lying ignominiously on the beach.[133] There is also a sly touch in using Cicero's own achievement (which encompassed the death of the conspirators) to undermine Cicero's case by bringing out how terrible was Pompey's end in contrast to theirs.

The expression is forceful in this final sentence. There is vehement alliteration, dactyls to sweep us along and emphatic placement of *cruciatu*, of *Lentulus* and *Cethegus*, and of *integer* ('unmutilated') and *toto* ('intact'), enfolding lines 287 and 288. A full three enemies of Rome are represented as being better off, building to the leader Catiline, who contrasts with the leader Pompey, the former dying on the battlefield as the latter would have wished. In addition, *cadaver totum* ('corpse intact') occurs elsewhere only at Lucan 8.700 (as something denied to Pompey), and the echo brings with it sombre associations, as it comes just after a picture of Pompey's headless body tossed to and fro in the shallows. But once again, for the reflective reader such forcefulness does not cover over the faults in J.'s logic. One wonders if Pompey, who accomplished so much and had an illustrious reputation in life and after his death,[134] was really worse off than traitors who achieved nothing and whose names lived on in infamy, something which J. himself ensures here, and at 2.27, 8.231ff. and 14.41. One also wonders if being strangled in a dungeon is much preferable to Pompey's end. And there was a (possibly true) tradition[135] that Catiline's head was cut off after the battle and sent to Rome to prove his death, so that the satirist would appear to be concluding on a controversial note with a provocative juxtaposition of *Catilina* and *cadavere toto* ('with his corpse intact'). All of this means that, amusingly and provocatively, J. builds to a problematical climax of the whole section.

John Dryden (1631–1700) produced not a literal translation but a paraphrase of several of J.'s satires, intended 'for the Pleasure and Entertainment, of those Gentlemen and Ladies, who tho they are not Scholars, are not Ignorant: Persons of Understanding and good Sense' and making Juvenal 'more Sounding and more Elegant than he was before in English'. Given such aims and the target readership, it is not surprising that in the lines on longevity (see Winkler, 2001, 158ff. for text), Dryden glosses over Phiale at 10.236ff., producing something inoffensive and also less hard-hitting. However, when it comes to the non-sexual material of the deaths at 10.240ff., Dryden matches and even at times outdoes J. in impact. Comparison of the Latin and English is illuminating in two directions, enhancing appreciation of both J. and Dryden.

Notes

1   For a positive attitude to old age in antiquity see esp. Cicero *De Senectute* and cf. also Cokayne, 12, 18, 91ff.; Parkin, 58ff.

2   The passage 11.201ff. intimates that J. was getting on himself when he wrote this poem.

3   See Campana.

4   On the controversy see esp. Mayor; Duff; Ebel; Tengström, 32ff.; Courtney; Campana.

5   See *OLD* s.v. *continuus* 2a, 2b, 3; s.v. *quantus* 2a, 2d; s.v. *malum* 1, 2, 7b.

6   For concern about physical manifestations of old age in antiquity see Cokayne, 15ff.

7   See *OLD* s.v. *deformis* 1, 3, *TLL* V.1.368.27ff., 83ff.

8   Cf. e.g. Sall. *Cat.* 1; Cicero *ND* 2.29; Pease, ad loc.

9   See *TLL* II.831.76ff.; *OLD* s.v. 9.

10   It is, of course, always possible to take a more positive attitude to wrinkles, to see them as indications of an old age invested with authority and deserving respect (cf. Cokayne, 21f.).

11   Cf. e.g. *OLD* s.v. *simia* 1b; Cic. *Div.* 2.69; *ND* 1.97; Pease, ad loc.

12   See Pease on Cic. *ND* 1.97.

13   Cf. e.g. Strabo 827.

14   Some scholars take *iam* (in the sense of 'already') with *mater* ('mother') and think the idea is that the ape has been disfigured by childbirth. This is possible, but that notion is adequately conveyed by *mater* on its own. Rudd and Courtney suggest 'long since' as the meaning for *iam* (for this cf. *TLL* VII.1.93.9ff.), and *iam* in this sense going with *scalpit* ('has ... been scratching') works very well by accentuating the prolonged (and damaging and deranged) nature of the scratching.

15   See e.g. http://neuro.psychiatryonline.org/cgi/content/full/18/2/242.

16   See above on lines 148 and 158.

17   See e.g. *OLD* s.v. *ater* 7, 8b and s.v. *niger* 7 and 8.

18   *OLD* s.v. 2.

19   See e.g. Virgil *Aen.* 6.282ff., 386, 451, 673.

20   See Urech, 264; Schmitz, 106f.

21   The text in line 197 is disputed and uncertain. Two manuscripts begin the line with *hoc atque alio*, which makes no sense. Most mss have *hoc atque ille alio*, which I have tentatively accepted. Many scholars question the latter reading (see Campana for the various emendations proposed), but I do not see strong enough grounds for rejecting it definitely. Some claim that it breaks a *pulchrior ille / hoc ... hic robustior illo* pattern at 196f. (of one man more handsome than another and one man stronger than another) and point to the similar doublet at Ovid *Am.* 2.10.7 (cited at the end of the paragraph in my main text). However, J. may well be going beyond the simple doublet to include a further contrast (in line

with the very many differences between young men mentioned in line 196) and be presenting a deliberate variation on Ovid, topping him with extra antithesis, right after talking of *discrimina* ('differences'). I cannot find an exact parallel for the intricate employment of triple *ille*, double *hic* and single *alius* to denote six different people; but it is not hard to work out the references to youths A, B, C, D, E and F in the Latin, and *TLL* VII.1.355.66ff. cites examples of triple *ille* denoting three different persons (Petron. *Sat.* 115.16; Sen. *Contr.* 3 *praef.* 9), and of triple *ille* plus *alius* (Sen. *Epist.* 59.15) or *hic* (*Aetna* 616ff.) denoting four different people.

22   Some mss have *labra* ('lips') instead of *membra* ('limbs'), and Ebel and a few other scholars accept *labra* on the grounds that in this subsection J. is talking only of the face. But the voice mentioned in line 198 is not a facial feature, and J. has gone beyond the face in 197, while a reference to lips is simply not as effective (in terms of impact, humour, etc.) as allusion to limbs.

23   For the ancients' sensitivity to baldness and their attitude to it as something ridiculous and unappealing see Cokayne, 14ff. and cf. 4.38.

24   See Campana for this concept in antiquity.

25   See *OLD* s.v. *miser* 1, 3a, 4.

26   *OLD* s.v. 13.

27   Cossus cannot be identified with certainty (cf. Campana).

28   See Parkin, 200f.; Cokayne, 115ff., 128ff., 140ff.

29   See Parkin, 200.

30   This is more forceful than taking *coneris* to be indefinite and meaning 'should one try'.

31   See *OLD* s.v. 2b, 3, 5, 6, 9.

32   See Cokayne, 120.

33   See Courtney.

34   Some critics think that the old man is playing with himself but, given the situation here (he is trying to have sex with a woman and is proving impotent), most naturally she would try to stimulate him manually; and only she would have the stamina to keep that up all night long. In addition, prolonged efforts by her would be more humiliating.

35   There may be a touch of pity as well (see Jenkyns, 190).

36   For *inguen* with this sense see Adams, 47, 224.

37   See Courtney.

38   See *OLD* s.v. 1, 2, 3.

39   See e.g. Mayor, ad loc.; Cokayne, 120.

40   For the attitude cf. Martial 4.50.

41   See Adams, 45, 56ff., 60f., 69f., 77, 93, 95, 115, 221, 224.

42   See Miller, 316.

43   Line 212 could also denote lyre players, but mention of pipers has more point, because it means that the old man misses out on another form of music. On elaborate costumes for pipers see Mayor; Courtney; Campana.

44   *TLL* VI.1.1511.28ff.

45   See Mayor, ad loc.

46   See Cokayne, 35, 76, 78; Parkin, 251f.

47   See *TLL* V.2.1825.15ff.; *OLD* s.v. *gelidus* 2a; Ovid *Met.* 6.277.

48   J. may be alluding to Martial 3.93.17. If so, he would be importing the extensively negative aura of that epigram into his satire.

49   The old man thus swamped by ailments may look to the idea of old age itself as a sickness. See Cokayne, 35.

50   See *OLD* s.v. 4, 5, 7, 8.

51   See Scott, 70; Campana; Jones, 101.

52   See Courtney and Campana. There are variants (Eppia and Ippia). Our poet may be thinking of the Vestal Virgin called Oppia who was condemned for unchastity, and presenting a degenerate present-day Oppia who is unchaste with countless men.

53   See Mayor; Adams, 188, 223; *OLD* s.v. 3a.

54   See Courtney; Campana.

55   *Exorbeat* ('sucks dry') could possibly refer to the draining of semen in copulation, but fellatio is more disgusting and would make for a larger number of diseases.

56   See Hom. *Od.* 18.247f.; Herodotus 1.60; Prop. 2.2.5f., etc.

57   Cf. e.g. Virg. *Aen.* 1.1, 2.373, 4.573; Ovid *Met.* 3.549; *OLD* s.v. 5.

58   Cf. 5.43ff.; Catull. 58.5.

59   For *sorbeo* ('gulp down') of Charybdis, cf. Sall. *Hist.* 4.28; Virg. *Aen.* 3.422.

60   See Homer *Od.* 12.105ff.

61   The order of the lines there is disputed. Clausen in his *OCT* places 308 before 307, which makes Maura rather than Tullia the subject of *sorbeat*.

62   See Adams, 139f., 192.

63   *OLD* s.v. 12.

64   Courtney on 1.24–5 takes *gravis* to be adverbial and to denote a rasping sound. The word could also mean (of J.'s beard) 'difficult to shift, clinging' and 'troublesome'. See *OLD* s.v. 5a, 10a; *TLL* VI.2.2290.80f.

65   Some scholars have needlessly suspected line 226 because it duplicates perfectly 1.25 (see Ebel; Courtney; Campana), but there are good reasons for the echo.

66   Cf. e.g. Braund (1996b), 120.

67   Cf. e.g. Courtney, 259.

68   See Cokayne, 2f.

69   See Ferguson.

70   See *TLL* X.1.130.35ff., 75ff.; *OLD* s.v. 1a, 3b.

71   Cf. Pliny *Ep.* 8.18.9 (cited by Viansino).

72   Cf. e.g. Virg. *G.* 4.307; Hor. *Ep.* 1.7.13; Ovid *F.* 2.853.

73   *Ceu* belongs especially to the high style. See Urech, 30ff.; *TLL* III.977.63ff.

74   For ancient horror at senility see Cokayne, 67ff., 70ff.; Parkin, 228ff.

75   *OLD* s.v. *magnus* 11, 12, 13, 14.

76   See Mayor for the relatives who could have inherited.

77   Cf. e.g. 6.51 (and Courtney, ad loc.).

78   See Courtney; Ferguson. Cf. Ovid *Am.* 1.8.2f.

79   See *OLD* s.v. *artifex* 1, 2, 3. J.'s unparalleled phrase may be a sneering variant on expressions for skilled hands and fingers. See Campana.

80   See Ferguson.

81   See Mayor.

82   *Iliad* 1.250ff.

83   For the loftiness of this kind of expression see Urech, 278.

84   See Urech, 278f.

85   Cf. e.g. Pliny *NH* 10.30.

86   See e.g. Ovid *Met.* 2.548 and *F.* 2.89 for the crow, and Hom. *Il.* 1.254ff. for Nestor.

87   See *OLD* sv. c.

88   It is possible that *saecula* means 'centuries' rather than 'generations', but the allusion to Homer in line 246 makes the latter the probable sense here.

89   J. may also have in mind the tradition (in Pindar *Pyth.* 6.28ff. etc.) that Antilochus was killed while saving his father's life in the fighting at Troy, so that in living on, Nestor was directly implicated in his own son's demise.

90   See *TLL* VIII.1713.59ff. Remember also the Sibyl's death wish at Petron. *Sat.* 48.

91   See esp. *Il.* 10.164ff. and 11.636f.

92   See e.g. *Il.* 2.370ff. and 11.627.

93   The phrase was largely restricted to high style and solemn contexts. See Urech, 280; Campana.

94   See *OLD* s.v. 2a, 2d, 4, 5, 6, 7, 9. For Antilochus's sterling qualities see Homer *Il.* 15.569ff., 23.306ff., *Od.* 3.111f. (where we also sense Nestor's feeling of deprivation) and 4.199ff.

95   See *OLD* s.v. *ardens* 3.

96   Cf. also *Il.* 24.538ff. and *Od.* 11.495ff. for Peleus's wretched final years.

97   11.187ff., 15.353ff., 24.226ff.

98   For *rapio* in this connection see Ovid *Am.* 2.1.32; and cf. the cognate *rapto* at Cic. *Tusc.* 1.105; Virg. *Aen.* 1.483 and 2.272.

99   See Courtney.

100   See Courtney.

101   Homer *Od.* 5.313ff. and 12.420ff.

102   See e.g. Courtney, ad loc.

103   Cf. e.g. the complaints of neglect by Cynthia's ghost at Prop. 4.7.23ff.

104   See e.g. Diod. Sic. 4.75 and Virg. *Aen.* 6.649f.

105   See Urech, 284.

106   See Urech, 284.

107   Cf. e.g. Homer *Il.* 24.253ff., 499ff.

108   See *OLD* s.v. *reliquus* 1 and 3b; cf. Homer *Il.* 24.255ff.

109   See Urech, 97f.

110   Statius also took over *audax carina* at *Silvae* 3.2.1, but he applied it to contemporary ships in general rather than a specific craft, so he will not be in the satirist's thoughts here.

111   See Campana, 290.

112   Cf. 265ff.; Virg. *Aen.* 6.325ff.

113   There is no reference to a funeral at Virg. *Aen.* 2.557f. either, at the end of a narrative picked up by J. at 265ff.

114   See *OLD* s.v. *everto* 3, 4, 5 and s.v. *cado* 2, 10 and 12.

115   See Campana.

116   Cf. *Od.* 11.412, where Agamemnon's death is described as most pitiful.

117   See Ovid *Met.* 13.533ff. It is possible that J. had Ovid in mind, as there are a few verbal similarities (on which see Mayor; Campana).

118   Cf. e.g. Ovid *Met.* 13.570f. and Seneca *Ag.* 705ff. For the various versions of Hecuba's metamorphosis see Frazer's note on Apollodorus *Epitome* 5.23 in his Loeb edition.

119   For Hecuba as long-lived see e.g. Seneca *Ep.* 47.12.

120   See Val. Max. 9.2 ext. 3.

121   See Herodotus 1.30ff.; Plutarch *Solon* 27.

122   Sen. *Contr.* 1.1.3, 5; Manil. 4.46ff.; Val. Max. 6.9.14; Lucan 2.69ff.

123   See e.g. Plut. *Marius* 43f.; Appian *BC* 1.70ff.

124   Cf. e.g. Sen. *Contr.* 7.2.6; Plut. *Marius* 40.

125   See e.g. Cicero *Paradoxa* 2.16; Val. Max. 6.9.14f.; Lucan 2.74.

126   *TLL* V.2.1404.43ff.

127   See *OLD* s.v. 1c, 3, 6.

128   For this meaning see Courtney.

129   *OLD* s.v. 8 and 9.

130   Cf. e.g. Lucan 8.678ff.; Val. Max. 5.1.10; Plut. *Caesar* 48.2.

131   *TLL* IV.1218.63ff.; *OLD* s.v. 2, 3.

132   As he was at Lucan 8.667ff.

133   J. may also be thinking of Pompey's shade being similarly disfigured (cf. Virgil *Aen.* 6.494ff. and Courtney).

134   See e.g. Duff.

135   Picked up by Cassius Dio 37.40.2.

CHAPTER EIGHT

Beauty (289–345)

The noun *formam* ('beauty') at the start of line 289 immediately makes clear the topic of this final section of prayers. Arrestingly, J. goes in for extensive antithesis, taking us from disfigurement to beauty, from corpses to live people, from men to children and a mother, from famous names to unnamed minor characters, and from dramatic public events to the mundane private sphere. At the same time, this is just another prayer, and verbal echoes reinforce that link – *opto* ('pray') in lines 289 and 284, *votum* ('petition') in 291 and 284.

This is another passage that relates directly to modern western society, with its obsession with attractiveness and whole industries based on it, and again the satirist raises some very relevant questions for us (for instance: is beauty so desirable, is it worth going to great lengths to secure it, does it necessarily make you happy and does the exterior appearance matter all that much in any case?) But there are several significant differences from the previous section, and as he approaches the end of his satire, J. is clearly trying to avoid being predictable and monotonous. This is a shorter passage with only one developed (and flawed) *exemplum* (at 329ff.). That example picks up and takes further the lines on Messalina in *Satire* 6 (see the appendix), and so amounts to a reprise, which is a novelty in this poem. Females figure more prominently here than they have so far in X, and in noticeable positions, at the start and end. This time the satirist sets up an interchange with the petitioner, and stresses and mocks her (very convenient) stupidity, intimating that anybody who makes such a prayer is foolish; and by way of a change, he makes her appeal not for herself but for her children, thereby bringing various troubles on her own flesh and blood as well as on herself, so that there is a double impact in this prayer. Finally, in his lines on old age, J.'s basic point was sound, but here we are back to blatant and major exaggeration and cynicism, as he closes the central part of the poem with strong satire on pessimism by means of his *persona*.

The poet's main thrust is that this prayer is harmful, because beauty entails various serious dangers, such as rape, near rape, castration, enforced effeminacy, sundry punishments for adultery, moral corruption and especially death, which appears at the start (293f.), in the middle (316) and prominently at the end (324ff.). The alternatives would appear to be degradation or death, and there is the paradox of an entreaty to acquire something resulting in the loss of many things (virginity, morality, reputation, life, etc.). In place of a broad investigation of the topic with a range of critical points, J. stresses harm again and again, with a single-minded insistence, and with a structural arrangement that highlights the worst scenario – in a tricolon crescendo, lines 289–95 deal with girls; 295–309 are concerned with dangers for boys; and 310–45 concentrate on the greater hazards for men, and contain the hard-hitting *exemplum* of Silius and Messalina). Our poet presents a dark world full of predators, especially powerful ones who are hard to resist, and these characters constitute a sinister presence, initially in the background, at 293f., but very much in the foreground at 304–9 and 326ff. However, the basic premise is patently flawed. There is little logic in saying that one should not pray for beauty because of the attendant perils mentioned by J., because they are far from inevitable accompaniments. With this dismal and one-sided world view (and again one wonders how the poet can know about the whole globe) beauty leads only to bad things for humans, and no allowance is made at all for positive outcomes for the beautiful person (like being liked and well treated by people, attracting a loving spouse and so on), and in fact there are, of course, lots of happy good-looking people. This is a blinkered outlook, and the more the satirist goes on, the more absurd the totally black picture seems. There is also an imbalance in the concentration on handsome men, with little said about the risks for lovely women, and in the emphasis on the harmful side of this prayer, the *supervacuus* (excessive, pointless) aspect being touched on only in line 291. Is J. deliberately and facetiously trying to militate against a serious protreptic thrust and create ambivalence?

> *formam optat modico pueris, maiore puellis*
> *murmure, cum Veneris fanum videt, anxia mater*   290
> *usque ad delicias votorum. 'cur tamen' inquit*
> *'corripias? pulchra gaudet Latona Diana'.*
> *sed vetat optari faciem Lucretia qualem*
> *ipsa habuit, cuperet Rutilae Verginia gibbum*
> †*accipere atque suum Rutilae dare. filius autem*   295
> *corporis egregii miseros trepidosque parentes*

semper habet: rara est adeo concordia formae
atque pudicitiae. sanctos licet horrida mores
tradiderit domus ac veteres imitata Sabinos,
praeterea castum ingenium vultumque modesto   300
sanguine ferventem tribuat natura benigna
larga manu (quid enim puero conferre potest plus
custode et cura natura potentior omni?),
non licet esse viro. nam prodiga corruptoris
improbitas ipsos audet temptare parentes: 305
tanta in muneribus fiducia. nullus ephebum
deformem saeva castravit in arce tyrannus,
nec praetextatum rapuit Nero loripedem nec
strumosum atque utero pariter gibboque tumentem.
i nunc et iuvenis specie laetare tui, quem   310
maiora expectant discrimina. fiet adulter
publicus et poenas metuet quascumque mariti
lex irae debet, nec erit felicior astro
Martis, ut in laqueos numquam incidat. exigit autem
interdum ille dolor plus quam lex ulla dolori   315
concessit: necat hic ferro, secat ille cruentis
verberibus, quosdam moechos et mugilis intrat.
sed tuus Endymion dilectae fiet adulter
matronae. mox cum dederit Servilia nummos
fiet et illius quam non amat, exuet omnem   320
corporis ornatum; quid enim ulla negaverit udis
inguinibus, sive est haec Oppia sive Catulla?
deterior totos habet illic femina mores.
'sed casto quid forma nocet?' quid profuit immo
Hippolyto grave propositum, quid Bellerophonti?   325
†erubuit nempe haec ceu fastidita repulso
nec Stheneboea minus quam Cressa excanduit, et se
concussere ambae. mulier saevissima tunc est
cum stimulos odio pudor admovet. elige quidnam
suadendum esse putes cui nubere Caesaris uxor   330
destinat. optimus hic et formonsissimus idem
gentis patriciae rapitur miser extinguendus
Messalinae oculis; dudum sedet illa parato
flammeolo Tyriusque palam genialis in hortis
sternitur et ritu decies centena dabuntur   335
antiquo, veniet cum signatoribus auspex.
haec tu secreta et paucis commissa putabas?

non nisi legitime vult nubere. quid placeat dic.
ni parere velis, pereundum erit ante lucernas;
si scelus admittas, dabitur mora parvula, dum res   340
nota urbi et populo contingat principis aurem.
dedecus ille domus sciet ultimus: interea tu
obsequere imperio, si tanti vita dierum
paucorum. quidquid levius meliusque putaris,
praebenda est gladio pulchra haec et candida cervix.   345

The anxious mother, when she sees the shrine of Venus, prays
     for beauty
with a moderate murmur for her sons, and with a louder one for
     her girls,   290
to the point of extravagance in her petitions. 'But why' she says
'should you censure me? Latona delights in beautiful Diana'.
But Lucretia forbids one to pray for good looks such as she herself
had, Verginia would love †to accept Rutila's hump and
give hers to Rutila. What's more, a son with a   295
splendid body has miserable and apprehensive parents
always: so rarely do beauty and chastity coexist
in harmony. Even though his family (austere and copying the
old-time Sabines) has handed on to him blameless morals,
and on top of that kind Nature with generous hand grants him   300
a pure disposition and a face that glows with
a modest blush (for what more can Nature, more powerful
than all guardians and vigilance, bestow on a boy?),
he's not allowed to be a man. For the corrupter's unbridled
unscrupulousness dares to work on the very parents: 305
so great is his confidence in his bribes. No tyrant in his
savage citadel has castrated a deformed youth,
nor did Nero rape any free-born boy who had disfigured feet
or was scrofulous or had a bulging belly and hump.
Go on now, take pleasure in the handsomeness of your
     young man,   310
whom greater dangers await. He will become a communal
adulterer and will fear whatever punishments the law owes to a
husband's anger, and he won't have a luckier star than Mars
did, so as never to fall into a trap. But that resentment
sometimes exacts more than what any law has allowed   315
to resentment: one man kills with a sword, another cuts with
bloody whips, and some adulterers the mullet actually penetrates.

But your Endymion will become the boyfriend of a married
   woman
whom he has fallen for. Soon, when Servilia has given him cash,
he'll also become the boyfriend of one he doesn't love, he'll strip
   her of all   320
the adornment of her body; for what would any woman deny
to her wet crotch, if she's an Oppia or a Catulla?
The worse kind of woman has her whole character there.
'But what harm does beauty do to a chaste male?' On the
   contrary, what
good did a stern lifestyle do Hippolytus or Bellerophon?   325
†To be sure, this one blushed like a scorned woman rejected
and Stheneboea flared up no less than the Cretan, and both got
themselves shaking with rage. A woman is most savage when
shame applies a goad to her hatred. Choose what on earth
you think should be recommended to the man whom the
   emperor's wife   330
is determined to marry. The most virtuous and also the
   most beautiful
member of the noble class, the poor man is hurried along to be
   snuffed out
by Messalina's eyes. She has long been sitting with her bridal veil
ready, and a purple marriage bed is being spread openly
in the gardens, and a million sesterces will be given according to 335
ancient custom, the augur along with the witnesses will come.
Did you think that this was a secret, entrusted to a few?
She wants only a legitimate marriage. State your decision.
Should you be unwilling to obey her, you'll have to die before the
   lamps are lit.
Should you commit the crime, you'll be granted a tiny delay, until
   the business   340
that is well known to the city and the people reaches the
   emperor's ear.
He will be the last to know the disgrace of his house. Meanwhile
submit to her command, if a few days' life is worth
so much. Whichever course you think is easier and better,
this pretty, white neck has to be offered to the sword.   345

To undermine the prayer for beauty from the start, J. opens by parading
before us his construct of the type of person who prays for it, and makes
her ambitious, pretentious and, in particular, stupid, foregrounding those

failings (which are not, of course, inevitable in people who make such entreaties). The first sentence contains graphic onomatopoeia (frequency of *m*, *p*, *u* and *e*) and black humour. The combination of *optat* ('prays for') and *anxia* ('anxious') recalls line 80, putting the mother here on a par with the misguided and despised plebeians there, as this woman in effect (according to J.) wishes misery on herself (cf. 295ff.) and terrible troubles on her children; and the plurals *pueris* ('for her sons') and *puellis* ('for her girls') conjure up some sort of latter-day Niobe destroying her whole family. *Anxia* is pointed in several ways: it mocks her desperate desire for something which is in fact harmful (in the satirist's view); she *should* be uneasy over making such a (pernicious) prayer, and she will be really worried if it is granted (295ff.); and there may well be ironical play on the adjective's sense of 'careful, cautious'.[1] The volume of the murmur is part of the mother's silliness: she appears to imagine that Venus will hear and better understand a louder mutter, and that beauty is more desirable for a girl (293ff. promptly depict it as very undesirable for more vulnerable females). Prayers which embarrassed the petitioner were murmured,[2] and here she is presumably uncomfortable about asking for good looks, especially for boys. But the woman should in fact be ashamed of being so foolish as to bring down disaster on her children. In addition, she is concerned about other people hearing her entreaty when she should really be bothered about the goddess hearing it (and hearkening to it), and she actually raises her voice so that she can be heard better by Venus. On top of that, she repeats her request often (on seeing a shrine of Venus). As well as bestowing beauty, Venus also had a cruel sense of fun,[3] and so might well be tempted (like the gods at 7f. and 111) to accede to the request and thereby cause sundry erotic problems (cf. 293ff. and 304ff.). There is a nasty close to this sentence in line 291. The phrase *delicias votorum* ('extravagance in her petitions') is unique and intriguing. It may mean that she is asking for extraordinary beauty and/or promising Venus singular offerings in return;[4] but in either case, within J.'s scenario she is going to great lengths to ensure catastrophe for her offspring and agony for herself.

In the second half of line 291 she appears to respond, having heard what J. has just said and taken in his disapproving tone.[5] Here we have the amusingly surreal situation of one of the poet's own characters talking back to him; and there is a joke at J.'s expense in her saying 'why should you censure me?' to the habitually censorious satirist. The words put in her mouth also (conveniently) bring out her stupidity further. The point assigned to her in line 292 is selfish (there is nothing wrong with my prayer because it will bring me maternal pleasure, like Latona's), and it is one to which J. can reply immediately and vigorously. In equating herself (who has just prayed to a goddess) and her equally mortal offspring to two *puissant* divinities, she produces an analogy that is risibly inept and hybristic. It is also pompous. The style is lapidary, there is eloquent juxtaposition of Latona and Diana, and there are grave spondees and assonance of long *a*. That sentence also recalls Virgil *Aeneid* 1.496ff., where the extremely beautiful Dido – *pulcherrima*; cf. *pulchra* ('beautiful') here – coming to the temple of Juno (compare Venus's shrine in line 290) is likened to Diana, in whom Latona takes delight – *gaudia*; cf. *gaudet* ('delights') here. There is some quirky humour, as it seems that this woman has read the *Aeneid* and is quoting solemn epic and the revered Virgil to bolster her case before the poet Juvenal. However, her citation sadly backfires by calling to mind Dido, a very lovely woman who endured such torment that she killed herself (cf. 293ff.), and who was caused great trouble by Venus (the very goddess prayed to in 290).

J. makes two historical allusions at 293–5. Firstly, he refers to Lucretia, the wife of Collatinus, whose beauty inflamed Sextus (son of the king Tarquinius Superbus), with the result that he raped her, and she committed suicide in shame. Next he mentions Verginia, the lovely daughter of L. Verginius: early in the republican period a senior magistrate called Appius Claudius tried to seduce her by bribes and promises, but she refused him; he then tried to acquire her by getting an accomplice to claim her as his slave, but her father killed her, to save her from falling into Appius's clutches. The satirist's point is that beauty engenders major problems for girls (attracting the attention of powerful men who are hard to resist, and leading to rape or near rape and death), and he makes a sharp progression from virginal Diana to violated Lucretia. He is also indirectly countering the picture of the rejoicing parent in line 292, because naturally in both of the cases he cites the fathers were deeply distressed, as his readers would recall[6] or could surmise. So to the mother's lone, unconvincing parallel J. forcefully opposes two well-known[7] and emotive examples which are much more pertinent, as they involve humans and Romans (then again he has very obviously set up this riposte for himself; and two *exempla* do not prove that beauty is always dangerous, so that in the process of coming out with an objection to the mother's argument he is leaving his own open to objection!). At 293f. the expression has a bizarre and grisly aspect, as it brings to mind an image of the ghost of Lucretia forbidding prayers. At 294f. there is also sombre wit in the application to Verginia of a set of words with erotic connotations. She did not long for Appius or accept him or his offers, or give him anything, and we are shown here what she would long for, accept and give instead, as our poet exploits the use of *cupio* ('love to') for amatory and sexual desire, of *accipio* ('accept') for taking bribes and lovers, and of *do* ('give') for granting favours to a man.[8] There is also the grotesque notion here of somebody (especially a beauty) actually wanting a hump (the unknown Rutila must have been a hunchback familiar to J.'s readers) and of people swapping body parts as if they were detachable (unfortunately, because of textual problems we cannot tell if Verginia would be giving Rutila her face, her good looks, her breasts or her derrière).[9]

At the end of line 295 J. starts to argue that the petition for good looks is harmful for sons as well as daughters. He builds a picture of a world of danger for them (due to themselves and others) and anguish for their parents. At 296f., by way of reinforcement, he now directly contradicts the notion of parental joy in handsome progeny, intimating openly that such selfish prayers backfire and are bad for mothers and fathers too. J. presents a grimly comic rebound of *anxia* at the start of this section, as the mother makes her mental state worse, joining the ranks of those who, amid nervous dactyls, are *miseros trepidosque* ('miserable and apprehensive', two adjectives now, topping the lone *anxia*, and juxtaposed for stress). In line 297 the run-over and the placement of *semper* ('always') give it great emphasis, and highlight the sweeping nature of the claim. While trying to convey how unperceptive the mother is, the satirist shows defective vision himself by means of this exaggeration! And he shows the same thing with the epigram which follows immediately after, which is cynical in general, and seems particularly questionable right after his own *exempla* of the chaste Verginia and Lucretia (and the mention of Diana in line 292). In addition, the poet's pronunciation at 297f., in terms of similarities of thought, language and (epigrammatic) form, clearly looks to Ovid *Heroides* 16.290, where Paris remarks to Helen *lis est cum forma magna pudicitiae* ('there is a major conflict between chastity and beauty'). J. is thus citing a handsome hero who himself shows that purity does not go hand in hand with good looks, who made his parents miserable and apprehensive, and who brought destruction on himself and many others. However, at the same time, J. is also citing somebody not renowned for morality or intelligence, a notorious philanderer who is using distinctly dubious arguments to seduce another man's wife, and this detracts further from the reliability of J.'s aphorism. In fact, by alluding to Ovid, the satirist is harming his own case, rather like the mother who referred to another bit of Augustan poetry with a Trojan War connection in line 292.

At 297f. there is an implication that a petition for handsomeness, as well as resulting in worry for the parents, may well be bad for the boy too, ruining his morals by facilitating promiscuity (whose dangers are paraded at 310ff.). Then, having maintained that beauty and purity coexist only rarely, at 298ff. J. progresses to the situation in which the son actually is chaste; but again he presents a pessimistic vision, to bring out the uselessness of the possession of purity, even to a very great degree. He begins a long sentence in line 298, and, especially after *licet* ('even though'), the more he goes on about the lad's virtue, the more we expect a negative pay-off (which finally comes at 304ff.). That sentence also makes the maltreatment of such a boy in 304 seem even more shocking and the parents at 304f. seem even worse in contrast to their family tradition, the Sabines, their very moral son and kindly Nature.

First at 298f. J. talks of the family instilling into the boy the highest morality, underscored by the conglomeration of *sanctos* ('blameless'), in emphatic position, *horrida* ('austere'), *veteres* ('old-time') – antiquity was synonymous with morality and piety[10] – and, also stressed by placement, *Sabinos* (Sabines', who were renowned for being severe types who led a simple and very virtuous life). However, when one reads about family members (the parents) betraying their son for money at 304f., in retrospect one can see appropriately critical hints here. *Horrida* is probably double-edged, meaning primarily 'austere' but also beneath the surface 'uncivilized' and 'dreadful'.[11] There is very likely play in *tradiderit* ('has handed on'), as the word can also be used of surrendering someone to an enemy,[12] and the family will be handing over the boy himself (to his corrupter) as well as handing on morals to him. So too *imitata* ('copying') initially appears to have the sense 'modelling itself on' but could also mean just 'simulating'.[13] There is also undermining by means of another Ovidian reminiscence here. The ending of line 299 calls to mind the close of *Amores* 2.4.15[14] – *rigidasque imitata Sabinas* ('copying the straight-laced Sabine women'), applied to a female whom he suspects in line 16 of wanting to have sex but concealing the fact. So the phrase has associations of dissimulation and hypocrisy. In that elegy Ovid confesses to loving all types of girls, so that in speaking of the family's morality J. is, aptly enough for such parents, using the words of a man in the grip of rapacious desire (and there is foreshadowing of the seducer at 304f. in such great lust).

At 300ff. J. adds nature on top of nurture, and again there is a flurry of adjectives to underline the extent of the boy's purity. There is a grim joke in well-meaning Nature, through the chaste blush, endowing the lad with the attractive redness of complexion that would actually draw the unwelcome attentions of a corrupter.[15] Lines 300–2 also set up some dispiriting twists at 304ff., where wickedness triumphs over morality: benign Nature's generosity is outdone by the malign seducer's gifts; giving Nature is succeeded by grasping parents; and where Nature grants the boy the blush of modesty and virtue, his parents will make such a youngster blush through shame (for himself and for them). The parenthesis at 302f. holds back the pay-off still further. Also by means of this aside, J. is subtly undermining the idea that chastity is in fact a great gift from Nature (prior to the total deflation in line 304) by intimating that it is great in a fashion that is decidedly questionable.

So the vehemently alliterative rhetorical question is undercut by the obvious answer: Nature could give him ugliness (cf. 293ff. and 306ff.). Nature is not more powerful than the seducer. Nor is Nature more powerful than all types of *cura*: the main meaning of the noun is 'vigilance' (on the part of those concerned for the boy's well-being), but the word could also refer to the amatory *cura* ('love') of the corrupter and his 'eagerness' to acquire the youth and the 'attention' he devotes to it[16] – all of which outweigh Nature. There is also a subversive Ovidian allusion. Line 303 calls to mind *Metamorphoses* 9.758: *at non vult natura, potentior omnibus istis* ('but Nature, more powerful than all of them, does not want [this]'). Those words are spoken by Iphis (thought to be a boy, but really a girl), who claims that he cannot embrace his beloved Ianthe, not because of guardians (*custodia*, 750) or the vigilance (*cura*, 751) of a husband, but due to his nature, and the 'them' than whom Nature is more powerful includes gods. But Iphis is wrong: after a prayer to Isis by his mother, the goddess turns Iphis into a boy, and he gains Ianthe as his wife. The echo of Iphis's ignorant and incorrect statement about Nature reinforces the wrongness of J.'s claims at 302f.[17]

After all the build-up in that long sentence, the (first) pay-off comes at the start of line 304 with a bleak brevity (just four words in the Latin). We have been kept waiting for the punch line, and (after 297f.) many of us will expect it to be that the boy grows out of his chastity and becomes promiscuous. But J. has something worse than that. With an engaging and chilling economy, he packs a lot into those four Latin words. The all-important *viro* ('man') is deliberately kept back until the very end and combines various possibilities, to stress the loss in the various things that the youngster cannot be. It denotes a 'man' as opposed to a catamite (so the lad would be forced into passive homosexuality) and a 'man' with sexual potency in contrast to a eunuch (so the youth would be castrated, to become a sexual object: cf. 307) and a 'husband' (of a woman) and a 'true man' (so he would not be resolute, courageous, etc., but be turned into something much less virile).[18] There is real impact in all of this, although one can object that these things are not inevitable.

There is another surprise and a second part to the pay-off at 304f., where the defilement of the boy is actually facilitated by his own father and mother for bribes. As that sentence progresses, we become aware of an unscrupulous corrupter who is audacious, and who is making an attempt to influence, but it is not something of the youth's (like his morals or feelings) that he is working on, as we might expect: held back as the final (emphatic) word is *parentes* ('parents'), for shock value (especially after lines 296 and 298f.) and comic effect. So, if the son is chaste, the prayer for beauty, as well as bringing misery on him rather than happiness, will shamefully debase the petitioners themselves (so says J., but, of course, it is not true that all such offspring are sold like this). At the start of the sentence, to stress the horror for the handsome boy and to make the acquiescence of the mother and father seem even worse, the expression brings out how evil the seducer is. In *prodiga corruptoris / improbitas* ('the corrupter's unbridled unscrupulousness') there is a collocation of negative words. The second and third are almost entirely prosaic[19] (and so are aptly down to earth); *corruptoris* forms an unusual spondee in the fifth foot, which attracts attention, and is also stressed by its position, as is *improbitas*; *prodiga* combines 'unbridled' and 'extravagant', while 'perverter', 'briber' and 'seducer' are all possible senses for *corruptoris* (he corrupts the father and mother as well as the youngster), and *improbitas* embraces 'unscrupulousness' and 'audacity'.[20] With *temptare* ('work on') in line 305 J. is exploiting to the parents' disadvantage the use of the verb in amatory contexts (*muneribus* ['bribes'] in line 306 is often applied to presents given to the beloved):[21] the idea is that because the lad is so chaste, the man is seducing with gifts not him but his mother and father. *Parentes* ('parents') at the end of line 305 directs us back gleefully to *parentes* at the close of 296. Now, instead of being protectively worried about their son's chastity, they have betrayed him and ensured his loss of chastity, and they must have inflicted misery and apprehension on *him*. And if it is true that a handsome boy always has wretched and nervous parents, as is maintained at 295–7, now they would be miserable over what they have done to their own flesh and blood, and apprehensive of retribution. J. adds yet another effective Ovidian reference in line 306. The only other surviving conjunction of *munus* and *fiducia* occurs in a parallel context at *Metamorphoses* 7.309f., where Medea tricks Pelias's daughters into killing their own father in the belief that she will rejuvenate him as a gift to them. She does this by cutting the throat of a ram with a knife and magically turning it into a lamb, and introduces this proof of her powers with the words *quo sit fiducia maior / muneris huius* ('so that you may have more confidence in this gift'). This is a very apt allusion: Medea too is winning over family members to do something undutiful and harmful to a relative by means of a gift, and a knife is involved (cf. 307). The echo increases the sinister menace by likening the corrupter to Medea, a malevolent, insidious, ruthless, irresistible and terrifying figure who was a great danger to children. There is also pointed antithesis: Pelias's innocent and well-meaning daughters were hoodwinked, whereas the lovely lad's wicked parents consciously and deliberately sell him off.

Towards the end of line 306 J. suddenly springs on us a new and even grimmer scenario, moving from the rich seducer to the much more powerful and ominous tyrant and Roman emperor, as the beautiful boy is now arbitrarily seized rather than bought, and we see that predators go all the way up to the top and operate over a broad area. Line 307, with its sombre spondees and assonance, gives us a dark sketch of a youth with no chance of escape or rescue permanently damaged and totally at the mercy of the ruler in his *saeva ... arce* ('savage citadel'), a unique and sinister coinage which implies that the man's cruelty is so great that it has permeated his very stronghold on high. Then, at 308f. there is intensification, as J. progresses from the vague monarch abroad to Rome and specifies the monstrous Nero. His main verbs spotlight two terrible acts, but he deliberately does not explain what happens after them, leaving us to fear the worst and fill in the picture ourselves, in the same way that the mother and father would be left apprehensive and in miserable ignorance of what was actually going on. Here too there is danger for the son and agony for the parents which a prayer for beauty might well have brought about, according to our poet. But here too he is exaggerating the menace: Nero's homosexual partners did not include free-born boys,[22] and a foreign tyrant and the long-dead Nero would hardly pose much of a threat to a Roman lad of J.'s own day. In line 307, *deformem* ('deformed') looks back to the cognate *formam* ('beauty') in 289, making the point that the absence of beauty is preferable to its presence. Such deformity saves boys from deforming castration, whereas good looks result in the deformity of the eunuch state; and while none of the castrated is deformed to start off with, but they all end up deformed.[23] At 308f., in the act of dismissing it, J. briefly conjures up an image of Nero raping ugly youngsters! There is paradox in such disfigurement being preferable to handsomeness, and the more the satirist goes on, the more he brings out the notion that it is better not to be good-looking. In line 309, a strikingly grotesque verse of swellings, *gibbo* ('hump') echoes *gibbum* in 294: the youth here is still more misshapen than Rutila, but even that is preferable to being attractive.

At 310f. J. seizes our attention by abruptly addressing the mother and moving on to further and even greater dangers for her son (specified at 314ff. and 339ff.). Again the relentlessly negative satirist envisages only bad things happening (although they are not inevitable for all handsome youths) and a prayer for beauty bringing about adultery, fear, capture and punishment. There are sardonic developments: if the son escapes castration, he will be sexually active to the point of immorality; in place of the undeserved hurt of castration and rape there is the deserved hurt of punishment (as he is anally penetrated with a mullet rather than a penis); instead of being prey he will be a predator; and the mercenary parents are replaced by their mercenary offspring. The mother taking pleasure in her child's beauty in line 310 recalls the same thing in 292, so that here is a sharp retort to the mother's claim there, and the point is made that this is just as inappropriate for a boy as it is for a girl. The contemptuous *i* ('go on'), plus another imperative in line 310, calls to mind line 166, thereby putting the mother on a par with the stupid, mad and destructive Hannibal, whose ambitions came to nothing. *Nunc* ('now') primarily means 'in the light of these circumstances', but the temporal sense will be intended too: in the future the woman will have no grounds for joy, and the youth's looks will be marred (316f.). I have translated *specie* as 'handsomeness', but the meanings 'outward appearance' (as opposed to inner nature), 'illusory appearance' and 'veneer'[24] are also apposite. Initially one imagines that the irony in *laetare* ('take pleasure in') looks to the preceding lines only, but then J. unexpectedly adds (and so stresses) other threats too. There is a mocking barb in *tui* ('your'), because he will soon be not just his mother's but the young man of many others too. Our poet's *quem / maiora expectant discrimina* ('whom greater dangers await') clearly echoes Seneca *Naturales Quaestiones* 6.33.2: *maiora me pericula expectant* ('greater perils await me'). As part of his argument in favour of contempt for death (which leads to tranquillity and happiness), Seneca asks why he should fear man, wild animals, arrows or spears, as greater perils await him, namely lightning, earthquakes and vast natural disasters, which one should face bravely and despise. In J. the greater dangers come from man rather than the awesome power of nature, are mundane and even sordid, and are the result of adultery; also, unlike the wise and undaunted philosopher, the stripling foolishly brings the perils on himself and fears punishment. The contrast demeans the son in whom the mother takes so much pleasure and undercuts the beauty which leads to him being a less impressive and attractive figure like this.[25]

At 311f. with *fiet adultery / publicus* ('he will become a communal adulterer') our pessimistic poet is brisk and definite, emphasizing all three words by placement. *Publicus* means 'available to the community at large', but the expression also flippantly suggests a position of 'state adulterer'.[26] In addition, notoriety as well as promiscuity is implied, which would damage the standing of the youth and his parents. Interpretation of the words that follow in the Latin is complicated by textual problems,[27] but there is clearly mention of punishment by an angry husband or husbands. At 313f. J. refers to an amusing story: Mars and Venus had an affair, but were caught by Venus's husband Vulcan, who suspended over the bed invisible netting, which dropped down and trapped them in the act; Vulcan then summoned all the other gods to witness their shame, and only let the pair go when Neptune agreed to pay the adulterer's fine if Mars reneged. The allusion deflates further the much-prized lad and the beauty that facilitates his immoral conduct by means of contrast between a divine love affair and his mean coupling, and between the warlike progenitor of the Roman race and this degenerate Roman, a fearful and lecherous pretty boy. There are several simultaneous jokes in *nec erit felicior astro/ Martis* ('and he won't have a luckier star than Mars did'). For one thing, the youth will be a *lot* less lucky than Mars: he will not go to bed with Venus; he will not have anyone to intervene for him; and he will not get off scot-free after a little embarrassment, but be liable to severe punishment at the hands of a much more vindictive husband. Then there is the droll idea of the god Mars having his own *astrum* (a star that affects one's destiny). That notion becomes even funnier when one reflects that Mars was a heavenly body himself (the planet Mars), and as such was not lucky for humans.[28] As a descendant of Mars, this Roman boy will be just as unlucky and fall into a trap like him! But where Mars was caught in a literal trap (Vulcan's nets), and his position in it was regarded as enviable by Apollo and Mercury, and aroused laughter from most of the gods,[29] the young Roman will be caught in an unenviable metaphorical trap with serious (in fact dreadful) consequences.

At 314f. the humour (in the Homeric allusion and the jokes about the star of Mars) gives way to grim reality, which thus hits harder. The son must fear not just legal punishment but worse (so parents should not expect the law to protect their boys). The doublet of *dolor* and (in emphatic position) *dolori* highlights the 'resentment' of the wronged husband and it encompasses in the word order and swamps the lone, brief *lex* ('law'). In fact, ominously, the expression depicts the husband as pure *dolor* or 'resentment' personified. *Exigit* ('exacts') is used of exacting money as well as punishment, and so brings out the idea that there is no payment of an adulterer's fine for the mortal but an illegal settlement of the offence; there is probably also sport with the verb's meaning 'thrust through', of a weapon, like the sword in line 316.[30] It also seems to me that there is a mocking jauntiness in the echoing *ille dolor – ulla dolori* (and *necat – secat* in 316). At 316f. with malicious glee J. spotlights three extreme punishments which the petitioner may bring on her son, by means of a prayer for beauty that leads to deformity. Death is foregrounded, and by way of another barbed contrast with Mars, this shows the stripling as all too mortal. The flogging has impact: there is stress in the placement of *cruentis* ('bloody') and *verberibus* ('whips'); in addition to the graphic 'bloody' sense *cruentis* will also mean 'savage'; and *secat* ('cuts') worryingly covers cutting with a lash, cutting up into pieces and cutting bits off (which includes castration, so that the son escapes the danger of that in 306f. only to succumb to it here).[31] The third punishment is a particularly painful and humiliating[32] one – the insertion into the adulterer's anus of a mullet, a fish with a large head and stiff, backward-pointing spines. This amounts to amusingly apt retribution for the penetration of the wife, and it summons up a grotesque picture. J. leaves to the end the drastic *intrat* ('penetrates'), which catches the awful moment as the fish is thrust in; and by saying 'penetrates' rather than something like 'is pushed in' he produces the bizarre image of the fish acting independently and of its own (twisted) volition (cf. 4.69). There also seems to be some comical onomatopoeia here: the repetition of *o*, *m* and *i* suggests to me the sounds made by the youngster as he is entered. In addition, J. obviously has in mind Horace *Satires* 1.2.37–46, on the great risks run by adulterers and the various penalties to which they are exposed, including flogging, death, anal rape and castration, and with *hic ... ille* ('one man ... another'). While reducing his predecessor's long list of punishments to three striking ones for more concentrated punch, J. also contrives by means of the echo to remind us of the others mentioned by his source, and so strengthens his point about the perils economically. At the same time, one now sees that there is an outrageous joke in *interdum* ('sometimes') in line 315: Horace spent the first two and a half lines of his passage dwelling on the constancy of the danger, suffering and pain for the adulterer, but with this word J. notably diminishes the frequency, and by toning down his model our hyperbolic satirist, who exaggerates as a matter of course, is thus actually correcting and tacitly criticizing hyperbole in Horace.

At 318f. J. comes out with a response by the mother to his claim at 311f. *fiet adulter / publicus* ('he will become a communal adulterer'). The retort which he assigns to her conveniently and most unrealistically accepts that her son will inevitably commit adultery, and merely protests that he will love his partner. He is designated as an Endymion, a very beautiful young man loved by the moon goddess, who was put into a permanent sleep by her so that she could forever kiss him at will, or who asked Jupiter for eternal sleep himself so that he could be deathless and ageless. This could be just a sneer by our satirist. But it has more bite if it represents the mother's point of view (compare the Diana analogy in line 292). J. would thus be mocking her preposterously romantic vision of someone who has just been classified as a *moechus* ('adulterer'), a blunt and stylistically low term, with the prospect of a fish stuck up his backside. This mundane and mean pretty boy is put on a par with a supremely handsome king who was a son or grandson of Jupiter. Endymion's lover was the moon goddess, who, in one tradition, gave him sleep,[33] not a lascivious Roman matron who gives cash. And Endymion's mother was the princess Calyce, not a stupid commoner who makes misguided prayers to the gods. It also suits J.'s case that the comparison of the Roman to a famously sleeping figure suggests that the former is in a dream world, not alert to problems and dangers, while the allusion to this rather lovely myth underlines how sordid and ugly the content of 319ff. is. *Tuus* ('your') again contains a dig, as the boy does not belong to the mother alone. Furthermore, the married woman is described as *dilectae* (literally 'loved'), and although the idea is that she is loved by the youth (hence my 'whom he has fallen for'), the expression also allows for her being loved by others (like her husband and children), to make the adulterer seem more despicable.

At 319ff. the poet counters the mother's response with a picture of her son's swift and definite degeneration; *mox* ('soon') and *fiet* ('he'll become') at 319f. are stressed by placement. The satirist is, as ever, forceful, but one wonders how he can be so sure about all this. In line 319 Servilia, a member of an ancient aristocratic family, may be the married woman just mentioned in 318, who is giving a present of money and thereby encouraging a mercenary streak in the boy; or (more probably), she is a successor of hers. In either case, the juxtaposition of *Servilia* and *nummos* ('cash') is eloquent, and the reference to coins depicts the relationship as a crude financial transaction and the son as little better than a male prostitute. There is a further echo of Horace *Satires* 1.2 on the perils of adulterers. At 1.2.43, Horace writes of one paying money to save his skin: *dedit hic pro corpore nummos* ('one gave cash to save his person'). Instead of giving cash, J.'s lad is given cash himself, and so (as well as denying him the possibility of escaping unharmed) our poet portrays him as not just a foolish and vulnerable adulterer (as in Horace) but also a gigolo, even more immoral and contemptible, and even less of an Endymion. In line 320 the prayer to the goddess of love results in an absence of love, as the youngster unscrupulously exploits the beauty thus acquired. Then, worse than just being given some cash, he greedily strips the woman of *all* her jewellery and clothing. The idea is that he will take these from her in payment for his services, but aptly enough the expression also makes one think of him stripping her naked prior to intercourse, thus closely linking coitus and remuneration. This is a degrading inversion of the normal scenario in love poetry of the female fleecing the male, and one which puts the youth on a par with the *puer delicatus*, the effeminate and grasping boyfriend of the love poets. There is mock-solemnity too, as J.'s words bring to mind the epic warrior who despoils his conquered foe.[34] This debased hero (Endymion) attacks a woman (regarding her as an enemy, and being aggressive and pitiless towards her), and he takes her belongings from her instead of the armour that proves a fighter's martial prowess and wins him respect and glory; and in place of an epic opponent he has the kind of low and lecherous female who is prepared to and/or needs to pay a lot for sex. At 321f.[35] there is sport with the common elegiac use of *nego* ('deny') of a woman denying her favours to a lover,[36] intimating that girls may often say no to a man when he wants intercourse but would never refuse their own urges when they are in the mood. The unpleasantly blunt *udis / inguinibus* ('wet crotch') demeans the woman and the young man who consorts with her; and here there is fantastic and expressive personification of the vagina, which is shown as having a life and desires of its own and as being demanding. There is also debasement in the reference to Oppia and Catulla. Oppia appeared earlier, in line 220, as an insatiable adulteress, and Catulla figured in 2.49 as a promiscuous female mentioned in the same breath as prostitutes.[37] So this Endymion's moral decline would now appear to be complete, with the idiotic mother's petition leading her son to sex with trash like this (in contrast to a romantic entanglement with the moon goddess). However, Oppia comes with associations of exaggeration (she was utilized in the very long list of countless diseases threatening the elderly), and there are connotations of dubiousness in Catulla (she was cited as part of a highly questionable claim that there was no female homosexuality in Rome). The epigram in line 323 is also problematical. It certainly has impact: it is a Golden Line, in connection with an immoral woman and her crotch; there will be ironical play on the 'virtuous habits' sense of *mores*;[38] and the novel and arresting expression suggests that the character is somehow stored in the receptacle of the vagina of such a type (reminiscent of the mullet in the adulterer's anus), and as such it would be unattractive and impaired. But there is again tunnel vision in line with the satirist's point here, because it is simply not true that all degenerate females are totally dominated by sexual desire or that their character is completely unaffected by other elements (such as spite, envy, greed and the will to survive).

At line 324 the mother who is moronic enough to pray for beauty is also apparently too obtuse to take in J.'s points at 304ff. about chastity not saving a good-looking boy from harm. This is funny and highlights the stupidity of the woman (but of course her question here is just a construct provided by the poet to suit his case). It is also amusing that she shoots herself in the foot by echoing Ovid *Metamorphoses* 2.572, where the daughter of Coroneus says *forma mihi nocuit* ('[my] beauty did harm to me'). Those words, on the lips of another unintelligent female who cannot control her mouth, affirm that beauty did cause harm to a chaste person. When she refused Neptune's overtures, he pursued her frighteningly and nearly raped her; she only escaped by losing her lovely human form and being turned into a crow. She also thus became a comrade of Minerva, but that turned out badly for her, as she herself says at line 589 – *quid tamen hoc prodest?* ('what good did that do?') – because, much to her regret, she fell out of favour with the goddess, and J. reminds us of that negative outcome with his corresponding *quid profuit* ('what good did it do') in line 324.

That brief remark by the mother is immediately swamped by a lengthy response on the poet's part, in which, reinforcing the dangerous males at 305ff., he moves on to powerful females posing a threat to handsome young men. He begins with two mythological *exempla* to show chastity causing

problems for its possessor, exploiting different senses of *grave* ('stern')
to underline that idea ('stern' and 'serious' and also 'painful' and 'grave'
are all feasible).[39] He frames line 325 with two bulky names in emphatic
position to get his point across strongly to the silly woman, but comically
is guilty of silliness himself, undermining his first example by means of the
ill-considered second one. Hippolytus, pointedly, was killed as a result of
a parent's prayer: when he rejected his stepmother Phaedra's advances, she
cried rape, and his father Theseus prayed to Neptune to punish him, and the
god caused Hippolytus to be thrown out of his chariot and dragged by his
horses to his death. His stern lifestyle did not benefit him, but Bellerophon's
situation is rather different. Falsely accused by the rejected Stheneboea of
trying to seduce her, he was sent by her husband to her father's kingdom
with a sealed letter ordering his own execution; her father set him a series of
dangerous tasks intended to kill him and had him ambushed by a large force,
but Bellerophon successfully handled all the hazards with such bravery that
the father rewarded him by giving him the hand of another of his daughters
and bequeathing him part of his kingdom. So, although his purity caused
Bellerophon toil and trouble initially, it *did* ultimately do him good, as
should be clear to anyone without a blinkered, pessimistic outlook.

Although the text of line 326 is unsure,[40] it is clear that at 326ff. J. is
dwelling on the ominous rage of the two women in the face of a chaste
refusal of their overtures. It is also clear that there are contemptuous barbs
here for the mother, as the poet parades before *her* women who are selfish,
misguided and destructive, shows his female addressee females in a bad
light (unreasonable, immoral, savage and dangerous) and implies that she
will expose her son to harm at the hands of her own sex. In line 327 *Cressa*
('the Cretan') is Phaedra, who was a daughter of Minos, king of Crete.
The periphrasis is effective: it is apt, because it was frequently claimed that
Cretans were liars;[41] and it also subtly increases the menace by bringing to
mind Phaedra's family – the powerful and stern Minos (who persecuted
Daedalus, imposed on Athens the tribute of fourteen youngsters to be killed
in the Labyrinth and became a dread judge in the Underworld) and also
the monstrous and deadly Minotaur. There is some ghastly verbal play too
in connection with the pair of pernicious heroines: *excanduit* ('flared up')
refers primarily to them burning with ire, but hints at the fire of passion
in both of them, which turned into rage and also at the 'bright' sense (the
Greek *phaidros*) in the name Phaedra. There is also, to my ear, a sinister
hissing sigmatism and angrily clattering *c* and *q* sounds at 327f. I have
translated *se / concussere* as 'got themselves shaking with rage', but the verb
combines various senses. It will mean 'upset' and 'aroused to action'; but one
should not exclude the idea of them literally shaking,[42] which conjures up

an intimidating picture and links with *excanduit* (fire when shaken blazes up dangerously and destructively), and Courtney suggests that they whipped themselves to fury like a lioness – *saevissima* ('most savage')[43] would tie in with that notion.

The rather debatable epigram at 328f., with its (to me) jangly dactyls and effective juxtaposition of *odio* ('hatred') and *pudor* ('shame'), contains a reminiscence of Livy. The only other surviving occurrence of *pudor* as the subject of *stimulos admovere* ('to apply a goad') is at Livy 7.15.3, where the dictator Sulpicius upbraids Roman troops for not fighting well against the Gauls, and as a result of his words, shame goads them into rushing on the enemy's weapons totally regardless of the peril in an almost frenzied assault, which throws the Gauls into disarray and leads to their pitiless slaughter. All of these associations attach to a woman's treatment of her enemy, and she is thus likened to Roman soldiers at their most ferocious. There are also demeaning aspects to J.'s employment of this phrase, which is now used in connection with a more sordid type of shame (at being rejected as a sexual partner) that has a dishonourable outcome in a shabby context. All of this degrades women in general (including the addressee) and, in particular, the females to whom she may well be exposing her son.

At 329ff. our poet supplements the mythological examples with a recent historical one. In 48 AD Messalina, wife of the emperor Claudius, had an affair with the consul-designate Silius, made him get rid of his wife and went through a wedding ceremony with him while Claudius was out of Rome; when the marriage was discovered by the emperor, Silius and Messalina were put to death. To drive his point home for the slow-witted mother, J. leaves this Roman *exemplum* till last and gives it an extended treatment. It reinforces and gives a fuller and more vivid version of the killing of the adulterer by the husband in line 316 and the threat of the predatory ruler at 306ff. (and this time the predator is female and the prey is not castrated or raped but killed, so if the handsome lad escapes the emperor's attentions, he may well be taken by the emperor's wife, and that will be the end of him). However, the satirist again exaggerates the peril for pure and good-looking Roman youths. They would hardly be likely to get involved with someone as powerful as the empress (or queens like Stheneboea and Phaedra, come to that); and J. puts his focus on the quandary facing Silius and the inevitability of execution, but few would be subject to such inescapable coercion and death. So too Messalina's unbalanced and self-destructive passion makes her an extreme case. And Silius is questionable as an exemplar of chastity, as according to another, respected account, he engaged in a liaison with the empress before the wedding, which was his idea.[44] In addition, the extended narrative about Messalina here immediately makes one think of that at 6.115ff (see the appendix). That earlier poem in general is notable for its cynicism, hyperbole and unreliable assertions, all of which helps militate against J.'s position here. In particular, the passage in *Satire* 6 on Claudius's wife was highly speculative, so that the reprise should alert us to look for that aspect in this passage too.

At the end of line 329 there is a sardonic joke in *elige* ('choose'), as there is no useful recommendation to be chosen in our poet's scenario. The word is directed at the mother and puts her on the spot, so that she might actually realize that her prayer for beauty could put her own son in such an impossible situation, at a loss, in great peril and beyond any advice or other help on her part. At the same time, *elige* also speaks to readers and draws them in, so they will become involved in the scene and perceive the awful predicament. With *suadendum* ('should be recommended') in line 330 J. is giving a nod to the *suasoria*, a rhetorical exercise in which one advised a course of action in a particular situation, and he is thus talking to the mother like a teacher to a pupil, an intellectual inferior who is ignorant, inexperienced and in need of guidance and instruction. J. represents the wedding as imminent rather than a past occurrence to achieve vividness and to put her and us in the midst of events for heightened awareness of the pressure on Silius. Unlike Messalina, Silius is never named, which downplays him in line with his inferior status. So too in line 330 he is denoted by the brief *cui* (translated as 'to the man whom') in contrast to the bulkier and more impressive *Caesaris uxor* ('the emperor's wife'); and Messalina is the subject of the verb (as she is also in lines 333 and 338) and so the active partner, whereas he is the object of *nubere* ('to marry') here and has a passive verb applied to him in line 332. As well as showing her ascendancy, *Caesaris uxor* accentuates the bigamous and treasonable nature of the wedding and brings into the picture the very powerful wronged husband. The whole sentence builds to the doubly emphatic *destinat* ('is determined'), as this forbidding figure reverses the normal roles (the female decides who she will marry) and is grimly set on having her way. The verb's sense 'fix as a target'[45] may well be hinted at too, as she is said to be responsible for Silius's death in the next sentence.

In line 331, responding to the mother's question in 324, *optimus* ('most virtuous')[46] picks up *casto* ('a chaste male') in 324, as *formonsissimus* ('most beautiful') takes up *forma* ('beauty') there, with a rhyme that links these two qualities, shortly before a demonstration of the harm that beauty does to a chaste male. In addition, as well as showing it being no help to him at all, the satirist minimizes Silius's morality by covering it in that single term, *optimus* (whereas Messalina is given precedence by being put first and being given more words at the end of the previous sentence), by juxtaposing *optimus* with her awful determination (*destinat*) and by following *optimus* up with a swamping series of words which again establish her predominance. The mention in line 332 of Silius's nobility[47] means that even somebody of high birth was not safe from a lustful and powerful female, and implies that ordinary Roman youths will certainly be vulnerable. There is a bleak collocation in the rest of that verse, as J. plunges us *in medias res*, depicting Silius at a crucial point, as events have started moving and he is already in the actual process of being swept along to the wedding and certain death – the gerundive *extinguendus* ('to be snuffed out') expresses necessity. *Rapitur* means he 'is hurried along' (and plays on 'is carried off as plunder' and 'is ravished'),[48] with a dispiriting inversion in the male being weak and helpless, while the female is in control. The same verb was used in an imperial context in line 308 with a different sense ('rape'), and there is a darkly comic twist here: if the chaste youth escapes rape (*rapio*) by a Nero, he may well be exposed to the verb in an even worse sense, being hurried along (*rapio*) to his doom by a Messalina. *Miser* will embrace 'poor' and 'sick at heart', and J. is probably sporting sarcastically with the meaning 'love-sick' that is found in love poetry[49] (he nowhere says that Silius felt passion, and he groups him with the chaste and unloving Hippolytus and Bellerophon). So too *extinguendus* ('to be snuffed out'), which makes for a solemn spondee in the fifth foot, refers to the putting out of the warmth of life, but suggests ironically extinguishing the 'fire' of love and metaphorically 'dying' of love. It is a striking touch to have Silius driven to destruction by Messalina's eyes (at the end and in a dominant position): the idea will be that Messalina took in through her eyes[50] her deadly passion for Silius, and she is now looking for him with them and so making him come to her and bringing about his demise.

The wording in 332f. recalls some lines of Propertius and Ovid. The gravity of Silius's real-life situation is brought out by contrast with the literary and lightweight world of love elegy, and while Propertius and Ovid present the girl's eyes as an attractive feature that makes the poet fall for her, in J. they don't inspire love but lead to death. At 1.1.1 Propertius announces *Cynthia prima suis miserum me cepit ocellis* ('Cynthia first took poor me captive with those eyes of hers') and then goes on to complain about the problems the affair is causing him. For Silius there are far more serious problems, and where Cynthia's eyes result in the poet living a reckless life (1.1.6), Messalina's eyes encompass Silius's end. Ovid at *Amores* 3.11.48 is in an amusing quandary over a woman he fancies but who maltreats him, and he playfully appeals to her *perque tuos oculos qui rapuere meos* ('and by your eyes which ravished mine'). In J. the predicament is a lot more drastic, and the female really evil, and *rapio* is used not of captivating but of sweeping off to destruction.

After this J. produces a selective sketch of the wedding, putting us right there, bringing this grotesque and perilous ceremony into focus and spotlighting various significant details. Dramatically, the event is already in train, and at 335f. there is a terrible sense of inevitability in the future tenses. At 333f. he gives us a grimly graphic picture of Messalina which conveys great pressure (she has got things moving, to force Silius into action), but which may well be his own invention, as it is not found in any other account. There is a reversal of roles here (as the bride was normally led to the groom), which reflects her predominance. Her long wait means that she is eager and determined, and will also be becoming impatient. *Sedet* ('has … been sitting') also suggests 'has been inactive',[51] but one fears that after all this time that inactivity will not continue for long. In line 334, with its bustling dactyls, attention is drawn via the word's position and rarity to *flammeolo* ('bridal veil'), a diminutive which has an affectionate nuance that fits with the empress's fondness for it (something that will lead to her downfall!) and intimates sneering on the poet's part. There is also a macabre pun: *flammeolum*, cognate with *flamma* ('flame'), denotes the flame-coloured veil which will help snuff out Silius. There is stress on Messalina's intimidating power at 334f.: purple was the imperial colour, and purple dye was expensive, while a million sesterces represents a substantial sum for her dowry. There is also stress on her dangerously crazy disregard of the risks of detection, with the wedding held *palam* ('openly'), and outdoors because it is a public ceremony attended by many.[52] Other elements increase the ominous aura. The presence of *genialis* ('marriage bed') alerts us to the sacrilege here that invites divine punishment. The *genialis*, linguistically connected with Genius (the god of the family), was spread in honour of that divinity and usually bore a representation of him, and he would be affronted by such bigamy.[53] The *horti* ('gardens') are not specified, but J. surely means the Gardens of Lucullus. To acquire them, Messalina had engineered the death of their owner, Valerius Asiaticus,[54] and so they remind us of her murderous ruthlessness. And they are where she was executed after Claudius found out about the marriage to Silius,[55] so that they also bring to mind the fatal outcome of this wedding. At the start of line 336, *antiquus* ('ancient'), with its connotations of the virtues of antiquity,[56] brings out the immorality of the empress in this perversion of tradition. In the rest of the line J. specifies some of those present at the ceremony, people who were potential gossips and informers – the augur, who pronounced the ritual formula, and the friends who witnessed the marriage contract, ensuring that there was hard evidence of the criminal offence in writing.

Most scholars maintain that in line 337 our poet is all of a sudden addressing Silius, but it seems to me most natural and obvious to see him speaking to the mother still; and he uses *puto* ('think') again, the same verb he applied to her in line 330, while *quid placeat dic* ('state your decision') in 338 seems to pick up the sentence at 329–31 which was directed at her. An address to her here also has more bite. It would appear that the foolish woman has been labouring under a sad misapprehension, and J. is now putting her straight. He ascribes to her an ignorance of the actual events and of the empress's character that seems particularly laughable after 331ff.; and, with contemptuous frequency of *p* and *c*, he mocks her obliviousness of the great danger by means of the doublet *secreta* ('secret') and *paucis commissa* ('entrusted to a few'). Line 338, while accounting for the absence of secrecy alluded to in 337, contains the joke of Messalina's wish for a legitimate marriage. She has already married legally, and what she wants now is illegal. This reflects her unbalanced and decadent outlook: for her, the wedding *will* be legitimate if it is one with all the formal trappings; and she wants a proper ceremony because of the infamy attendant on bigamy.[57] In my opinion, with *quid placeat dic*, J. is returning insistently to his request at 329–31, now with a brisk and staccato brevity to put pressure on the mother too, browbeating her to expose her idiocy, as there is nothing useful that she could recommend in the situation presented by J., the sort of situation that she might well help bring about for her own child. *Dic* ('state') is barbed: the woman was not short of words earlier (at 289ff., 291f. and 324), so let's see what she has to say now; and this time the poet gives her no response, depicting her as reduced to silence by aporia.

Many critics believe that Silius is the one spoken to in line 339 and in the following verses, but again a continuation of the address to the mother is more pointed. Arrestingly and effectively, this would put her in Silius's shoes, in the kind of danger that her petition for handsomeness may well create for her own son, so that she might really grasp the harm that beauty does. It also puts readers, who might make such a prayer, in Silius's position. The dactylic rhythm in 339 conveys a chilling notion of speed, and there is sick humour in the empress killing somebody she supposedly loves and wants to marry. There are probably also sarcastic spins to some other topoi of love poetry – the image of somebody 'dying' of love and the connection of the lamp with lovemaking.[58] Here the lover would literally die, and the lamps are connected with death rather than an assignation and would not be shining for him in bed, as they conventionally did. To create pressure and a dilemma, the satirist is very definite there about what will happen in the event of non-compliance and allows for no other possibilities, but his gloom and doom are open to question. Messalina's murderous vindictiveness when thwarted has to be speculation on the poet's part. And one wonders how he knows that she would want to kill Silius *before dark*, how she could in fact kill him so quickly and whether he would actually have to die at all (for instance, why could he not turn to her enemies, Claudius's freedmen, for protection, or just flee and go into hiding?).

At 340f. J. creates a darkly comic quandary. According to him, death is certain; it's just a matter of how soon you choose to die. There is also the grim inversion of innocence resulting in rapid execution and guilt winning a delay. However, if you do marry, the delay will be short and unimportant,[59] and you will die anyway, as a criminal. In line 340 *si scelus admittas* ('should you commit the crime'), with its hissing sigmatism, is a blunt and unsympathetic way of putting it, given the coercion, but it represents the official and legal point of view. In line 341 the postponement of *principis aurem* ('the emperor's ear') wittily recreates the delay of the news reaching him but, ominously, in the Latin it does not take long to come to his ears. There is a dig at the mother in the line too. The general knowledge of the wedding here accentuates the ignorance assigned to her in line 337, and her late discovery of the truth puts her on a par with Claudius, that imbecilic and contemptible figure of fun.[60] There is also an intertextual aspect to the line, as J. echoes some words in Seneca *Epistles* 66.34, where the philosopher talks about minor differences (of age, looks and circumstances) within the overarching virtue of good men and says that one of them is influential, powerful and well-known to cities and peoples (*urbibus notus et populis*), whereas another is obscure and unknown to most. There is a mischievous transfer of the Senecan phrase from a moral person to an immoral deed. In addition, while we have in mind Seneca's discussion of the righteous, we note that J.'s good man – cf. *optimus* ('most virtuous') in line 331 – is, by way of contrast, himself now under the influence of another, powerless, and will soon become notorious. So the echo highlights the weakness and failings of Silius, who does not live up to the Senecan picture of the upright person, because his morality is ineffectual and has been undermined by his handsomeness.

In the first part of line 342 J. underlines the severity of the crime and the inevitability of punishment, while working in a sneer at Claudius. The dactyls fit with the news not taking long to reach him. *Ille* ('he') is encompassed by *dedecus* and *domus* ('the disgrace of his house'), and *ultimus* ('the last') is wittily left to the end of the sentence. The expression *scire ultimus* ('to be the last to know') is paralleled only at Lucan 5.779, which also has a spouse as the subject of the verb: *eventus rerum sciet ultima coniunx* ('your wife will be the last to know the outcome of events'). Those words are spoken to Pompey by his wife Cornelia. He wants to send her to Lesbos for her safety, but she does not want to be parted from him, and complains movingly in the same line that on Lesbos, if the gods grant her prayers, she will only hear very late of his victory over Caesar in the coming battle. J. switches the phrase from a noble wife being the last to learn of her husband's glorious triumph to the despicable Claudius being the last to learn of his ignoble wife's bigamy and the disgrace of his house, so as to demean him further. By bringing to mind the loving and faithful Cornelia who could not bear to be parted from her husband, the allusion also points up the corrupt nature of Messalina (the type of mercenary female who preys on handsome youths).

In the goading sentence that follows at 342–4, J. disparages the alternative to almost immediate death by sniping at survival for just a few days[61] and representing the delay as being secured by means of subservience to a woman (as well as involving a criminal act). Her forbidding dominance is brought out by *imperio*, which I have translated as 'command', but which also embraces 'authority' in general and the 'power' of the Roman emperor in particular[62] – with another role reversal, she is as powerful as Claudius, for now. There also seems to be a mocking twist to the standard obsequiousness of the elegiac lover[63] and the imperiousness of his mistress: here in real life, the male's submissiveness is a far more serious matter and the female's dominance is far more deadly than anything found in the world of love poetry.

At 344f. J. ends the *exemplum* and the whole section forcefully. He answers the mother's question in line 324 with a supremely harmful outcome of beauty for the chaste – a horrible form of death (decapitation) after an awful predicament. And with savage humour he shows the prayer for beauty leading not just to loss of life but also to loss of beauty (after its brief possession) for the rest of eternity, as the ghost would be permanently disfigured.[64] Assonance and lilting short syllables draw attention to *quidquid levius meliusque* ('whichever course ... easier and better') with its bleak joke. *Levius* could mean more 'easy to perform', 'easy to bear' or 'trifling', and *melius* covers more 'virtuous', 'commendable', 'appropriate' and 'advantageous',[65] but neither course merits either adjective in any of these senses. The collocation of *levius* and *melius* occurs elsewhere in the surviving literature only at J.'s *Satire* 2.55f., in connection with the ridicule of girlish pathics spinning better than heroines, as a hypocritical homosexual moralist is attacked by Laronia: *fusum / Penelope melius, levius torquetis Arachne* ('you people turn a spindle better than Penelope, more deftly than Arachne'). As employed here in line 344, the phrase relates to Silius and has sneering connotations of a despised male who is effeminate and browbeaten by a woman, which fits with the humiliating gender inversion in J. So too Silius resembles the females Penelope, who was virtually helpless and in a quandary in the face of great pressure to marry, and Arachne, who fell foul of a superior power and as a result came to the end of her human existence (she engaged in a spinning contest with Minerva, enraged her with her weaving and was turned into a spider by her).

In line 345, with its gloomy spondees (especially noticeable after all the short syllables in 344), J. presents a grimly graphic picture, focusing on the vulnerable neck stretched out and just waiting for the *coup de grâce*, whether administered by an agent of the emperor or the empress (putting to death one she supposedly loves and wants to marry!). The gerundive *praebenda* ('has to be offered'), placed at the start of the line, emphasizes the fact that there is no escape, and *haec* ('this') aims at empathy, to make the mother and the reader feel that their own neck is about to get the chop, while the frequency of *p* and *c*, as well as being vigorous, creates a hacking sound. The primary sense of *pulchra* is 'pretty', and *candida* ('white') implies attractiveness,[66] so there is a twofold stress on beauty leading to death, as well as an eloquent juxtaposition of *gladio* ('to the sword') and *pulchra* ('pretty'). In *pulchra* there will be play on the sense 'morally beautiful, honourable'[67] (cf. line 331): being moral and refusing Messalina only ends in death, whereas giving in to her results in loss of honour and extinction anyway. *Candida* suggests the whiteness of fear (prior to the redness of blood) and foreshadows the pallor of death. There will be similar play on the meaning 'morally pure', and also cruel sport with the sense 'lucky' for the adjective.[68] The only other example of *candida cervix* ('white neck') is found at Horace *Odes* 3.9.1ff.: *donec gratus eram tibi / nec quisquam potior bracchia candidae / cervici iuvenis dabat* ('as long as I was attractive to you and no more favoured young man put his arms around your white neck'). These words are spoken by a man to a woman called Lydia with whom he has had an affair, and in the course of the poem he proposes that they drop their current partners and resume their liaison, and after some teasing banter she happily accepts. Again there is a move from the trivial and harmless world of love poetry to the real world, which seems still harsher by contrast; and the phrase is transferred from an amusing poem of love, tolerance and reconciliation to the opposite of all that, the neck being hacked rather than embraced (and in Horace the neck was Lydia's, so that giving it to Silius here fits with the reversal of gender). There is some effectual antithesis: in Horace, the more favoured rival is not hurt, and the male and Lydia (unlike Silius and Messalina) apparently live on, happy in their love. The killing of the bigamous pair also means that there is a gruesome link to the final line of the *Ode*, where Lydia says that she would willingly die with her lover.

Notes

1   See *OLD* s.v. 4, *TLL* II.203.11ff.

2   See Mayor.

3   See e.g. Nisbet and Hubbard on Horace *Odes* 1.33.12.

4   See Courtney.

5   The speaker quoted at 291f. might be an imaginary interlocutor (see Courtney; Campana), but it is much more startling and funny, and pointed, if it is the mother.

6   For Lucretia's father see Ovid *Fasti* 2.822, 835f.; for Verginia's father see Livy 3.47.1, 48.4, 50.4ff.

7   See e.g. Mayor; Ebel.

8   See Pichon s.v. *cupere* and *dare*, and *OLD* s.v. *accipio* 2b; McKeown on Ovid *Am.* 1.3.5. For the bribes offered by Appius cf. e.g. Livy 3.44.4.

9   On the textual controversy in line 295 see Tengström, 36ff.; Campana. It seems impossible to decide with any certainty what J. wrote there. Some manuscripts read *atque suam*, to which a few editors would supply *faciem* from line 293, so that Verginia is giving Rutila her 'good looks' (but *faciem* in 293 seems rather distant to be understood in line 295). Other mss have *atque suum*, to which *gibbum* could be supplied. Several scholars do so, taking the word to mean 'swelling' and to refer to Verginia's bosom or backside (there is no parallel for *gibbus* denoting those parts, although this would be a bold and sardonic expression of the kind often found in Juvenal). There has been emendation too, with *osque* (denoting Verginia's 'face') being conjectured for *atque*, which provides good sense and is palaeographically plausible – *otque* was written by mistake in place of *osque*, and then became *atque*.

10   Cf. my commentary on Tibullus 1.1.39–40.

11   See *TLL* VI.3.2992.82ff., 2994.5ff.; *OLD* s.v. 6.

12   See *OLD* s.v. *trado* 3.

13   *OLD* s.v. *imitor* 1, 3.

14   There too a trisyllabic epithet for the Sabines precedes the almost identical phrase *imitata Sabinas* (found nowhere else in extant Latin), and there is similar sport with the two senses of *imitor* (see McKeown's commentary, ad loc.).

15   For the appeal of redness see e.g. Ovid *Am.* 3.3.5f., *AA* 3.200 (and Gibson, ad loc.) and *Met.* 3.423. So too certain men found chastity titillating and a challenge (cf. e.g. Ovid *F.* 2.765f.). For the corruption of a youth in satire cf. especially Petron. *Sat.* 85ff.

16   See Pichon s.v. *cura* and *OLD* s.v. 2, 3, 6.

17   The story of Iphis also has apposite associations of homoeroticism and a sex change, and there is a depressing contrast between the myth with the marvellous divine intervention (thanks to the loving mother) that ensures a happy ending and the sordid picture at 304ff. which presents no help, no happiness and parents who sell their child.

18   See *OLD* s.v. *vir* 1c, 1d, 2, 3.

19   See Ebel.

20   See *OLD* s.v. *prodigus* 1c and 3; s.v. *corruptor* 2a, b, c; s.v. *improbitas* 1 and 2; *TLL* VII.1.685.27ff., 686.10ff.

21   See Pichon s.v. *temptare* and *munera*.

22   See Courtney.

23   For *deformis* applied to a eunuch see Amm. Marc. 14.6.17.

24   See *OLD* s.v. *species* 3b, 5, 6, 7.

25   There may be play by J. on the 'differences' sense of *discrimina*, reflecting these variations from his model. The Senecan allusion picks up neatly the mention of his ward Nero at 308f.

26   See *TLL* X.2.2458.61ff., 2465.60ff.

27   The mss have various readings, and scholars have proposed many different emendations. See Ebel; Campana. In common with Housman, I read *lex irae*, but with no real confidence.

28   Cf. e.g. Cicero *De Re Publica* 6.17; Servius on *G.* 1.335.

29   For *laquei* of Vulcan's netting see Ovid *AA* 2.578, 580, *Met.* 4.177. For the divine envy and laughter see Homer *Od.* 8.335ff., 343 and Ovid *AA* 2.585f.

30   See *OLD* s.v. *exigo* 3a, 8b.

31   See *OLD* s.v. *seco* 2, 3a, 3c, 4c.

32   See Campana on the humiliation.

33   Cf. e.g. Ovid *Am.* 1.13.43f.

34   See *TLL* V.2.2120.4ff. for *exuo* ('strip') of taking arms as spoil from an enemy, and IX.2.1019.45ff. for *ornatus* ('adornment') of armour.

35   There is controversy over the punctuation and interpretation of 321–3 (see Ebel; Campana). Others place a question mark after *inguinibus* in line 322 and a comma after *Catulla* in 322 or *deterior* in 323. The punctuation in Housman is preferable because it combines all the following benefits: the logic is clearer; the youth's mistress is thus designated as an Oppia or a Catulla; and line 323 refers directly to her and presents a neat epigram in a single, end-stopped line.

36   See Pichon s.v. *negare*. For the personification of the vagina in X, compare that of the penis at Lucilius 307M; Hor. *Sat.* 1.2.68; Petron. *Sat.* 132; Persius 6.72.

37   See Braund's commentary, ad loc. There is a beautiful but lascivious Catulla in Martial 8.53, and the name may be intended to make us think of Catullus's whorish Lesbia too.

38   See *OLD* s.v. *mos* 4c.

39   See *OLD* s.v. *gravis* 10b, 11, 12, 14; *TLL* VI.2.2288.40ff.

40   There are very complex textual problems here (see Ebel; Courtney; Campana), which cannot be resolved with any certainty. The mss have variant readings in line 326, and scholars have suspected several words there and offered different conjectures. Some would delete the line, while others believe that a line has dropped out after 325.

41   See Ovid *AA* 1.298; Hollis, ad loc.

42   See *OLD* s.v. *concutio* 1, 4, 5.

43   *OLD* s.v. *saevus* 4.

44   Tacitus *Annals* 11.26.

45   See *OLD* s.v. *destino* 7.

46   'Highest born' and 'most estimable' are also possible meanings. See *OLD* s.v. 2, 6, 8.

47   For which cf. Tacitus *Ann.* 11.28.

48   See *OLD* s.v. *rapio* 2 and 4.

49   See *OLD* s.v. *miser* 1 and 3a and my commentary on Tibullus 2.6.17–18. Because of the allusion here to Propertius and Ovid (for which see below in the main text) it is easy enough to feel the amatory nuance in *miser* and in *extinguendus*.

50   See Pichon s.v. *oculi*.

51   *OLD* s.v. *sedeo* 7.

52   Cf. Tacitus *Ann.* 11.30.

53   See 6.21f. and Courtney, ad loc.

54   Tac. *Ann.* 11.1ff.

55   Tac. *Ann.* 11.37; Cassius Dio 60.31.5.

56   See *TLL* II.179.24ff.; *OLD* s.v. 9a.

57   See Tacitus at *Ann.* 11.26.

58   For *pereo* of the lover 'dying' see Pichon s.v. *perdere*, and for lamps cf. e.g. *AP* 5.4, 5, 7, 8; Prop. 2.15.3f., 4.8.43. Campana sees a play on words in *parere* ('to obey') and *pereundum* ('you'll have to die').

59   *Parvula* ('tiny') has both these senses. See *OLD* s.v. 1a, 1c.

60   Cf. 5.147f., 6.115f., 620ff., 14.330f. for this view of the emperor.

61   Cf. 357ff. and 8.83f.

62   *OLD* s.v. *imperium* 1c, 2c, 8.

63   Cf. my commentary on Tibullus 1.4.39–40.

64   Cf. e.g. my commentary on Tibullus 1.10.37–8.

65   See *OLD* s.v. *levis* 9, 10, 13; s.v. *melior* 2, 6, 7, 9.

66   See *OLD* s.v. *candidus* 5; *TLL* III.241.10ff.

67   See *OLD* s.v. *pulcher* 3.

68   See *OLD* s.v. *candidus* 7 and 8b.

Appendix

J. had already expatiated on Messalina at 6.115–32, while trying to persuade
the addressee of that poem from marrying by parading before him a series of
awful Roman wives. When reading *Satire* 10 that earlier passage immediately
comes to mind, especially because at 329ff. we find another extended narrative
about Messalina with thematic links (see below) and with close similarities
in the very negative treatment of the empress, combining criticism of her
(as corrupt, perverse, adulterous, etc.) with hard humour. The impact of
the Messalina *exemplum* in 10 is heightened by her earlier appearance. The
picture of her already established in *Satire* 6 at quite some length and in
memorable detail means that she brings to 10 other repulsive associations
by way of reinforcement. In *Satire* 6 she was so depraved that she worked
as a prostitute in a foul brothel, dirtying herself and demeaning herself by
association with the pimp and his clientele, while proving unable to satisfy
her lust with a series of customers. Silius was in fact but the last in a long line
of men, including the low characters who frequented brothels. So, bearing in
mind what we have been shown at 6.115ff., at the first mention of Messalina
in X we are led to infer that the petitioner's prayer for beauty is exposing
her supposedly chaste son to the very opposite of chastity, to disgusting,
degraded and insatiable persons who will certainly have no respect for his
purity but will very probably be offended and angered by it.

The criticism of Messalina in VI is dense and hard-hitting:

respice rivales divorum, Claudius audi	115
quae tulerit. dormire virum cum senserat uxor,	
sumere nocturnos meretrix Augusta cucullos	118
ausa Palatino et tegetem praeferre cubili	117
linquebat comite ancilla non amplius una.	
sed nigrum flavo crinem abscondente galero	120

intravit calidum veteri centone lupanar
et cellam vacuam atque suam; tunc nuda papillis
prostitit auratis titulum mentita Lyciscae
ostenditque tuum, generose Britannice, ventrem.
excepit blanda intrantis atque aera poposcit.   125
[continueque iacens cunctorum absorbuit ictus.]
mox lenone suas iam dimittente puellas
tristis abit, et quod potuit tamen ultima cellam
clausit, adhuc ardens rigidae tentigine volvae,
et lassata viris necdum satiata recessit,   130
obscurisque genis turpis fumoque lucernae
foeda lupanaris tulit ad pulvinar odorem.

Take a look at the rivals of the gods, hear what Claudius   115
endured. Whenever his wife realized that her husband
   was asleep,
the Whore-empress, daring to put on a night-time hood   118
and to prefer a piece of matting to her bed in the palace,   117
used to leave with no more than a single maid accompanying
   her.
Yes, and with a blonde wig hiding her black hair   120
she entered a brothel warm with old curtains
and an empty cubicle of her own. Then naked, with gilded
nipples, she stood for hire, under the false name of 'She-wolf',
and displayed the belly that bore you, noble Britannicus.
She welcomed those entering seductively and asked
   for money.   125
[Lying there, she repeatedly absorbed the thrusts of them all.]
Later, when the pimp was now dismissing his girls,
she was sad to leave, but (all she could do) was the last to close
her cubicle, still hot, with her clitoris swollen and stiff,
and she went away exhausted by men but not yet sated,   130
and, repulsive with her filthy cheeks and dirty from the smoke
of the lamp, she took the stench of the brothel to the emperor's bed.

In the mock-solemn line 115 (with its spondees, alliteration and assonance)
rivales divorum ('the rivals of the gods') will refer ironically to the moronic
emperor Claudius, but Messalina will also be meant.[1] This fits with context: J.
is here moving on from the private individual Eppia, a bad wife (mentioned
in line 115), so allusion to another bad wife at a higher level would smooth
the progression, and mention of the subject of the section at its start would

be natural. This would also begin the whole passage with a sneer at the empress, who hardly deserves to be classified with divinities, especially in view of the behaviour attributed to her in the following verses.

In line 116, *cum* ('whenever') brings out the great frequency of her trips to the brothel (and her insatiability), while the presence of *virum* ('her husband') and *uxor* ('his wife') accents the adulterous nature of her conduct. The striking *meretrix Augusta* ('Whore-empress') in line 118, with its cutting juxtaposition, powerfully condemns her debasement of her lofty position, with the noun *Augusta* denoting 'the emperor's wife' and also containing sarcastic play on the senses 'worthy of honour' and perhaps 'majestic in appearance' in the adjective *augustus*.[2] The expression recalls *meretrix regina* ('whore-queen') at Propertius 3.11.39 and Pliny *Natural History* 9.119 and so puts Messalina on a par with a hated foreign despot and enemy of Rome. That phrase is wittily enfolded by the *nocturnos ... cucullos* ('a night-time hood'), which is worn for concealment, because she knows that her goings-on are disgraceful and dangerous for her, should she be found out. And that is reinforced by the single maid in line 119 (she does not mark herself out as a great lady with a large retinue) and the disguise of the blonde wig in 120, so that there is a threefold stress on her underhand furtiveness. In line 117 the empress is pointedly reduced to the level of beds, and her preference for the brothel's matting (the brief *tegetem*) over a luxurious bed in the palace (the longer and grander *Palatino ... cubili*) shows how perverse and lecherous she is, and also how much she lowers herself and besmirches the imperial family.

There is an *ersatz* gravity again in the spondees of line 120, and a powerful collocation of *nigrum* ('black') and *flavo* ('blonde'). The former adjective can also mean 'filthy', 'sombre, funereal' and 'evil',[3] while blonde was the hair colour favoured by courtesans and prostitutes,[4] and real goddesses were blonde. The brothel she enters in line 121 is obviously a low-class one, as the curtains covering the doors are not replaced, and it is easy to imagine how soiled and stinking they must be. The brothel is warm, quite possibly because it also sold hot food and drinks,[5] but one thinks in particular of body heat due to sexual activity – and *calidus* ('warm') has connotations of passion.[6] Certainly it will be stuffy and will smell of sweat (and other secretions). Remarkably, Claudius's wife is such a regular performer there that she has her own cubicle for copulating with clients. *Vacuam* ('empty') suggests the unadorned cubicle of a very cheap brothel[7] and also contains a joke (it is empty for now, but will soon be constantly filled by the empress and a long succession of men). Her nakedness means that she is keen to entice customers, and to get down to business quickly; it also marks her out as the lowest class of prostitute.[8] The gilded nipples (a vivid touch) would certainly attract men's attention. They also represent debasement of a noble metal[9] and an obscene perversion of the gold jewellery worn by high-class Roman ladies; and they have an ironical aspect, as gold was especially associated with divinities in general,[10] and Venus in particular.[11] The false name is yet another sly attempt at concealment. The name attributed to her is appropriate – the wolf is a wild animal, hated, ruthless and rapacious, and in Latin *lupa* ('she-wolf') also had the sense 'prostitute'[12] – and it calls to mind the creature that suckled Romulus and Remus, so that we sense a sordid degeneration from Rome's singular and marvellous origins. In line 124 the unexpected address to Claudius's son Britannicus drags him into all this squalor, and reminds us that the vagina that gave birth to an imperial prince is now presented for contemplation and penetration by the scum of Rome. To increase the shock and outrage in the allusion to Britannicus in such a context, *generose* ('noble') will mean not just 'of noble birth' but also 'noble-spirited'.[13]

In the spondaic line 125 the emperor's wife is depicted as so wrapped up in her role that she wheedles (the lowest of the low) and asks for cash (as if she needed it!). There seem to be derisive puns there too, in *intrantis* ('those entering') (of men entering the brothel and her),[14] and in *excepit* ('she welcomed'), as this verb can also mean 'take the weight of, support' and 'receive' (blows), or the thrusts of a penis,[15] a notion picked up in the next line, if 126 is genuine.[16] I am inclined to think that this verse was written by J. because it is so effective. It is a single end-stopped line that bleakly reduces the act of love to obsessive and mindless repetition, with no reference to any warmth or pleasure or satisfaction. This would have been the only direct description of Messalina coupling and, as such, would really add to the overall impact because it is disgusting, disturbing and depressing. To my ears, there is onomatopoeia here, in the frequency of *c*, *q*, *t*, *u* and *o*, to ensure vividness. In addition, *iacens* ('lying') combines 'being in a recumbent position', 'having sexual intercourse' and 'being in a mean or lowly situation',[17] while (*ictus*) 'thrusts' (often used of violent blows) implies vigorous activity, and *absorbuit* ('absorbed') suggests taking in semen, over and over again.[18]

In the following lines Messalina leaves the brothel (unlike the palace) unwillingly. Still in her role as one of his girls, the empress actually obeys a pimp, showing more respect for him than for the emperor and her husband, and believes that all she can do is close her cubicle last, desperate to squeeze in as much sex as she can (and thus lower than the real whores, who are readier to call it a night). In line 128, *tristis* ('sad') is economically condemnatory: as well as 'sad', other possible senses are 'ill-humoured', 'dreadful', 'having an unpleasant appearance' and 'having an unpleasant smell'.[19] The crudity at 129f., while suiting such a crude character, is also meant to make her seem grotesque and repellent. *Ardens* ('hot') suggests eagerness (for more intercourse), the flames of passion and the heat of the genitalia.[20] The zoom-in on the clitoris is an apt focus for the nymphomaniac presented by our satirist. That it should still be in an advanced state of arousal after lots of energetic coition (hence her exhaustion) is abnormal; so too the words for tumescence (*rigidus* and *tentigo*) are usually applied to the penis,[21] and the rhyme in *lassata necdum satiata* ('exhausted ... but not yet sated') also highlights her unnaturalness.

Lines 131f. crown Messalina's repulsiveness. Appealing to the senses of sight and smell, there is stress on stench and filth in a flurry of words whose alliteration adds to their forcefulness. There are two pregnant adjectives that reinforce each other – *turpis* ('repulsive'), which embraces 'offensive to the senses', 'unsightly' and 'guilty of disgraceful behaviour',[22] and *foeda* ('dirty'), which combines 'offensive to the senses', 'atrocious' and 'disgraceful'.[23] In line 132 *foeda* and *odorem* ('stench') frame the line in emphatic positions, and in the word order the emperor's bed (*pulvinar*) is encompassed by the smell of the brothel (*lupanaris ... odorem*). The empress's revolting outer appearance matches her inner nature, and she has played the prostitute so wholeheartedly that the brothel is now part of her, imprinted on her skin and accompanying her as a miasma (and making her stink, of smoke, dirt, sweat, semen, etc., is a telling detail). There is effective ring structure too. The passage ends as it began, in the emperor's bedroom, where the imperial bed is again juxtaposed with a brothel (cf. 117), but it is now soiled after all the intervening misconduct of Claudius's wife in another bed. *Pulvinar* also picks up *rivales divorum* ('the rivals of the gods') in line 115: the word was used of a couch on which images of the gods were placed at a festival of supplication, and also of one occupied by a divinity or person(s) of quasi-divine status. This reminder of Messalina's celestial connection is particularly tart after all the lines on her acting as a member of one of the lowest ranks of mortal society and consorting with the dregs of humanity.

There is another important aspect to this link between the two narratives about her. As well as exploiting all the associations of 6.115ff., in *Satire* 10 the poet is building on the earlier passage and portraying the empress as even more monstrous, to make the threat of such predators to handsome lads seem all the greater. Now, instead of being disgusting she is intimidating, dangerous and actually harmful. Rather than putting herself under the control of a pimp, here frighteningly she is the one in control, pressurizing Silius, taking the male role and exploiting her position of power. She now poses a real hazard too: in place of the furtive adultery in *Satire* 6, she is set on a bigamous marriage and is crazily open about it. This time, fatally, her conduct is discovered, and from being lustful (but not endangering her customers) she becomes deadly, capable of murdering Silius, and ultimately responsible for his demise. And instead of just copulating with the rabble, she inflicts harm on a noble and (before her advent) very virtuous young man.

There are also many minor variations to underline the worsening of the situation in X. Where Messalina had been *tristis* ('sad') at leaving the brothel in 6, she is responsible for Silius being *miser* ('poor man') and having grounds for real dejection in line 332 of 10. Various details spotlight the pernicious progression from prostitution to marriage: in 6 the empress is naked, but she is dressed up as a bride at 333f., and her blonde wig and gilded nipples give way to a flame-coloured veil; and at 334–6 a marriage bed replaces the mat in the brothel, she provides a cash dowry for Silius rather than asking men for money, and the brothel's old curtains are succeeded by an ancient wedding custom. In addition, there are macabre twists in line 339, where the brothel's lamp becomes death before the lamps are lit, and in 345, where Messalina's display of her belly is taken up in the offering of the neck to the sword, and the cheeks blackened by smoke are given a spin in the white neck stretched out for execution.

Notes

1   For the divine status of imperial females see e.g. Cassius Dio 60.5 (deification of Augustus's wife Livia) and Suet. *Gaius* 24 (Caligula swears by the godhead of his sister Drusilla). On the clash between high style and low subject matter, see Nadeau, 100.

2   See *OLD* s.v. *augustus* 2 and 3.

3   *OLD* s.v. *niger* 5, 7, 8.

4   Cf. e.g. Winkler (1983) 197 n. 37. For blonde goddesses see e.g. Pease on Virgil *Aen.* 4.590.

5   See Courtney.

6   *OLD* s.v. *calidus* 9, *caleo* 6; *TLL* III.148.30ff.

7   See Winkler (1983), 196 n. 33.

8   See Courtney, ad loc.

9   Cf. e.g. Pindar *Ol.* 1.1f., 3.42f.

10   See Pindar *Pythian* 1.1; Bacchyl. 3.28; Virgil *G.* 2.538, *Aen.* 10.116; Ovid *Met.* 1.697, etc.

11   Cf. e.g. Homer *Il.* 3.64; Virgil *Aen.* 10.16.

12   Cf. Winkler (1983), 197 n. 35

13   *TLL* VI.2.1799.44ff., 1800.72ff.; *OLD* s.v. *generosus* 1 and 2.

14   Cf. *TLL* VII.2.61.35ff. There is no classical parallel for a sexual sense, but it is easy enough to see, and various verbs of motion had erotic currency in J.'s time and before. See Adams, 175f.

15 See *OLD* s.v. *excipio* 5b, 11; Horace *Sat.* 2.7.49.

16 On the issue see Courtney.

17 *OLD* s.v. *iaceo* 1, 2b, 5b.

18 Cf. Adams, 139f., 148f.

19 See *OLD* s.v. 1, 3, 5d, 5e, 8a, 8b.

20 Cf. Adams, 87.

21 See Adams, 103f.

22 *OLD* s.v. 1, 2, 4.

23 *OLD* s.v. *foedus* 1, 3, 4.

CHAPTER NINE

Conclusion (346–66)

There is a surprise here, as J. abruptly drops examples of misguided prayers and moves on to his conclusion, with a silly question by an interlocutor in line 346 that suddenly breaks in on the poet's voice and the grim picture in 345. The satirist thus gets our attention; and he keeps it, because this is only the first in a series of surprises. First of all, he tells us that instead of praying we should leave it to the gods to decide what is good for us, now presenting them with disturbing inconsistency as essentially benevolent rather than the malicious jokers of 7f. and 111. Then he does allow us to supplicate heaven after all, and in fact gives a long list of things that we can ask for. But he goes on saying that we don't need to request them at all, as we can get them by our own efforts. And he concludes with a totally unexpected assault on Fortune.

So this is a lively conclusion. It is also an appropriately powerful ending for what has, so far, been a powerful poem. It is amusing, interesting and provocative, and has real bite. We are, as it were, eavesdropping on an exchange between the poet and a slow-witted reader, and we are entertained by J.'s mockery and digs at him. But we can take a message for ourselves too, because what the satirist has to say to one is relevant for all his readers (and, so as not to alienate them, his barbs are directed at the interlocutor only, and he includes the disarming *nos* ('we/us') in lines 348, 350 and 365f., to align himself with them as another inferior mortal). He takes the whole issue of prayer much further here. After outlining various entreaties that should not be made in the previous sections, he now progresses to what we *can* ask for, listing at 356ff. various things which he believes will lead to our happiness. But he also undermines prayer, by saying that we should leave it to the gods themselves to give us what is best for us without directing ill-judged petitions at them (347ff.), by poking fun at the offerings that accompany requests to heaven (355) and by claiming that we can secure such blessings ourselves without recourse to deities (363f.). And in the final two lines, in connection with the recipients of entreaties, he calls into question the whole idea of divinity, maintaining that it is only our foolish supplication to Fortune that makes her a goddess. So it would appear that people are stupid not only in what they ask for but also in making requests at all, and J. is here attacking prayer as a general concept in a challenging climax that complements and goes beyond the earlier part of this *Satire*.

The internal structure is subtly effective, underscoring key points. The conclusion breaks up into three parts (346–53; 354–62; 363–6). J. highlights things that he sees as truly good for us, so that we will take them in and ponder them, by placing them at the centre of this section and devoting the longest subsection (nine lines) to them. And he surrounds them with the idea of prayer being unnecessary and misguided, and with encouragement not to pray, repeated in two subsections positioned for emphasis at the start and end of the conclusion. So, after telling us at 1ff. that few humans can distinguish *vera bona* ('genuine blessings'), J. now specifies what they are and thrusts them upon us, and he ends his poem on prayer by urging us not to pray for them (we should let the gods provide them unasked or acquire them by ourselves).

After all the negativity earlier in X, and even while criticizing prayer, the conclusion does have a positive aspect (so too there is much less pessimism here). This constructive element was promised in line 55, and the extensive retardation makes for a great build-up to it. Now at last we are told what it is right to ask the gods for (especially internal qualities rather than external things like military glory). We are also told that we can obtain all that without deities, most obviously by taking in the messages of philosophy, rhetoric and moralizing literature.[1] Here we see the preaching element of satire, and it is diverting and pointed preaching, which should really reach readers and be remembered. Much in J.'s recommendations is useful, and he usefully makes us think by raising major questions once again (in fact, aptly for a climax, this is the most thought-provoking section of the whole poem) – in particular, does god love people and give them what they need most? Are offerings to heaven (and similar religious paraphernalia) absurd? Do we accept all of J.'s *bona* here as blessings? Do we want to add more of our own to them? Is a peaceful life so desirable (or just boring)? And is there really a god (or gods)? But in addition to all that, does this section make you wonder who on earth the (bigoted, cynical, blinkered, etc.) J. of the earlier part of this poem is to lecture and instruct you like this?

Ring structure rounds off the whole satire neatly and provides a satisfying sense of closure. On the thematic level, most notably J. picks up from the introduction the mockery of human stupidity with men not knowing what to pray for (347ff., 365f., 1ff.), entreaties turning out badly (352f., 7ff.), true blessings (356ff., 3), philosophy (356ff., 28ff.), wealth as something undesirable (362, 12ff.) and disrespect for Fortune (365f., 52). The most pertinent verbal echoes (reinforcing, making twists, inverting and so on) are, in line 346, *ergo* ('so then') in a question about praying at the beginning of the section (cf. 54 at the end of the section) and *opto* ('request', cf. 7 in the Latin, 8 in my translation); in line 349, *di* ('gods') interacting with humans (cf. 8 in the Latin, 7 in my translation); in line 352, *peto* ('pray for') of foolish petition (cf. 8 in the Latin, 9 in my translation); in line 354 *voveo* ('vow', cf. the cognate *votum* ['prayer'] in 23); and, in line 360, *cupio* ('desire', cf. 5 in the Latin, 4 in my translation). So too, *caelo* ('heaven') in the final line looks to *terris* ('lands') in the opening verse.

> *'nil ergo optabunt homines?' si consilium vis,*
> *permittes ipsis expendere numinibus quid*
> *conveniat nobis rebusque sit utile nostris.*
> *nam pro iucundis aptissima quaeque dabunt di,*
> *carior est illis homo quam sibi. nos animorum*   350
> *inpulsu et caeca magnaque cupidine ducti*
> *coniugium petimus partumque uxoris, at illis*
> *notum qui pueri qualisque futura sit uxor.*
> *ut tamen et poscas aliquid voveasque sacellis*
> *exta et candiduli divina thymatula porci,*   355
> *orandum est ut sit mens sana in corpore sano.*
> *fortem posce animum mortis terrore carentem,*
> *qui spatium vitae extremum inter munera ponat*
> *naturae, qui ferre queat quoscumque dolores,*
> *nesciat irasci, cupiat nihil, et potiores*   360
> *Herculis aerumnas credat saevosque labores*
> *et venere et cenis et pluma Sardanapalli.*
> *monstro quod ipse tibi possis dare; semita certe*
> *tranquillae per virtutem patet unica vitae.*
> *nullum numen habes, si sit prudentia: nos te,*   365
> *nos facimus, Fortuna, deam caeloque locamus.*

'So then, will humans request nothing?' If you want [my] advice,
   you'll leave it to deities to estimate by themselves what
   is appropriate for us and advantageous to our circumstances.
For the gods will give all that's most fitting/useful instead of what's
      pleasurable,
   man is dearer to them than he is to himself. We, led on by   350
   an emotional impulse and by a blind and great desire,

pray for marriage and offspring from a wife, but they
know what our children will be and what kind of wife she'll be.
However, to give you something to ask for and a reason to vow at
    shrines
entrails and sausages fit for the gods made from a white pig,   355
you should pray to have a sound mind in a sound body.
Ask for a brave heart that is free from the fear of death,
which counts a long period of life as least important among
nature's gifts, which can endure any pain,
doesn't know how to get angry, desires nothing and believes   360
Hercules's troubles and cruel labours to be preferable to
the loves and dinners and feathers of Sardanapallus.
What I'm pointing to, you can give yourself; undoubtedly the only
path to a peaceful life lies through moral excellence.
You have no divinity, if we were sensible: it is we, we,   365
Fortune, who make you a goddess and place you in heaven.

In line 346 *nil ergo optabunt homines?* ('So then will humans request nothing?') could be a rhetorical question posed by J. But it is livelier and has much more force if it is an interruption by a reader,[2] amusingly exasperated by all J.'s negativity, and breaking in with an impatient question based on the assumption (doubtless shared by many) that it simply cannot be the case that humans should pray for nothing. Comically, according to our poet's following lines, in fact that *is* the case, and on top of that the protest facilitates the subsequent undermining of the whole concept of prayer.[3] In the rest of 346, *vis* ('you want') replies directly to this simple-minded interlocutor and introduces the barbed *consilium* (there is no word for 'my' in the Latin, and J. exploits that absence: such a person really *needs* advice, and 'discernment' and 'intelligence' too, which are also feasible senses for *consilium*).[4] There is another barb in *expendere* ('to estimate') in line 347: the gods will weigh things up and exercise judgement, unlike the reader (cf. 350f.). The influence in that verse of Valerius Maximus 7.2 ext. 1a has already been discussed in Chapter 2; but the use of *permitto* ('leave it to'), with a word for deities as its indirect object, directed at an addressee who is receiving advice, also recalls Horace *Odes* 1.9.9, where the poet says to Thaliarchus *permitte divis cetera* ('leave the rest to divinities'). Again there is subtle needling, since the reminiscence puts J.'s dumb reader on a par with Thaliarchus, who is a (naive and inexperienced) *puer* ('lad'), in need of lots of counsel, which he gets in the ode.[5] Keeping up the entertaining mockery, at 348f. the poet implies that his dull-witted addressee would just not be capable of seeing for himself and asking for what is appropriate and advantageous, but would be so shallow and short-sighted as to opt for what seems pleasurable (even after the lessons of the earlier part of this satire!). And there is bitter humour in the fact that those things (like the objects of prayer already mentioned in X) will not turn out to be pleasurable in the long run. In fact, as the poem has intimated, the idea is that they will be *supervacua* ('pointless', 'excessive') and *perniciosa* ('harmful'); and to that negative pair in the introduction J. pointedly opposes here in the conclusion the positive pair of *conveniat* and *sit utile* ('is appropriate' and 'advantageous'). He also disdainfully diminishes the lone, short *iucundis* ('what's pleasurable') in line 349 by swamping it and surrounding it with *conveniat, utile* and *aptissima* ('most fitting/useful'), which economically combines the senses of *conveniat* and *utile*,[6] and with judicious divinities.

There are wider implications too. J. has shown prayers turning out badly. Here, with a step up and a great joke about human blindness and stupidity, he claims that not only do we appeal for things that are in fact evils, but if we didn't pray in the first place all would be fine and well for us; we ruin that desirable situation by making entreaties. If left unharassed, divinities will generously give us what is best for us (the alliteration and rhythm at the end of line 349 are forceful), and we actually subvert their generosity and spoil things with our cretinous requests, which the gods grant.[7] Worse than that, and even funnier, the gods actually love us very much,[8] as is highlighted by the epigram in line 350, but we mess that up too, turning their essential benignity into malignity (cf. 111). There is another pawky touch in an inference to be drawn from the progression here: deities love us more than we love ourselves, and we can't love ourselves all that much, because we want to get married and have children (as well as making other disastrous prayers).

At 350f. the poet takes more than a line to spotlight derisively our lack of rationality (cf. 4): there is twofold reference to the emotions; amid mock-solemn spondees *inpulsu* ('impulse') and *ducti* ('led on') in emphatic positions frame line 351; there is (to me, contemptuous) frequency of *c* and *q* in this line; nouns and verbs are arranged chiastically here, and *caeca* ('blind') and *magna* ('great') are juxtaposed forcefully; there is also pregnant diction, with *caeca* embracing 'lacking sight', 'stupid', 'not prescient' and 'misdirected',[9] while in *magna*, which primarily denotes intensity, there is probably ironical play on the sense 'lofty'.[10] There is also drollery in a great desire for something which (according to J.) will wreck your life. Comically, too, humans are being led by something blind, which is hardly going to turn out well, and major emotional problems are likely to result from being dominated by the emotions. There is also a scoffing sandwiching, as mortal irrationality at 350f. is made to look even sillier by being enfolded by the gods' superior perception at 347–9 and at 352f., with the authoritative *notum* (translated as 'know') emphatically placed in 353.

When we reach the actual prayer in line 352 there is an in-joke in the very idea of asking for a spouse after the extensive attack on Roman wives in *Satire* VI, and humour too in entreating for offspring after the previous section, which dilated on the miseries of children and their parents. With *nos* ('we') in 350 J. means 'mortals', but the expression flippantly suggests the satirist also, after all his ranting and revelations, seeking a bride and progeny; and *caeca* in line 351 adds to the fun, as it would be a really blind desire that impelled J. to do so. Not only are we fools to make such a request but, as elsewhere in this poem, the gods will actually grant it. It is easy enough to picture them, with their insight into the future, laughing as they do so, and the implication is that the wife and children – presumably to be included among *iucundis* ('what's pleasurable') in 349! – will be awful, so that once again the petitioner is ruining his own life. The prayer is dismissed in the cutting line 353, with the scornfully suggestive *qui* ('what') and *qualis* ('what kind of'), which make for an insistent fulness and contemptuous alliteration. The grim jesting is funny, but again there is pessimism here. Although problems could be caused by a spouse and offspring,[11] lots of people were (and are) perfectly happy as husbands and fathers, and there was in any case the possibility of divorcing spouses and abandoning and disowning children; in addition, the misery intimated here is at variance with J.'s own 240ff., where wives and progeny are loved and sorely missed when dead.

In line 354 the poet moves on to things the addressee *can* pray for. The derision continues, as the implication is that the reader who cannot believe that humans should ask for nothing is so slow and so set in his ways on the question of petition that even after the satirist has clearly instructed him to leave it to the gods to decide what's best for us, and even after he has shown at length various entreaties turning out badly, the fool will still pray, and pray for something that is not appropriate or advantageous. So J. steps in with some damage limitation, informing him of requests that he can make which won't cause him problems. There is a joke too in *aliquid* ('something'). The singular *aliquid* succeeded by the prayer in line 356 makes it look as if that is all he should ask for, but then comes a whole series of further appeals at 357ff. It appears that the poet is giving him a lot to pray for so that he won't demand other things besides but will feel that he is asking for a substantial amount and will be getting a fair return for his offerings (as J. constructs him, lines 360 and 362 suggest that he is rather greedy). At 354f. the satirist also pokes fun at those offerings, which are part of the whole praying process. Undercutting is achieved by means of a full three disrespectful diminutives – *sacellis* ('shrines'), *candiduli* ('white') and *thymatula* ('sausages'). There is diminution too in the associations of *candiduli*: the only earlier instance of this extremely rare word is at Cicero *Tusculan Disputations* 5.46, where in a discussion of *bona* ('blessings'), he refers to *candiduli dentes* ('white teeth'), which he specifically designates as *minima* ('insignificant'). *Divina* means 'fit for the gods', but there will be frivolous play on other senses – 'divine', 'superlative', 'having supernatural power' and 'foreseeing'[12] (of sausages!). There is also deflation in *thymatula*, a word of a low stylistic level,[13] for a mundane object. There may well be a dig in the choice of a pig in particular for this reader to sacrifice, as that animal had connotations of ignorance and stupidity.[14] Line 355 is also a comically elegant one to describe guts and sausages, with its alliteration, assonance, homoeoteleuton and internal rhyme, and (in *candiduli ... porci*) its balance of adjectives and nouns and chiasmus of genitives and accusatives. As well as undermining the sacrifice that is the concomitant of supplication, J. thus casts doubt on the whole religious convention of the *quid pro quo*, by making these gifts to the gods seem quite negligible (especially in return for all the blessings at 356ff.) and even rather grotesque;[15] and if the gods can be won over by such things, they seem odd and even somewhat absurd,[16] so that J. is briefly questioning divinity here prior to the more substantial debunking below.

At line 356 the list of blessings that one can pray for begins. On one level, this is a serious recommendation of qualities which various philosophers and moralists endorsed[17] and which J. sees as important to help one lead a good life, and his advice is applicable generally, to the great mass of humanity, who misguidedly pester the gods for power, eloquence, military glory and so on instead. But there are also humorous aspects. J. is addressing the silly interlocutor, so that the specification in line 356 of *mens sana* ('a sound [i.e. sane and sensible] mind') is tart, as this is something which he singularly lacks. And he is apparently so obtuse that he actually needs to be told in this line to request mental and physical health (surely an obvious thing to pray for)[18] and in 358 not to value longevity – this after 188–288, hence *spatium vitae* ('a long period of life') deliberately echoes 188). So too the addressee will for the most part be asking for what he does not already possess, so at 356ff. J. builds up a satirical portrait of him as a foolish coward who cannot cope with pain and is prone to anger, greed and sensuality. At the same time, there is also some disarming wit at the poet's own expense. It is a bit rich for him to tell another person to ask for a heart which is brave and free from the fear of death (357) and which can endure any pain (359), when at the end of his first poem he was warned of the dangers of a painful death if he named the objects of his satire and promptly stated that in view of that, he would attack only the dead.[19] J. is also a fine one to urge on someone else the avoidance of rage in line 360, after writing the angry first two books of *Satires*, and showing irritation with the mother in the previous section of this poem and with the reader in this one. It would seem that the poet himself is not perfect and is here mentioning some qualities that he also needs to acquire.

Line 356 is made memorable by its spondees, alliteration, repetition of *sanus* ('sound') and balance (of mental and physical health, of nouns and adjectives). It also has a subtle point: one should ask for a healthy body rather than a beautiful or long-lived one, in view of all the trouble that good looks and longevity cause. Line 357 is also striking, with its solemn rhythm, stress by position of the rhyming *fortem* ('brave', a block spondee) and *carentem* ('free from'), iteration of *-or* and assonance of *e*. In addition, there may well be some sly joking at the pessimism in X: you really would need to be courageous to cope with the kind of world that is depicted here, and death could be seen as a welcome release from such hazards and horrors. At 358f. the grave spondees persist, and there is also a very unusual (and therefore arresting) absence of a caesura in the third and fourth feet of 358[20] and forceful alliteration in 359. But again there is pawkiness beneath the surface. In 358 it is droll of the poet, after 188ff., to call a long life a 'gift'.[21] He is also having fun here with *extremum*: its primary sense is 'least important', but in view of his earlier remarks on old age there will also be play on 'extremely distressing'.[22] Similarly, in line 359 with *quoscumque dolores*[23] ('any pain'), which embraces both physical and mental distress, J. makes another jibe at the interlocutor, having in mind *inter alia* anguish caused by fools like him for themselves, the satirist and others; and there is probably a continuation of the jesting about the bleak world portrayed in this poem (and there is still more hardship in line 361). In 360 our poet is recommending the Stoic virtue of *apathia* (freedom from the passions). But with *nesciat irasci* ('doesn't know how to get angry') there is again teasing of this reader, whose ignorance should include ignorance of anger. And *cupiat nihil* ('desires nothing') has its frivolous side too. The phrase denotes an absence of cravings, and after all that has gone before in this poem J. apparently still has to tell this person not to long for things. In addition, if you pray for something, you desire it, so here he would be desiring the ability to desire nothing! At 360f. J. moves on to the Labours of Hercules. Philosophers considered them services to mankind, so Hercules was revered by Stoics and Cynics, and his Labours were seen as suitable for emulation.[24] The satirist has these serious views in mind, but there has to be some scoffing at the addressee too, in the idea of this cowardly idiot as a would-be second Hercules (and line 361, with its ponderous rhythm and wearisome echoing of the ending *-ores* at the end of lines 359 and 360, underscores his hardships), and also as somebody on a par with the emperor Trajan – *saevos labores* ('cruel labours') occurs elsewhere only at Pliny *Panegyricus* 14.5, where Trajan is likened to the demi-god for his military activities in Germany, and is said to have inspired great admiration for his feats there. Hercules is mentioned first to give him precedence over Sardanapallus, who figures in the very voluptuous line 362 (with its languorous assonance of *a*), and who, at the end of his line, is in tension with Hercules at the start of his verse, widely separated from that very different character by starkly contrasting nouns. Sardanapallus is an entertainingly crafty choice as a symbol of the most extravagant luxury and lechery. The last king of Assyria (668–29 BC), he was, according to Greek and Roman sources, very wealthy but also disgracefully decadent and effeminate, and led a life of such disgusting dissipation that there was a successful conspiracy against him and he committed suicide after mounting a funeral pyre along with his treasures and his women.[25] So his lifestyle is redolent of excess (*supervacuus*), and turned out to be very harmful (*perniciosus*), leading him to a bad end. On top of that he is non-Roman, and seems even more despicable (inactive and unmanly) beside the labouring Hercules. Adding to the deflation is *pluma* ('feathers'). This word brings one up short after *venere* ('loves') and *cenis* ('dinners') and, on first reading, it briefly conjures up a surreal and absurd picture of a plumed human. Of course, J. is actually thinking of cushions and mattresses stuffed with down, which connote enervating indolence, indulgence and sensuality. And the feather was proverbially lightweight and soft,[26] so these associations also attach to the king.

Line 362 mocks the interlocutor by again targeting wealth (even after 12ff. the point needs to be repeated for him), and the ribbing continues in line 363, where he is represented as so slow as not to realize that he can acquire all the desired blessings by himself. Again sobriety (in connection with the self-sufficiency that was prized by various moralizers and philosophers) is combined with levity. As the foregoing list consists of things that we can achieve on our own, if we will only act and do something for ourselves, its length brings out how fine we can make our lives without turning to deities and prayer; and the gods are diminished by not being necessary for humans in general and in particular by the idea that even the fool of a reader can bypass them. In addition to this sardonic touch there is the joke of the prayers just recommended by J. being themselves superfluous (*supervacuus*), as are the gods. At 363f., engagingly, the progression of thought is not spelled out, but the idea will be that the qualities at 356ff. which people can get for themselves constitute *virtus* ('moral excellence'), and that is the only way to a *tranquilla vita* ('a peaceful life'), which is viewed as an ideal by J. (and by many others, including poets and philosophers). The idea is put across vigorously and memorably: *certe* ('undoubtedly') is stressed by placement; *per virtutem patet* ('lies through moral excellence'), in an important central position, is enfolded by a chiastic arrangement of nouns and adjectives; line 364 is framed by the rhyming *tranquillae ... vitae* ('a peaceful life'), and has alliteration. There is also significant literary allusion. The phrase *semita ... vitae* ('path to a ... life') appears elsewhere only at Horace *Epistulae* 1.18.103: *fallentis semita vitae* ('the path of a life unnoticed'). The echo comes with apposite associations that support J.'s argumentation here: it occurs in a passage in which Horace rejects greed, fear and desire for things that are not really useful, and champions moral excellence and a peaceful life. There is also diverting bite in directing the reminiscence at J.'s reader: the Horatian expression comes at the end of a lengthy epistle packed with advice and is addressed to a naive person in need of extensive instruction from a knowledgeable expert (reinforcing the barbed allusion to Thaliarchus in line 347).

There is an arresting conclusion at 365f. Initially one assumes that J. is still talking to his reader in line 365, so that surprisingly and comically the poet seems to feel the need to deny divinity to that moron. Actually, as we come to realize, there is an attack on Fortuna here, which we did not anticipate. Our attention is also seized by the fact that the thought is really elliptical, and makes demands on us to work it out, involving us. The idea seems to be that, as well as it being unnecessary to entreat the gods in general, it is particularly foolish to pray to Fortune (as many did)[27] and thus turn her into a deity.[28] This will be because Fortuna cannot give us all the inner qualities that lead to a peaceful life (they are not all a matter of luck), and should not be able to affect that happy existence via external events, if we are brave, enduring and so on (as at 356ff.).[29] Fortune only gives extrinsic things like wealth and power, the false blessings which are so often superfluous and harmful, and also unstable,[30] so that Fortuna is beside the point and should be ignored by sensible people.[31] In addition to rejecting again the need for prayer and heaven, J. here goes further and brings the very concept of divinity into question. He denies celestial status to Fortune, forcefully, with vehement alliteration, repetition and, in 365, weighty spondees, emphatic position for *nullum* ('no') and the very definite *habes* ('you have' instead of 'you would have'). And he leaves us to wonder if that status is dubious in other cases too, for personifications like Pecunia ('Money'),[32] and perhaps even for full gods. J. also undermines the immortals in other ways. Normally they are the ones who deify people and place them in the heavens,[33] but here mortals are actually on a par with the gods (cf. line 363), because they do all this themselves, in the case of Fortuna (and also with personifications and the imperial family). So too Fortune's divinity depends not just on humans but on human foolishness. The final words of the poem, *caeloque locamus* ('and place [you] in heaven'), mean that heaven contains at least one charlatan. They also effectively echo Virgil *Aeneid* 12.145 (*caelique libens in parte locarim*, 'and I willingly placed [you] in part of heaven'), words spoken by Juno to Juturna in the process of making it clear to that being of lesser divine standing that she cannot offer a human (her brother Turnus) any real, lasting help.[34] There is definite punch in the apostrophe too, as J. ends a poem on prayer (a respectful address to a deity, tacitly acknowledging their divinity, and asking for something) with a disrespectful address to one widely viewed as a deity, openly repudiating her divinity and asking for nothing (for, in fact, it is humans who her grant her favour).[35] The satirist also ends, as he began, by poking fun at human ignorance. Not only do we not know what to ask for and fail to realize that we don't need to make such entreaties at all, but in our supreme stupidity we even create a deity to pray to where there is none.[36] We cannot distinguish true *bona* ('blessings') (1ff.), and we cannot distinguish true divinities either, elevating to heaven a false deity who cannot give us the *bona* we need, and praying to a non-goddess for non-blessings!

Notes

1   See Chapter 2 above.

2   So I have added inverted commas (not found in Housman) around the question. This also means that the numerous jibes in the following lines are directed at this particular person and not at J.'s readers in general, and so are diverting for us rather than infuriating. For the interjection cf. 291f., 324; 1.150.

3   With *nil* ('nothing'), the satirist may also be playing on the senses 'nothing of importance' and 'nothing sensible'. See *OLD* s.v. *nihil* 8 and 9.

4   See *OLD* s.v. 7 and 8; *TLL* IV.455.61ff.

5   There may be some implicit correction of Horace here as well. In that poem, he recommends as a way of life enjoying oneself with wine and love and not worrying about the future, whereas J. is rather dismissive of pleasure (349) and love and partying (362), and at 356ff. presents a fuller and sterner vision of what is needed for the good life.

6   See *TLL* II.329.18ff.; *OLD* s.v. *aptus* 8, 9.

7   As they do, for example, in Socratic thought (Plato *Alc. II* 138b) and in the myth of Midas and the golden touch (Ovid. *Met.* 11.100ff.). Our poet does not explain here why the gods grant these prayers, but earlier they seemed to have a harsh sense of humour (7f., 111); they could also be acting in irritation and/or to punish our silliness.

8   For the idea cf. e.g. Sen. *Ben.* 2.29.6: *carissimos nos habuerunt di immortales habentque* ('the immortal gods have regarded us and still regard us as very dear'). But the gods, who operate on a different plane, can be hard on people they love:

e.g. Venus distresses her son Aeneas by appearing to him in disguise (Virg. *Aen.* 1.407ff.), and allows an affair with Dido to begin even though she knows it cannot last and he will be hurt by it (*Aen.* 1.257ff., 4.105ff.).

9   See *OLD* s.v. *caecus* 1, 2c, 2d, 3a.

10   See *TLL* VIII.135.23ff.; *OLD* s.v. *magnus* 14. The reading *magna* has been suspected (see Courtney; Campana), needlessly.

11   See Campana for ancient philosophical thought about this.

12   See *OLD* s.v. *divinus* 1, 3b, 4a, 5, 6.

13   Urech, 163.

14   See Otto s.v. Minerva 1; cf. also Suet. *Gram.* 23 (p. 117 Re).

15   For the sneer at offerings cf. esp. Persius 2.30.

16   Compare 6.539–41. Some scholars suggest that the mockery here also extends to the entreaties recommended at 356–62. I just cannot see this, particularly as J. champions the blessings of 356ff., at 363f. and also in *Satires* 11 and 12 (see the next chapter).

17   See the commentators (especially Mayor; Ebel; Courtney; Campana) and also my Chapter 2 above, Highet (1954), 276; Lawall, 31; Dick, 242–5; Plaza, 125.

18   For this very widespread prayer see e.g. Mayor; Campana.

19   Even though the dead stand for the living in his poetry, he did formally and openly back down at 1.155ff.

20   On which see Mayor; Courtney.

21   On the interpretation of this line see Courtney; Campana. The considered echo of *spatium vitae* in line 188 makes the translation 'a long period of life' certain here.

22   See *OLD* s.v. *extremus* 4b, 5; *TLL* V.2.2003.46ff.

23   Some mss read *labores* instead of *dolores* (see Campana). In line 361, in view of the reference to Hercules there, *labores* is secure, and there is no reason for J. to use the same word here, so *labores* in 359 will be a mistake, quite possibly under the influence of *labores* at the end of 361.

24   See especially Mayor. It is a neat touch that Hercules, who fought against and in company with gods, and who was himself deified, is presented as a role model for one who can dispense with deities (363f.).

25   See Mayor; Courtney.

26   Otto s.v. *pluma*.

27   Cf. e.g. Pliny *NH* 2.22.

28   So Martial (8.24.5f.) says it is not the person who sculpts divine statues who makes gods but the one who directs requests to them.

29   For this notion cf. 52f.; Sen. *Dial.* 5.25.4, *Epist.* 98.14.

30   For this instability and for the fickleness of Fortune see 285f., 3.40, 6.605ff.; Sen. *Epist.* 66.23, 74.6f.; Otto s.v. *fortuna* 5.

31   Cf. 52f. and 13.19f.

32   Cf. 1.112ff.; Courtney on 1.112; Mayor on 1.113.

33   E.g. Hercules, Aeneas, Romulus, Juturna, Flora and Leucothea.

34   See *TLL* VII.2.1564.75ff. for this and similar expressions. Common to Virgil and J. are *te* ('you'), *caelum* ('heaven') and *loco* ('place', at the end of a hexameter line), and in both the phrase is addressed by one person to another, whose position in heaven is due to the speaker, and who is called *dea* ('goddess') (in J.'s 139 and Virgil's 366). Cicero *Leg.* 2.19 also has *caelo locare*, but it is not employed in such an address, the subject of the verb is *merita* ('merits') and its object is plural.

35   The repeated *nos* ('we') and singular *te* ('you') could be an inversion of du-Stil (the iteration of 'you' addressed to a god or goddess in prayers).

36   See Mayor for ancient denial of Fortune's divinity. Our role is mockingly stressed by the repetition of *nos* ('we'), by the fulness in 'make you a goddess' plus 'place you in heaven' and by the enfolding of *te* ('you') by *nos* ('we') in lines 365 and 366.

CHAPTER TEN

(Satires 11 and 12)

A study of *Satire* 10 on its own would provide an incomplete picture because it is closely related to and has a distinct bearing on the two other poems in J.'s fourth book. *Satires* 11 and 12 are, of course, distinct pieces in their own right and exhibit many substantial differences from 10 that make for a lively variety.[1] But there are numerous verbal and thematic links that draw the three poems together, and J. also makes X an apt introduction to XI and XII in terms of tone and thrust, and in the latter two *Satires* he reinforces and takes further important points made in the first of the trio.

The poet ensures that the fourth book has structural neatness and forms a coherent whole. The three poems make up a tricolon diminuendo, as XI is 208 lines long and XII has 130 verses. As will become clear below, 12 is harder and more extreme than 11, so that with 10 it provides a harsh frame around the milder 11. There is also ring composition, as 12 ends with a flurry of clear allusions to 10: at 128ff. J. closes the whole book with a prayer, one which incorporates various themes from X (see the final paragraph of this chapter), and in particular the wish for a long life and wealth recalls the entreaties for same in 10;[2] Nestor in line 128 looks to 10.246ff.; Nero in 129 takes up 10.15 and 308f.; and there are linguistic echoes in *possideat* ('possess', line 129; cf. 10.225), *rapuit Nero* ('Nero stole', 129; cf. 10.308, where the same phrase means 'Nero raped'), *aurum* ('gold', 129; cf. 10.27) and *amet* ('love', 130; cf. 10.68, 220, 241, 320). There are binding verbal reminiscences elsewhere too. Most significantly, in all three pieces we find *deus* ('god', 10.8, 55, 129, 184, 349; 11.107, 113, 12.2, 114), *argentum* ('silver', 10.19; 11.109; 12.43, 49) and *belua* ('beast') of the elephant (10.158; 11.124; 12.104);[3] 11 picks up *cenis* ('dinners', 10.362; 11.1, 12, 78, 120), *arca* ('strongbox', 10.25; 11.26) and *coniugium petimus* ('we pray for marriage', 10.352; 11.29); and 12 recalls *amicus* ('friend', 1.46, 234; 12.16, 96) and *captator* ('will-hunter', 10.202; 12.114). There are many common themes as well, and these connections are often interesting and enlivening. They can provide added support for ideas via iteration. So at 11.27 and 111ff. we find the gods caring for us (cf. 10.347ff.); at 11.45 the misery of old age (cf. 10.190ff.); at 11. 93ff., 121ff., 136ff. and 193ff. deflation of pretentiousness and display (cf. 10.34ff.); at 11.162ff. disapproval of immorality (cf. 10.208f., 223f., 304ff. and 318ff.); at 11.201ff. the positive presentation of the quiet life (cf. 10.364); at 12.24ff. danger created for himself by a fool (cf. 10. 139, 311); and at 12.44f. expensive drinking cups as something undesirable (cf. 10.26f.). There is also entertaining and effective point in these connections. So at 11.60ff. the reference to Hercules in connection with a simple dinner is a deft allusion to his Labours being preferable to an extravagant dinner at 10.360ff.; at 11.186ff. the detailed picture of the bad wife represents a droll development of 10.352f.; at 12.15ff. Catullus lacks a disregard for death and many of the other qualities championed at 10.356ff., thereby neatly illustrating how deplorable is their absence; at 12.118ff. the betrayal of a child for mercenary motives looks back to 10.304ff. but tops the earlier passage because it is more drastic; and 12.128f., calling to mind the sad figure of Nestor at 10.246ff., the horrors of longevity at 10.190ff. and the sinister figure of Nero at 10.15 and 308f., underscores the negative aspect of the wishes for Pacuvius there and makes for real bite.

On top of these structural considerations, X functions in various ways as a programme poem for the rest of the book. Continuing in the vein of 10, *Satires* 11 and 12 are also thought-provoking compositions that snipe at their addressees, and they also have a calmer, mocking tone,[4] parade and pillory human stupidity with humour and wit, include much absurdity and grotesquery (especially 11.93ff., 120ff., 126f., 136ff., 12.20ff., 34ff., 102ff.) and present a gloomy picture of Rome, with cynicism and exaggeration (particularly at 11.50ff., 120ff., 199ff., 12.95ff.). In addition, at 11.152f., where a young slave sighs for his mother, whom he has not seen for a long time, and for his home, we see the admixture of pathos that was a feature of the preceding poem; and we find at 12.48f. the global vision and at 12.95ff. the sweeping generalization that were prominent in 10.

Some major issues of 10 are also taken up and developed further in an interlocking complex of ideas spread over 11 and 12. I will begin with 11. This is, of course, a satire which has much of interest and significance independently of 10. So, for example, scholars have commented on its relationship to Martial[5] and Horace,[6] and examined its connection with the invitation poem[7] and its treatment of the satirical theme of the dinner party, with particular reference to J.'s fifth poem;[8] others have explored it as a tract on the need to recognize all people and all things as they really are[9] and as a study of moral ambiguity.[10] But *Satire* 11 also, and importantly, functions *vis-à-vis* 10. Given the nature of this book, I will be concentrating on that aspect, which actually provides an interesting new way of looking at XI. Before doing so, I need to establish the background situation and the overall drift of the piece, as these important elements are quite problematical.

At 11.1–55 J. describes how people laugh at and gossip about Rutilus for putting on costly dinners and thus ruining himself financially, so that he has to sign up as a despised gladiator to earn some money. You see (the poet says) many others seriously in debt who end up in the gladiatorial school as a result of dining extravagantly, for their taste in fine food, and also because they like spending. Genuinely rich people are admired for this type of expenditure, but Rutilus is regarded as a crazy spendthrift. You should know yourself, being aware of your limits, living according to your means and not desiring pricier food than you can afford. Otherwise what kind of end awaits you, as your appetite increases and your resources decrease and you spend all that you have on meals? Such persons end up begging or bankrupt and fleeing from Rome and their creditors there. Next, at 56–64, J. reveals that his satire has a specific addressee (Persicus), who will soon see if J. practises what he preaches, because he has accepted the poet's invitation to dinner that day. In fact, it will be a simple dinner. At 65–89 the satirist lists the good plain food from his Tiburtine farm that he will be serving, the kind of fare that the early Romans ate. At 90–135 he moves on to the simplicity of the furniture in the dining room during those virtuous times, when wealth was not prized, in contrast to the ludicrous affectation of the rich of his day, who cannot enjoy a meal unless it is served up on a huge table with an ornate ivory support. J. himself has no ivory in his home. He doesn't have a ridiculous professional carver either, or expensive foreign slaves, just ordinary lads from the country who speak Latin (136–61). At 162–82 he tells Persicus that he may be expecting the titillating and obscene Spanish dancers prized by the well-heeled, but J. will offer instead readings from Homer and Virgil as the entertainment at his meal. In the conclusion (183–208) the poet urges Persicus to come and leave behind his worries about money matters, ungrateful friends and his blatantly unfaithful wife, who spends all day out and returns home at night, her clothes suspiciously wrinkled and damp, her hair dishevelled, and her face and ears flushed. While the rest of Rome is at the races, Persicus should join J. quietly sitting out in the sun; but he should not take this simple pleasure to excess.

Intriguingly the background is revealed only gradually, and we are left to work out the big picture for ourselves; but all the pieces do come together coherently. Some critics describe Persicus as a friend of the poet, but it is clear that, whether or not he actually existed, he is not supposed to be that. The graphic revelations at 186ff. about his wife's infidelity are not the kind of remarks that one addresses to a friend[11] and then publishes; there is also extensive, and at times harsh, ridicule of Persicus (see below); and, as will become obvious shortly, he is hardly the type of person whom the satirist seems likely to befriend or would want to be seen as befriending. In fact, the invitation to him is just a peg, a way of attacking contemporary extravagance in general and getting at Persicus in particular.[12] It has been claimed that Persicus is wealthy. But someone who is worried about business, interest and breakages at home (as he is said to be at 183ff.) is not likely to be really rich; and J. does not include his addressee among the well-off when he mentions them at lines 120, 168, 171ff. and 177f., where he talks of 'the rich' or 'they' rather than 'you people', and appears to be giving Persicus information about a different section of society. But it does seem that Persicus, whose name has connotations of luxury and wealth,[13] aspires to the lifestyle of the affluent. When we learn in line 57 that *Satire* 11 is addressed to Persicus, we have to assume that the remarks at 1–55 about ruining oneself by dining beyond one's means have pertinence for him: otherwise J. would be opening with a long section in a prominent position that is quite pointless, and over a quarter of the poem would be irrelevant digression.[14] In particular, the apostrophe in line 57 means that the 'you' at 1–55 is not the general reader (as some might have assumed) but (as we learn with a surprise that makes for impact) specifically Persicus, so J. is saying to Persicus that he should ponder the divine injunction to know himself and should not exceed his limitations and crave food that he cannot afford (27ff.), and J. is asking Persicus what end awaits him as his wallet fails and his appetite grows and he squanders all he has on meals (38ff.). So Persicus is to be included among those who, like Rutilus, overstretch themselves and borrow money and risk financial disaster to indulge in expensive dinners. Persicus's worries about business affairs and interest (presumably owed by him, and perhaps to him as well) and things broken or lost in his house (183ff.), and the implication at the very end that he has a tendency to excess in pleasure (206ff.) obviously fit with that scenario. So too J. will be stressing the simplicity of his meal and the absence of various forms of luxury (at 131ff., 136ff., 142ff. and 162ff.) because they are what his guest has grown used to and what he sees as constituting a dinner and may anticipate receiving from his host (cf. *forsitan expectes*, 'perhaps you expect', in line 162).

To move on to the main satirical thrust of 11, J. mocks his addressee for his stupid behaviour and misguided aspirations, giving him (and others like him, and the general reader) food for thought, and showing him at the start of the poem that his way of life may well lead to much greater problems in the future, and at the end that it does not bring him happiness now. As well as spotlighting the trouble caused by adopting the lifestyle of the rich when one is not rich and deriding those who do that at 1ff. and 183ff., in the middle of *Satire* 11 J. undermines the coveted wealth and the envied wealthy people, disparaging the possessions (as trivial, excessive, absurd, etc.) and the possessors (their pretensions, immorality, repulsiveness, etc.). He also holds out another option for Persicus which is sensible and upright – the simplicity of early Rome evinced in the poet's own meal. J. gets his satire across in a new way here, by means of an inversion of the topos of the awful dinner party and a variation on the invitation poem. Line 60 makes it clear that the addressee has already agreed to come, so this is not an actual invitation poem (a composition which issues an invitation) but one which makes a follow-up before Persicus leaves home that day (cf. 204ff.) on his way to J.'s house. Actually, what we have here is an anti-invitation poem, because instead of encouraging the recipient to come by showing affection, complimenting him and promising him a good time (standard features of the genre), J. would turn him off by lecturing him in a superior fashion, making gibes and holding out the prospect of a dinner that he would not enjoy. In fact, he rubs Persicus's nose in what he will get, repeatedly denying him the kind of thing he wants, and criticizing it; and the poet mischievously puts him on the spot, by stressing the moral aspect of his meal, so that his guest would look bad if he tried to back out now. While doing so, J. also picks up and deftly ties together four elements from X, employing the lavish dinner (cf. 10.362) as a way of attacking people with cravings (cf. 10.360) and wealth itself (cf. 10.12ff., 362), and providing an alternative which bolsters and expands on the virtue recommended at 10.356ff.

J. now brings out the point that the *cena* ('dinner', a small word, which was just one component in the list at 10.356ff.) actually has major significance, and so deserves a major expansion, a whole poem devoted to it. According to the satirist, the *cena* is a statement, an affirmation of lifestyle and a way of putting oneself across to the world (see the next paragraph); it is also a giveaway, an indication of one's intelligence and morality (or lack thereof). In XI the poet explores further the negative associations of *cenis ... Sardanapalli* ('dinners ... of Sardanapallus') at 10.362 (decadence, sensuality, indulgence, excess, self-destructiveness, etc.) and provides a concrete form for them that is full and vivid; he also tries to show how unimpressive and even repellent are contemporary equivalents of Sardanapallus and his dinners, to strengthen his earlier dismissal. J. here acts in accordance with his prior stance by offering a modest meal, and also builds on that bald rejection, trying to justify it at length and in detail. While presenting his own dinner as a preferable alternative invested with the moral authority of old Rome, J. fills out the picture of the lavish *cena*, covering many components to ensure extensive disparagement. As well as the food itself he mentions couches, tables, the carver, costly foreign slaves, Spanish floor shows for entertainment and fine marble flooring.[15] He provides an impressionistic sketch of the expensive dinner by means of scattered touches, each of which is attended by criticism and/or contrast (with J.'s meal and revered Roman ancestors). Essentially, after stating briefly in 10 that such a *cena* is not admirable, he now presents one for our contemplation, so that we can see the many reasons why it is not admirable; and he censures and derides people who put on this kind of meal – the rich[16] and those who ape their way of life.

J. also takes his injunction against desiring things at 10.360 much further, by giving a concrete example of such a desire and expatiating forcefully on its negative effects in a twofold attack in prominent positions at the start and end of the satire (1ff., 183ff.). Again we see the elements of excess, pointlessness and harmfulness (such cravings beyond what one can afford destroy happiness, financial security and, for those who are reduced to being gladiators, quite possibly life too). And again, we see stupid and irrational humans – those who feel the longing (and who clearly lack a sound mind and cannot distinguish between true blessings and things very different from them). J. shows himself as free from such yearnings, in line with his programme at 10.356ff.

Our poet analyses facets of these misguided souls' desire and provides indications of their motivation, so that he can undermine it all. There is the gourmet aspect: they want fine food because they relish its flavours (11, 14, 19f.). They also favour it simply because it is expensive: in line 16 J. maintains that the more it costs, the more pleasure they get out of it[17] – they like spending lots of money, feeling rich and enjoying the lifestyle of the affluent. And, of course, they want other people to think that they really are wealthy on the basis of their extravagant repasts[18] (the *cena* was often for guests; the gossip at 2ff. and 21f. makes it clear that people were invited to be over-awed and to pass on information about the dining in the case of Rutilus, who is an exemplar of such aspirers; and line 47 implies public display too). So they hunger for the reputation of being rich and elegant, so that they will be admired as great men (like Atticus in line 1 and Ventidius at 22f.). J. represents them as acquiring instead notoriety and ridicule, any brief pleasure more than offset by the general unhappiness of their existence, when he considers the outcome of their cravings, which is where he places his main stress. Of course, as we know from modern western society, many people get great enjoyment from living beyond their means, and some manage to do it without too much trouble, but J.'s viewpoint is entirely negative, as he packs in the darkly comical drawbacks and ironical reversals.

At 1–8, in his first attack on desire, with the character Rutilus (who is not affluent) J. depicts a costly *cena* put on by such people as not impressing or winning respect (such as that accorded to the well-heeled Atticus) but achieving the exact opposite – widespread mockery for lunacy. As well as pointlessness there is also harmfulness, because as a result of spending like a moneybags, Rutilus is impoverished and has to raise cash by signing on as a gladiator, and thereby losing his liberty, legal rights, status and dignity (he is now anything but a grand man!) and possibly his life too in combat. At 9–11 our satirist moves on to the gourmet element, again casting aspersions on the sanity of such persons (by claiming that their sole reason for living is the taste of food), and reinforcing the public humiliation by representing them as being pursued by moneylenders, who know that the best place to catch their debtors is at the entrance to the food market, and who make it clear to onlookers that their targets are not in fact well off. At 12f. our poet pokes fun at the unconvincing façade built up by such extravagant dining, likening it to a badly cracked house on the point of collapse,[19] and at 14–16 he conjures up an absurd picture of the gourmet on an international quest, for flavours, unconcerned about the expense, and in fact happier the more he has to pay for mere food. At 17–20 the man (neither dutiful nor intelligent) pawns silver dishes and melts down a statue of his mother to raise money which he squanders on fine food, that now has to be eaten off cheap earthenware (ruining the effect); and in this way he ends up in the grim surroundings of the gladiatorial school reduced to the coarse stew served there – a cruel rebound for a gourmet who wants to cut an imposing figure. At 21–3 J. repeats the belittling contrast at 1f. between Rutilus and a genuinely rich person (bringing in another plutocrat, Ventidius, to diminish Rutilus further), and maintains that as a result of putting on a lavish repast, Ventidius achieves the reputation and esteem to which Rutilus aspires, whereas the latter is simply seen as being guilty of excess and extravagance.

Lines 23–55 are initially not so closely focused on the unpleasant outcomes of these people's desire, but J. brings in significant additions at 42ff., making a progression to begging, miserable penury in old age, bankruptcy and flight from Rome (and its creditors and pleasures).[20] Before that, at 38–41, he effectively highlights the aspect of excess in lines addressed to Persicus:

> quis enim te deficiente crumina
> et crescente gula manet exitus, aere paterno
> ac rebus mersis in ventrem faenoris atque   40
> argenti gravis et pecorum agrorumque capacem?

For what end awaits you as your wallet fails
and your throat grows, after you've gulped down

inherited cash and belongings into a belly capable of holding   40
interest and heavy silver plate and herds and estates?

This is an engaging question, which leaves it up to Persicus (and the general reader) to come up with a bleak scenario by way of answer. Unsettlingly, *exitus* ('end') in line 39 combines 'final state, fate' and 'end of life' and 'departure'[21] (cf. the departures of the ring that symbolizes equestrian status in line 42 and of bankrupts from Rome at 49ff.). In *deficiente crumina* ('as your wallet fails') in line 38, the noun denotes a small money bag, whose decrease contrasts ominously with the increase in *crescente gula* ('your throat grows'), while attention is drawn to these two linked and goading phrases by means of balance, alliteration and homoeoteleuton. In the latter expression, *gula* stands for 'appetite', but with its literal sense suggests a simultaneously funny and repellent image of a throat growing larger and larger (apt for a devouring gourmet). This is then taken up and developed with the surreal picture of a belly to match, making for a savage caricature of Persicus as all (huge, yawning) throat and (massive, distended) stomach. This is an arresting and memorable way of conveying the idea that a vast amount of money is spent on food which is swallowed down, and *mersis* ('gulped down') has connotations of destruction and financial ruin.[22] All of this calls to mind Erysichthon, an impious man who cut down a sacred tree in a grove of Ceres and was punished with a frenzied and insatiable hunger, which led him to spend all that he had on food, and then to raise more cash by selling his daughter, and finally to eat himself. So Persicus is associated with a figure who was immoral, stupid, destructive, obsessive and unbalanced, and who came to a bad end through his own actions. Echoes of Ovid's version of that myth in *Metamorphoses* 8 (noted by various scholars) underline the connection: compare (of Erysichthon) *iamque fame patrias altique voragine ventris / attenuarat opes* ('and now though hunger and the abyss of his deep belly he had diminished the wealth he inherited', 8.843f.) and *demisso in viscera censu* ('his fortune sent down into his innards', 8.846). But J. makes his Erysichthon even more voracious and grotesque by adding to the items consumed by him in a list that pointedly goes on and on with vigorous polysyndeton and reaches a climax in quaintness with the ingestion of heavy silver plate, herds and estates. There is another notable allusion here by our author. Horace, at *Epistles* 1.4.11, described one of Albius's many blessings as *mundus victus non deficiente crumina* ('a stylish way of life as your wallet does not fail'). J. produces a twist with bite by making the wallet fail and transferring the phrase from someone who has an elegant lifestyle within his means to one who tries to be stylish and in so doing exceeds his resources. The reminiscence also calls to mind the rest of Horace's sketch of Albius at the start of 1.4 – an admirable figure who led a quiet, relaxed existence, who was wise, moral and sensible, and who knew how to enjoy his resources properly. By way of contrast, J.'s addressee seems even more foolish and despicable, and next to the normal Albius, the misshapen Persicus of 39ff. appears even more monstrous.

At 183ff., in his second attack on desire, J. considers the effects of Persicus's aspirations on his life now rather than in the future:

> sed nunc dilatis averte negotia curis
> et gratam requiem dona tibi, quando licebit
> per totum cessare diem. non faenoris ulla   185
> mentio nec, primo si luce egressa reverti
> nocet solet, tacito bilem tibi contrahat, uxor
> umida suspectis referens multicia rugis
> vexatasque comas et vultum auremque calentem.
> protinus ante meum quidquid dolet exue limen,   190
> pone domum et servos et quidquid frangitur illis
> aut perit, ingratos ante omnia pone sodales.

But now shelve your worries, put aside business matters
and give yourself a welcome rest, as you'll be able to take
a break for the whole day. Let there be no mention of   185
interest, and don't let your wife provoke you to silent rage, if she's
in the habit of going out at dawn and returning home at night,
her thin dress damp and suspiciously wrinkled,
her hair dishevelled, and her face and ears flushed.
Right before my doorstep strip off whatever upsets you,   190
forget your home and slaves and whatever is broken or lost
by them, above all forget your friends' ingratitude.

For a start, there is again a strong sense of pointlessness, as these lines put across the idea that, far from being widely admired as a great man on the basis of his dinners, Persicus does not win respect even from his own wife and friends (J. places great emphasis on the latter in line 192, and, as one naturally invited friends to dine and this is a poem so concerned with the *cena*, their ingratitude may well operate in that context, with Persicus's attempt to win their regard for him and support for his reputation backfiring). On top of that, the mockery and public branding by the poet here would militate against widespread esteem. But, in particular, J. conveys the notion that any brief pleasure derived from such dining by the fool Persicus is totally negated by the general unhappiness of his existence while exerting himself to pay for his aspirational meals. With cumulative impact, and some graphic touches at 188f., J. takes a full ten lines to build up a picture of an empty and unpleasant life, which seems even more mean and agitated within the frame of the reading of sublime poetry as entertainment for J.'s *cena* at 180f. and the relaxation in the sun at 202f. The passage stresses Persicus's obsession with money (while financing his craving), his inability to relax properly, his extensive worries and his serious problems with relationships (one's spouse and friends have a great bearing on a person's contentment; and the slaves add to his domestic woes). With a flurry of details J. dwells on the wife, who is quite possibly misbehaving because her husband is so anxious and so focused on cash as to neglect her sexual needs, and who certainly has only contempt for his feelings and disregard for his status, as she is so blatant that word about her goings-on must get around. She flaunts her infidelity: dressed in provocative clothing[23] and habitually unfaithful, she devotes whole days to adultery, coming home with five clear indications of her vigorous activities on her person[24] and her clothing, which will be damp from sweat, semen and female secretion.[25] All of that is followed by some cruel jests in line 190: *exue* ('strip off') is a witty choice of word after the reference to the fornicating wife; and Persicus could hardly put his troubles out of his mind after J.'s vivid depiction of them at 186–9. There is also a functional reminiscence of Horace *Epistulae* 1.5.8f.,[26] where the poet invites Torquatus to a simple repast and tells him to cast off other concerns, which are defined (in one and a half lines) as hopes, the struggle for wealth and his defence of Moschus at his trial. The fact that Persicus has many more and much worse things to forget (spread over ten verses) underlines how disagreeable his life is.

At the start and end of XI J. presents the drawbacks of desire, and in between (at the heart of the poem) he addresses the object of the aspirations – wealth – and tries to show that it is simply not worth desiring anyway. He exposes the expensive things that money buys as trappings for the *cena* and impugns the rich themselves, undermining their standing and the attitudes, morals and intelligence evinced at their dinners. He represents them as in fact not admirable and stylish figures, but risible, despicable, affected and tasteless (once more with a one-sided and pessimistic point of view). At 10.12–27 wealth was depicted as entailing worry, danger and especially death, and at 10.362 (the dinners and feathers of Sardanapallus) it was associated with disgraceful dissipation (and death again) and opposed unfavourably to the virtuous Labours of Hercules. In 11 there is a further onslaught on opulence by way of reinforcement, and the attack is strengthened by more frequent digs at greater length. The satirist does not see the need to reiterate the points made forcefully at 10.12ff., but he does pick up on the criticism at 10.362, subverting additional pricey possessions extending the contrast with superior morality (now represented by the early Romans, J.'s simple *cena* and the Spartans in line 175) and really building on that brief allusion to shameful dissolution. He brings out more failings of the wealthy, to fill out the negative picture of them, and with much humour and mockery (in place of the undiluted seriousness at 10.362) he depicts them as so absurd, freakish and repulsive as to constitute the kind of person that only a moron would want to be.

He begins with disparagement of the furniture (couches for dining) and pretensions of the rich. At 90–2 he summons up the austerity and virtue of old Rome by talking of the time when people feared the censure of stern characters like the Fabii, Cato, the Scauri and Fabricius. At 93–5 he goes on to say that in those days:

> *nemo inter curas et seria duxit habendum*
> *qualis in Oceani fluctu testudo nataret*
> *clarum Troiugenis factura et nobile fulcrum.*   95

nobody thought it should be considered a matter of serious
    concern
what kind of tortoise was swimming in the ocean's waters,
about to become a splendid and illustrious head-rest for the sons
    of Troy.   95

At 96ff. he adds that their couches back then were small and inexpensive. So contemporary extravagance is pointedly swamped by early Roman morality and simplicity. The disdainful line 93, sneering at skewed values, is succeeded in 94 by the deflating tortoise, which seems perfectly banal and irrelevant, so that a concern about what kind of tortoise swam in the sea appears quaint in the extreme. Having worked in that joke, in line 95 J. suddenly reveals that in fact the shell of the tortoise will be used as a headrest (and so be a foreign import, something non-Roman), and he leaves us to wonder how significant the distinction between different kinds of tortoise really is. He sarcastically describes what is, to him, a mere couch support as 'splendid' and 'illustrious' (in contrast to its owner) and the precious types who bother about such fripperies as 'the sons of Troy',[27] thereby spotlighting their degeneration.

At 117ff. J. moves on to another item of furniture (tables), again with eloquent antithesis. At 117–19 he describes the simple, frugal and adequate tables of their ancestors, made from local wood, if the wind had brought down an old walnut tree, and then at 120ff. he progresses to his own day:

> *at nunc divitibus cenandi nulla voluptas,*   120
> *nil rhombus, nil damna sapit, putere videntur*
> *unguenta atque rosae, latos nisi sustinet orbis*
> *grande ebur et magno sublimis pardus hiatu*
> *dentibus ex illis quos mittit porta Syenes*
> *et Mauri celeres et Mauro obscurior Indus,*   125
> *et quos deposuit Nabataeo belua saltu*
> *iam nimios capitique graves. hinc surgit orexis,*
> *hinc stomacho vires; nam pes argenteus illis,*
> *anulus in digito quod ferreus.*

But these days for the rich there is no pleasure in dining –   120
the turbot has no taste, the venison has no taste, the perfumes
and roses seem to stink – unless the broad tabletop rests on a
massive piece of ivory and a rampant leopard with a great gaping
    mouth
made from those tusks which the gateway of Syene sends
and the swift Moors and the Indians darker than the Moors,   125
which the beast shed in a Nabataean forest when they'd grown too
big and heavy for its head. That's what makes for a good appetite
and a strong stomach; for in their eyes a silver table leg is
as bad as an iron ring on the finger.

At 120–7 J. produces a long sentence with cumulative impact, wittily dwelling on the table to match its size, and also because the rich make much of it. The first two and a half lines are intriguing, with their vigorous negation and striking inversion of normal sensations of taste and smell; and then it turns out that this very strong reaction is based on something as trivial as the table (as if that could affect those senses, for any reasonable and sane person!). Its importance to these ludicrously fastidious plutocrats is brought out, with more sniping, at 122ff., where what is essentially just a receptacle for food is ridiculously vast, elaborate and expensive, and also foreign. The magnitude is conveyed by a full three adjectives in rapid succession at the start – *latos* ('broad'), *grande* ('massive') and *magno* ('great') – and by the huge tusks emphatically placed at the end of the sentence and presented with comic hyperbole. The ornateness lies in the decoration of the carved leopard (with a gaping mouth that frivolously seems to mimic the diners), although the expression initially conjures up a bizarre picture of a real leopard holding up the table. In line 123, *sublimis* means primarily 'rampant', but the senses 'grand' and 'exalted'[28] may also be intended to be felt, for sarcastic effect, and to bring out, by way of contrast, the absence of such qualities in the rich.

The costliness is evident in the size of the wooden tabletop[29] and the piece of (expensively sculpted) ivory used as a support, and again there is the notion of excess, in *nimios* ('too big') in 127. There is also much here that is not Roman, and this alien taint is meant to attach to the opulent owner who prizes such stuff. With regard to provenance and ornamentation, the elephant and the leopard are foreign animals and are supposed to look bad beside the Roman wolf and the ass and soldier's horse mentioned recently at lines 97, 103 and 104. The *per se* grotesque elephant is designated by means of the pejorative *belua* ('beast') in 126,[30] and the outlandish (but in fact inaccurate) shedding of the tusks intimates that the well-heeled with their twisted viewpoint attach value to the mere refuse of this monster.[31] At 124ff. J. dwells with distaste on the extraneous sources of ivory.[32] *Obscurior* ('darker') has negative connotations: the adjective can also mean 'gloomy', 'undistinguished', 'secretive' and 'incomprehensible',[33] while blackness in ancient thought was connected with ill omen, evil and death.[34] Line 125 also brings to mind Lucan 4.678–80: *concolor Indo / Maurus ... / Marmaridae volucres* ('Moors of the same colour as Indians ... speedy Marmaridae'). There the men are tribesmen in a list of formidable fighters, so that the echo has a touch of off-putting menace and creates antithesis to affected rich people indolently dining.

In the next sentence, at 127ff. there is the crazy idea of a table inspiring hunger and affecting digestion (compare 120f.). In line 127 *orexis* ('appetite') is a Greek word (even their appetite is foreign)[35] and a very unusual word (for a very unusual attitude); it has repellent associations too, as before here it only appears at *Satire* 6.428, in connection with a wife who drinks two pints of wine to build up a raging appetite and then vomits copiously. As a last dig, the sentence also contains the laughably unbalanced snobbery that views a table support made of silver rather than ivory as being as mean and vulgar as the iron ring that marked out the plebeian.

In the lines that follow, J. states that he has no ivory at all in his house, and even the handles of his knives are bone, but the food is not spoiled because of it. He then puts the focus on a different possession, expensive slaves – the Phrygian and Lycian of line 147 and especially the expert *structor* ('carver') of 136ff. In another sentence of quite some length that adds point after point, J. targets the rich and their fare as well as the carver. One can easily infer that only a mad fool would pay lots of money for someone just to cut meat, especially after 5.120ff., where the satirist openly derided the showy gyrations and flourishes of the trained *structor* and the notion that the proper gestures for the carving of hares and hens were vitally important. At 10.136ff. the carver is shown as practising at his instructor's studio on a whole host of (in particular large, exotic and expensive) animals – hare, boar, a big sow's udder, antelope, pheasants, a huge flamingo and a gazelle.

This is the food of the wealthy, and taken all together it constitutes the kind of (excessive) feast that they put on, and is described as a *lautissima* ... / ... *cena* ('really stylish dinner') at 140f. But again the seeming stylishness is punctuated. The food is belittled by being designated by (to our poet) distasteful .Greek words[36] and references to its alien provenance, and by a deflation at the end of the sentence that also discredits the *structor*. For at 140f. it is suddenly revealed that these carcasses are only wooden models for him to practise on with a blunt carving knife, and he is making such a racket fatuously hacking away at this *ulmea cena* ('elmwood dinner') that he can even be heard in the noisy Subura (and the vulgarity of that district adds to the bathos).[37] Then at 142ff. J. states that his own slave, an ordinary local lad, only pinches tiny cutlets from dinner and does not know how to steal a hunk of venison or a slice of guinea fowl; so the expert carver is an expert thief, and this costly purchase engages in costly depredation.

At 162ff. J. progresses to the entertainment at dinners of the well-to-do, the kind of thing they buy with all their money, when he remarks to Persicus that he may be expecting sexy Spanish chorus girls. This is the only type of mealtime recreation ascribed to the rich, and it is meant to portray them as woefully deficient in morals, intellect, dignity and taste, although in reality some were refined (like Seneca) or at least had intellectual pretensions (compare Trimalchio and Habinnas).[38] These Spanish dances with their castanets (172) are also non-Roman. From the start J. reduces them to pure eroticism, with no mention of any skill in singing or dancing. Initially we are shown obscene actions, as the females sink to the floor with shimmying bottoms. Then we see the effect of this, in the erections and secretions of the onlookers. After a brief aside in line 171 describing such performances as frivolous and negligible trash,[39] J. moves on to the obscene words in the girls' songs – according to him, the kind of language avoided by even the lowest whore standing for hire in a stinking brothel. He says that he leaves the enjoyment of such pornography to the moneybags who tastes wine and spits it out on to his floor of fine Spartan marble, thereby making us think of the starkly contrasting discipline, austerity and militarism of the Spartans. At 176–8 J. adds gambling and adultery to the faults of the wealthy, complaining of the lack of logic and fairness whereby for such scandalous behaviour they, unlike lesser mortals, are called elegant and full of fun. With a final thrust at 179ff. he moves on to the much quieter and calmer entertainment at his own *cena* – readings from the *Iliad* and *Aeneid*. Once more there is functional antithesis: the recitation of lofty and morally improving[40] poetry with stimulation for the mind rather than the penis underlines how debased and debasing (in J.'s eyes) the Spanish dancing is; the active fighting heroes of the epics are opposed to the passive, aroused spectators at the dinner party; and the allusion to their illustrious Trojan ancestors points up the degeneration of contemporary well-heeled Romans.

The fourth major element of *Satire* 10 taken up here is *virtus* ('moral excellence'), which now receives further examination and definition. J. listed various qualities that lead to a peaceful life at 10.356–62. By way of support in 11, as we have seen, he presents a strongly negative picture of some of their opposites – cravings, extravagant dinners, luxury and an unsound mind. There is also expansion, as J. fills out the picture by parading for our edification several other virtuous traits and depicting them in a good light – recognizing and keeping within one's limits (27ff.), honesty (56ff.), hospitality (65ff.), simplicity (64ff., 96ff., 117ff., 131ff., 145ff.) and moderation in one's lifestyle (64ff., 78ff., 131ff.). In line with his position at the end of 10, the poet is here practising *virtus* himself, as his *cena* incorporates all these traits, and at 201ff. he shows himself, the champion and possessor of these moral qualities, enjoying a peaceful life.

Although not everybody will see a tranquil existence as particularly desirable, and some may feel that the moralising in 11 is rather trite, J. does attempt to convey his advocacy of *virtus* in a vigorous and engaging fashion. He claims divine support for these traits twice (in 27 and at 111ff.), and he associates them with revered Roman prehistory (Evander and Aeneas at 60ff.) and with the early Romans, at length and in a central position (77ff.). He also tries to make his virtuous dinner seem attractive to the general reader by means of all the wholesome and tasty food (65ff.), the recitation of great poetry as entertainment (179ff.) and the appealing and touching servants (142ff.). He employs wit and humour too, in an effort to ensure that his case is palatable for us and punchy. As has been noted, in general the satirist is mischievously taunting Persicus by stressing how much the *cena* will not be to his taste and putting him on the spot over withdrawing at this stage from such a moral meal. There are also many individual instances of ridicule and jesting. For example, at 58f. J. has fun with the idea that all his fine talk might just be hypocrisy, and he might sing the praises of beans while being a secret glutton, and make a show of asking his slave before others to serve him porridge but slyly whisper in his ear that he wants pastries; at 103ff. there is the grisly joke about the last thing that a dying enemy sees being a Roman helmet's decoration depicting Mars descending to rape Ilia, naked (possibly erect) and about to father the progenitor of the enemy's own killer; and at 134f. J. derides Persicus's pretensions by (mock-)solemnly informing him that the bone handles of J.'s knives do not adversely affect the food that he serves and make it rancid.

A good extended instance of the bite that our poet thus achieves in this connection occurs at 27–38, where he not only adds knowing and staying within one's limits to the definition of moral excellence in 10, but also revisits its theme of desire:

> *e caelo descendit* γνῶθι σεαυτόν
> *figendum et memori tractandum pectore, sive*
> *coniugium quaeras vel sacri in parte senatus*
> *esse velis; neque enim loricam poscit Achillis*   30
> *Thersites, in qua se traducebat Ulixes;*
> *ancipitem seu tu magno discrimine causam*
> *protegere adfectas, te consule, dic tibi qui sis,*
> *orator vehemens an Curtius et Matho buccae.*
> *noscenda est mensura sui spectandaque rebus*   35
> *in summis minimisque, etiam cum piscis emetur,*
> *ne mullum cupias cum sit tibi gobio tantum*
> *in loculis.*

> From heaven comes down 'KNOW YOURSELF',
> which should be fixed and pondered in your unforgetting heart,
>   whether
> you are looking for a wife or want to have a seat in the sacred
> senate; for Thersites does not demand Achilles's   30
> breastplate, in which Ulysses made a fool of himself.
> If you aspire to defend a difficult and highly critical
> case, take stock of yourself, tell yourself who you are –
> a forceful orator or a Curtius or Matho (mere mouths).
> A person must know his measure and pay regard to it   35
> in important and trivial matters, even when a fish is bought,
> so you don't desire a mullet when you have only a gudgeon
> in your cash box.

The sentence before this had just ended with mention of a treasure chest and a money bag, so the progression in line 27 to the weighty maxim inscribed in Apollo's temple at Delphi is striking. That line is in itself arresting and mysterious – are we to imagine 'KNOW YOURSELF' coming down in verbal or written form? All of this, and the authoritative provenance of the injunction, means that it should receive attention; and line 28 remarks on the need for that openly and fully, with grave spondees. At the same time, there is the flippant touch of quoting Greek to Persicus (whose name means 'Persian'). There are barbs for him too, starting in 29, as we subsequently realize. There J. has him looking for a spouse (after the warning at 10.350ff.!), and the necessity of careful deliberation in this matter and awareness of one's nature and limitations represents an obvious dig in view of the contempt for him demonstrated by the wife he has chosen at 186ff. J. also raises mockingly the possibility of this ridiculous fool, who cannot even regulate his own home properly, aspiring to a place on the august and revered senate. The mythological *exemplum* at 30f. refers to the famous contest for the arms of Achilles after his death, which was won by the crafty Ulysses rather than the brave Ajax. The implication is that Persicus might overreach himself, and he is thus likened to Thersites (a repulsive and contemptible figure, who got above himself in criticizing Agamemnon, until humiliated by a thrashing)[41] or at best Ulysses making an exhibition of himself in divine armour that he does not measure up to (and Ulysses, who was also fond of food and possessions, was often depicted in a hostile light).[42] There is also the joke of comparing Persicus to a *Greek* hero, indeed to any epic hero. At 30ff. J. has him perhaps fancying himself as a lawyer, in a very difficult case at that (stressed in 32), and sneeringly tells him to work out whether he is a forceful speaker (this man who cannot even influence his own wife and friends) or just a windbag. The definition of such a person as a 'mouth' is well aimed at the gourmet Persicus. As examples of the windbag, J. cites Curtius and Matho. The former is unknown, but the latter, significantly, figures in 1.32f. as a dubious lawyer, prospering much to the poet's annoyance, but only temporarily, because by 7.129 he has gone bankrupt. After the solemn restatement of the importance of 'KNOW YOURSELF' at 35f., J. comically[43] but pointedly brings it down to the level of cash and food. Actually he brings it down to the level of fish, distinguishing between the expensive mullet and the small and cheap gudgeon which was eaten by the poor. With the final words of the sentence J. means having only the price of a gudgeon in one's cash box, but the expression creates a bizarre image of an actual fish in the cash box (which would render one absolutely unable to pay for a mullet). In addition, *ne mullum cupias* ('so you don't desire a mullet') represents a playful twist to *cupiat nihil* ('desires nothing') at 10.360.

To move on to XII, again this is a satire that has much of interest and significance in its own right. So, for instance, scholars have studied its relationship to Martial,[44] and generic aspects, looking at it as a prosphoneticon (a poem of welcome to a traveller)[45] and commenting on how epic and tragic sublimity are deflated by elements of lower genres;[46] others examine its treatment of the topics of *captatio* ('will-hunting') and friendship[47] or consider it as a poem about the ties that bind men to gods and gods to men[48] or an explanation of lost masculinity linked with greed.[49] But again a major function of *Satire* 12 lies in its close connection with 10 (and also 11). Before we look at that aspect it is necessary to clarify the background situation and the overall thrust of 12, controversial issues that have a vital bearing on overall interpretation.

At 12.1–16 J. tells the addressee (Corvinus) that this day, on which he will pay his vow to the gods, is sweeter to him than his own birthday. The victims (sacrificial animals) consist of a lamb each for Juno and Minerva and a spirited calf for Jupiter, and the poet says that if he had the money to match his feelings he would be offering a prize bull fatter than Hispulla. The offerings (made on the Capitoline Hill in Rome) are made on behalf of his friend Catullus, who is still trembling after a terrible experience and is amazed to be alive. At 17ff. J. reveals that Catullus is a merchant who got caught in a bad storm during a recent trading trip. There was dense darkness and a thunderbolt suddenly struck the yardarms, setting the sails on fire and causing general panic. J. remarks that this is what happens whenever a poetic storm blows up. He then moves on to more danger, which he says is of the kind experienced by many people at sea and depicted in votive offerings by survivors. When the tossing ship was half-full of water and beyond the helmsman's help, Catullus began to do a deal with the winds by jettisoning cargo, like the beaver, which, to escape capture, bites off its own testicles (containing a valuable secretion used in medicine) and leaves them behind for those hunting it. Catullus hurled overboard the most beautiful items, such as a purple robe fit for Maecenas, fabrics made from the finest wool, silverware, expensive salvers, a huge mixing bowl, a thousand plates and many embossed goblets. The poet wonders who else has the nerve to set his own life above his possessions. When even throwing things overboard did not help, Catullus chopped down the mast. Go, says J., entrust your life to the winds and place confidence in a ship's thin planks of wood; in future, when you sail, take axes with you for use in a storm. But the sea grew calm, thanks to the kindly Fates, and the gale dropped to a moderate breeze, and the pitiful ship ran on propelled by its single surviving sail and clothes spread out in place of sails. It passed Mount Alba (which Aeneas's son Iulus named after a marvellous white sow he saw there), where he founded the city Alba Longa. Finally it entered the *portus Augusti*, the wonderful harbour near Rome with its safe, calm water, where they landed. At 83ff. J. returns to his vow, telling his slaves to go silently and see to the preparations, so he can make offerings on the Capitoline Hill and then at home to Jupiter and the Lares as well. At this point (line 93) the satirist assures Corvinus that there is nothing suspect about his actions because Catullus has three sons and heirs (so J. can't be trying to worm his way into Catullus's will). Nobody would waste even the cheapest of offerings on a 'friend' who is a man with children. But if a rich person with no children starts to feel a fever, the entire colonnade is covered with tablets containing vows by those hoping to be named as heirs, and some people even promise to sacrifice a hundred oxen in return for the recovery of the wealthy person. They would readily vow elephants if they could, but those in Italy belong to the emperor. One of these will-hunters (Pacuvius), if it were allowed, would offer up his slaves or even his daughter, if he had one at home (like Agamemnon sacrificing Iphigenia). J. praises Pacuvius, because if the sick man escapes death, he will include him in his will and perhaps make him his sole heir, so the loss of the daughter will be well worthwhile. The poet prays that Pacuvius lives as long as Nestor and has masses of money, loving nobody and loved by nobody.

We cannot tell if Corvinus and Catullus are real or invented. Critics generally agree that Corvinus is a *captator* ('will-hunter'): his name is connected with *corvus* ('raven'), and will-hunters were quite often compared to carrion-eating birds;[50] J. attributes to him the mindset of a *captator* in line 93, when he has him automatically suspect that the satirist is trying to get himself named in Catullus's will; and there would be real pertinence in addressing to such a character a poem attacking greed in general and will-hunting in particular (with a sharpening of focus for the onslaught at 93ff.). However, there is disagreement among scholars about Catullus, and although many feel that he is not really a friend of the poet,[51] some assume that he is. It is in fact highly unlikely that Catullus was, or was supposed to be, a friend or that J. would want to parade him publicly as one, especially after X and XI. The satirist's highly critical attitude to traders is evident at 14.265ff.[52] Catullus has on board lots of the kind of luxury items that were impugned in 11, and he obviously prizes wealth highly, is certainly not free from cravings or fear of death, but does lack a sound mind in J.'s view. He is not portrayed sympathetically here, and is in fact disparaged and ridiculed extensively. As J. is presented as not having been personally on board the ship, his narrative of the storm at 17ff. must be actually or supposedly based on Catullus's own version of it, and comically the merchant does not show himself in a good light at all. The more he goes on about how terrible the tempest was and how serious his losses were, the more stupid and crazy he is meant to seem for exposing himself to such peril and financial damage; and this point is underlined at 57ff., where J. scoffs at the idea of entrusting one's life to the winds and a ship's flimsy wooden structure. Catullus is far from dignified too, panicking during the storm, and (15f.) still fearful long after it is over. J. also subverts Catullus's description of the incident, puncturing the solemnity and ruining the impact by breaking up the flow of the account from early on and throughout with asides of his own, which are not only distracting but also often derisive. So, most notably at 22–4, when he says this is what happens when a poetic storm arises, he is accusing Catullus of exaggerating and building up his storm into an epic tempest (compare the crew telling long-winded stories about the danger they went through after they land in line 82). Right after that, at 25–8, he remarks essentially that this was just a normal risk of the voyage (not something extraordinary, as Catullus seems to present it), since many people have experienced storms, and survived. At 33–6 there is the joke of the trader doing a deal with the winds, which represents him as a bankrupt and the gales as creditors (!) who want his life, body and goods, but would be satisfied with partial payment (just the possessions);[53] and there is also the demeaning comparison of Catullus to a self-castrating beaver, which mocks his desperation and the pain he must have felt over the loss, and intimates that he values his luxury goods on a par with his testicles, so that now he has lost a major part of himself and is a contemptible eunuch, and equal to an animal. At 38ff. the long list of things thrown over the side takes one away from the storm, and one is also sidetracked by the implicit criticism there of Catullus's greed and funk and by the schadenfreude (over the jettisoning of so many expensive items and the fact that they are all hurled away in vain). Lines 57–61 also interrupt the narrative of the tempest, and laugh at Catullus's madness in entrusting himself to winds and a frail ship, and imply that the fool will actually do it all over again, not having learnt his lesson, and so should take axes with him the next time he sails.[54] At 62ff., when talking of the calm that ensued and the wonderful harbour reached by the ship, the poet will still be quoting Catullus, so the effusiveness and prolixity there represent his cowardly relief as he burbles on and on, and J. is jeeringly reproducing his maundering verbiage. The epic allusions at 70ff. in connection with Mount Alba[55] also make Catullus look bad by way of contrast.

All of the above means that when J. calls Catullus an *amicus* ('friend') in line 16 he is using the word ironically, as he does elsewhere.[56] It also means that the satirist's vow and offerings are fabrications[57] (on the many good reasons for this, see below). In line with this, J. pokes fun at them, so that the alert reader will not take them seriously. Although most readers will initially be misled into thinking that J. is being sincere at 1–16, there are hints that he may not be so solemn in those lines. On a first reading the earnestness and elaborate detail about the sacrifices should strike us as suspicious so soon after the ridicule of that religious practice at 10.354f.; and there is obvious frivolity in the notion in line 8 of an embarrassed calf (ashamed to pull at its mother's teats) and in the reference in line 11 to a bull fatter than Hispulla, who was presumably an extremely large lady, and figured in 6.74 as a slut, so that the tone is lowered here. In retrospect, after we learn the truth about J.'s attitude to his 'friend', we can see more undermining. It is clearly excessive to offer quite expensive victims to the revered Capitoline triad of Juno, Minerva and Jupiter for the return of this despised fool. And in line 1, where J. claims that the day of sacrifice is sweeter to him than his own birthday, there is flippant topping of Horace *Odes* 4.11.17f., where the poet says that the birthday of his beloved and respected patron Maecenas is *almost* more special than his own. At 83ff., when J. returns to the vow and offerings after the revealing passage on the storm, the irony should by now be obvious. It is underscored by a couple of verbal twists that point back to the lines on the tempest. In line 83, *ite* ('go', plural) recalls *i* ('go', singular) in line 57, where Catullus was told to go and entrust his life to winds, reminding us of the satirist's contempt for him; and in 90, when J. talks of himself throwing flowers as part of his offerings, he uses the verb *iacto*, which had been employed in line 52 of the terrified trader throwing his goods into the sea. In line 83, when he orders his slave boys to maintain ritual silence, there may well be a dig at the very recent garrulity of Catullus (and the rest of the crew). And at 93f., when he mentions putting up laurel branches on the door of his house and lighting lamps in rejoicing, he talks of the door itself putting up long branches and performing rites in a festive mood with its morning lamps and thus employs a personification which is quaint and also makes for droll inversion of Catullus cutting down the wooden mast of the ship.

The main satirical thrust of XII is an attack on greed, as seen in the trader Catullus and the *captator*, who are depicted at 48f. and 95ff. as representatives of a malaise found throughout Rome and the whole world (another questionable generalization). There is impact in the twofold assault, with sensational illustration each time, and the second half of the poem (93ff.), far from being a pale repetition, is more forceful with its sinister figure of the will-hunter and his much more horrific character and conduct. Corvinus is addressed twice, in lines 1 and 93, in prominent positions at the start of each half,[58] so the whole piece is directed at him, criticizing his outlook and way of life; but, of course, there is a message for other readers too and criticism of society generally. Here J. resumes and develops further three elements from X – wealth, desire and prayer[59] (also picking up from the treatment of the first two in XI). And he weaves them together dexterously: the desire is for wealth and in the first half the (invented) prayer is for a trader who sailed off in his craving for riches, while in the second half the prayers are made by will-hunters yearning for lots of money.

J. further reinforces the onslaught on opulence begun in *Satire* 10. As in 11, he disparages the things bought by cash and impugns the rich themselves. While listing at 38–47 the luxury goods cast overboard by Catullus during the storm, J. works in attacks on pricey possessions. He subverts them at 40–2, when talking of the provenance of expensive woollen fabrics, by bloated and bombastic expression for mere sheep, and also at 44f., by means of the notion of excess in a mixing bowl big enough to hold three gallons. He attaches pejorative associations to them as well: in line 39, a robe is said to be fit for soft types like Maecenas, who was notorious for indolence, luxury and effeminacy; at 43f. there are dishes made (most probably) for Parthenius, the treacherous chamberlain of Domitian; in line 45 there is a mixing bowl worthy of the hard-drinking and violent Centaur Pholus and of Fuscus's wife, who is obviously a drunkard; and at 46f. there are goblets which once belonged to Philip II of Macedon, with allusion to his cunning and use of bribery to take the town of Olynthus.[60] As for the wealthy, they are presented as far from enviable or admirable figures at 98ff., where the will-hunters care not for them but only for their money. There is some highly unflattering (and dubious) speculation at 122ff., where J. repeats the idea found in *Satire* 11 of the rich being stupid and immoral, but gives those failings a more extreme and outrageous form. There he imagines Pacuvius vowing his own daughter in return for the recovery of a sick moneybags and claims that if the latter does survive, he will change his will to include Pacuvius and might leave everything to him, taken in by this obvious ploy and acquiescing to human sacrifice and the man's murder of his own daughter. In *Satire* 12 J. also adds something not found in 10 or 11 with the humiliating and sardonic imagery in line 123, which describes the well-heeled invalid who has been fooled like this as caught in a fisherman's trap. This portrays him as a *fish*, rather than a grand man who is stylish and respected, and also mere prey, ignorant of what is going on, a vulnerable and unloved source of sustenance trapped by an efficient and indifferent operator.

After recommending that we desire nothing at 10.360, and showing the bad effects of a particular craving (for fine food) in 11, J. here presents another concrete example of desire (for wealth itself) and its drawbacks, adding more aspirants (the representative trader Catullus and various will-hunters), to suggest how widespread this failing is, and providing detailed and memorable illustration for impact. As in 11, J. depicts himself as free from yearning, makes a twofold attack and includes the key themes of harmfulness (Catullus very nearly loses his life; the *captator* would kill people), excess (in Catullus's luxurious possessions, and in the will-hunters' sacrifices) and pointlessness (Catullus loses a huge amount of money in the attempt to make more, and rich possessions and the wealthy themselves are represented as not at all admirable anyway). The satirist repeats some of the criticisms of desire found in 11 to bolster them, and aims at intensification, bringing in new points, to extend the assault.

In the first half of XII, as in XI, the aspirant is put across as a stupid, undignified and ridiculous figure, likely to become notorious (because of his own exaggeration and J.'s poem), and also as a madman, crazy for having exposed himself to the storm and (60f.) being ready to do so all over again for the sake of riches. But Catullus is even more of a moronic lunatic than Persicus and co. Here, instead of life being generally unpleasant and the unstated possibility of being killed as a gladiator, we find the great terror to which the aspirant subjected himself (caught at length from line 15 onwards) and a very real danger of death conveyed graphically. In addition, because Catullus has three little sons (94f.), he also ran a risk of orphaning them and ruining their lives too.[61] There is also a wry connection with 10.12ff., on the perils of the actual possession of wealth: you nearly kill yourself acquiring it, and, if you do get it, your life is put in danger all over again.

At 93ff. the *captator* is again painted as foolish (for wanting to join the rich, who are just unloved prey) and unbalanced (fully prepared for human sacrifice and the murder of his own daughter). But now, climactically, the stress is on his supreme immorality; and he is repulsive rather than just absurd and lacking in dignity. He is portrayed as more appalling than Catullus (and anyone in XI), potentially bringing death to others rather than himself, ready to end the life of his own daughter (rather than disregarding the risk of his sons being orphaned) and prepared to commit horrific acts himself instead of enduring a horrific storm (15). Desire here has a variously criminalizing and dehumanizing effect, corrupting friendship, kinship and religion, and the will-hunters subject to it are shown to be more and more evil as part of the climactic effect. At 95-8 they are mean and calculating in not being prepared to make offerings for a 'friend' with children and heirs. At 99-101 they are deceitful, cunning and extravagant, as they hurry to make vows for childless rich people who are sick and even promise a hecatomb. The extravagance goes over the top at 111-14, where two will-hunters are ready to sacrifice an elephant, if it would ensure they inherited. There is a sinister progression at 115-17, where the murderous and irreligious Pacuvius would vow to sacrifice his slaves, and then, still more shockingly, at 118-20 he would offer his offspring as victim. Finally, 125f. depict that ploy as working and Pacuvius being named heir, and then demonstrating arrogance and a callous lack of remorse and concern about the death of his daughter. Essentially, the *captator* is depicted as being prepared to go to any lengths to satisfy his desire, with forceful (and problematical) conjecture and hyperbole.

When reprising the topic of prayer, J. keeps up the mixture of flippancy and seriousness found in X, but the frivolity takes a novel form at 1ff., and there is harsher criticism of the petitioners and the requests they make at 93ff. In the first half of the satire, J. has fun with the *votum* ('vow'), sacrifice and the *quid pro quo* in a manner reminiscent of 10.354f. in particular, but this time he deftly employs them in a great variety of ways. Since Catullus was not really a friend and the *votum* is a fabrication, there is irony here, the poet being aptly and wickedly slippery in connection with a trader given to exaggeration. He is also wittily providing poetic offerings (just described in poetry, not actually made) in return for survival of a poetic storm; and he is matching and parodying Catullus's extravagance and prolixity over the tempest (in particular, running on and on about the ceremony all over again at 83ff. looks like a send-up of the way in which the trader burbled on and on about the storm's aftermath just before that at 62ff.). The pretence of friendship and concern for a person's well-being evinced in a *votum* also mimics and mocks such pretence by the *captator*;[62] and in addition there is the subtle joke of the satirist being insincere and just using a vow like such a character, but doing it not in a reprehensible way but to work in a dig at the will-hunter's misuse of the *votum*. J. may be assumed to be teasing Corvinus too, parading before him a prospective victim and a means of getting to him, only to dash his hopes by finally revealing that he has three sons at 94f. There is teasing of the reader as well: at 1–16, J. intimates via the promised sacrifice that he is absolutely delighted at the survival of a good friend, only to invalidate all that subsequently; and at 83–92 the return to the vow provides ring structure, which suggests that the poem is over, so that the continuation and new direction at 93ff. catch one's attention.

The picture at 93ff. is much darker, with hard-hitting censure of Corvinus and his ilk, and mounting hypocrisy and horror. Again there is amplification and intensification in connection with a topic of *Satire* 10. The criticism is now stronger: here prayer is not misguided and foolish, as in X, but immoral and irreligious, and those praying are repellent and depraved rather than laughable. Further contrasts with 10 underline the bleaker vision and greater condemnation of the petitioners. The appeals made in X were sincere, if poorly judged; here they are merely made for show. Prayers for others were uttered out of genuine concern for them at 10.289ff. (appeals for beauty for offspring), but here are entirely selfish; and they brought harm to others in an accidental way there, but do so in a decidedly deliberate fashion here (the human victims at 116ff.). It is all very calculating and mercenary, which represents a grim twist to the *quid pro quo* notion, presenting it in a grubby light; and the sacrifice that J. poked fun at in 10.355 becomes something grotesque in the case of the elephant and heinous in the cases of the slaves and daughter. In addition, the satirist is here accentuating the value and importance of his advice in the conclusion of the tenth satire by sketching in lurid colours more of the kind of thing that happens when people don't leave it to the gods to give them what is fitting and don't ask heaven for or acquire by themselves the qualities listed at 10.356ff., especially a sound mind and a freedom from desire and from regard for wealth.

The conclusion of the poem repays a closer look, as it is an instructive example of the vigour, humour and point in J.'s treatment of the interwoven themes of wealth, desire and prayer. After mentioning Novius and Pacuvius, two will-hunters who would readily sacrifice elephants in order to inherit, at

115ff. J. considers Pacuvius on his own (a character who bears the name of a highly respected Roman tragedian!):

> *alter enim, si concedas, mactare vovebit*   115
> *de grege servorum magna et pulcherrima quaeque*
> *corpora, vel pueris et frontibus ancillarum*
> *inponet vittas et, si qua est nubilis illi*
> *Iphigenia domi, dabit hanc altaribus, etsi*
> *non sperat tragicae furtiva piacula cervae.*   120
> *laudo meum civem, nec comparo testamento*
> *mille rates; nam si Libitinam evaserit aeger,*
> *delebit tabulas inclusus carcere nassae*
> *post meritum sane mirandum atque omnia soli*
> *forsan Pacuvio breviter dabit, ille superbus*   125
> *incedet victis rivalibus. ergo vides quam*
> *grande operae pretium faciat iugulata Mycenis.*
> *vivat Pacuvius quaeso vel Nestora totum,*
> *possideat quantum rapuit Nero, montibus aurum*
> *exaequet, nec amet quemquam nec ametur ab ullo.*   130

For the latter, if you allowed it, will vow to sacrifice   115
from his band of slaves full-grown ones, and the most handsome
  of them,[63]
or he'll place sacrificial headbands on slave boys and
slave girls' foreheads, and if he has at home an Iphigenia
of marriageable age, he'll offer her at an altar, even though
he has no hope of a secret expiatory victim (the deer of tragedy). 120
I praise my fellow citizen and don't regard a thousand ships as
on a par with a will: for if the invalid escapes Libitina,
he'll destroy his testament, imprisoned in the fisherman's trap,
after that truly amazing service, and perhaps in a short
will he'll leave everything to Pacuvius alone. He will strut about, 125
proud at the defeat of his rivals. So you see how
very worthwhile is the slaughter of the girl from Mycenae.
May Pacuvius live, I pray, even as long as Nestor did,
may he possess as much as Nero stole, pile up his gold as high
as mountains, and not love anyone or be loved by anybody.   130

The will-hunters' employment of vows had been depicted as widespread at 95ff. and took a drastic turn (the hecatomb) at 101, but at 111ff. it is shown as not far from being totally out of control, where the *captator* would offer an elephant if he could, but would not stop at that, being ready to slaughter humans in a form of sacrifice which is appalling rather than grotesque, and which represents a climax of extremity, immorality and insanity. In line 115 *si concedas* ('if you allowed it') may be addressed to a general 'you', but has most bite if it is flippantly directed at the will-hunter Corvinus, who very probably *would* allow such conduct. At the end of that line the religious language of *mactare vovebit* ('will vow to sacrifice') enhances the impact of the (carefully delayed) sacrilegious victims who follow. To show his concern for the recovery of the well-off invalid, Pacuvius will offer a plurality of humans, beginning with handsome adult slaves and also young ones, and then moving on to the still greater concession of his own offspring (again deliberately postponed). The scenario is meant to arouse in us feelings of sadness and abhorrence. There is the loss of beauty, the lives cut short and the snuffing out of a girl who will now never marry at the hands of her own father, and the spondees at the end of line 117 and in 118 have a mournful air. There is also the wily expenditure in expectation of a greater return and the step up in profiting from death, as the *captator* now does not simply wait for his rich prey to die but actually inflicts death as well, and becomes in the process a mass murderer guilty of supreme *impietas*, with no sense of duty to his family or the gods.

J. designates Pacuvius's child by allusion to Iphigenia, the daughter of Agamemnon, who had to offer her up in atonement for offending Diana, so that the Greek force could sail off to Troy after Helen. In one version of the story (found in tragedy), at the moment of sacrifice Diana stealthily substituted a deer for Iphigenia, who was transported to Tauris and subsequently reunited with her brother and returned to Greece. The mythological reference turns the will-hunter's daughter into a similarly innocent and touching figure, but there is no escape and no happy ending for that poor girl, who *will* be killed by her father. All this makes Pacuvius look bad, as does the correspondence between that selfish wretch and the noble, famous and powerful king who performed the rite out of concern for others, and who went on to the major exploit of taking Troy, in contrast to Pacuvius's mean little victory over his rivals (126). In line 120 J. adds substantially to the condemnation. This is a full line to stress that the will-hunter acts in the knowledge that there is no hope of a miraculous substitution, with homoeoteleuton, balance and chiasmus in the final four words drawing attention. The mention of tragedy highlights the sordidness of his behaviour, and there is also point in *non sperat* ('he has no hope') – he has hopes of inheriting instead – and *furtiva* ('secret') – the only secrecy here is on the part of the *captator*, who is concealing his real feelings and motives.

Someone driven to such lengths by his yearning for money seems truly barbaric, and so there is a surprise at 121ff. in J.'s praise of Pacuvius (which is in fact ironical) and in the opulent invalid (genuinely) being taken in by and condoning such conduct. The will-hunter's ploy is patent, the offerings of such victims clearly aimed at the moneybags rather than the gods. It should make the wealthy man feel revulsion and shun the *captator*, who is thus betraying the fact that he has no feeling for his fellow humans, and so must be stalking him. Such wickedness and sacrilege would not appeal to deities, so the recovery from illness can hardly be due to them, and it might even involve the well-heeled prey in divine retribution, as well as ruining his reputation, for approving of murder. When, despite all this, Pacuvius is included in the will at 123f., we see the stupidity and depravity of the rich.

At 121f. there is heavy irony not only in the praise of the *captator* but also in the notion that his petty and grubby achievement of having himself included in a testament is on a par with securing the Greek expedition's departure for Troy, as the poet juxtaposes the thousand ships with the singular will, denoted by *testamento*, with spurious gravity in the fifth-foot spondee. The insincerity is mischievously appropriate in a statement about one will-hunter addressed to another. With *meum civem* ('my fellow citizen'), whom he applauds in contrast to Agamemnon, J. may even be having fun with the anti-Greek and pro-Roman stance in his earlier satires.[64] *Laudo* ('I praise') looks back to 4.18f. and the ironical approbation there (expressed with *laudo*) of a trick assigned to the Egyptian Crispinus for getting himself named as the heir of a rich person. J. thus associates Pacuvius with a foreigner while calling him a fellow citizen, and ties him in with a hated and sinister upstart to boot.[65] In line 122, with *si Libitinam evaserit aeger* ('if the invalid escapes Libitina' – a goddess of death) J. recalls *Odes* 3.30.6f., where Horace, claiming that his first three books of lyric poems will last as long as Rome does, constantly fresh with the praise of posterity, says *non omnis moriar, multaque pars mei / vitabit Libitinam* ('I will not wholly die, and a large part of me will elude Libitina'). J. is thus likening the inane and immoral rich man who is a reviled target of his poetry, and who will live on temporarily as a dupe, to wise and morally improving poetry which will win approval and live on forever in glory.

At 123-5, amid mock-solemn spondees, as part of this broadened-out attack on the representative of wealth as well as the exemplar of desire, J. includes a cutting image from fishing (on which see above) and depicts the plutocrat as idiotic enough not just to change his will so that it now includes Pacuvius but perhaps even to leave everything to the *captator* (which would entail dropping his family and friends, who would have genuine affection for him) and also, with an equally unbalanced outlook, to regard the murder of the girl as a meritorious action, and a really marvellous one at that – with play by the satirist on the less positive senses 'extraordinary' and 'bewildering' in *mirandum* ('amazing').[66] Given the mythological allusion in this passage, at 125f. the detail of the proud strutting readily brings to mind the ominous scene in Aeschylus *Agamemnon* 910ff. in which the victorious king walks on purple vestments, a misguided and sacrilegious act of hybris. In addition to these negative connotations there is the fact that things subsequently went badly for Agamemnon (cf. 128ff. below), when he was assassinated. The actual wording of 125f. echoes Horace *Epodes* 15.17f. (addressed to a despised rival who has supplanted Horace in the affections of the fickle Neaera): *meo nunc / superbus incedis malo* ('you now strut about, proud because of my misfortune'). The reminiscence comes with an aura of hatred and contempt, and with tawdry associations (of infidelity); and again there is a suggestion of comeuppance ahead, because Horace went on immediately to maintain that even if the man had great wealth he would be unloved (by Neaera) and unhappy (cf. 128ff.). Lines 126f. put craving for cash in a really bad light by presenting the point of view of the *captator* in connection with the murder of his child (again likened to Iphigenia, daughter of the king of Mycenae). J. brings out the awfulness of that deed by means of *iugulata* (translated as 'the slaughter of'), a callous[67] and grimly graphic word (the verb means 'to kill by cutting the throat, kill by violent means'), next to the rare and poetic *Mycenis* ('girl from Mycenae').[68] But the unrepentant Pacuvius sees the act purely in financial terms, and considers it a great deal: *grande* ('very') is emphatically positioned at the start of line 127.

Lines 128–30 form a powerful and playful conclusion that addresses wealth, desire and prayer simultaneously. Continuing to be suitably slippery in connection with the *captator*, J. begins at 128f. with what are on the surface good wishes, while working in digs and negative undertones. The mention of Nestor in line 128 sets up a contrast between Pacuvius and that heroic character, a revered, wise and moral king. There is a barb in the idea of living as long as Nestor, because in *Satire* 10 there was nothing pleasant about old age in general or Nestor's in particular (cf. 10.250ff.), and this is also a reminder that the will-hunter will die eventually, so all his exertions might seem somewhat futile in the long run. In line 129 Pacuvius is linked to the despicable Nero, another greedy monster who killed his own relatives. The possession of as much as Nero stole and mountains of gold, as well as amounting to excess, would naturally attract attention, and one immediately thinks of the major risks involved in being rich, as outlined at 10.12ff. In line 130 J. now openly attacks, with vehemence in the repetition of words, the frequency of *q*, *n* and *a* and the placement of *ullo* ('anybody'). J. is praying that Pacuvius continues to be unloving and that, in a symmetrical repayment, he is not loved himself,[69] which seems quite probable in view of his conduct and character and his possession of a fortune (cf. 10.25ff.). J.

wants that totally loveless (and so pointless) existence to go on and on (cf. 128), the craving for riches satisfied but bringing no joy. The sketch of the affluent and unloved person here makes one think of the invalid targeted by Pacuvius, so we can easily envisage this *captator* ending up as the prey of will-hunters himself in a comical rebound.

There is much more to the humour at 128–30. Here at last the satirist himself prays! And what prayers! The first two, at 128f., are ones which he criticized as bad in 10. Then he adds two new requests in line 130. Here again, as in X, he undercuts wealth and longevity via their drawbacks, reminding us of one posited in 10 (the well-off and the elderly are not loved), and tacking on another (with the rich old man himself not loving), to make for an even bleaker scenario that represents still more clearly opulence and long life as not constituting genuine blessings. But this time J. does not just describe the disadvantages; he makes use of them, to turn the prayer into an anti-prayer, and in particular he employs the petition for wealth against somebody desirous of wealth. So there is a deft and amusing redeployment of the appeals for riches and longevity, as curses. And the poet gives them validity at last, by using them to inflict damage by way of punishment on a thoroughly immoral character. So too here J. himself prays for things which are excessive, pointless and harmful, but wishes them on another. All of this produces a clever, complex and very funny conclusion to this satire and to the whole fourth book.

Notes

1   Cf. e.g. Coffey, 133.
2   See Braund (1988), 189.
3   On the elephant as a linking thread see Braund (1988), 188; Plaza, 313ff.
4   Cf. Anderson, 287ff.; Bellandi, 82f.; Braund (1988), 184ff.
5   Adamietz, 131ff.; Courtney, 491; Bracci, 9ff.
6   Anderson, 289; Adamietz, 119; Braund (1988), 186f.: Plaza, 238ff.; Bracci, 20ff.
7   Ferguson, 287; Courtney, 490f.; Bracci, 15ff.
8   Highet, 132f., 278f.; Adamietz, 119ff.; Ferguson, 277f.; Bracci, 33ff.
9   Felton and Lee.
10   Weisinger; Plaza, 238ff.
11   See Courtney, 491.
12   Cf. McDevitt; Courtney, 491.
13   See Courtney, 492; Jones, 186f. n. 85; Nisbet and Hubbard on Hor. C. 1.38.1 *Persicos odi, puer, apparatus* ('boy, I dislike Persian extravagance').
14   McDevitt rightly rejects the suggestion by Highet (1954, 130f.) that those lines are an introductory gossipy chat. It is highly improbable that such a chat would run on for so long in what is after all a piece of satirical writing.

15   See 93ff., 120ff., 136ff., 147f., 162ff., 175.

16   At 1f. and 22f. the poet allows that people think that the rich who dine very well are stylish and laudable, but he does not express approbation on his own part, and at 175ff. he criticizes popular approval of the wealthy and their conduct.

17   See Mayor, ad loc. for parallels for this attitude.

18   Cf. e.g. Virro in *Satire* 5 and Trimalchio in Petronius's *Satyricon* for the use of the dinner party to parade opulence.

19   Cf. Romano, 169 on the irony at 12f.

20   See Romano, 169.

21   See *OLD* s.v. *exitus* 1, 3b, 4; *TLL* V.2.1532.13ff., 1535.58ff.

22   See *OLD* s.v. *mergo* 10b; *TLL* VIII.832.3ff., 835.18ff. Compare the picture at 10.176–8.

23   See Mayor on line 188.

24   For the hair dishevelled and the face flushed from sex see Mayor on line 189.

25   Cf. Courtney on lines 186–9. Persicus's wife is reminiscent of Messalina at 6.131f.

26   On the various connections between the two poems cf. esp. Braund (1988), 187.

27   *Troiugena* (see *OLD* s.v.) is an elevated word.

28   See *OLD* s.v. 7b and 8.

29   For which see Mayor on 1.137.

30   See *OLD* s.v. 2, and cf. Plaza, 313ff.

31   See Courtney.

32   Cf. 10.148, 158, 194 and my comments on those lines.

33   *OLD* s.v. *obscurus* 2b, 5, 7b, 8.

34   See e.g. *OLD* s.v. *ater* 7, 8b and *niger* 7, 8, 9.

35   See Courtney.

36   The point is made by Courtney on line 138. So too the carver's teacher has a Greek name (Trypherus).

37   Cf. Romano, 171f.; Ferguson on line 141.

38   See Petron. *Sat.* 55, 59, 68.

39   See *OLD* s.v. *nugae* 2, 3, 4.

40   Cf. e.g. Keith (2ff., 8ff.) for the edifying aspects of epic poetry.

41   Homer *Il.* 2.211ff.

42   See Stanford, 17, 67f., 76, 90ff.

43   Cf. Romano, 169; Plaza, 240.

44   See e.g. Colton, 414ff.

45   Courtney, 516f.

46   See Littlewood.

47   See e.g. Highet (1954), 134ff.; Ramage; Stramaglia, 231; Keane (2015), 160ff.

48   Ronnick (1993). Uden (176ff.) sees a satire on mercenary concepts of the relationship between men and gods.

49   Larmour.

50   See Braund (1988), 274 n. 46.

51   See e.g. Coffey, 133; Ferguson, 294; Romano, 174ff.; Courtney, 516f.; Smith; Littlewood; Hooley 125f. I pick up several arguments from them.

52   Cf. the disapproval of commerce at 1.103ff.

53   See Mayor and Courtney on the deal in line 33.

54   Lines 57–61 are hardly an injunction to Corvinus or the general reader but must be directed at the greedy merchant who will go to sea again for profit.

55   On which see Mayor; Ferguson.

56   See Smith, 289f.

57   Ferguson (294) opines that J. is giving thanks for Catullus's deliverance no matter how undesirable he is. But it is not likely that he would have made vows in advance for such a person, and subsequently sacrificed quite pricey victims (costly enough to make Corvinus think that the poet is trying thereby to wheedle his way into Catullus's will), or be ready to offer a much more expensive bull if only he could afford it, and describe the day on which he repays a vow for the greedy merchant as sweeter than his own birthday.

58   The poem does consist of two halves (1–92; 93–130), but it does not fall apart, as some have claimed. Transition is made carefully at 93–8. There are links between the two parts as well: in addition to the addresses to Corvinus and the shared theme of greed, Catullus features at 93–5 as well as at 1–92, and there are various other aspects in common, like hyperbole (concerning the storm and the will-hunters' sacrifices), epic allusion (at 70ff. and 118ff.), friendship, with the ironical *amicus* ('friend') in lines 16 and 96, sacrifice (1ff., 100ff.), escape from death (in the storm and at 122) and ships (19ff. and 122).

59   Vows are, of course, a form of prayer. See Pulleyn, 17 and 30f.

60   For explanation of the references in these lines see the commentators, and for Parthenius cf. Suet. *Dom.* 16.2 and 17.2. It is far more pointed if there is allusion to that minister rather than to a craftsman. See Courtney on line 44.

61   That selfish disregard for other family members recalls but is even worse than the wife's contempt for Persicus at 11.186ff.

62   Cf. Hooley, 126.

63   I accept tentatively Housman's explanation of the text here, Cf. Courtney, ad loc.

64   See e.g. Courtney, 28.

65   On Crispinus see 1.26ff., 4.1ff., 108f.

66   See *TLL* VIII.1064.15ff., 1068.76ff.

67   See Courtney.

68   Before here only at Ovid *Met.* 12.34.

69   There is a pertinent allusion to *De Amicitia* 52, where Cicero says that nobody would want to have great wealth if it entailed not loving anyone and not being loved, and describes the miserable plight of tyrants, who lead such a life.

Select Bibliography

I list below only works which are cited in this book and works which I found particularly helpful in the writing process.

Adamietz, J. (1972). *Untersuchungen zu Juvenal.* Wiesbaden.

Adams, J.N. (1982). *The Latin Sexual Vocabulary.* London.

Anderson, W.S. (1982). *Essays on Roman Satire.* Princeton.

Beardsley, G.H. (1979). *The Negro in Greek and Roman Civilization.* New York.

Bellandi, F. (1980). *Etica diatribica e potesta sociale nelle Satire di Giovenale.* Bologna.

Bracci, F. (2014). *La Satira 11 di Giovenale.* Berlin.

Braund, S.M. (1988). *Beyond Anger.* Cambridge.

—— (1996a). *The Roman Satirists and their Masks.* London.

—— (1996b). *Juvenal Satires Book 1.* Cambridge.

—— (2004). *Juvenal and Persius.* Cambridge, MA.

Campana, P. (2004). *D. Iunii Iuvenalis Satura X.* Florence.

Clausen, W.V. (1992). *A. Persi Flacci et D. Iuni Iuvenalis Saturae.* Oxford.

Coffey, M. (1976). *Roman Satire.* London.

Cokayne, K. (2003). *Experiencing Old Age in Ancient Rome.* London.

Colton, R.E. (1991). *Juvenal's Use of Martial's Epigrams.* Amsterdam.

Courtney, E. (1980). *A Commentary on the Satires of Juvenal.* London.

de Decker, J. (1913). *Juvenalis Declamans.* Ghent.

Dick, B.F. (1969). 'Seneca and Juvenal 10', *HSPh* 73: 237–46.

Dubrocard, M. (1976). *Juvenal-Satires Index verborum Relevés statistiques.* Hildesheim.

Duchesne, J. (1933). 'Une petite comédie dans Juvénal, Satire X', *LEC* 2: 149–52.

Duff, J.D. (1898, repr. 1970). *D. Iunii Iuvenalis Saturae XIV.* Cambridge.

Ebel, D.N. (1973). *Iunii Iuvenalis Satura Decima*. Diss. Wien.

Edgeworth, R.J. (1999). 'Passages in Juvenal Four and Ten', *C&M* 50: 179–87.

Felton, K. and Lee, K.H. (1972). 'The Theme of Juvenal's Eleventh Satire', *Latomus* 31: 1041–6.

Ferguson, J. (1979). *Juvenal The Satires*. New York.

Fishelov, D. (1990). 'The Vanity of the Reader's Wishes', *AJPh* 111: 370–82.

Freudenburg, K. (2001). *Satires of Rome*. Cambridge.

—— (ed.) (2005). *The Cambridge Companion to Roman Satire*. Cambridge.

Freudenburg, K., Cucchiarelli, A. and Barchiesi, A. (2007). *Musa Pedestre*. Rome.

Friedländer, L. (1895). *D. Iunii Juvenalis Saturarum libri V*. Leipzig.

Gauger, F. (1936). *Zeitschilderung und Topik bei Juvenal*. Bottrop.

Gérard, J. (1976). *Juvénal et la Réalité Contemporaine*. Paris.

Green, P. (1998). *Juvenal The Sixteen Satires*. London.

Griffith, J. (1988). *Festinat Senex*. Oxford.

Henderson, J. (1997). *Figuring Out Roman Nobility*. Exeter.

Hendry, M. (1988). 'Three Cruces in Juvenal', *CQ* 48: 252–61.

Highet, G. (1949). 'The Philosophy of Juvenal', *TAPhA* 80: 254–70.

—— (1954). *Juvenal the Satirist*. London.

Hooley, D.M. (2007). *Roman Satire*. Oxford.

Housman, A.E. (1931). *D. Iunii Iuvenalis Saturae*. Cambridge.

Iddeng, J.W. (2000). 'Juvenal, Satire and the Persona Theory', *SO* 75: 107–29.

—— (2005). 'How Shall We Comprehend the Roman I-poet? A Reassessment of the Persona Theory', *C&M* 56: 185–205.

Jenkyns, R. (1982). *Three Classical Poets*. London.

Jones, F. (2007). *Juvenal and the Satiric Genre*. London.

Keane, C. (2006). *Figuring Genre in Roman Satire*. Oxford.

—— (2015). *Juvenal and the Satiric Emotions*. Oxford.

Keith, A.M. (2000). *Engendering Rome*. Cambridge.

Larmour, D.H.J. (2005). 'Lightening the Load: Castration, Money and Masculinity in Juvenal's Satire 12', *Syll. Class.* 16: 139–72.

Lawall, G. (1958). '*Exempla* and Theme in Juvenal's Tenth Satire', *TAPhA* 89: 25–31.

Lelièvre, F.J. (1958). 'Juvenal: Two Possible Examples of Wordplay', *CPh* 53: 241–2.

Lindo, L.I. (1974). 'The Evolution of Juvenal's Later Satires', *CPh* 69: 17–27.

Littlewood, C. (2007). 'Poetry and Friendship in Juvenal's Twelfth Satire', *AJPh* 128: 389–418.

Maier, B. (1983). 'Juvenal – Dramatiker und Regisseur. Am Beispiel der zehnten Satire', *AU* XXVI.4: 49–53.

Marmorale, E.V. (1938). *Giovenale*. Naples.

Martyn, J.R.C. (1979). 'Juvenal's Wit', *GB* VIII: 219–38.

Mayor, J.E.B. (1886–9). *Thirteen Satires of Juvenal*. London.

McDevitt, A.S. (1968). 'The Structure of Juvenal's Eleventh Satire', *G&R* 15: 173–9.

Miller, P.A. (2005). *Latin Verse Satire*. London.

Nadeau, Y. (2011). *A Commentary on the Sixth Satire of Juvenal*. Brussels.

Nisbet, R.G.M and Hubbard, M. (1970). *A Commentary on Horace: Odes Book 1*. Oxford.

Otto, A. (1964, repr.). *Die Sprichwörter und sprichwörtlichen Redensarten der Römer*. Hildesheim.

Parkin, T.G. (2003). *Old Age in the Roman World*. Baltimore.

Pichon, R. (1966, repr.). *Index Verborum Amatoriorum*. Hildesheim.

Plaza, M. (2006). *The Function of Humour in Roman Verse Satire*. Oxford.

—— (ed.) (2009). *Oxford Readings in Classical Studies Persius and Juvenal*. Oxford.

Powell, J.G.F. (1999). 'Stylistic Registers in Juvenal' in *Aspects of the Language of Latin Poetry*, ed. J.M. Adams and R.G. Mayer, 311–34. Oxford.

Pulleyn, S. (1997). *Prayer in Greek Religion*. Oxford.

Ramage, E.S. (1978). 'Juvenal Satire 12. On Friendship True and False', *ICS* 3: 221–37.

Ramage, E.S., Sigsbee, D.L. and Fredericks, S.C. (1974). *Roman Satirists and their Satire*. Park Ridge, NJ.

Ramelli, I. (2008). *Stoici Romani Minori*. Milan.

Reckford, K.J. (2009). *Recognizing Persius*. Princeton and Oxford.

Romano, A.C. (1979). *Irony in Juvenal*. Hildesheim.

Ronnick, M.V. (1992). 'Juvenal Satire 10.150: *atrosque non aliosque (Rursus ad Aethiopum populos aliosque elephantos)*', *Mnemosyne* 45: 383–6.

—— (1993). 'Juvenal, Satire 12,32 Catullus' Shipwreck', *MH* 50: 223–4.

Rudd, N. (1986). *Themes in Roman Satire*. London.

Rudd, N. and Barr, W. (1991). *Juvenal The Satires*. Oxford.

Rudd, N. and Courtney, E. (1977). *Juvenal Satires I, III, X*. Bedminster.

Schmitz, C. (2000). *Das Satirische in Juvenals Satiren*. Berlin.

Scivoletto, N. (1963). 'Presenza di Persio in Giovenale', *GIF* 16: 60–72.

Scott, I.G. (1927). *The Grand Style in the Satires of Juvenal*. Northampton, MA.

Serafini, A. (1957). *Studio sulla Satira di Giovenale*. Florence.

Shackleton Bailey, D.R. (2000). *Valerius Maximus Memorable Doings and Sayings*. Cambridge, MA and London.

Smith, W.S. (1989). 'Greed and Sacrifice in Juvenal's twelfth Satire', *TAPhA* 119: 287–98.

Snowden, F.M. (1970). *Blacks in Antiquity*. Cambridge, MA.

Stanford, W.B. (1954). *The Ulysses Theme*. Oxford.

Stocks, C. (2014). *The Roman Hannibal*. Liverpool.

Stramaglia, A. (2008). *Giovenale, Satire 1, 7, 12 16 Storia di un Poeta*. Bologna.

Sullivan, J.P. (ed.) (1963). *Satire Critical Essays on Roman Literature*. Bloomington and London.

Tengström, E. (1980). *A Study of Juvenal's Tenth Satire*. Gothoburg.

Uden, J. (2015). *The Invisible Satirist*. New York.

Urech, H.J. (1999). *Hoher und niederer Stil in den Satiren Juvenals*. Bern and Frankfurt am Main.

Viansino, G. (1990). *Decimo Giunio Giovenale, Satire*. Milan.

Weisinger, K. (1972). 'Irony and Moderation in Juvenal 11', *CSCA* 5: 227–40.

Wickham, E.C. (1967). *Q. Horati Flacci Opera Editio Altera curante H.W. Garrod*. Oxford.

Winkler, M.M. (1983). *The Persona in Three Satires of Juvenal*. Hildesheim.

—— (1988). 'Juvenal's Attitude toward Ciceronian Poetry and Rhetoric', *RhM* 131: 84–97.

—— (2001). *Juvenal in English*. London.

Index